The Microsoft Windows XP Professional Handbook

The Microsoft Windows XP Professional Handbook

Louis Columbus

FIREWALL MEDIA
(An Imprint of Laxmi Publications Pvt. Ltd.)
22, Golden House, Daryaganj
New Delhi-110002

Published by :
FIREWALL MEDIA
(*An Imprint of Laxmi Publications Pvt. Ltd.*)
113, Golden House, Daryaganj,
New Delhi-110002

Phone : 011-43 53 25 00
Fax : 011-43 53 25 28

www.laxmipublications.com
info@laxmipublications.com

This economy edition is for sale in the following countries :
India, Bangladesh, Nepal, Pakistan, Sri Lanka and Bhutan.

Economy Edition Price : **Rs. 295.00** *Only.* *Edition* : 2008

OFFICES

India

✆ **Bangalore**	080-26 61 15 61
✆ **Chennai**	044-24 34 47 26
✆ **Cochin**	0484-239 70 04
✆ **Guwahati**	0361-254 36 69, 251 38 81
✆ **Hyderabad**	040-24 65 23 33
✆ **Jalandhar**	0181-222 12 72
✆ **Kolkata**	033-22 27 37 73, 22 27 52 47
✆ **Lucknow**	0522-220 95 78
✆ **Mumbai**	022-24 91 54 15, 24 92 78 69
✆ **Ranchi**	0651-230 77 64

USA

Boston
11, Leavitt Street, Hingham,
MA 02043, USA

FMS-2761-295-MS WINDOWS XP PROF HANDBOOK **C—14731/07/09**
ISBN: 81-7008-342-7 *Printed at* : Ajit Printers, Delhi.

Table of Contents

Introduction

Thank you for using this book as a guide in your exploration of the Windows XP Operating System. Microsoft has created both Windows XP Professional and Windows XP Home editions. This book is written for intermediate-to-advanced Windows NT and Windows 2000 users who are looking to see how best to get up to speed with Windows XP Professional. Many of the chapters take the approach of assisting system administrators in both supporting Windows XP Professional and also assisting users in learning how to support themselves. This book focuses on how to make the most out of Windows XP Professional from first introducing users to key concepts and progressing to steps showing how to best manage this operating system.

This book is also specifically created for universities, schools, and learning centers seeking to assist their students in learning the fundamentals of Windows XP. Stressing the concepts behind the key features and then providing hands-on examples of key tasks, it is specifically written with the goal of making learning Microsoft's latest operating systems as efficient as possible. If you are teaching courses on Windows XP you will find this book invaluable for the hands-on exercises and a chance to see how Windows XP Professional is changing how companies globally do business electronically. You will also find plenty of useful tips and hints on teaching Windows XP Professional if you are a company trainer, or even a system administrator who supports a department of computer users.

WHY LEARN WINDOWS XP PROFESSIONAL?

Information technologies are changing the landscape of how jobs get created and the direction jobs take over time. Knowing as much as possible about operating systems and how they work, being able to assist others in learning about them, and becoming proficient in a new skill such as working with and configuring Windows XP Professional makes one more marketable. From an industry standpoint, Windows XP represents the melding of both personal- and business-oriented operating systems. The fact that Microsoft has chosen to create both Windows XP Professional and Windows XP Home Editions shows that there are fundamental differences that exist at the operating system level between business and home users. The goal of *The Microsoft Windows XP Professional Handbook* is to explain how you can get the most out of the business-oriented version of the Windows XP operating system for both your own productivity and that of others you teach, support, work with, and work for.

WHOM THIS BOOK IS FOR

Developed specifically for intermediate users, power-users and system administrators, this book focuses on the aspects of Windows XP Professional that are important for managing either a small workgroup or an entire enterprise. In completing this book I have strived for a conversational tone that is focused on speaking to a Windows XP user at any level, with the hands-on exercises giving the intermediate and advanced user a refresher on how to accomplish tasks in this new operating system.

For the beginning user, these exercises are meant as tutorials. It is my hope this book adds to the knowledge of all levels of users, and for the intermediate and advanced users of NT, I drill down into subjects and provide you with background information you need to excel at your job as it relates to using Windows XP. For the system administrator who has a group of users to support in addition to keeping servers and workstations humming, this book provides tips and tricks that will give you a chance to get more done in less time. This book is also aimed at the system administrator who needs a useful desk reference on how to set up and manage various aspects of the Windows XP Professional operating system. If you are a system administrator and are frequently asked to teach short courses on how the users you support can get more out of Windows XP, this book's exercises give you a chance to create entire mini-courses on selected areas of the Windows XP Professional operating system. Above all, I hope you find this book significantly contributes to your knowledge of Windows XP Professional, and that after reading it you find you are more productive than ever in your job or position.

1 Introducing Windows XP Professional

INTRODUCTION

The development efforts surrounding Windows XP Professional and Home Editions have been marked by the rapid integration of key features, the quick progression from beta versions to finished product, and the depth of feature support for both editions. The wealth of features that are now included in Windows XP Professional are described throughout this book, starting with an overview of the operating system. In looking at

Windows XP Professional, it is a good idea to step back and look at the design objectives that led to the development of the first versions of Windows NT. Looking at these design goals gives you a good idea of just how quickly the progression has occurred from Windows NT to Windows 2000 and now to Windows XP Professional. Creating an operating system that could scale or grow with the needs of an organization, having a platform that can securely handle transactions and protect data, and delivering an operating system that is compatible with previous generation applications were all initial goals of the first Windows NT development. Today the capability to scale across the needs of an enterprise—called scalability—is critical for any operating system. Security of an operating system is an essential design objective, and as the events in the world show, it is an area where constant development is needed to further secure operating systems from outside threats. Making an operating system that is capable of running applications from other development environments, including previous generations of the same operating system family, is also critical. Often called interoperability, this and security are considered two essential elements of any operating system.

Microsoft's approach is to develop their operating systems to accomplish each of these objectives. As you read through this book and learn more about Windows XP Professional, keep in mind these design goals as the core design requirements of any operating system. Microsoft also worked through many other design requirements and worked extensively with focus groups, customer interviews, and even a lab to check the ergonomics of the Windows XP interface.

This chapter also covers Windows XP Professional's improved networking capabilities and also compares Windows XP Professional to UNIX. You may also be interested in the capabilities of Windows XP Professional to coexist with UNIX, and the transition path for migrating from UNIX to Windows XP.

SIMILARITIES BETWEEN WINDOWS XP PROFESSIONAL AND XP HOME EDITIONS

For the first time, Microsoft is releasing both a business and home-oriented version of a networked operating system. While this book is primarily focused on the Windows XP Professional operating system, there is going to be much said and written about Windows XP Home Edition as well. To make sure you have a chance to get caught up on the differences between these operating systems, a summary of the common features each share follows. As this chapter will illustrate, Windows XP Home Edition is actually the same basic system as the Professional version, except with fewer features.

Features Shared by Windows XP Professional and Windows XP Home Edition

There are many shared features between both operating systems, including:

- **New user interface**—This includes a more intelligent Start area of the desktop.
- **32-bit multitasking operating system components**—This was first developed for Windows NT 3.51. Both also support Win16- and Win32-based applications.
- **The newest version of Windows Media Player**—This is superior to Real Audio's products in that there is a more efficient storage of media and better support for organizing and playing digital media.
- **Network setup wizards**—These wizards streamline the process of getting connected to the Internet and working with home networks.
- **Windows Messenger**—Windows Messenger is a collaboration tool that includes instant messaging, voice and video conferencing, and application sharing. What is interesting is the market research that shows how often business users are using instant messaging for both business and personal use. Windows Messenger has the capability to share applications as well—an innovative tool for companies with employees distributed worldwide.
- **Help and Support Center**—This is improved over the help functions in previous versions and includes seamless integration of information from Microsoft's Web site.
- **Laptop Support Enhancements**—Microsoft has created support for ClearType, a font technology making laptop screens easier to read, in addition to Dualview, which is support for two monitors at once, plus support for multiple monitors. There are also significant enhancements to power management features in both versions.
- **Support for wireless networking**—Microsoft has done an outstanding job in this area. This area of networking is entirely new to

Microsoft's operating systems, and their work with the 802.11b standard is very good.

- **Start-up support**—Both operating systems include OnNow support, ensuring quicker boots. In tests, Windows XP boots at least 40 percent faster than Windows 2000.
- **Multitasking support**—Both Windows XP Professional and XP Home Edition are based on the same platforms as Windows NT and Windows 2000, all of which support multitasking of applications and balancing processing loads between processors. This, in conjunction with the Performance tool, gives Windows XP Professional and Home Edition equivalent functionality to many versions of the UNIX operating systems.
- **Internet Connection Firewalls**—Both versions of Windows XP support Internet Connection Firewalls configured through the network configuration settings. The firewalls are used for protecting a workstation or PC while the users are accessing the Internet.
- **Internet Explorer 6.0 Privacy support**—This feature is aimed at making sure your personal data both entered into the browser and gathered via the Internet is secure. Internet Explorer 6.0 is the version shipped with Windows XP.
- **Binary Language support**—This allows text to be entered in any language and Win32 applications in any language to be used on any version of Windows XP.

EXPLORING WINDOWS XP PROFESSIONAL

Now in its fourth generation, Windows XP Professional signals a milestone in the Windows NT roadmap. It is a milestone because it brings together the design requirements of both business and home users on the same platform. Let us first take a look at the essentials of how the Windows XP Professional operating system is put together.

An operating system actually functions to provide a "wake-up call" for a computer system in that its role is to coordinate all the activities in a computer system. The focus on operating system design has changed dramatically from twenty years ago, when designers focused almost exclusively on the needs of a hardware platform to have streamlined code to maximize system performance. With the introduction of DOS there was a reliance on providing the core features necessary for making a computer work. The lessons learned in operating systems in the DOS years continue to impact the development of compatibility features in Windows XP Professional among other operating systems being developed today.

The needs of both people who design products and people who develop new software, and those using workstations for mainstream applications including creating documents and presentations, are exerting the biggest influence on the direction Microsoft is taking with Windows XP Professional. Windows XP Professional indeed signals an entirely new direction for Microsoft, as the design objectives shift toward providing greater desktop management, advanced security, advanced networking, power-user features and a stronger focus on user interface and design than has ever been the case before. In developing Windows NT and 2000, Microsoft was focusing on building a foundation for handling multiple applications well through preemptive multitasking, developing a platform that could scale across thousands of users, and providing compatibility for previous-generation applications. With Windows XP Professional, Microsoft has moved into an entirely new dimension—more of a focus on administrative ease of use and support of key features that users are asking for.

Like Windows NT Workstation and Windows 2000 Professional, Windows XP Professional also uses preemptive multitasking memory management to ensure reliability and consistency of performance across applications. Windows XP Professional is truly a 32-bit operating system that has TCP/IP as its networking foundation. The goal of making Windows XP Professional more accessible than previous operating systems was accomplished by using a new graphical user interface for the desktop.

Let us now tour the features of Windows XP Professional. Keep in mind that if you are an experienced user of any previous Windows version, you will find Windows XP Professional easier than ever to navigate. Microsoft has taken great efforts in the area of ergonomics to make Windows XP Professional one of the easiest operating systems to work with. The desktop itself is organized more like a home appliance than a computer's operating system. Figure 1.1 shows the Windows XP Professional desktop.

Microsoft focused on interoperability and making the architecture of Windows XP Professional stronger at handling the tasks of working with other operating systems, and within the Internet environment. The features in Windows XP Professional are specifically developed to provide system wide reliability, productivity tools for both technical professionals and office users, and a much-expanded approach to automating the tools

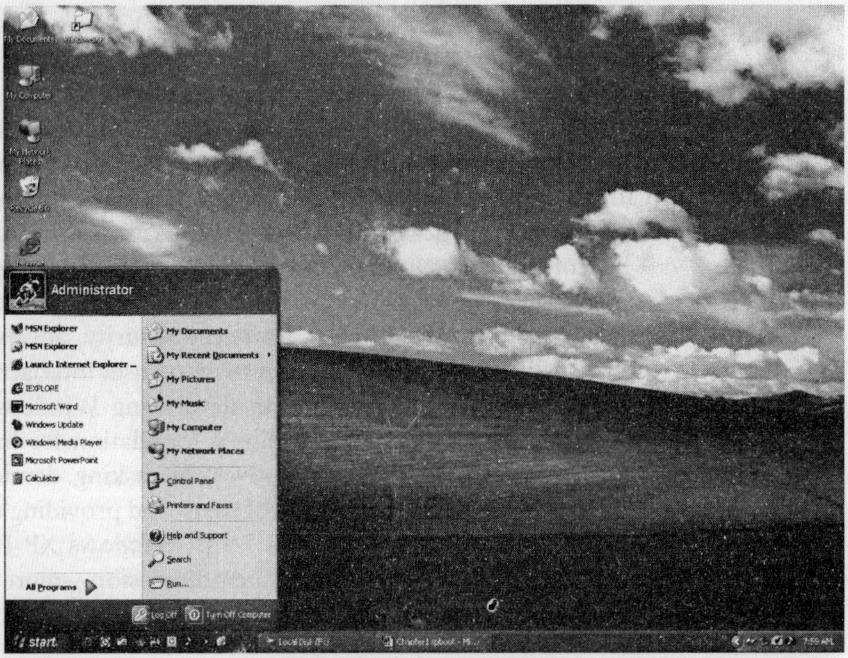

FIGURE 1.1 The Windows XP Professional desktop.

administrators use for handling the deployment of thousands of workstations and servers at any given time.

Windows XP Professional Features

More features of Windows XP Professional are described here:

- **32-bit, preemptive multitasking platform**—This architecture has been proven in Windows NT and Windows 2000 operating systems. The continued refinement of such key features as Plug and Play functionality and the ability to support applications from multiple memory models including the Win16 and Win32 API platforms makes Windows XP Professional the most stable operating system available for handling applications designed for various systems.
- **Driver Verifier**—Microsoft has struggled with the widely varying quality of device drivers in previous versions of their operating systems. For the first time, Microsoft has introduced the Device

Driver Verifier as part of the baseline in Windows XP Professional. It had been included in Service Pack 4 for Windows NT 4.0, and has just begun to be used in many corporate accounts. Device Driver Verifier initiates a series of tests to make sure the device drivers being installed in Windows XP Professional are suitable enough to keep the main operating system stable.

- **Kernel data architecture is now read-only**—As in UNIX, Microsoft's decision to make the core processes of Windows XP Professional at the kernel level read-only is an effort to stop programming efforts by some applications to change the fundamental architecture of an operating system while it is running. This can provide for greater security and stability of the operating system.
- **Side-by-Side DLL support**—Given the fact that every version of Windows NT, Windows 2000, and now Windows XP supports the flexboot option of being able to boot into any installed version of an operating system at any time, there has always been the need to match DLL files with the appropriate operating system. Microsoft has created a parallel DLL architecture that does so.
- **Support for the Plug and Play IEEE 1394 standard**—This is present in Windows 2000 and now in Windows XP Professional. Figure 1.2 shows a diagram of the Plug and Play subsystem that has been integrated into Windows XP Professional's kernel architecture.
- **OnNow ACPI power management on laptops and portables**—Power Management in Windows XP Professional stands out as being an area where Microsoft has made a concerted effort to get greater innovation into the depth of product functionality and also provide greater options for the many ways users work with laptops. Microsoft seems to have accomplished the vision they have had starting with Windows NT—a power management application that could handle a multitude of scenarios. Power management functions in Windows XP Professional will be explored in greater depth later in this book.
- **Support for the Intelligent I/O (I^2O) architecture**—This focuses on specialized board support for storage cards, extensive support for redundant array of inexpensive disk (RAID) cards, and built-in support for software RAID.
- **Support for Infrared (IR) devices**—IR support began in Windows 2000 and is continued in Windows XP Professional. The Network

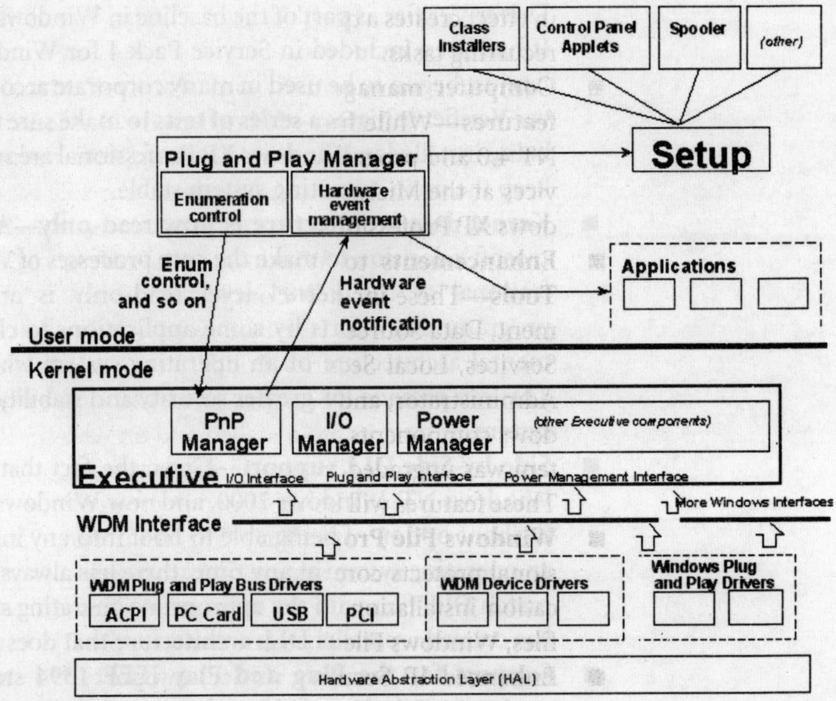

FIGURE 1.2 Plug and Play architecture.

Driver Interface Specification (NDIS) 4.0 is used as the basis for an expanded support for the IR interface.

- **IntelliMirror management capabilities**—Provides for synchronizing the data on local clients with servers. This was first included with Windows 2000.
- **Task Scheduler**—One of the key advantages UNIX has over Windows NT 3.51 and 4.0 is UNIX's capability to schedule batch-oriented tasks for completion at a later time. This is a strong feature in UNIX, in which many applications, most of which are client/server-based, initiate their communications to other systems at a time when network traffic is low. Task Scheduler is accessed by going to Start > All Programs > Accessories > System Tools > Scheduled Tasks, or from Task Scheduler in Control Panel. Task Scheduler can be a very useful tool for system administrators. You can use this tool to schedule tasks to occur during the evening or weekends when you are out of the office. The Task Scheduler uses the Scheduled Task Wizard to configure tasks. Once a task has

been added using this process, Task Scheduler saves the tasks and in effect creates a queue of them. This is very useful for completing recurring tasks.

- **Computer management and Microsoft Management Console features**—While first included in the Service Packs in Windows NT 4.0 and progressing to Windows 2000, the integration of services at the Microsoft Management Console is now part of Windows XP Professional.
- **Enhancements to Windows XP Professional Administrative Tools**—These include Component Services, Computer Management, Data Sources (ODBC), Event Viewer, Internet Information Services, Local Security Policy, Performance, Server Extensions Administrator, and Services. These can vary based on which Windows components are installed and on whether the operating system was upgraded from a previous version or was a clean install. These features will be explained in greater detail later in this book.
- **Windows File Protection**—This feature in Windows XP Professional protects core system files from being overwritten by application installation. If an application does overwrite one of these files, Windows File Protection will restore it to the correct version.
- **Enhanced IP Security (IPSec) support**—Microsoft has significantly added depth to this function as their focus with Windows XP drives toward security as a key design goal. IPSec is being brought to the forefront of Microsoft's design strategies so that security on VPNs and intranets can be made more robust. IPSec is a technology that provides secure tunnels between two peers, such as routers.
- **Smart card support**—As security has become one of the key design objectives of Windows XP, support for smart cards is included to make it possible for more secure logging onto computers and networks. A smart card is a tamper-resistant device the size of a credit card that stores logon and other authentication data. It allows a user to be authenticated on the network when away from the home office, as long as there is a smart card reader wherever the user is.
- **Dualview and multiple monitor support**—This shared feature between Windows XP Professional and Home Edition makes it possible to have a single computer desktop spread out on two monitors, driven off a single display adapter that supports two monitors, such as on a laptop with a built-in monitor and a VGA connector for an external monitor. The desktop can be expanded up to ten monitors by using an additional video adapter for each

additional monitor. Different windows can be displayed on different monitors. This is especially useful for business laptop users who complete product demonstrations.

- **ClearType**—This is a new font technology that makes reading fonts on smaller screens, such as those on laptop computers, more efficient. ClearType triples the horizontal resolution for rendering text and graphics.
- **Synchronization Manager**—A vast improvement over the Briefcase application found in earlier versions of Windows, Microsoft has included Synchronization Manager in Windows XP Professional to make it possible for comparing files both online and offline, then updating to the latest version.
- **Hot Docking**—Windows XP Professional is the first operating system to provide for hot docking and undocking of your notebook computer without having to change hardware configuration or having to reboot.
- **Network Location Awareness**—Windows XP Professional and Home Edition also can report the location of your workstation or laptop from its location throughout a network. This Network Location Awareness is one of the features that, along with wireless networking, makes Windows XP Professional adaptable for distributed work environments.
- **Device Driver Rollback**—One of the most innovative features in Windows XP Professional and Home Edition, this feature provides administrators with the ability to roll back to the set of device drivers of a previous configuration. This is particularly useful when working with new device driver installations, especially when new drivers cause problems on the system.

Pervasive Internet Access in Windows XP Professional

From the Internet Explorer icon on the desktop to the capability of making a Web site be your desktop background, resources on the Internet or on an intranet are just a click or URL away. The integration of HTTP and ActiveX technology in the Windows XP Professional desktop is as thorough as any company building an intranet site for hundreds of employees or any group of students needing access to the Internet for research from their dorm rooms would need.

- **Off-line Web Browsing**—In conjunction with Internet Explorer 6.0, Windows XP Professional includes the option of downloading

Web pages while online and setting them to be available offline. These pages can be viewed while offline, saving downloading time and phone line use.

Ergonomic Desktop Features

- **Quick Launch Toolbar**—In streamlining the ways users work with Windows XP Professional, Microsoft learned from speaking with customers that adding shortcuts to the taskbar would increase productivity. This toolbar is improved in Windows XP, allowing a whole stack of shortcuts to be accessible by clicking an arrow symbol on the toolbar.
- **Improved Control Panel contents**—Applets in the Control Panel have had their feature sets increased allowing users to complete many administrative and user preference tasks from there. There are many new features included in the Control Panel, all of which are described in later chapters of this book. Figure 1.3 shows the contents of the Windows XP Professional Control Panel.

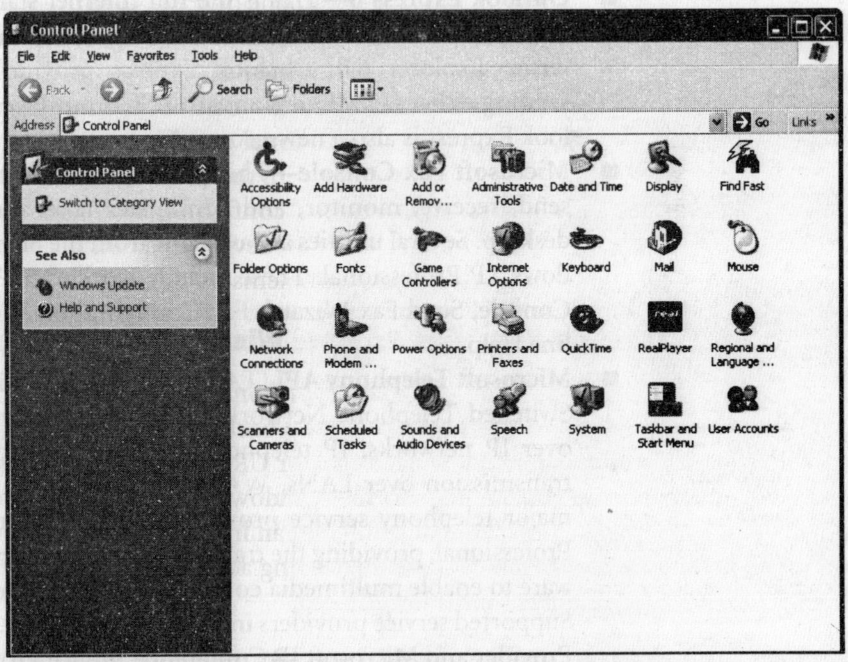

FIGURE 1.3 The contents of the Windows XP Control Panel.

NOTE

RealPlayer and QuickTime are not supplied by Microsoft, and certain other installed applications, such as Microsoft Office, place applets (Find Fast, for example) in Control Panel.

- **Significant use of wizards**—There are several key new wizards in Windows XP Professional that have been developed to streamline the tasks of getting connected to the Internet, home network, or corporate network. These wizards will be covered throughout the book.

New Communication Tools in Windows XP Professional

With over 60% of personal computers networked and a higher percentage of Windows 2000 Professional workstations being networked, the need for streamlining communications has been given priority. Presented here are the new communications features in Windows XP Professional:

- **Internet Explorer 6.0**—Inclusion of this browser includes support for sending e-mail, entering and participating in chat rooms, and also viewing and participating in newsgroups.
- **Outlook Express 6**—This is the full Internet standards-based e-mail client that is included with standard or full installation of Internet Explorer 6.0. Outlook Express provides flexibility for sending either HTML or standard ASCII messages, or both. Outlook Express is also a newsgroup client.
- **Microsoft Fax Console**—This provides users with the ability to send, receive, monitor, and administer faxes directly from the desktop. Several utilities are available from the Start menu in Windows XP Professional. These include Fax Cover Page Editor, Fax Console, Send Fax Wizard, Fax Configuration Wizard , and Online Help.
- **Microsoft Telephony API (TAPI) support**—Provides both Public Switched Telephone Network (PSTN) telephony and telephony over IP networks. IP telephony enables voice, data, and video transmission over LANs, WANs, and the Internet. Support for major telephony service providers is provided in Windows XP Professional, providing the translation between hardware and software to enable multimedia computers to act as telephony devices. Supported service providers include Microsoft H.323 TAPI Service Provider and Microsoft IP Conference Service Provider.

- **Textual Find File support**—Built-in indexing support is accessible from the Search command on the Start menu. The advantage to XP's search function is that the user can more easily select from many categories in which to search, (pictures, music or video, documents, etc.). This saves the user from having to memorize certain file extensions in order to search for a file if he doesn't remember the name of the file.

Additional Tools in Windows XP Professional

- **OnNow Power Management for Laptops**—This feature is specifically aimed at laptops or even desktops where the user wants to have the workstation go into a state of "hibernation." After a period of computer inactivity, OnNow puts the workstation in an off-but-ready mode that in effect makes the workstation look like it has been turned off. The OnNow API prevents systems from drive wear and reduces drive noise. This support is compatible with ACPI-compliant workstations and laptops. Power management also includes power schemes, standby, automatic monitor and hard drive shut-off, automatic hibernation and standby, and more.
- **Accessibility tools**—Included in Windows XP Professional are three accessibility tools. The Accessibility Settings Wizard helps you adapt Windows options to the needs and preferences of those users wishing to customize their systems for easier access. The Microsoft Magnifier enlarges a portion of the screen for easier viewing. The Microsoft Screen Reader uses text-to-speech to read the contents of the screen. There are several other features in this applet.
- **Windows Scripting Host**—This is a language-independent scripting host for 32-bit Windows platforms that includes Visual Basic Scripting Edition (VBScript) and Jscript scripting engines. Performing functions comparable to batch files in MS-DOS, the Windows Scripting Host was developed for Windows 95 and continues to be used in XP.
- **Device Manager snap-in**—Resides in the MMC and provides for configuring of devices on your workstation.
- **Hardware Wizard**—A well-done wizard that makes it possible to configure Plug and Play devices on your workstation. It allows you to add, remove, repair, upgrade and customize hardware. You can

also manually set up non-Plug and Play devices as well. This wizard will be extensively explored throughout this book.

Storage, Security and Windows 9x Compatibility Features

- **Upgrade support**—Windows XP Professional includes an upgrade wizard for seamlessly moving from the following Windows versions: Windows 98, NT 4.0 Workstation, 2000 Professional, and XP Home Edition.
- **FAT32 support**—Support for this file system originally appeared in Windows 95 OSR2. Support for this file system gives Windows XP Professional users the flexibility of using FAT-based file systems to their fullest performance extent. FAT32 is typically preferred to FAT 16 due to its support for disk volumes larger than 2 GB and more efficient storage.
- **NTFS enhancements**—This version of NTFS, first used in Windows 2000, offers many performance enhancements and a host of new features, including per-disk quotas, file encryption, distributed link tracking, and the capability to add disk space to an NTFS volume without rebooting. NTFS also has many advantages over FAT and FAT32 file systems including support for larger drives, the capability of setting permissions at the file level that apply even on the local machine, and better resistance to fragmentation.
- **UDF**—Support for the first time is included for the Universal Disk Format, a new file system used on DVD-ROM and DVD video discs.
- **Encrypting File System**—Using Public Key technology, this file system provides transparent on-disk file encryption for NTFS files and was first introduced in Windows 2000.
- **Quotas**—Administrators can set disk quotas and monitor and limit disk space use. If you are an administrator, familiarize yourself with this feature, as it can spare you the hassle of reallocating used space when servers' storage devices get filled up.
- **Disk Defragmentation Utility**—This utility is provided for defragmenting FAT, FAT32 and NTFS disk volumes and was first introduced in Windows 2000.

Printing Features in Windows XP Professional

- **More thorough support for Internet printing and other printing enhancements**—There have been major improvements in the area of printing including a simplified user interface, Active Directory integration, and image color management APIs (Application Programming Interfaces). The major enhancements to Windows XP Professional printing include capabilities of printer sharing over the Internet or an intranet, installing HTTP printers using Point to Point Protocol (PPP), installing printer drivers from a Web site, and even changing printer status using HTML-based forms. User interface changes include a Web view of the Printers folder and the queues on each printer, and an enhanced Add Printer Wizard that allows users to search for printers in the directory as well as browse a network. There are also expanded printer properties associated with printers. The Image Color Management series of APIs provide for a mechanism to send high-quality color documents from a Windows XP Professional computer to a printer or to another system more efficiently and with greater image quality. Internet printing has replaced faxing in some enterprises—instead of faxing documents, users can print documents on remote Internet printers. This allows a first-generation copy of a document to be produced, eliminating any degradation that can occur due to the faxing process.

- **Active Directory Integration**—Windows XP Professional makes all shared printers in a domain available in the directory. Publishing printers in the Active Directory allows users to quickly locate the most convenient printing resources.
- **Image Color Management 2.0 API**—Using Image Color Management 2.0, you can send high-quality color documents from your computer to your printer or to another computer quickly and easily, and with a high level of consistency.

Hardware Support in Windows XP Professional

- **Plug and Play**—Windows XP Professional supports Plug and Play, making it easy to install and troubleshoot new hardware. Plug and Play support includes a Hardware wizard, the Device Manager, and improved support for laptops.
- **USB support**—Automatically detects the new device and installs the appropriate device driver.
- **Win32 Driver Model (WDM)**—Drivers that adhere to this standard provide a common architecture of I/O services and binary-compatible device drivers for Windows NT, 2000, and Windows

XP Professional operating systems. Included in the Win32 Driver Model is the IEEE 1394 (FireWire) standard for still image and motion video cameras and storage, and scanner support for parallel, SCSI and USB interfaces. Input support includes DirectX, HID layer, and support for multiple joysticks.

Additional hardware support includes:

- Graphics and multimedia support
- I2O Fibre Channel and smart card support
- Media changer support for CD-ROM, tape, and optical disc changers
- Multiple joystick model support, with WDM support for HID-class devices. HID (Human Interface Devices) is a uniform way to access input devices.

Customizing the Windows XP Professional Desktop

If you have ever used Windows 9x, NT 4.0, or Windows 2000 you will find your way around Windows XP Professional quickly. The actual appearance of Windows XP Professional is comparable to Windows 2000, yet the navigation is easier than any other operating system to date. You will find a similar but improved taskbar and Start menu, and many of the same Control Panel applets.

One of the key features is the role of the desktop; it can be customized to a high degree with Internet content. You can have the wallpaper on your Windows XP Professional be your favorite Web site.

What Is New in the Taskbar?

The taskbar groups key functional applications by their use, and also includes a centralized navigation area for using the operating system. Figure 1.4 shows an example of the Start menu. Windows XP streamlines the tasks of finding information, launching applications, and more by allowing great flexibility in adding icons to the desktop and customizing the Start menu. The taskbar provides shortcuts to applications, files, even the Internet, and also gives you the option to customize the selections that appear in it. The taskbar is the rectangular bar that by default is located at the bottom of the screen in all Microsoft desktop operating systems since Windows 95.

FIGURE 1.4 The Start menu can be used to complete navigation tasks throughout Windows XP Professional.

COMPARING WINDOWS XP PROFESSIONAL AND UNIX

Many companies, universities, and institutions of all types worldwide have standardized on UNIX as their operating system of choice. Why does UNIX continue to have a strong following? What are the strengths and weaknesses of UNIX relative to Windows XP and vice versa? These questions and more are discussed in detail throughout this section. Let us begin by looking at the primary differences between UNIX and Windows XP, and then progress through the considerations companies make when transitioning from UNIX to Windows XP.

How Do UNIX and Windows XP Professional Compare?

Of all operating systems being used by corporations today, UNIX is most often considered the one that most closely resembles recent versions of

Windows in terms of device support, security and the networking capabilities each possesses. While many see UNIX and Windows XP Professional to have very comparable architectures, there are fundamental differences between the two. For example, the Windows XP Professional kernel is modular and extensible by nature, while the many variants of UNIX have kernels compiled and predefined according to one of the many target audiences they serve. Windows XP's kernel is consistent across hardware platforms due to the role of the Hardware Abstraction Layer (HAL). What is truly differentiating for XP relative to UNIX is that the former also has a consistency in terms of learning time spent. Experience with UNIX shows that with every version you work with, there is a learning curve to understand the specific command syntax and structure. XP's consistency of interface across the Intel, and in previous versions, PowerPC and MIPS processors, was the learning curve accelerator. UNIX is just as powerful from a command standpoint yet there is so much variation between versions many administrators specialize in their specific version and know it very well, to the exclusion of other versions.

Both Windows XP Professional and UNIX are 32-bit and both have versions that support the evolving 64-bit standard. Hewlett-Packard is working with Intel to ensure the Itanium processor will be compatible with the latest generation of HP's version of UNIX, which is called HP-UX. Both operating systems also have strong security provisions inherent in their architectures, and are multi-user capable from the start.

In the area of specialized imaging applications such as CAD/CAM design and drafting, and in 3D animation, UNIX had built a strong reputation for years. Companies such as Intergraph Corporation had build their strongest products relative to HP and Sun Microsystems on the latter's display subsystems and imaging technology called the Intergraph Graphics Design Systems, or IGDS for short. With the en masse migration from UNIX to Windows for many of the applications being used on the technical desktop, the migration of imaging technologies has followed. This has included a surprising move in 1999 by Intergraph Corporation to partner with Compaq on the Intergraph graphics subsystem. The development of high-end 3D protocols including Open GL and Raydream point to Windows XP Professional becoming the platform of choice for design and animation professionals. The role of UNIX has diminished in the area of graphics, once its stronghold, due to a wide variety of market factors which are in turn making the market for Windows grow at a rapid pace. One of the primary drivers or initiators of change in the migration of users from UNIX to Windows XP Professional is the total cost of ownership of

UNIX-based systems. Manufacturers of hardware designed to run UNIX have seen Intel-based systems running Windows penetrate and capture market share in their larger accounts with increasing frequency. Many customers transition from UNIX to Windows due to the maintenance costs they save; others transition due to the increased level of performance for the price. Still, there are increasingly more software companies basing their development decisions on the strength Windows is showing as a viable platform for development.

In summary, UNIX and Windows XP Professional share many comparable features and traits as operating systems. The truly differentiating aspect is the uniformity and standards-based approach to XP. UNIX has many variations, each with a specific series of needs and target customers in mind.

A BRIEF HISTORY OF WINDOWS XP PROFESSIONAL

The origins of Windows XP Professional emanate from a joint development agreement between Microsoft and IBM on a version of OS/2 originally developed in the late 1980s. Microsoft and IBM failed to complete the project due to differences in architectural direction, and both companies parted before the operating system could be finalized. IBM took over OS/2 for its own development, and Microsoft decided to redesign the operating system to create what would become Windows NT. At first, Windows NT struggled to gain market acceptance, and with the release of version 3.51, Microsoft targeted users of their competitor's products. The result was an operating system that is much different from OS/2.

The first releases of Windows NT 3.51 were met with mixed reviews. As the majority of business PCs became networked, Microsoft continued to refine NT with the goal of capturing market share from Novell, UNIX and DOS users. In 1995, Windows NT began to gain momentum, increasing market share in the very competitive network operating systems marketplace.

Windows is now rapidly becoming a market standard for businesses worldwide due to its reliability, multi-threaded capabilities, and proven networking. The success of Windows has been brought about partly from aggressive marketing, partly from market leverage to the large Microsoft base, but mostly because the very discriminating buyer—the CIO, system administrator, or the client/server manager—have all tested Windows NT, Windows 2000, and Windows XP Professional according to their requirements and they have proven to be satisfactory.

With Windows XP Professional, Microsoft is bringing together the lessons learned from Windows 9x and the enterprise selling lessons learned from selling Windows NT 3.51, 4.0, Windows 2000, and the entire server product line. Windows XP Professional becomes the unifying operating system in terms of development experience in Microsoft's product strategy.

ADDITIONAL RESOURCES AND WEB SITES PERTAINING TO THIS CHAPTER

To help you to stay current on Windows XP, there are several Web sites to monitor periodically for new content.

- **www.bhs.com**—The Web site for Beverly Hills Software, bhs.com is perhaps one of the best-supported third-party Web sites dedicated to Windows 2000 and Windows XP Professional topics. Resources on this site include utilities for performing key tasks. There is also a listing of jobs for those interested in working in the IT field. One of the most valuable areas of the site is the listing of user's groups. These listings at times include copies of the handouts provided at the meetings. This is a very useful site overall for staying current with Windows XP.
- **www.win2000mag.com**—Formerly the Windows 2000 Professional Magazine Web site, it is now called the Windows & .NET Magazine Network. You will find this an invaluable aid in making sure you stay current with the latest technologies, including articles that describe how best to navigate the intricacies of the operating system and also how to manage a Windows-based network if you are a system administrator.
- **www.brainbuzz.com**—A must-visit site for your continuing efforts to stay current with both the technology and press-related events in the industry. This site has a wealth of information. This is one of the better vertical portals (called vortals by Internet analysts) and worthy of your time.
- **www.labmice.net**—One of the better portals on Windows 2000/XP and .NET servers, this site is worth a visit once a week or more as it has an impressive amount of new content.

CHAPTER SUMMARY

With the latest generation of this powerful operating system, Windows XP Professional has embraced the World Wide Web and its applications both inside and outside businesses. Windows XP Professional has features that include support for Plug and Play, extensive printing and file system enhancements, and also hardware support for the ACPI standard. This chapter has provided a focus on the key features of Windows XP Professional, and the following chapters will include key hands-on exercises and insights that will maximize the value of Windows XP Professional in your school, business, or organization.

2 Touring the Windows XP Professional Desktop

INTRODUCTION

One of the truly differentiating aspects of Windows XP Professional is the new approach to navigating the desktop. Using the tools and applets described in this chapter you will be able to customize both your desktop and how you manage applications. You will also notice when you first start Windows XP Professional that the desktop has a very comparable appearance to both Windows 98 and Windows 2000 desktops. Any references to properties have references to Internet resources as well, making the steps to researching any aspect of Windows XP Professional much more efficient than having to switch over to a browser and look up information. The intent of this chapter is to give you a thorough overview of the properties customizable directly from the Windows XP Professional graphical interface. Figure 2.1 shows the Windows XP Professional desktop.

FIGURE 2.1 The Windows XP Professional desktop.

TAKING A TOUR OF THE WINDOWS XP PROFESSIONAL DESKTOP

The approach Microsoft continues to take on their operating systems is to make accessing Internet-based resources transparent to the user. This provides users who have T1 or ISDN lines to the Internet quick access to resources that are hopefully as up to date as possible (at least as up to date as the Web sites on which the resources are found). It is clear that the level of Web integration in Windows XP is one of the features that Microsoft hopes to use to differentiate this operating system from its earlier versions, in addition to its competitors' systems. Customizing the desktop is easily accomplished using the procedure shown in this section. If you are a Windows XP Professional user who is using a laptop or supporting a series of systems that dial out frequently to the Internet, you will probably want to change the desktop from being Internet-centric to being more standalone in nature. You have the option of centrally managing Internet access so that access is permitted only to specified Web sites.

EXPLORING THE TASKBAR

Windows XP continues the desktop approach to presenting applications and operating system resources to users. An essential element of this approach to organizing the desktop is through navigational tools such as the taskbar, the shortcut, and the pervasive use of properties on many aspects of the operating system.

What is the taskbar? And how customizable is it? As a system administrator you will need to be able to customize this tool for users. Let us take a look at the taskbar and the properties you can use to customize it for yourself and others you support. The taskbar is by default located along the bottom of the screen, and as applications are started, they are added to it. Figure 2.2 shows the taskbar.

FIGURE 2.2 The Windows XP Taskbar.

The taskbar also includes the Start button, time, and icons representing utilities and tools as they are installed on the computer. As an administrator you will be able to see which utilities are initialized during boot-up by looking at the right hand section of the taskbar.

The taskbar was developed in Windows 95 as a method for quickly changing between applications from the desktop. In versions of Windows prior to Windows 95, you would have used the Alt+Tab keystroke sequence to toggle between open applications. Windows XP Professional continues to support this keystroke sequence as well.

Probably the best new feature of the taskbar is "application stacking." On previous versions of Windows, every open application gets its own block on the taskbar. When there are many programs open, the blocks get small enough so that it is impossible to determine which applications they represent. The Windows XP desktop, however, stacks different instances of the same programs once they get to a minimum size. For instance, if the taskbar is full and you have three Web sites open, there will be one block for Internet Explorer displaying the number 3. Clicking on the block calls up a menu listing each Web site and giving the option to restore or close individual instances. Right clicking on the block gives the options to minimize or close the entire group of instances. When there are multiple folders open, they are stacked as instances of Windows Explorer. But what if there are still too many applications open to fit on the taskbar? A second page of the taskbar becomes available, accessible from up and down arrows to the right of the program blocks.

Hands-On with the Taskbar

The best approach to learning about how to manage the taskbar is to complete the series of hands-on tutorials presented here. These tutorials are structured to assist you with learning how to customize the taskbar along with some tips to make it easier.

The taskbar can be aligned along the right, top, left or bottom edges of the screen. Click on the taskbar and drag it to the right. You can now size the taskbar to any width you want. Click on the taskbar again and drag it up to the top of the screen. You can use this method to move the taskbar to any edge of the screen. Windows XP includes a new feature that allows you to lock the taskbar so you will not be able to relocate the taskbar by accident. To activate the lock, right-click on an empty portion of the taskbar and click the Lock the Taskbar command. A check mark will appear next to the command and the taskbar will remain stationary until this check mark is cleared.

Exploring Taskbar Properties

As a system administrator you will sooner or later encounter the need to understand how to customize the taskbar for a specific user, group of users, or even for yourself. How do you do it? Options are available for the Taskbar and Start menu programs. To explore these capabilities, follow the steps described here.

1. Right-click on the taskbar. A menu appears showing various selections. Figure 2.3 shows the menu.

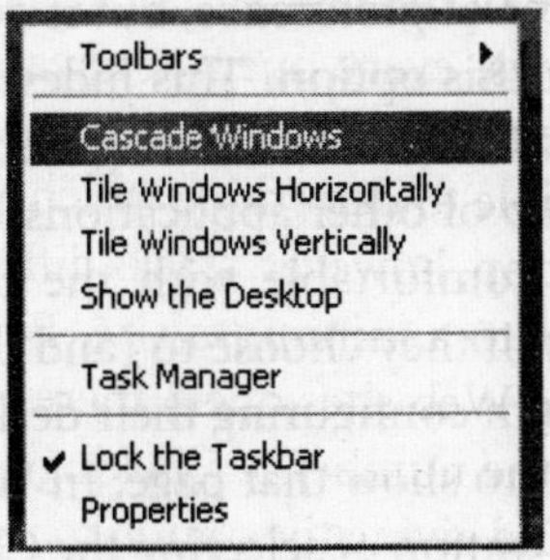

FIGURE 2.3 The Taskbar Options menu is opened by right-clicking on the taskbar.

2. Click Properties on the menu. The Taskbar and Start Menu Properties dialog box appears, and is shown in Figure 2.4.

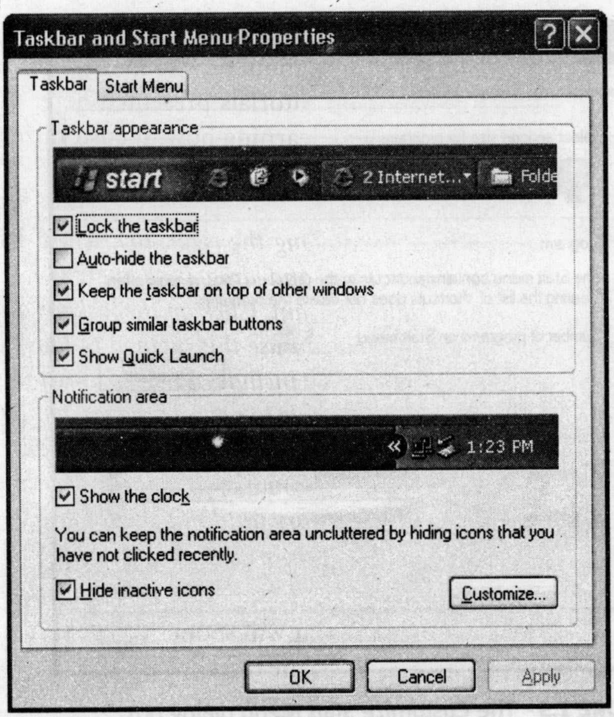

FIGURE 2.4 The Taskbar Properties dialog box.

3. By default the Taskbar page of the Taskbar and Start Menu Properties dialog box is shown. To make sure you have the largest amount of workspace possible, it is a good idea to toggle the auto-hide feature. It is a matter of preference, but it does free up space on your monitor. Select this option. This hides the taskbar. This dialog box also contains the option of having the taskbar always in the foreground, or on top of other applications. As the users you support become more comfortable with the taskbar they can change this on their own if they choose to (and the administrator has not blocked users from configuring their desktops).
4. Click the Start Menu tab to show that page. In Windows XP, Microsoft has provided the option of selecting the Classic Start menu (the same as in previous versions of Windows) or the customizable XP Start menu.
5. Click the Start menu radio button. This selects the new XP customizable Start menu.
6. Click the Customize button next to the Start menu radio button. The Customize Start Menu dialog box appears as shown in Figure 2.5.

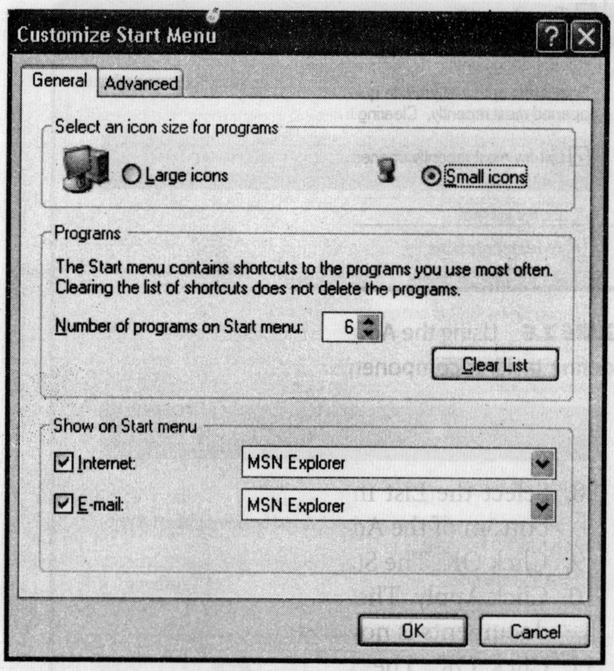

FIGURE 2.5 The Customize Start Menu dialog box.

7. Notice that the Customize Start Menu dialog box contains two tabs. The first is General, and the second, Advanced. Click the Advanced tab. Microsoft's commitment to personalized taskbars is very strong. Notice that in the Start menu items scroll box there are options for customizing the taskbar's many components. Figure 2.6 shows the Advanced page of the Customize Start Menu dialog box.

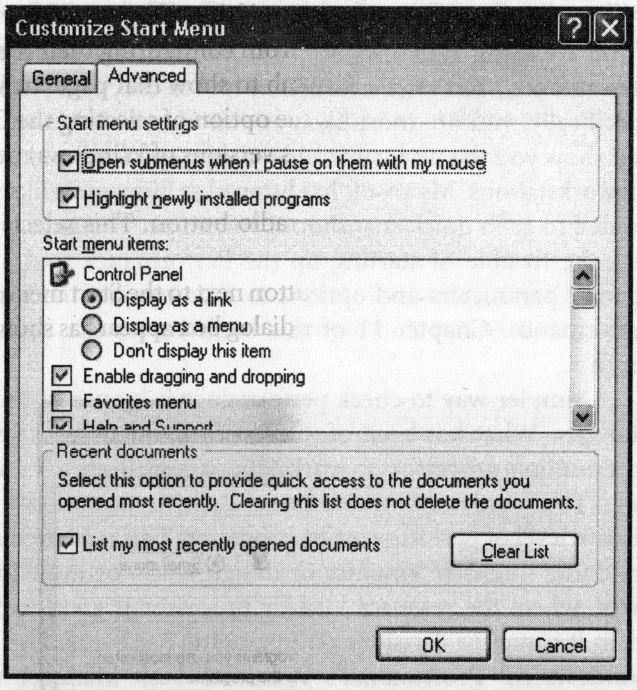

FIGURE 2.6 Using the Advanced options in the Customize Start Menu dialog box to define taskbar components.

8. Select the List my recently opened documents check box at the bottom of the Advanced page.
9. Click OK. The Start Menu tab is again shown.
10. Click Apply. The option for the Start menu to list the most recent documents is now enabled.
11. Click OK. The Taskbar and Menu Properties dialog box now closes.

As you could tell from going through the procedure, there are many alternatives for creating a customized Start menu. You can choose as many or as few of these alternatives as you wish. There is much more depth to the Properties dialog box and there are many possible combinations of configuration options for the taskbar and Start menu. So experiment with the options on the taskbar and see what works best for your approach to getting work done in Windows XP Professional.

Getting a Handle on System Performance–The Windows XP Task Manager

If you are using Windows NT or Windows 2000 you are probably using Performance Monitor/Performance tool to check on system performance. Specifically, you are most likely monitoring object/counter relationships that show you the performance level of your server, network and individual workstations. Microsoft has listened to customers like you and me who wanted to get a quick snapshot of system performance without having to take the trouble of starting up the Performance tool, checking object/counter parameters and options to monitor just the local workstation's performance. Chapter 11 of this book covers the Performance tool in depth.

A simpler way to check performance is by use of the Windows Task Manager. What has been of interest to many users is graphically seeing how multiple processors in workstations contribute to handling processing tasks. The Windows XP Professional Task Manager allows you to check the relative level of performance by processor. This is particularly useful if you are doing intensive graphics or design work, or even software development, where the resource load by processor is good to know, especially when it comes to decisions on upgrading hardware. Figure 2.7 shows the Windows XP Professional's Windows Task Manager monitoring two CPUs and also tracking Page File Usage History. A page file is what Windows XP Professional creates to store virtual memory. The page file is actually a virtual memory swap file that gets assigned the title *pagefile.sys* when created during XP installation.

The Windows XP Task Manager is a very useful tool for checking system performance and tracking the tasks running on a workstation at any time. Unlike the Performance tool, Task Manager doesn't provide TCP/IP connectivity across a network so as to measure performance of other systems—it is standalone but very convenient for measuring the performance of your individual workstation. When Task Manager is active, a small green graph appears on the taskbar. This is the CPU usage meter. This meter will change to reflect the resource load on your system as resource use varies.

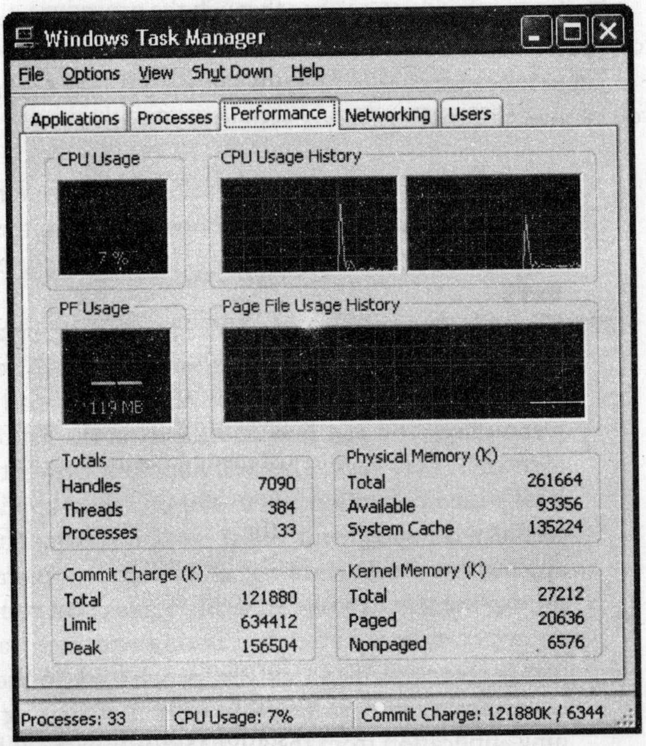

FIGURE 2.7 **Viewing multiple processor performance in Windows XP Task Manager.**

The Task Manager is a tool for administrators and power users for quickly troubleshooting performance issues on an individual system level. This utility is very useful for checking how each application is running. Figure 2.7 shows the Performance page of the Task Manager. Notice that there are five pages in the Windows Task Manager. Notice also the series of metrics shown on the bottom part of the Performance page. These pages and metrics will be discussed in detail later in this chapter.

You can access the Task Manager from any of the three approaches provided below:

- Right-click on the taskbar and click Task Manager from the menu.
- Type **taskmgr** from the Run dialog box in the Start menu.
- Press Ctrl+Alt+Delete to open the Task Manager directly. (In Windows NT and Windows 2000, pressing Ctrl+Alt+Delete opens the User Manager of which the Task Manager is a part.)

Task Manager is divided into five tabs, Applications, Processes, Performance, Networking, and Users.

Let us take a quick tour of the Windows XP Task Manager and see how you can use this tool to analyze system performance.

1. Right-click on the taskbar and select Task Manager. The Windows XP Professional Task Manager opens showing the five tabs for accessing applications, processes, performance, networking, and users.
2. Click the Applications tab. This lists all running applications and their current status. An application's status will be either Running or Not Responding. In the case of an application in a state of not responding, you can first select it from the list on this page and then click End Task. This will hopefully prevent the need to reboot your workstation just to stop an errant application from potentially bringing your entire system down. This will stop the application from running, providing an interim dialog box prompting you to make sure this is an action you want to take. If an application is correctly running and you want to exit, it is highly recommended that you switch back to the original application and close it, saving your work first. Exiting a properly running application from the Task Manager without first saving your work can lead to losing work that has not been saved, so be careful when you exit applications using this approach. Virtual DOS Machines, described later in this book, provide you with "insurance" against errant 16-bit applications causing the entire operating system to crash.
3. Click New Task. The Create New Task dialog box is shown. It is a nonmodal dialog box, meaning it always stays in the forefront of your screen and other applications unless you either click OK or Cancel, type in an application to launch and create a new task, or browse for an application to launch. Note that the New Task dialog box is virtually identical to the Run dialog box from the Start menu. You can also launch applications from the Applications page in the Windows XP Task Manager as well as use a series of dialog boxes provided with this procedure. Figure 2.8 shows the New Task dialog box, which provides you with the option of browsing for executables.
4. Type **REGEDIT** in the Open text box and click OK to launch the Registry Editor. Notice that in the Applications view in the

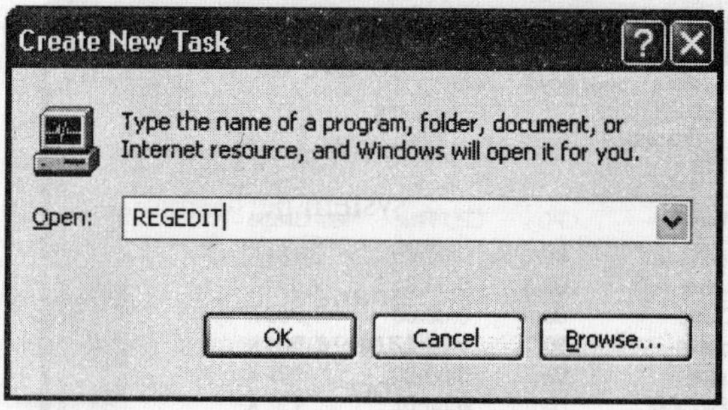

FIGURE 2.8 Using the New Task options in the Task Manager to launch the Registry Editor.

Windows XP Task Manager (Figure 2.9) that the Registry Editor has now been added.

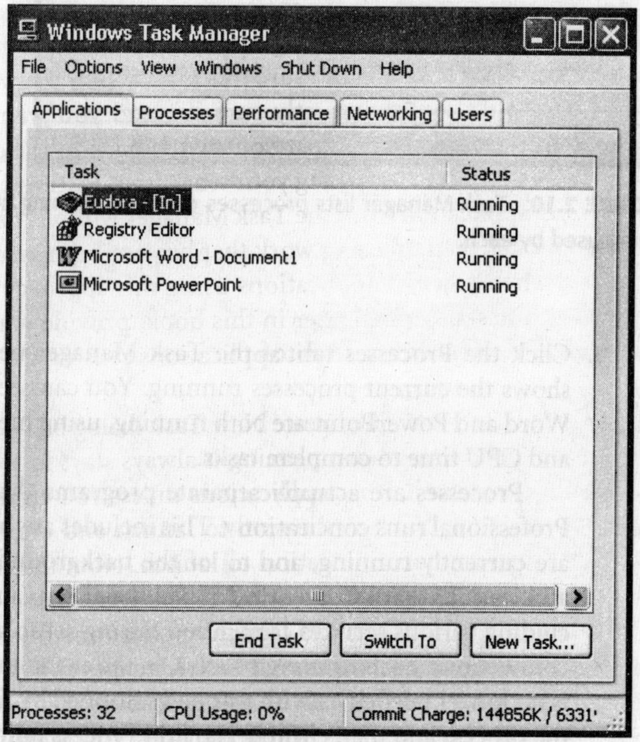

FIGURE 2.9 The Applications page of the Windows Task Manager showing the Registry Editor among other applications.

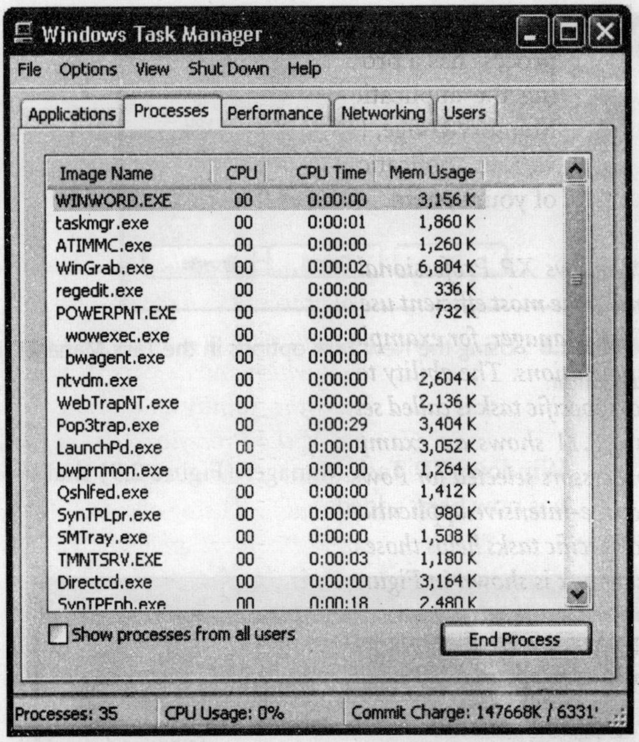

FIGURE 2.10 Task Manager lists processes currently running and the resources being used by each.

5. Click the Processes tab of the Task Manager next. Figure 2.10 shows the current processes running. You can see that Microsoft Word and PowerPoint are both running, using memory resources and CPU time to complete tasks.

   Processes are actually separate programs that Windows XP Professional runs concurrently. This includes any applications you are currently running, and all of the background programs and applications that Windows XP Professional runs automatically, including various services configured during setup and for network connections. Each running process, in the event it malfunctions or is no longer needed, can be manually stopped by first highlighting the process and then clicking the End Process button.

   Processes can be sorted using any of the headings shown along the top row including Image Name, CPU Usage, CPU Time (A measurement showing how much real time, in seconds, that a process has a processor's attention), and Memory Usage. By sorting the applications and processes running by CPU Time and Memory Usage, (Mem Usage for short) you can learn about how various applications and processes impact the overall performance of your system.

Windows XP Professional has the capability on multiprocessor systems to make the most efficient use of processors. In the Processes page of the Windows Task Manager, for example, right-click on any of the third party or nonsystem applications. The ability to set which and how many processors are dedicated to a specific task is called setting the Affinity level for a specific application. Figure 2.11 shows an example of the Processor Affinity dialog box with two processors selected for PowerPoint. Users working with several large, more resource-intensive applications will find being able to apply multiple processors to specific tasks helps those tasks run more smoothly. The Processor Affinity dialog box is shown in Figure 2.11.

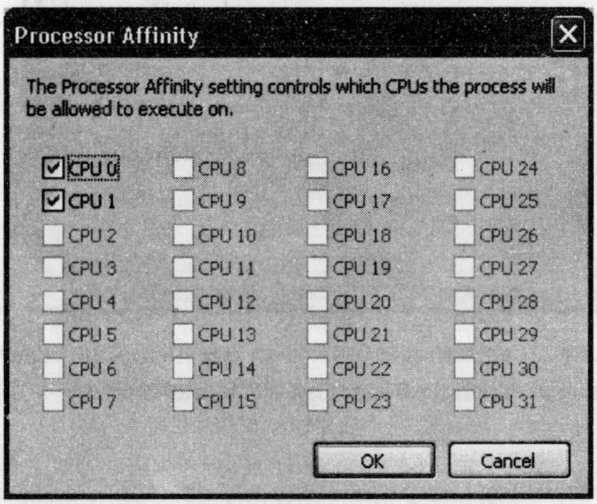

FIGURE 2.11 Using the Processor Affinity dialog box to assign multiple CPUs to a given application or process.

6. Click the Performance tab, and that page of the Windows Task Manager is shown. This page of the Task Manager records the performance of your system with regard to CPU Usage, Memory, Page File System (PF Usage for short), and a trending graph that

shows Page File Usage History. Below the graphs of both processor and Page File performance there are key metrics associated with the usage of Physical and Kernel Memory. Figure 2.12 shows the Performance page of the Windows XP Task Manager utility.

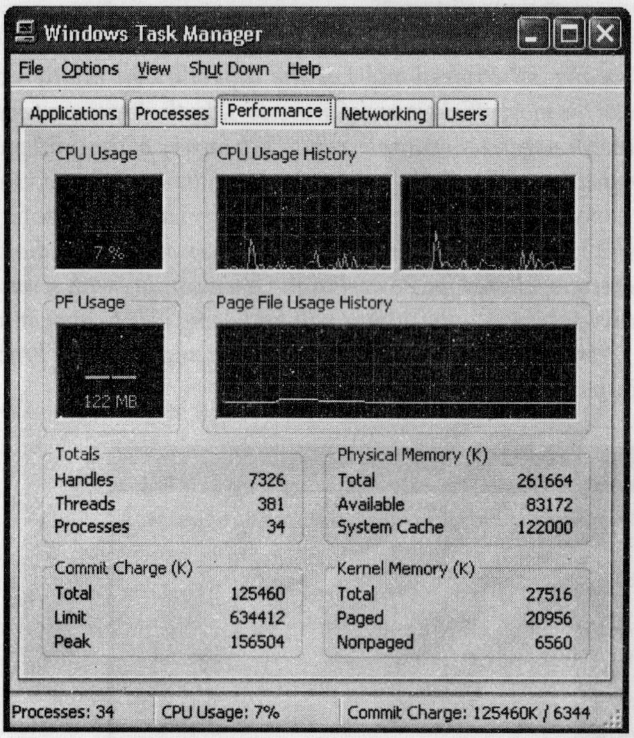

FIGURE 2.12 Task Manager reports on key metrics of performance including threads being used, physical memory, and kernel memory.

The remaining two pages of the Windows XP Task Manager are entitled Networking and Users. Both are self-explanatory and can be easily understood, so instead of going into detail on them, let us get into the many features in the Windows XP Professional Control Panel.

Windows XP Professional Control Panel

With both a new look and several new additions, the Control Panel in Windows XP Professional is a big improvement in the design of common utilities and applets used in this latest generation operating system. The intent of this section is to provide you with a quick tour of the key applets and tools within the Control Panel. Figure 2.13 shows the contents of the Control Panel.

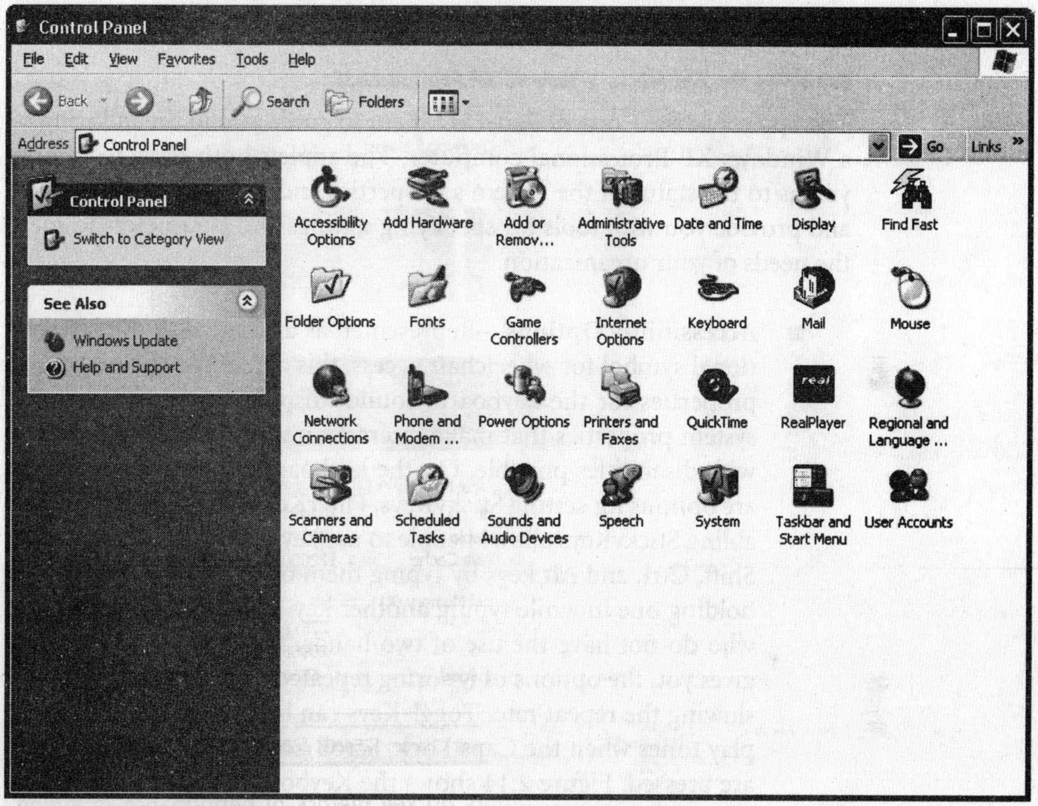

FIGURE 2.13 Windows XP Professional's Control Panel.

Certain installed applications such as RealPlayer and Microsoft Office place their own icons in the Control Panel—these icons are not placed there by Windows XP.

Notice that along the left side of the screen there are two navigation areas, one for getting around in the Control Panel and another for getting the latest additions to XP through the Windows Update button. There is quick access to the Windows Help files as well. Notice along the top of the Control Panel window there is an address box for entering a URL or file path you may want to navigate to. When a URL is entered, Internet Explorer will start and, if there is an Internet connection available, the Web site should appear. If you enter a file path, Windows Explorer will access the file, and if you click the arrow to the right of the address bar, a Windows Explorer display will allow you to browse to any part of the computer or network.

Exploring the Applets in Windows XP Professional

The applets in the Control Panel are there to guide you in the tailoring of a Windows XP Professional computer. The applets both serve to inform you as to the status of the system's properties and performance variables, and provide you with tools for specifying settings and parameters to meet the needs of your organization.

- **Accessibility Options**—Represented as an icon with the international symbol for wheelchair access, this applet focuses on setting properties for the keyboard, sound, display, mouse and general system properties that make interaction with a system for people with disabilities possible. On the keyboard properties page there are options for setting StickyKeys, FilterKeys, and ToggleKeys. Enabling StickyKeys allows people to use key combinations using the Shift, Ctrl, and Alt keys by typing them one at a time rather than holding one in while typing another key (this is useful for people who do not have the use of two hands, for example). FilterKeys gives you the options of ignoring repeated or brief keystrokes and slowing the repeat rate. ToggleKeys can be set to have the system play tones when the Caps Lock, Scroll Lock, and Num Lock keys are pressed. Figure 2.14 shows the Keyboard page of the Accessibility properties dialog box.

  The Sound tab contains options for toggling on SoundSentry and ShowSounds functions, which make visual representations of sounds produced by Windows and by installed programs. The Display tab contains useful options for configuring the display on systems where visually challenged users need to work. Clicking the Settings button provides a large number of options for high-contrast text including black on white text, white on black text, text of various sizes and even different background colors and patterns. The Mouse page allows enabling of the numeric keypad on your keyboard to move the pointer, freeing the user from having to use a mouse. The General page provides you with the option of toggling the automatic reset on or off (it is set for 5 minutes of in-

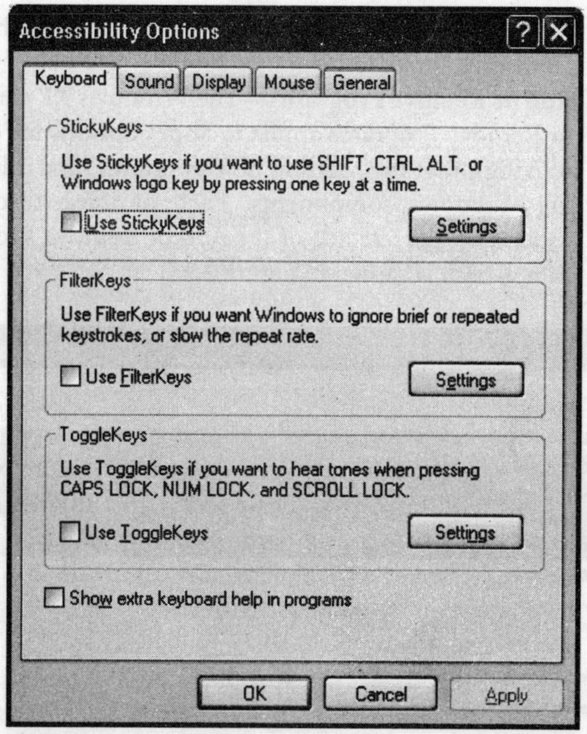

FIGURE 2.14 Keyboard page of the Accessibility Properties dialog box.

activity by default). SerialKey options are also included. SerialKey devices are input devices connected through a serial port that allow alternative methods of computer input. The features of the Accessibility applet are easily configured and can be of great assistance to disabled Windows XP Professional users.

- **Add Hardware**—Represented as a disk drive with a mouse overlaying it, the Add Hardware Wizard is used for finding and installing new and existing hardware on a Windows XP Professional system. The key to the Add Hardware Wizard is the Plug and Play Wizard that was first introduced in Windows 95, and has made significant strides since that point. Double-clicking the Add Hardware Wizard icon launches the Add Hardware Wizard and makes it possible to integrate hardware components into Windows XP Professional. If you have been involved with Windows 2000 as an administrator or even power user, you have most probably spent time in this applet. This applet is very similar to the Add/Remove Hardware applet in Windows 2000.

- **Add or Remove Programs**—The Windows XP edition of the Add or Remove Programs applet includes options for changing or removing programs, adding new programs, and adding or removing Windows components. Each of these three selections is located on the left side of the Add or Remove Programs application, which is shown in Figure 2.15.

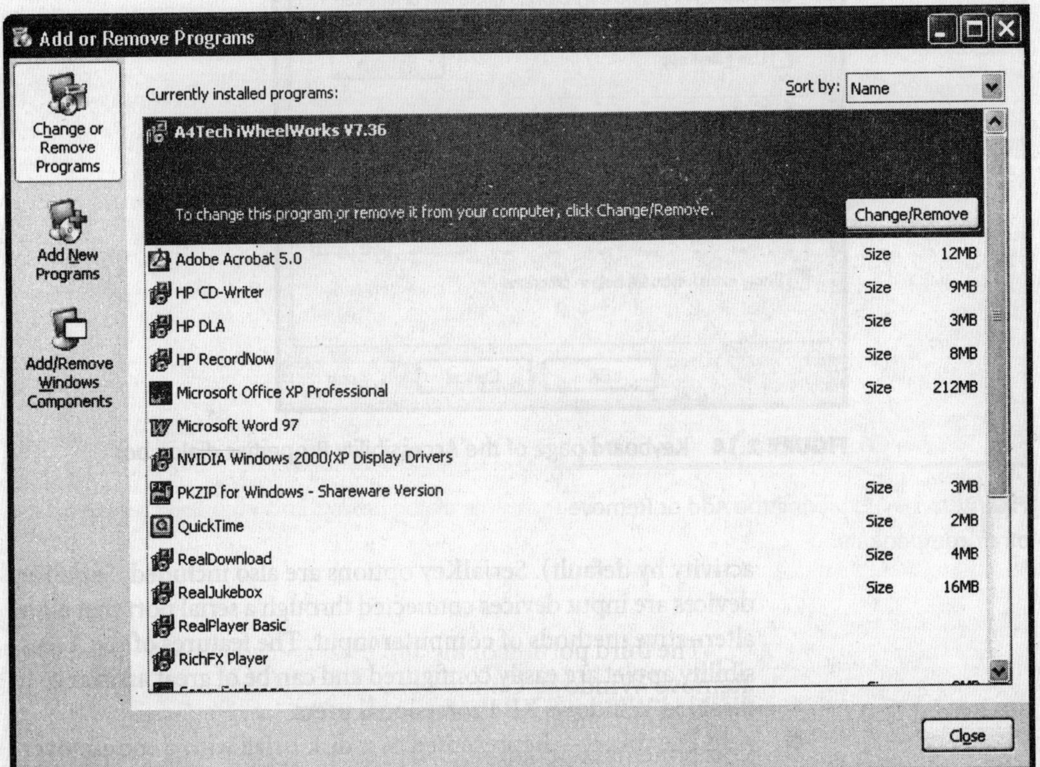

FIGURE 2.15 Exploring the Add/Remove Programs applet.

By default, the view shown in the Change or Remove Programs page is shown first when the Add or Remove Programs applet is selected. Clicking the Add New Programs icon on the left side of the screen gives you the option of adding a program from CD-ROM or floppy. There is also a selection for adding programs from Microsoft, including updates for Windows XP. The Add New Programs screen is shown in Figure 2.16.

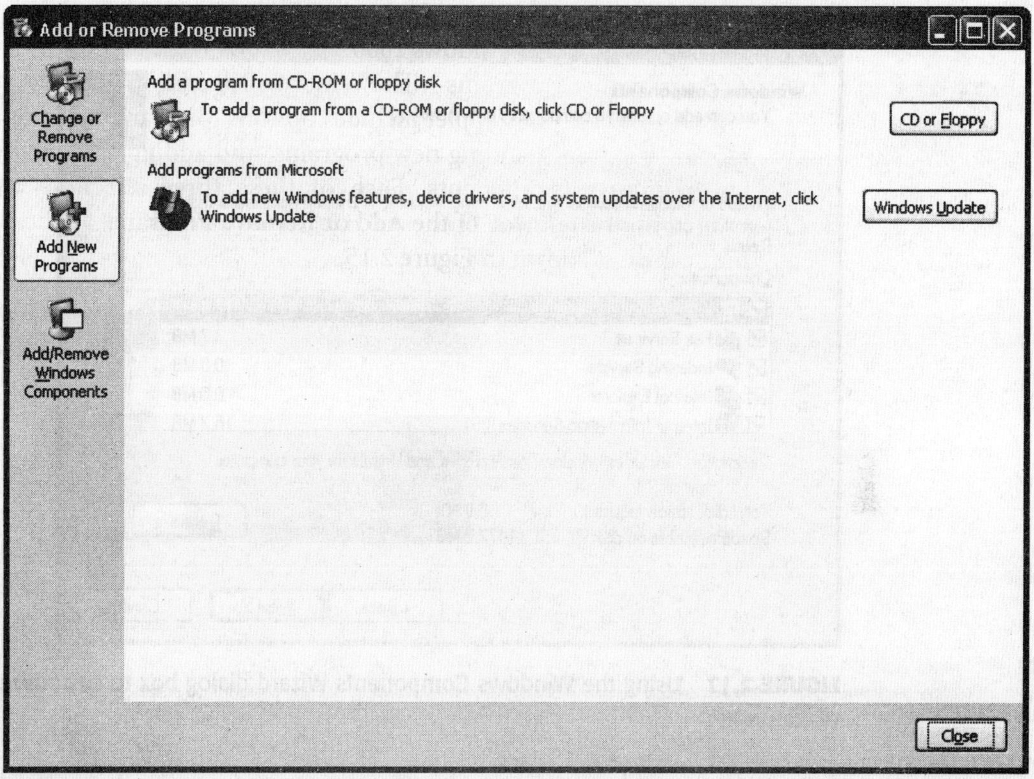

FIGURE 2.16 Exploring the Add or Remove Programs dialog box options for adding programs and other components.

The third portion of the applet is reached by clicking the Add/Remove Windows Components icon. This brings up the Windows Components Wizard which is used for determining which components supplied with Windows are to be installed or uninstalled. Figure 2.17 shows the Windows Components Wizard dialog box.

In the Components scroll box you will see various categories of Windows components. Selecting the check box next to each category instructs the wizard to install all of the subcomponents in that category. To view a list of the individual programs that make up a category, highlight the category and click Details. A new page appears with the category's subcomponents listed. You can select individual subcomponents if you want only those subcomponents to be installed. If you have, after you click OK you will notice that

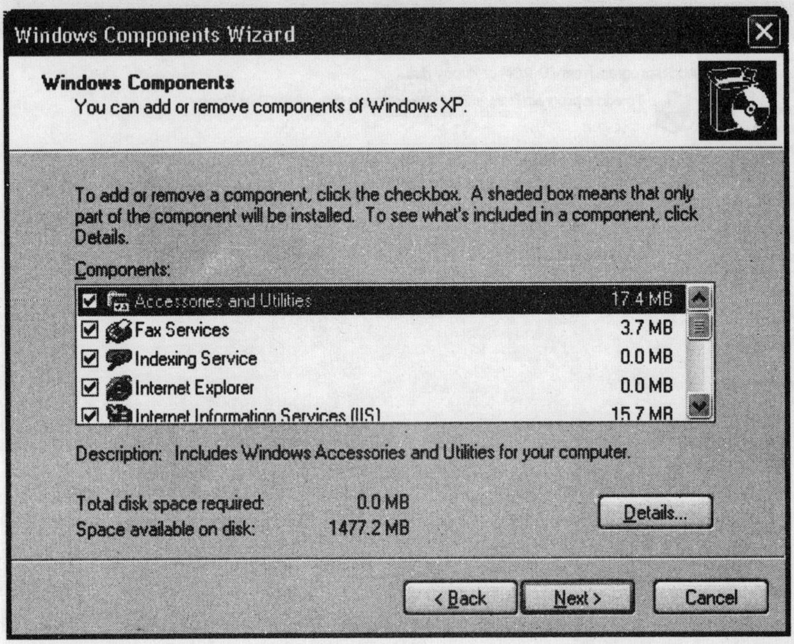

FIGURE 2.17 Using the Windows Components Wizard dialog box to customize Windows XP.

the check box for the component category is checked and shaded, indicating that some but not all of the subcomponents are set to be installed. Go through all of the components and subcomponents to fully familiarize yourself with the many Windows programs you can install.

- **Administrative Tools** –Represented as an icon with a file folder in the background and a hammer and screw driver in front of the disk drive, the Administrative Tools in Windows XP Professional show an improvement over those in Windows NT and Windows 2000. There are the comparable applications you may be accustomed to seeing in the Administrative Tools of Windows NT in addition to several new applications. Figure 2.18 shows the contents of the Administrative Tools in Control Panel. Notice that every one of the tools in this dialog box is actually a shortcut. By default, Windows shortcut icons including the ones in Administative Tools have a small arrow pointing towards two o'clock on their lower left-hand corner (you may also notice that next to each

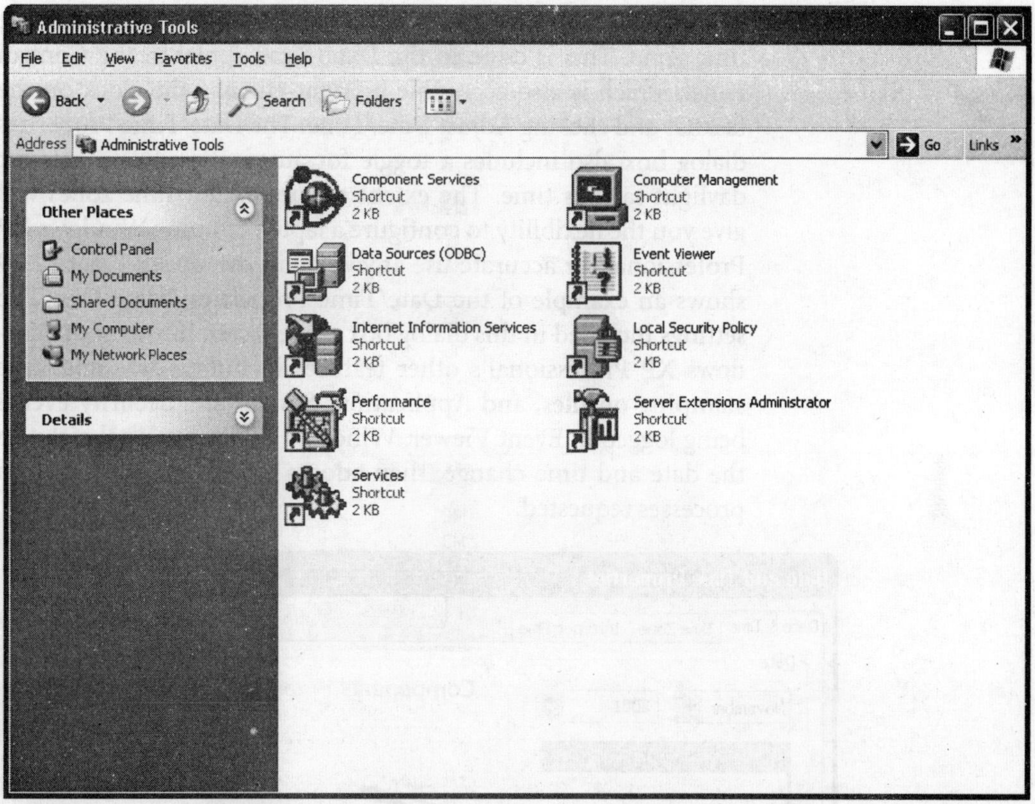

FIGURE 2.18 Contents of the Administrative Tools applet in the Control Panel.

icon is the word "Shortcut"). This signifies that the applications are not actually stored in this location; they are stored in subdirectories of the <system_root> folder.

The various default components of Administrative Tools, Component Services, Data Sources (ODBC), Internet Information Services, Performance, Services, Computer Management, Event Viewer, Local Security Policy, and Server Extensions Administrator are all discussed in detail in later chapters of this book. Other components may appear in Administrative Tools depending on the Windows components that are installed on the computer.

- **Date/Time**—Many Windows XP Professional-based workstations, when first shipped, have the date and time already set from the manufacturer's time zone. As an administrator you will in the majority of cases need to reset the date and time, specifically the time zone. This is done in the Date/Time applet in the Control Panel, which is also accessible by right-clicking the clock on the taskbar and clicking Adjust Date/Time. The Date/Time Properties dialog box also includes a toggle for automatic adjustments for daylight savings time. The extent of support for time zones will give you the flexibility to configure a laptop running Windows XP Professional for accurate use anywhere in the world. Figure 2.19 shows an example of the Date/Time Properties dialog box. The settings included in this dialog box are reflected throughout Windows XP Professional's other features including date and time stamping on files, and Application, System and Security events being logged in Event Viewer. Windows XP Professional picks up the date and time change, then adopts the revised settings into processes requested.

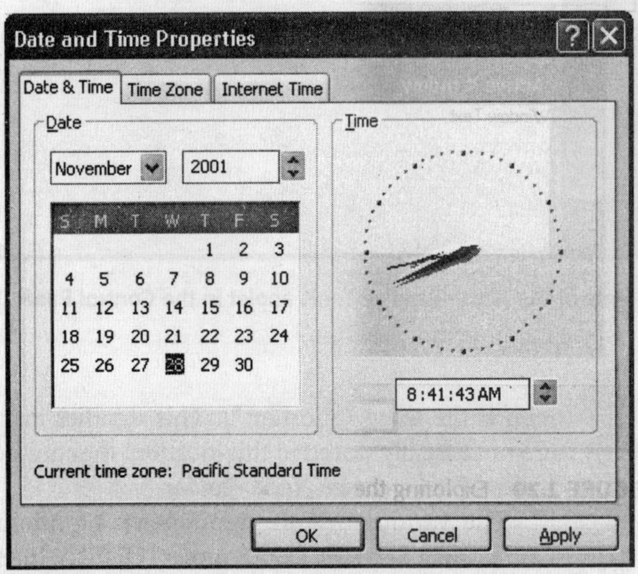

FIGURE 2.19 Using the Date/Time Properties dialog box.

- **Display**—One of the most commonly used applets or utilities in Windows XP, the Display applet includes many useful options for customizing the appearance of the desktop. The contents of this applet are also directly accessible from the desktop by right-clicking on a portion of the screen with no icons and selecting Properties.

You can use the Display dialog box to set many options including Themes (collections of appearance and sound settings), Desktop (the background), Screen Saver, Appearance (the styles and colors of windows and buttons, plus font size), and Settings (hardware options). Figure 2.20 shows the Display Properties dialog box with the five tabs across the top.

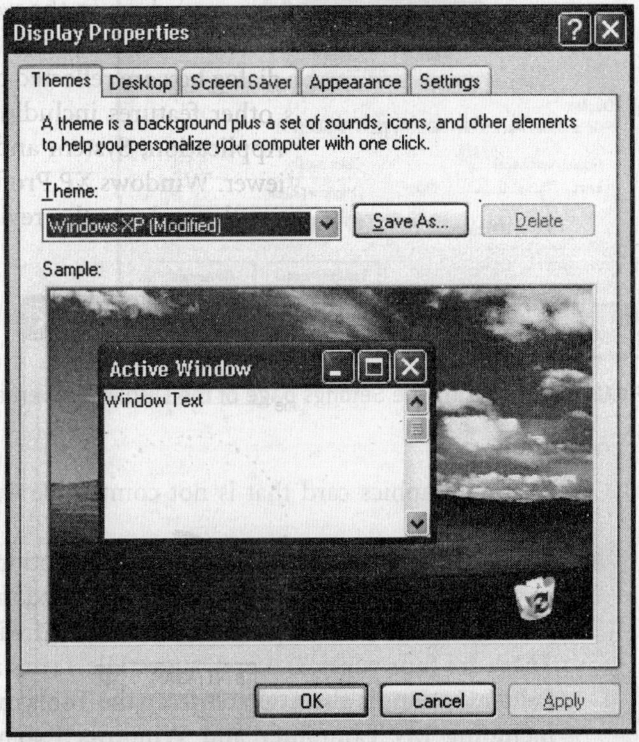

FIGURE 2.20 Exploring the Display Properties dialog box.

Clicking the Settings tab of the Display Properties dialog box causes the settings for configuring your monitor's resolution and color quality to be shown. Figure 2.21 shows this page.

One of the new developments in Windows XP Professional is the greatly expanded support for the nVidia chipset that is used in many of the graphics cards in distribution today. Microsoft's support for the GeForce chipset, another high-quality device, is outstanding, and is worth considering as an upgrade if you have an

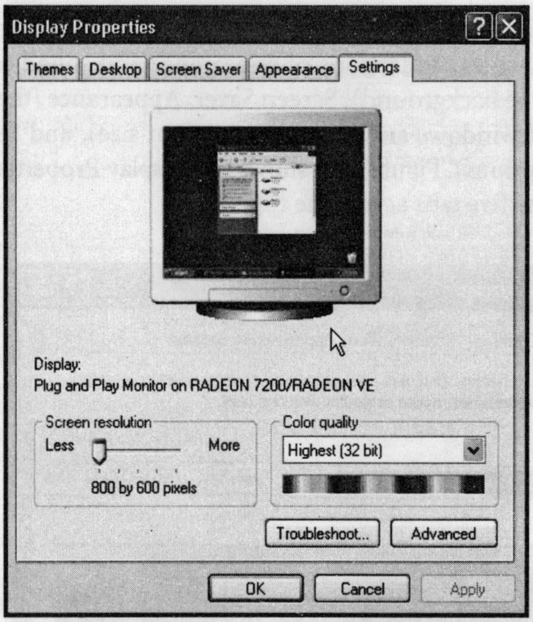

FIGURE 2.21 Using the Settings page of the Display Properties dialog box.

existing graphics card that is not compatible with Windows XP Professional.

- **Folder Options**—Folder Options includes options for configuring how folders and files appear and are opened, browsed, and accessed, and also which program is associated with each file type. There are four pages, General, View, File Types and Offline Files. Folder Options is also available from the Tools menu of any folder including My Computer and Windows Explorer. Figure 2.22 shows the Folder Options dialog box
- **Fonts**—This is not actually an applet, it is a subfolder containing font files. File icons with 'TT' or 'O' on them are TrueType fonts, while the ones with an 'A' are Adobe fonts. Clicking Install New Font from the File menu presents a dialog box for locating and installing font files. The Details command and option to hide or display font file variations (in the View menu) are useful when managing a larger set of fonts. Figure 2.23 shows the Fonts folder.
- **Game Controllers**—Microsoft includes an applet specifically for configuring game controllers in an operating system. An easy dialog box to navigate, the Game Controllers box is shown in Figure 2.24. There is an abundance of support for the many game

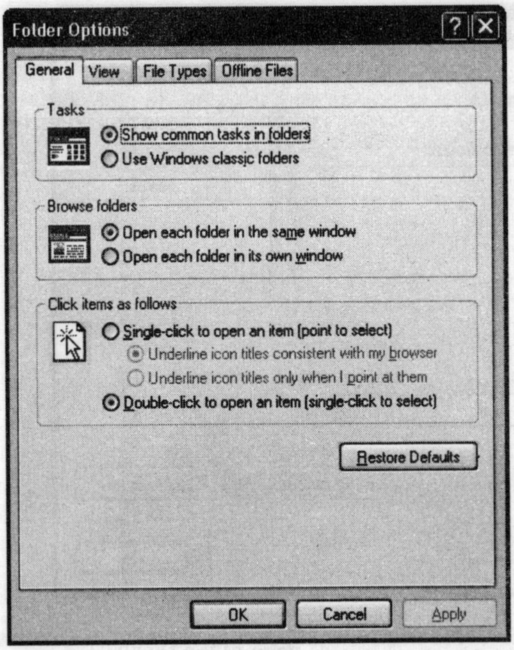

FIGURE 2.22 Exploring the Folder Options applet in the Control Panel.

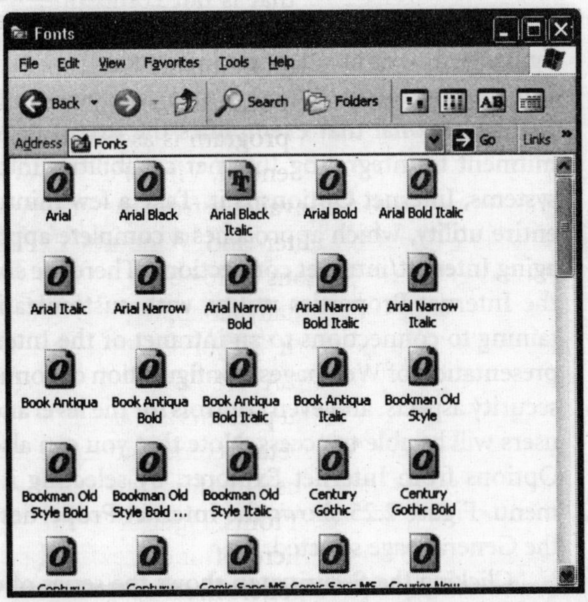

FIGURE 2.23 Using the Fonts folder to review all available typefaces in Windows XP Professional.

FIGURE 2.24 Game controller support is available in Windows XP Professional.

controllers on the market today, accessible through the Add button in the Game Controllers dialog box. Plenty of options for configuring game controllers are included.

- **Internet Options**—If there is a single applet or utility in Windows XP Professional that exemplifies the extent of Microsoft's commitment to integrating Internet capabilities into their operating systems, Internet Options is it. Take a few minutes and tour this entire utility, which approaches a complete application for managing Internet/intranet connections. There are six specific areas of the Internet Properties utility, with customization options pertaining to connections to an intranet or the Internet, storage and presentation of Web pages, configuration of connections and their security aspects, and even controls for the level and type of content users will be able to access. Note that you can also access Internet Options from Internet Explorer, by selecting it from the Tools menu. Figure 2.25 shows the Internet Properties dialog box with the General page selected.

  Clicking the Security tab shows the series of different security settings for different "zones" of Web content. There are four zones

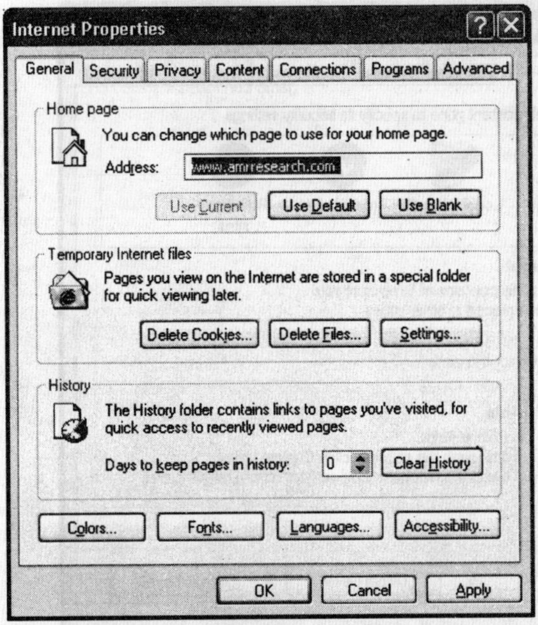

FIGURE 2.25 Setting home page parameters and managing Internet files is easy using the Internet Properties utility.

included in this dialog box by default. These four zones include one dedicated to general Internet access, one to local intranet access, one for trusted sites, and a fourth for restricted sites. Each of these can be configured for High (most secure), Medium, Low, or Custom. Figure 2.26 shows the Security page with options selected for the Internet Zone access profile. This profile will be used when the system accesses Internet sites located outside the firewall of a network.

Clicking the Custom Level button causes the Security Settings page to appear, showing the available options. There are options for Active X controls, downloads, Java permissions, navigation, scripting, user authentication, and many other areas.

Settings in this applet are determined by the version of Internet Explorer installed. Windows XP comes with Internet Explorer 6.0. As Explorer is updated, these settings are also subject to change.

The Privacy tab is new and contains many options for restricting cookies. Cookies are files that are placed on computers by Web sites in order to keep track of information pertaining to individuals' use of that Web site.

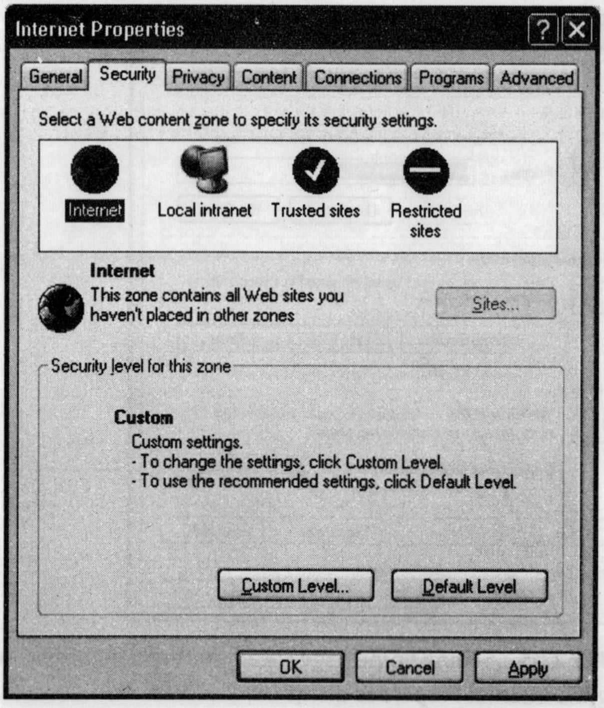

FIGURE 2.26 Setting Security for Internet Access.

The Content tab is shown in Figure 2.27. The Ratings options on the top of this page provide you with the flexibility of controlling the Internet content viewable on the workstation.

From within the Ratings area of the Content dialog box it is possible to filter access to Web sites using the rating service developed by the Recreational Software Advisory Council on the Internet. Based on the work of Dr. Donald F. Roberts of Stanford University, who has studied the effects of media for nearly 20 years, Microsoft has given system administrators the ability to configure computers to filter Internet content based on these standards.

Also included on the Content page are options for viewing certificates for individuals, sites, or publishers. Certificates verify that Web sites are what they purport to be.

Connection, Programs, and Advanced are the three remaining tabs. Additional chapters of this book will cover these areas of the Internet Properties dialog box in the contexts of creating Web sites and home pages, and enabling intranets within your organization.

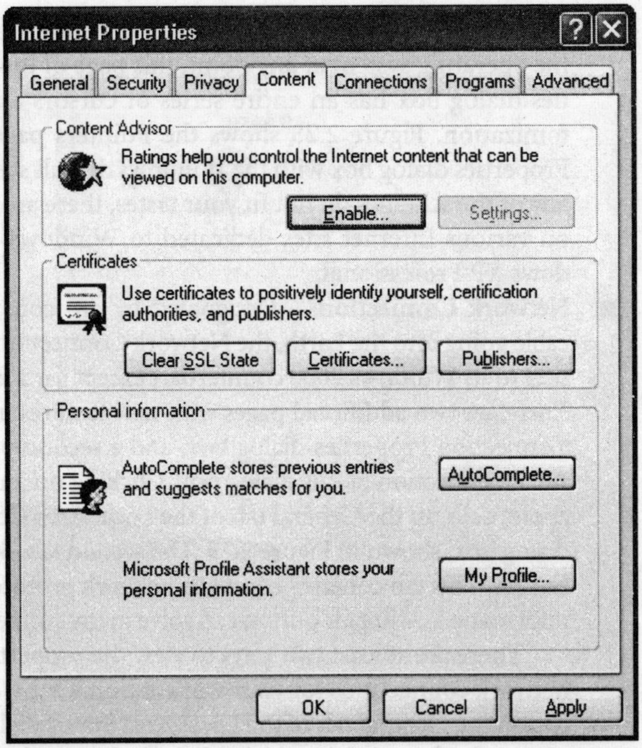

FIGURE 2.27 Content customization is possible through the use of the Internet Properties dialog box.

- **Keyboard**—Provides customization options for the keyboard and related items. There are two pages in the Keyboard Properties dialog box. The first is dedicated to speed parameters and includes sliders for adjusting the character repeat delay, character repeat rate, and cursor blink rate. The second page contains hardware properties.
- **Mouse**—This is familiar ground for any of you who have set up mice before on any other Microsoft operating system. By default, there are four tabs in this applet. Other tabs may appear depending on the type of mouse installed. By default, the first tab is for configuring buttons on the mouse. This page focuses on configuring the mouse for left- or right-handed use, and the setting of the double-click speed for the buttons. The Pointers page is used for customizing the specific scheme you want to use for your cursors.

Since cursors can be in multiple states depending on the activity of the operating system at any point, this page of the Mouse Properties dialog box has an entire series of cursors available for customization. Figure 2.28 shows the Pointers page of the Mouse Properties dialog box with the Windows default scheme selected. If any of the schemes do not fit your tastes, there are plenty available on various Internet sites dedicated to Windows 2000 and Windows XP Professional.

- **Network Connections**—Designated by an icon with a network cable going into the Earth, the Network Connections applet is identical to its Windows 2000 counterpart except for a few new features. There are two additional pages with new features in the Local Area Connection Properties dialog box, and a second page in the Local Area Connection Status dialog box. Clicking on an icon within the applet calls up the General tab of the Local Area Connection Status dialog box, shown in Figure 2.29. The second tab, Support, is a new feature. This tab contains complete network protocol configuration information. A Repair button can solve many connection problems.

  There are at least two ways to view the properties of any of the network connections for your workstation. One is to click Properties on the General tab of the Local Area Status dialog box (see Figure 2.29). The other is to right click on the Local Area Connection icon. Click Properties on the menu that appears. Either method brings up the Local Area Connection Properties dialog box, which is shown in Figure 2.30.
- **Phone and Modem Options**—This utility is used for installing a new modem or changing properties for an existing modem. The three pages that comprise this utility include Dialing Rules, Modems, and Advanced. Figure 2.31 shows the Modems Properties dialog box with the General page visible.
- **Power Options**—Power management in Windows XP Professional is comprehensive and easy to use, and very complete in its implementation. Figure 2.32 shows the contents of the Power Options Properties dialog box showing the Power Schemes page.

  From the Power Schemes page, there is a menu for selecting from the following power schemes: Home/Office Desk, Portable/Laptop, Always On, Presentation, Minimal Power Management and Max Battery. In conjunction with these options there are options for configuring the turn-off times for monitors and hard disks.

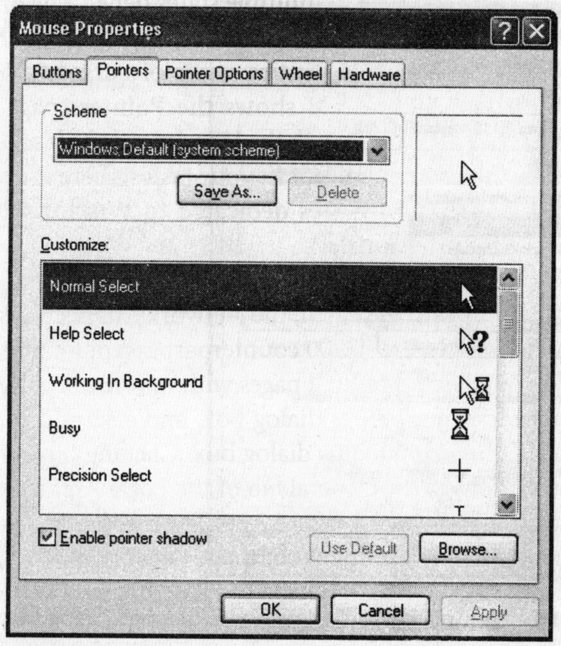

FIGURE 2.28 Configuring Pointers using the options in the Mouse Properties applet.

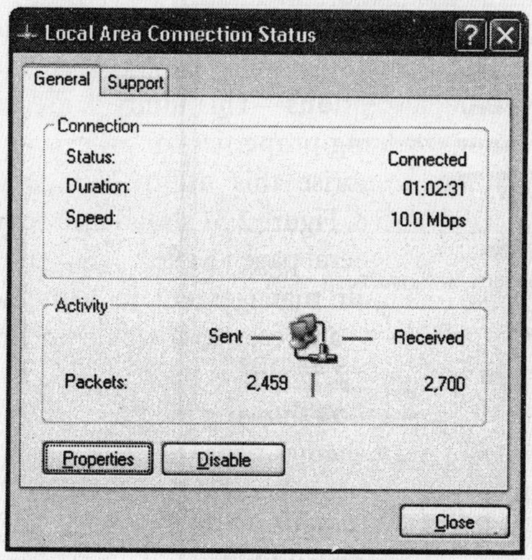

FIGURE 2.29 Windows XP Professional includes the capability to monitor the status of network connections.

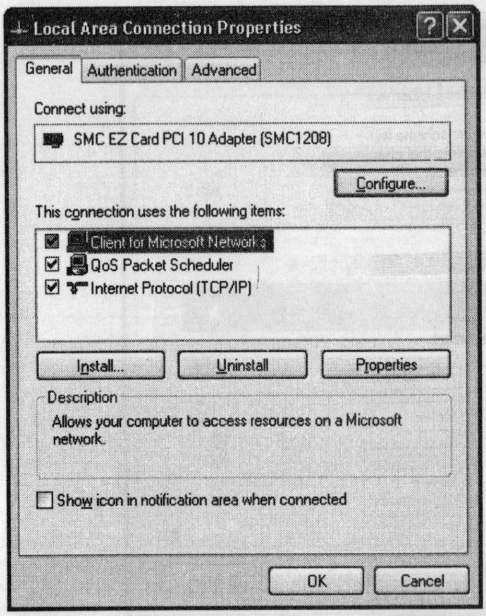

FIGURE 2.30 The Local Area Connection Properties dialog box contains three pages.

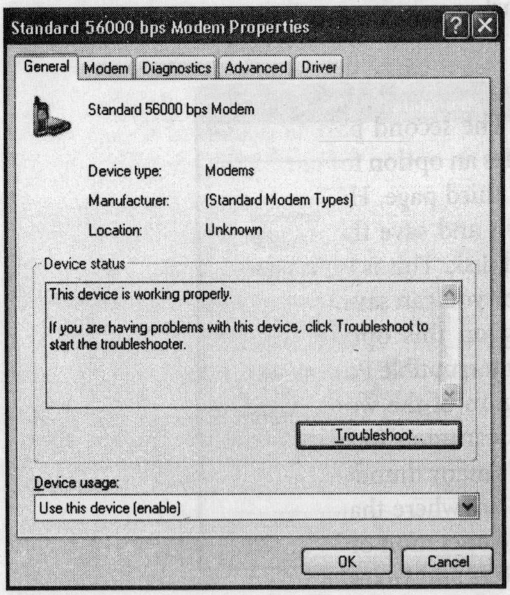

FIGURE 2.31 Using the Modems Properties dialog box to manage modem connections.

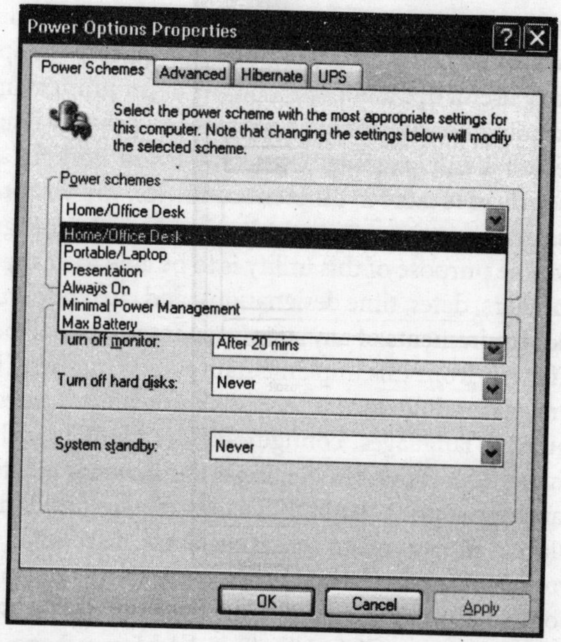

FIGURE 2.32 Extensive Support for Power Management is available in Windows XP Professional.

The second page is dedicated to advanced functions and includes an option for having the power meter appear on the taskbar. The third page, Hibernate, provides for your system to shut itself down and save the memory's current contents to your system's hard disk. This is very useful for laptops, and as a system administrator you can save the people you serve a lot of headaches by toggling on this option. The fourth page, UPS, which stands for Uninterruptible Power Supply, is invaluable, especially if you live in a region of the world that has sporadic power outages. UPSs are very common in the Midwestern United States because of that area's many thunderstorms, for example. However, UPSs should be used anywhere that power failures can cause significant problems to the operation of an organization.

- **Printers and Faxes**—In Windows NT and Windows 2000, this was referred to as just "Printers." Chapter 5, *Working with Printers in Windows XP Professional,* explains in detail how to use this applet. Installing support for a new printer using the Add Printer Wizard is actually pretty easy to do, and as an administrator you will be able to teach others how to accomplish this quickly. Chapter 5 provides many useful tips and tricks on how to get printers up and running, including how to troubleshoot network printing issues.

- **Regional and Language Options**—If you work for a company that has offices located in different countries, you will probably need to customize settings using the Regional and Language Options utility. The purpose of this utility is to be able to change the format of numbers, dates, time designations, and currency symbols to match the requirements of any supported international location. What is different from this implementation in Windows XP Professional? One major difference is the ability to read and write documents in multiple languages, configurable on the Regional Settings page. Figure 2.33 shows the Regional Options tab of the Regional and Language Options utility. The second page of this dialog box, Languages, allows you to select keyboard drivers for every language from Afrikaans to Uzbek (there are 94 languages and language versions supported). Click Details to call up the Settings page. In Installed Services, click Add. The Add Input Language dialog box appears. Between the two drop-down list boxes there are hundreds of options for languages/countries and keyboard layouts.
- **Sounds and Audio Devices**—Previously entitled *Multimedia*, in Windows XP Professional the same series of tools is now referred to as the *Sound and Audio Devices* applet. It includes a series of options for configuring audio, video, MIDI, CD Music and multimedia devices. You can configure the sound mixer for both playing and recording to determine relative levels of different sound sources, such as microphone, system sounds, and CD audio. Other settings include options for playing back video files, designation of a drive as the default player for audio CDs, and configuration options for multimedia devices, including MIDI devices. Figure 2.34 shows the Hardware page of the Sounds and Audio Devices applet.
- **System**—Provides a comprehensive series of pages for defining the system parameters, options, and performance enhancements you can choose to include in a system's profile. This is an area of the Control Panel where any administrator needs to take some time and get familiar with the many features included. This is useful from the standpoint of getting new and existing hardware up and running quickly. If you are a system administrator who gets a lot of requests for troubleshooting slow performance or hardware incompatibilities, the System applet is the place to begin looking.

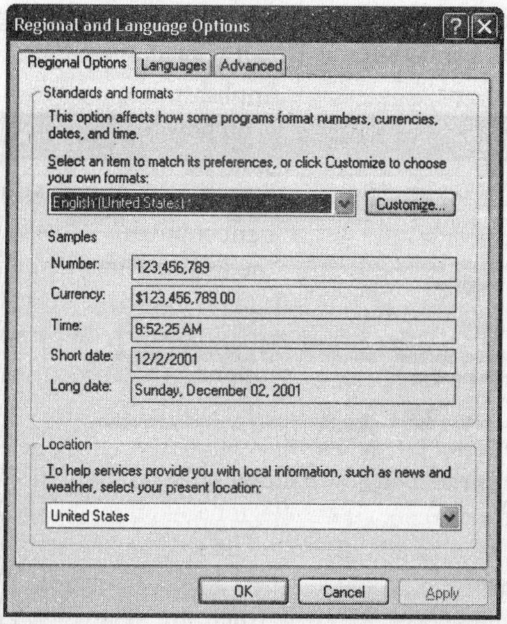

FIGURE 2.33 Using the Regional and Language Options Properties to set filters for displaying numbers, currencies, dates and time in formats for different countries.

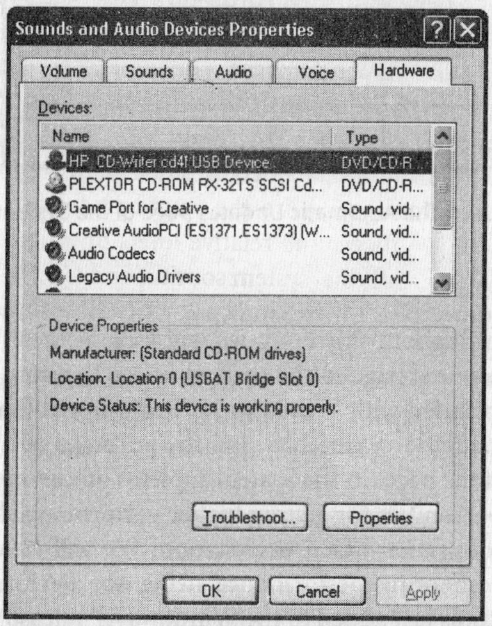

FIGURE 2.34 Configuring multimedia devices with the Devices options in the Sounds and Audio Devices applet.

Figure 2.35 shows one of the more advanced pages of the System applet, the Automatic Updates page.

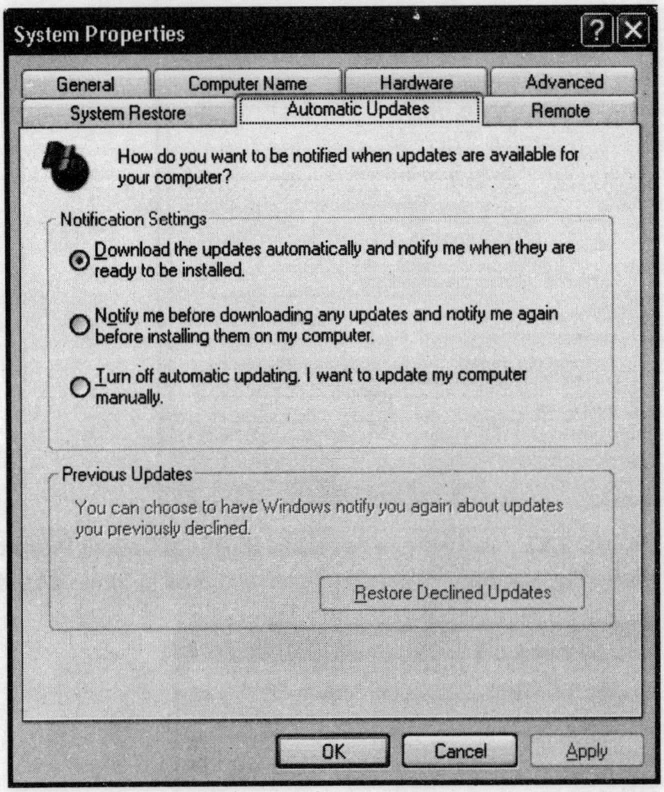

FIGURE 2.35 Using the Automatic Updates page of the System Properties dialog box.

Throughout this book we will look at these variables on the Environment page in the context of the Registry, which is a database included with Windows XP Professional that is used for setting system-level variables. For the purposes of our tour, click on each of the pages in the System applet. You can see there are plenty of opportunities for getting higher performance from a Windows XP Professional-based workstation. We will cover the aspects of troubleshooting performance using the Performance tool and other tools just added to the Windows XP release that provide you insights into a system's and networks' performance.

The next time you are in front of a dual-boot computer containing Windows NT, 2000, or XP Professional as one of its operating systems while it is booting up, you will see a complete list of all the operating systems loaded on that system. This is called FlexBoot. Originally developed on the UNIX platform, FlexBoot gives you an opportunity to choose the operating system you want to use for a given session. Notice how the FlexBoot is organized. You control the sequence of the operating systems list by using the Startup/Shutdown page of the System applet. There are a multitude of reasons why this is a very useful tool if you have a dual or multiple-boot system. Perhaps the best is that it gives your users an easy way to choose the desired operating system. Figure 2.36 shows the System Startup option on the Startup/Shutdown page of the System applet.

Two more applets, Taskbar and Start Menu, and User Accounts are covered elsewhere in this book.

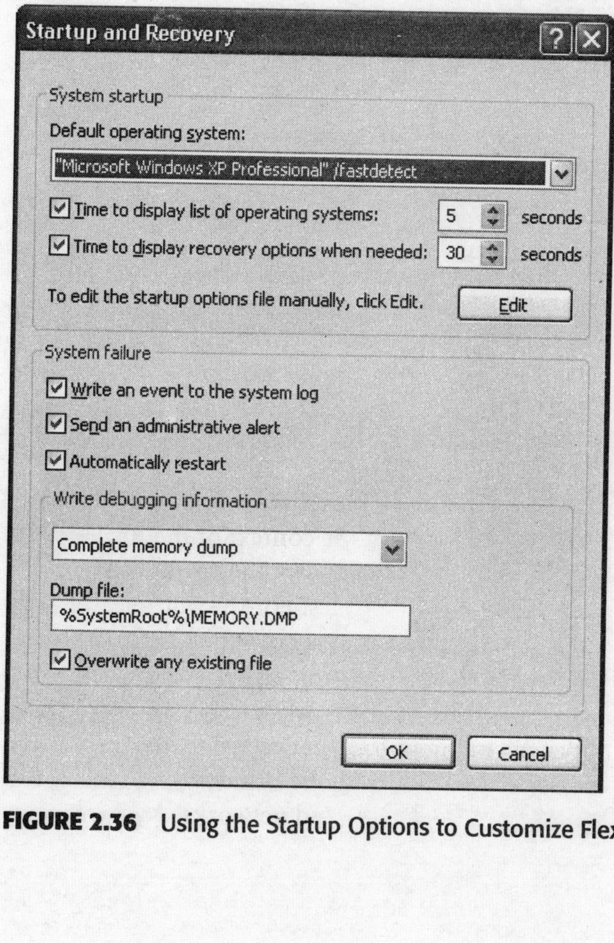

FIGURE 2.36 Using the Startup Options to Customize FlexBoot.

CHAPTER SUMMARY

What truly differentiates Windows XP Professional from previous versions of this operating system? The addition of new features and enhancements to existing utilities and applets in the Control Panel and enhancements to the taskbar is the answer. The integration of Internet and intranet-based capabilities is stronger than ever—especially in the Internet Options applet that is found in the Control Panel. There are options within this applet for configuring security aspects of Web surfing and toggling on the use of Java and scripting.

This chapter focused on the hands-on aspects of configuring a Windows XP Professional desktop, and includes a roadmap for getting around in the Control Panel. Many of the more detailed aspects of troubleshooting and working with Windows XP Professional are covered in later chapters of this book.

3 Customizing the Desktop and Exploring Commonly Used System Properties in Windows XP Professional

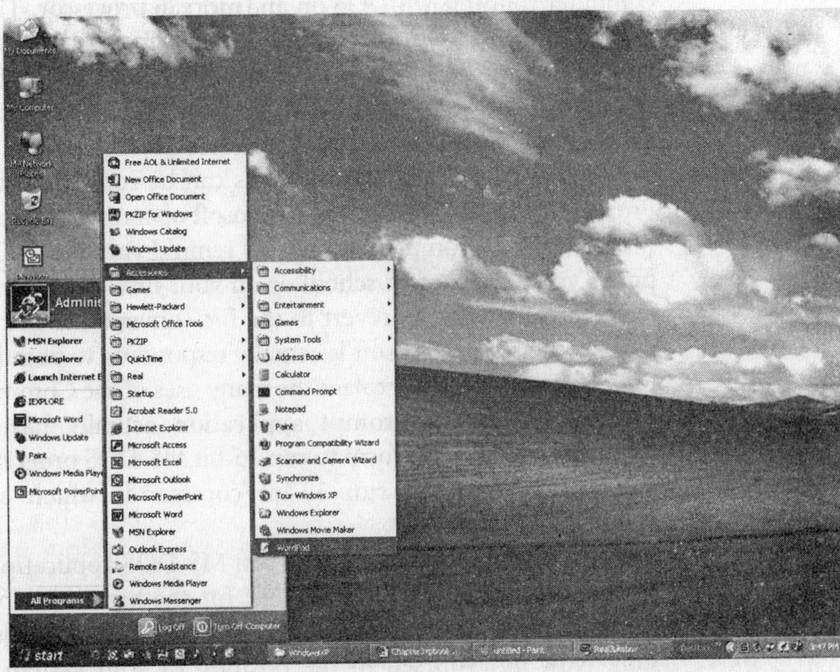

INTRODUCTION

There are a host of changes in the tools of Windows XP Professional and Windows XP Home Edition, many of which provide users with more flexibility than has been possible before for managing networks and distributed environments, and accessing the Internet.

The intent of this chapter is to provide you with a thorough understanding of the role properties play in Windows XP Professional. If you are a systems administrator you will find this chapter a useful tour for teaching others how to manage the features of Windows XP Professional.

THE COMMAND PROMPT

The Command Prompt, found on all versions of Windows NT since 3.1, plus Windows 2000 and XP, is a 32-bit application that simulates a whole computer running MS-DOS on an Intel x86 processor. This is an updated version of the MS-DOS prompt found on Windows 3.x and 9x. The difference is that the MS-DOS prompt actually used the MS-DOS shell under those versions of Windows. When the Command Prompt is opened it starts a virtual DOS machine (VDM). Many TCP/IP, network administration, and system maintenance commands can be run through the Command Prompt. If you have been using Microsoft operating systems for a long time the Command Prompt window may remind you of MS-DOS-based computers you have used in school or on your first job. Why, you might ask, would anyone want to revert to the file conventions and command lines that time forgot? Microsoft is actually responding to popular demand. The rest of this section will explain the many uses of the Command Prompt.

The Command Prompt application actually has two functions. One is to provide a platform to run 16-bit MS-DOS programs on Windows XP. The other is to run 32-bit commands which are available in Windows XP.

Given a choice of whether to run MS-DOS applications on your own workstation, you would mostly opt for the higher-performance, multi-threaded version of your favorite applications instead of the MS-DOS version. Now put yourself in the position of your system administration colleagues at companies that used MS-DOS based applications for communicating between various systems. You will find that Windows XP supports running MS-DOS applications either directly from the Command Prompt window or alternatively by clicking on the application from within Windows Explorer. Do you wonder if one of those approaches provides better performance on your MS-DOS applications? The Command Prompt window actually is a shade faster due to overhead saved by not running the program through the Windows XP graphical interface.

Is Windows XP Professional actually loaded on top of MS-DOS? No. Windows NT, 2000, and XP are not loaded on top of MS-DOS. So where do the applications actually run? The answer is in a protected memory subsystem, which is a key component of the architecture of the Windows XP operating system. Within the set of Microsoft operating systems, protected memory subsystems are specific to Windows NT, 2000 and XP, and ensure that each type of application supported has its own memory address space to complete calculations. There are protected memory subsystems within Windows XP Professional built specifically to support MS-DOS, Win16, and Win32.

Using Properties to Customize the Command Prompt

You will find that many of the utilities included in Windows XP Professional have properties associated with them. The Command Prompt has a series of properties you can use to customize the font, colors, and layout, in addition to setting cursor size and the amount of command history to save. You can adjust these properties to make the Command Prompt easier to use.

These steps illustrate how to access the Command Prompt's properties.

1. Click the C:_ icon in the upper left corner of the Command Prompt window. A menu appears, as shown in Figure 3.1.

FIGURE 3.1 Accessing the Command Prompt Properties.

2. Click Properties. The "Command Prompt" Properties dialog box appears as shown in Figure 3.2.

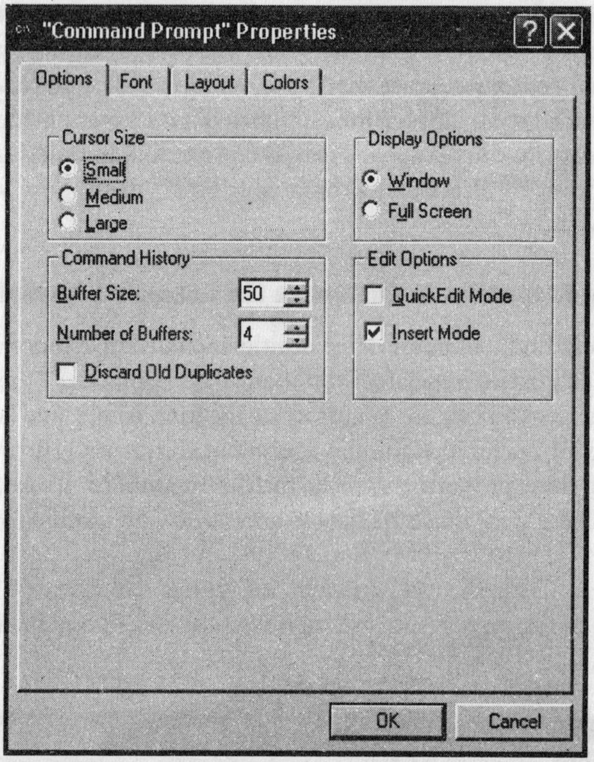

FIGURE 3.2 The "Command Prompt" Properties dialog box.

3. Click the Layout tab. The Screen Buffer Size, Window Size, and Window Position variables are all shown. You can also override the system's default locations for the Command Prompt window by clearing the Let System Position Window check box.
4. Click the Colors tab. This is the page where you can set the colors of the Command Prompt window's background and text. Figure 3.3 shows an example of the Colors page of the "Command Prompt" Properties dialog box.
5. Click the Font tab. This is the page that is used for setting the font of the characters used in the Command Prompt window. You can

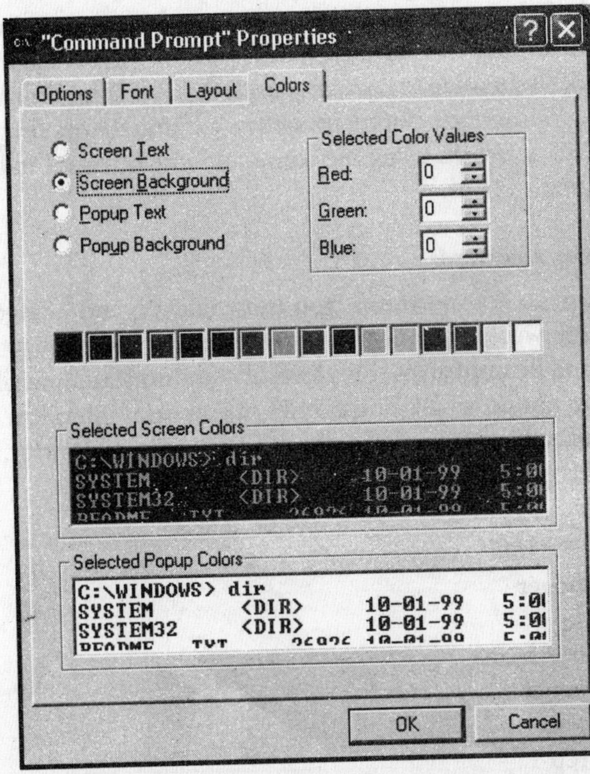

FIGURE 3.3 Exploring the Colors page of the "Command Prompt" Properties dialog box.

see that there are options available. Choose the one that is most readable for you.

6. Click OK. The "Command Prompt" Properties dialog box closes, showing the Active Desktop.

What Can You Use the Command Prompt For?

If your organization has standardized on an MS-DOS application, you will find the Command Prompt a useful utility for getting these programs up and running on your workstation. Increasingly, the Command Prompt is being used as a mechanism for troubleshooting network connections, completing file transfers using the ftp (file transfer protocol) command, or using the Telnet command to log onto another workstation. It is true that there are utilities that have been developed for the Windows environment that make it possible to complete both ftp and Telnet commands through a graphical interface, but many system administrators first learned how to work with networks using the command line interface in both UNIX and mainframe systems.

Networking Commands

If you are an administrator, you most likely spend a large percentage of your time working with the networks in your organization. Using the Command Prompt gives you a level of communication flexibility that quite frankly is not possible using a series of graphical interfaces for completing the same tasks. Some of the commands compatible with the Command Prompt application are:

TCP/IP Commands

- finger
- ftp
- hostname
- netstat
- ping
- rcp

TCP/IP Utilities

- lpq
- lpr

Networking Commands

- net help
- net computer
- net file
- net helpmsg
- net print
- net start

ACCESSORIES IN WINDOWS XP PROFESSIONAL

Getting familiar with the WordPad and Paint features of Windows XP Professional can assist you in getting everyday tasks done more efficiently than before. In the case of WordPad, you will find that there are many features that make this utility comparable to Microsoft Word. Think of WordPad and Paint as "everyman's" tools for handling basic tasks.

Exploring the WordPad Features

This is really a scaled-down word processor, and is backwards-compatible (thankfully)! with Microsoft's Word 6.0 and Office 95-generated documents. You will find WordPad in the Accessories group, accessible from the Start menu. It is a de-featured Word for Windows-like application that is useful for creating documents that you can save as text documents and/or export to existing Word documents. WordPad bridges the gap between text editor and fully defined word processor successfully by integrating key elements of more advanced word processing applications.

Creating New Documents Using WordPad

Provided here is a procedure for creating a document using WordPad. You will find this a simple process, useful for creating note files for yourself, and then either mailing the file or saving it to diskette and taking it with you.

1. From the Start menu, select Accessories, then WordPad. Figure 3.4 shows the path from the Start menu to the Accessories applet.
2. Launch WordPad. Unmistakable in its resemblance to Word, notice that the toolbars are smaller with fewer commands and the menus are shorter.
3. You can enter text, and emphasize it using Bold, Italic, and/or Underline commands. You can also change the alignment of the text using the left, middle, and right text alignment buttons. There is also an option for taking text and creating a bulleted list from it. Figure 3.5 shows the Formatting Toolbar.
4. WordPad also has settings for determining how the program and document is viewed on the screen. Clicking Options on the View menu brings up the Options dialog box, as shown in Figure 3.6.

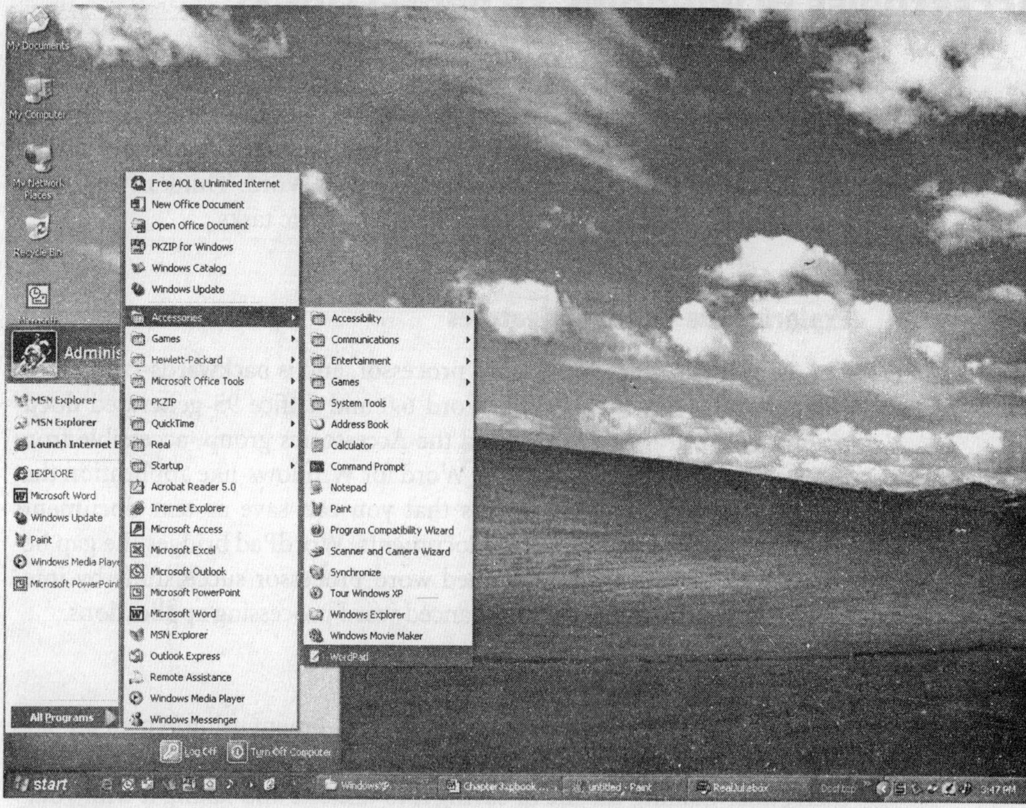

FIGURE 3.4 Finding your way to the WordPad applet.

5. After creating your document, click Print from the File menu. You will find that printing in WordPad follows the same process as does every other application.

Importing and Exporting Documents from WordPad

One of the most valuable features of WordPad is its ability to import and export documents. This can come in very handy when you create documents on a new workstation that does not yet have Word or another full-featured word processor installed. In the event you need to import files, you will find that WordPad supports Microsoft Word, Windows Write, rich text format (rtf), MS-DOS text and Unicode. You can export files in rtf, text, MS-DOS text, and Unicode formats. Accessing the import and

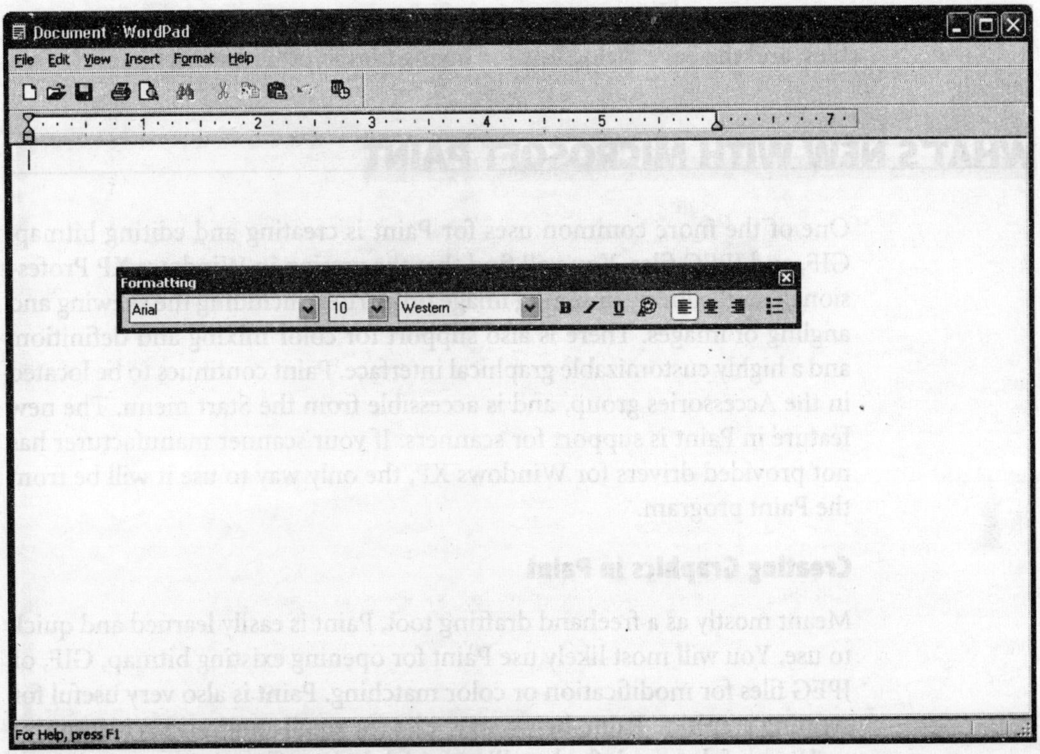

FIGURE 3.5 Exploring the Formatting toolbar.

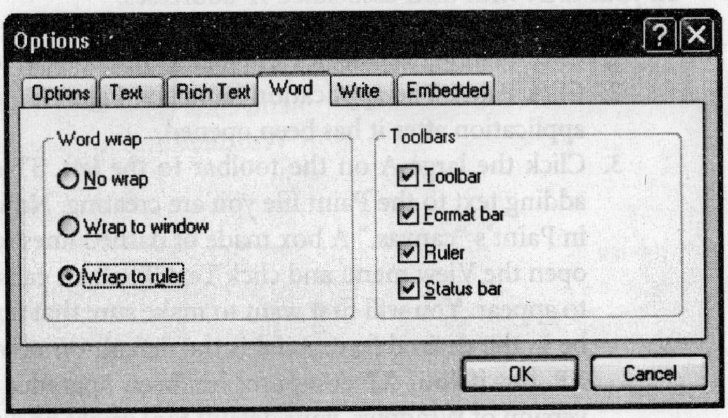

FIGURE 3.6 Using the Options dialog box for customizing the appearance of the program and documents on the screen.

export capabilities are as easy as using the Open dialog box for importing files, and the Save dialog box for saving files in other formats.

WHAT'S NEW WITH MICROSOFT PAINT

One of the more common uses for Paint is creating and editing bitmap, GIF, and JPEG files. You will find that the version in Windows XP Professional has flexibility in setting image properties, including the skewing and angling of images. There is also support for color mixing and definition, and a highly customizable graphical interface. Paint continues to be located in the Accessories group, and is accessible from the Start menu. The new feature in Paint is support for scanners. If your scanner manufacturer has not provided drivers for Windows XP, the only way to use it will be from the Paint program.

Creating Graphics in Paint

Meant mostly as a freehand drafting tool, Paint is easily learned and quick to use. You will most likely use Paint for opening existing bitmap, GIF, or JPEG files for modification or color matching. Paint is also very useful for creating graphics. Paint, being an applet (or small application) is intuitive and powerful enough for handling initial design efforts.

The process of creating a document in Paint is entirely up to the creative or graphics goals you have in mind. Let us take, for example, the task of creating a network topology diagram that shows the locations of systems on your LAN with their associated IP addresses.

1. Click Start > Accessories and locate the shortcut to Paint.
2. Click Paint. The application launches. Figure 3.7 shows the Paint application after it has been opened.
3. Click the large A on the toolbar to the left. This is the tool for adding text to the Paint file you are creating. Now click anywhere in Paint's "canvas." A box made of dashed lines will appear. Now open the View menu and click Text Toolbar, causing that toolbar to appear. You will first want to make sure that text you enter will be in the desired font. Arial is the default on new installations of XP, but if your XP computer has been upgraded from an earlier version of Windows, your default font might be different. You will probably want to use a font such as Arial or Times New Roman that is easy to read at lower resolutions and/or small sizes.

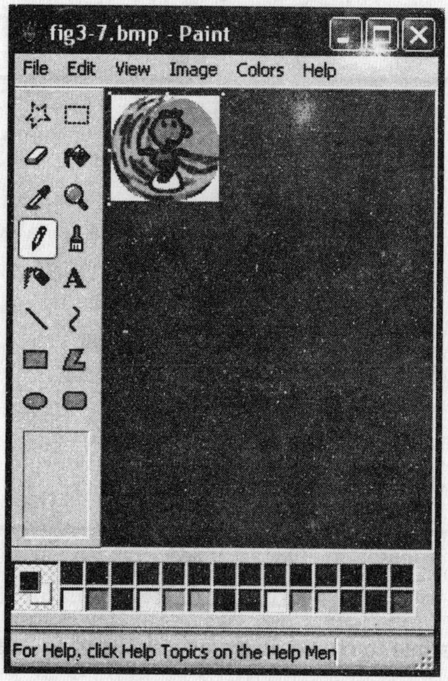

FIGURE 3.7 Microsoft Paint.

4. Using the pull-down Font selection bar, peruse the different fonts and make your selection.
5. Click on the canvas so that the cursor is visible.
6. Type in the title, "IP Address Definition."
7. Next, click the rectangle tool and draw boxes, each representing a system on the network.
8. Click the text tool to select it.
9. Clicking on one of the rectangles in the diagram, stretch the text box until it covers an entire rectangular box.
10. Next, type in the IP addresses of each system. Figure 3.8 illustrates an example of what this graphic would look like.

Importing and Saving Graphics into Paint

As with every Windows-based application, you can save your diagrams using the Save As command from the File menu. You will have the option of saving the file you have created in one of several formats, including four

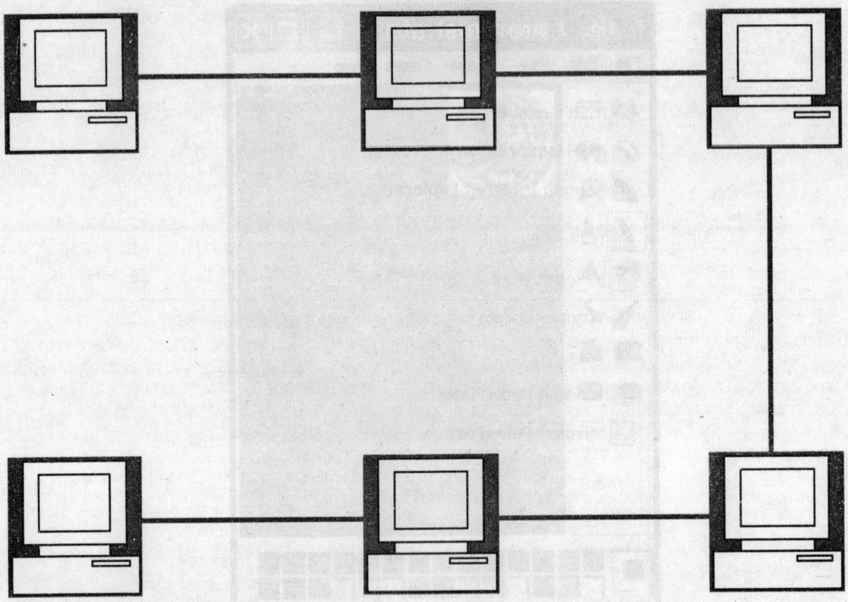

FIGURE 3.8 It is possible to create diagrams quickly using Paint.

choices of bitmaps ranging from monochrome to 24-bit, GIF, TIFF, PNG, or JPEG. The majority of applications on the Windows platform can accept each of these formats. In terms of importing files into Paint for editing, the same file formats are available.

INTRODUCING THE SEARCH COMPANION

The Search Companion is a browser-type applet used to find just about anything. The Search command is located on the Start menu and is represented by a magnifying glass icon. It is used just as the Search Assistant is used in Windows 2000. You can search for files and folders, printers, computers on the network, anything on the Internet, and personal address book entries in your Outlook and e-mail folders. Figure 3.9 shows the location of the Search command.

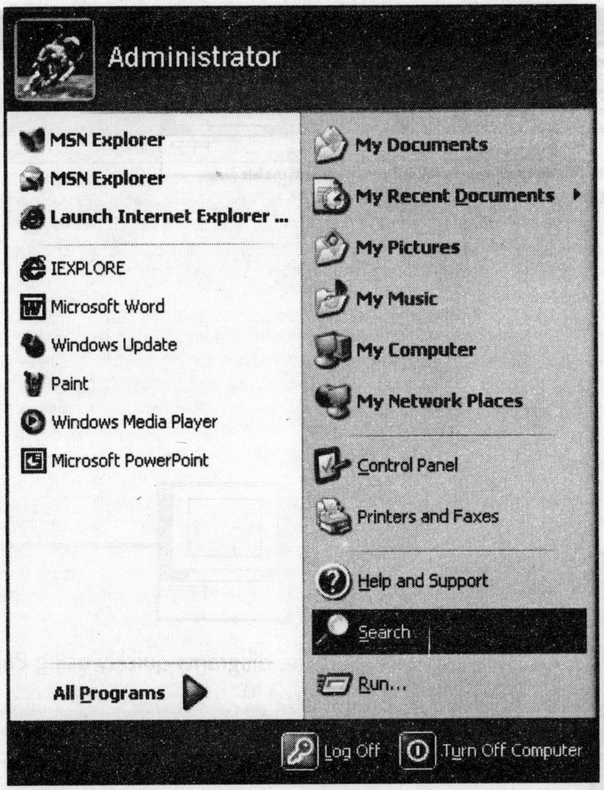

FIGURE 3.9 The Search command.

How the Search Companion Works

This application is unique within Windows XP Professional in that it is very command-like but also has a graphical interface associated with it. The Search command works in the same way a browser window does. This application gives you the opportunity to search for files by name, date created, or even application originally used to create the file. You can also search for files that contain a specific textual phrase or word, regardless of the file the text is in. Figure 3.10 shows an example of the Search Companion dialog box.

The majority of the time you are looking for a file you know the contents but not the name. Say for example you need to locate a report you have written that described how Hydra works and its implications on your

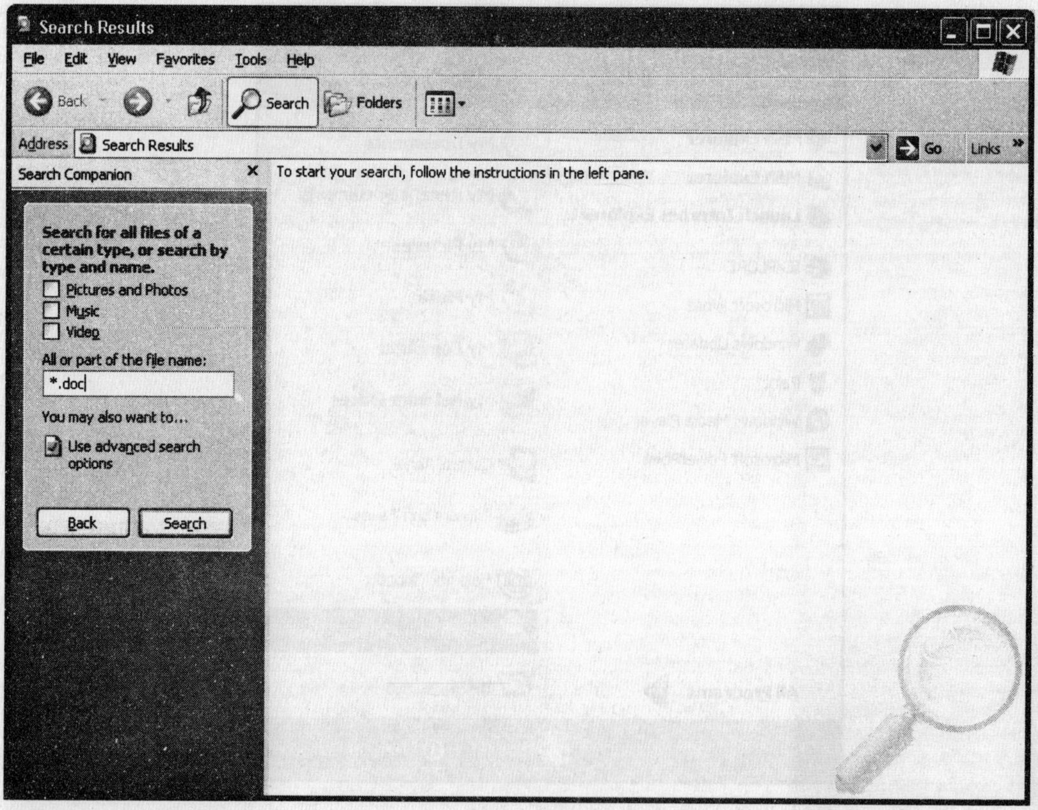

FIGURE 3.10 Introducing the Search Companion dialog box.

organization. You would enter the word "Hydra" in the A word or phrase in the file text box. Search Companion would then query every single file on your workstation, showing the results. Figure 3.11 shows the Search Companion searching for the word "Hydra" in files on the computer.

Search Companion includes options for locating files created during a specific period, and also gives you the option of searching for all files of a specific size. New for the Search Companion are tools that make searching easier than ever before. Instead of having to search the entire computer, or remember dozens of file extensions, Search Companion gives you easy ways to narrow down your search. Let us say you are looking for a video file. Click the arrow next to Pictures, Music or Video. On the next page, click Video and enter as much as you can remember of the file name. The search will be a good deal faster than in previous versions of Windows. If

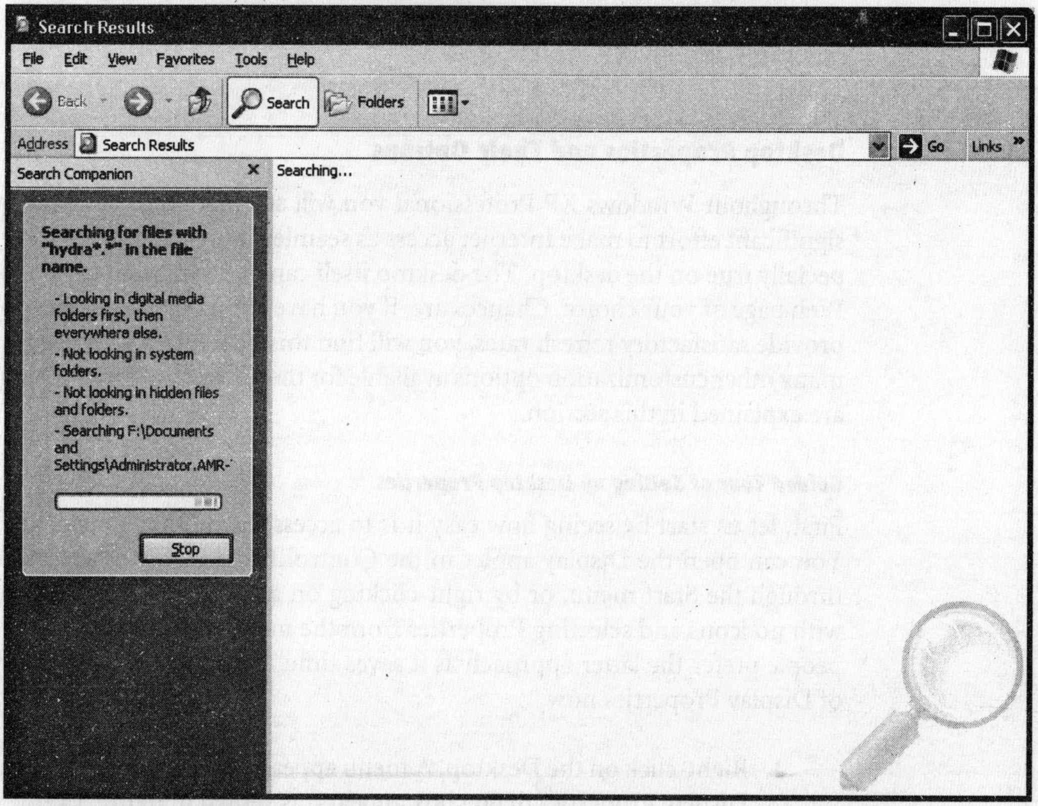

FIGURE 3.11 Using Search Companion to retrieve all files with the word "Hydra" in the text.

you need more help, click Use advanced search options. This provides virtually every conceivable option for finding your file. These options are all configurable in the box on the left side of the Search Companion window.

EXPLORING SYSTEM PROPERTIES IN WINDOWS XP PROFESSIONAL

There continues to be more and more of an emphasis in each subsequent version of Windows to focus on the properties of key resources within the operating system. This properties-centric approach gives you more of an opportunity to customize the operating system with greater flexibility than ever before. Throughout this section, we will look at setting system properties in Windows XP Professional.

Desktop Properties and Their Options

Throughout Windows XP Professional you will see that there has been a significant effort to make Internet access as seamless as possible. This is especially true on the desktop. The desktop itself can be configured to be the Web page of your choice. Chances are, if you have sufficient bandwidth to provide satisfactory refresh rates, you will find this a useful tool. There are many other customization options available for the desktop, a few of which are explained in this section.

Guided Tour of Setting up Desktop Properties

First, let us start by seeing how easy it is to access the desktop properties. You can open the Display applet in the Control Panel, which is accessed through the Start menu, or by right-clicking on a portion of the desktop with no icons and selecting Properties from the menu that appears. Many people prefer the latter approach as it saves time. Let us take a quick tour of Display Properties now.

1. Right-click on the Desktop. A menu appears. Click Properties. The Display Properties dialog box appears, as shown in figure 3.12.

Notice along the top of the Display Properties dialog box there are five tabs, each containing different properties that can be customized.

2. Click the Settings tab in the Display Properties dialog box. For many system administrators, this is the series of properties in this dialog box where they spend the majority of their time. Figure 3.13 shows the Settings page of the Display Properties dialog box.
3. Note that the slider is set to a particular screen resolution. There are two ways to move the slider. You can click and hold on the slider knob and drag it to the desired setting, or you can click on another part of the slider's path, causing the knob to move to the spot where you clicked. Notice how the image on the monitor illustration on this page changes to reflect the changed resolution setting. Certain resolution changes you make may be implemented as soon as you click Apply or OK, but more extreme changes will likely show you the screen but prompt you to accept or reject the

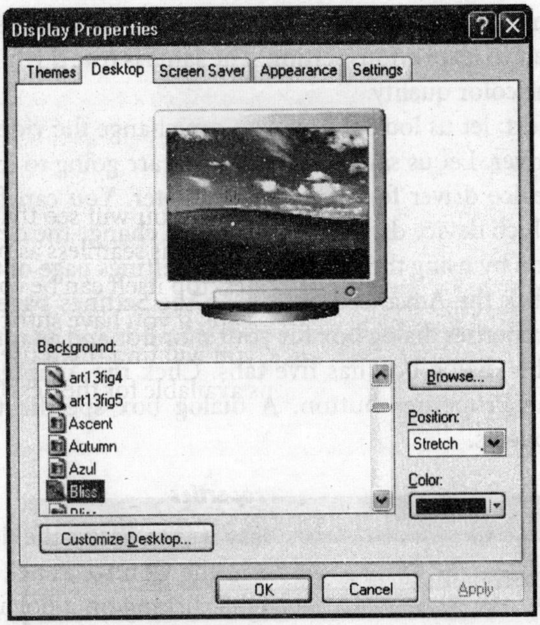

FIGURE 3.12 Use the Display Properties dialog box to customize the desktop.

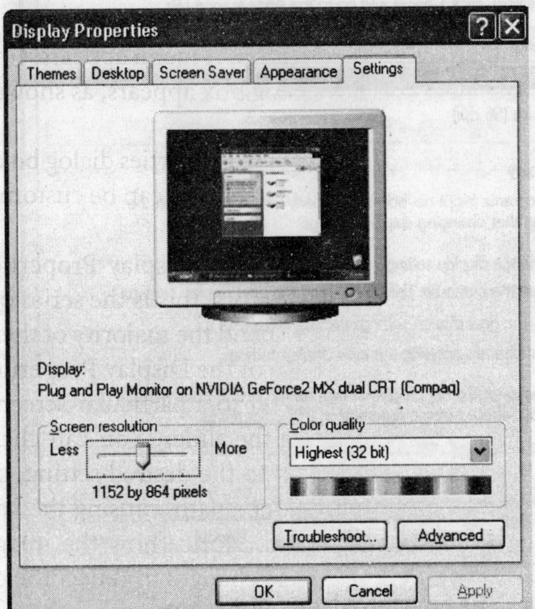

FIGURE 3.13 Use the Settings page of the Display Properties dialog box to set your screen's resolution.

change. If you fail to respond within 15 seconds, the screen will revert to its previous setting. The same is true if you make changes to the color quality.

4. Next, let us look at how you can change the video adapter device driver. Let us say for example you are going to install an updated device driver for your video adapter. You can first check to see which device driver is loaded, then change the device driver selection by using the options on the Settings page of the dialog box.
5. Click the Advanced button on the Settings page. This calls up a properties dialog box for your monitor and adapter (Figure 3.14). This dialog box has five tabs. Click the Adapter tab, then click the Properties button. A dialog box specific to your adapter appears.

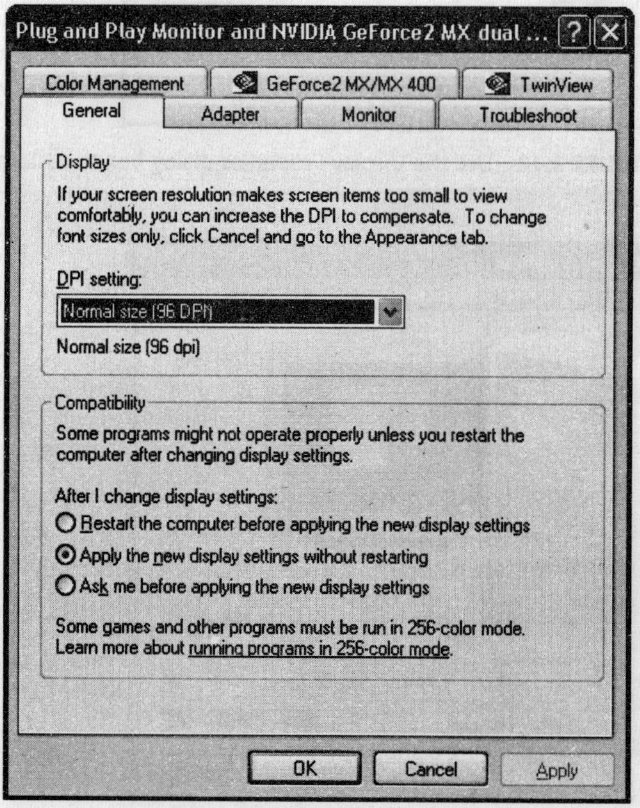

FIGURE 3.14 The monitor/adapter dialog box.

6. Click the Driver tab and then the Driver Details button. You can now view the file names and locations of the adapter driver. Click OK.
7. Click the Update Driver button. The Hardware Update Wizard appears, ready to update your video driver. Cancel this and close all open dialog boxes.

How Shortcuts Are Added to the Desktop

Look at the desktop of your workstation, or any system running Windows 98/Me, Windows 2000, or Windows XP. You will notice small icons with an arrow coming up from the lower left corner. This is a *shortcut*, which is a direct link to an application, folder, file, or applet. Shortcuts are very useful for streamlining access to commonly used applications. Let us take a quick tour of how to create a shortcut on the Windows XP desktop.

1. Right-click on the desktop. A small menu appears. Click New, then Shortcut from the next menu that appears. The Create Shortcut Wizard starts, as shown in Figure 3.15.

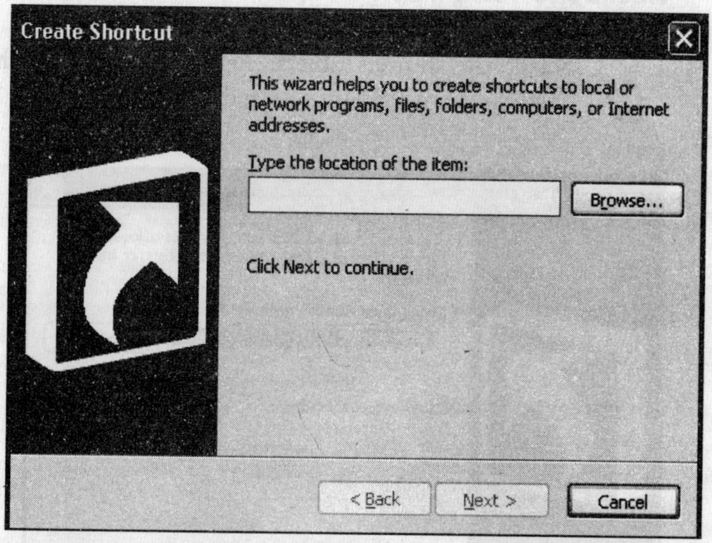

FIGURE 3.15 Creating a shortcut for the Windows XP Professional desktop.

2. Click Browse. The Browse dialog box is used for finding the object for which you want to create a shortcut. Figure 3.16 shows what your screen looks like at this point.

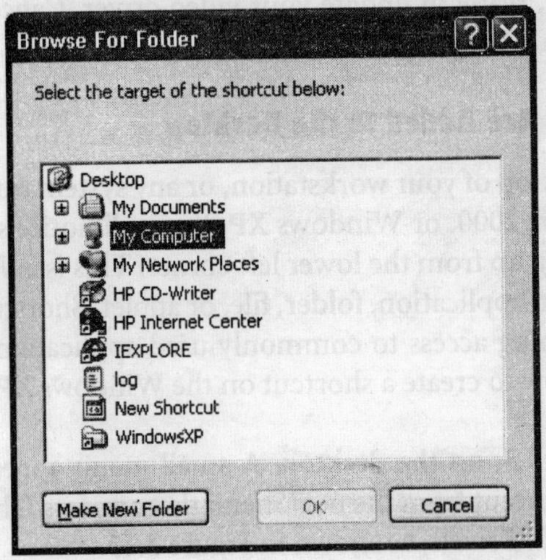

FIGURE 3.16 Using the Browse option in the Create Shortcut Wizard.

3. Select the desired object. Figure 3.17 shows the wizard with Microsoft PowerPoint selected.

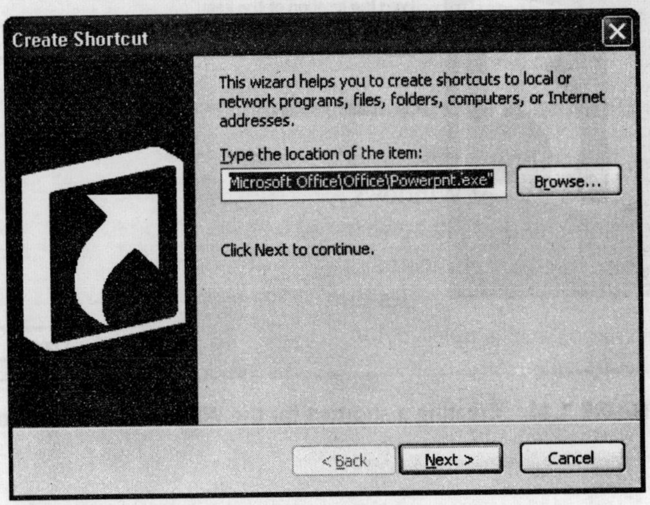

FIGURE 3.17 The object is selected.

4. Click OK. The object you have selected is now displayed in the wizard page. Figure 3.18 shows what the wizard looks like.

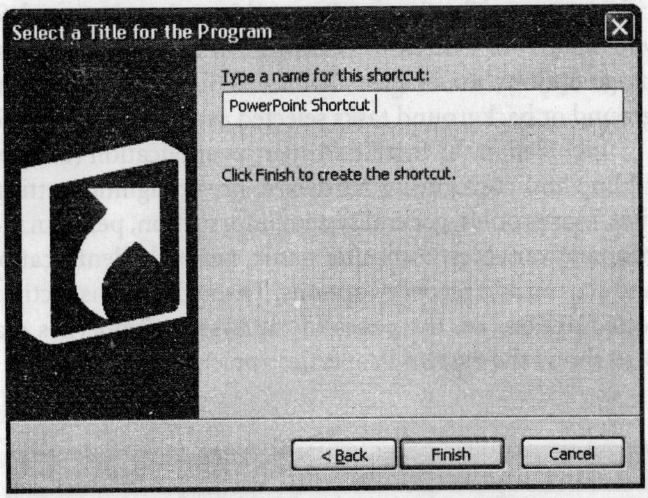

FIGURE 3.18 Selecting a name for the shortcut.

5. Click Next. The final page of the Create Shortcut Wizard is shown.
6. Click Finish. The shortcut is then finished and ready for use directly from the desktop.

Desktop Properties and Their Many Uses

Display Properties provide a wealth of customization options for you as both a user of Windows XP Professional and also as an administrator. A book could easily be written covering the myriad of option combinations and their implications on user productivity. Take some time to explore the Display Properties dialog box as time permits. It has a rich feature set that includes options for configuring Web site integration directly to your desktop.

Defining System Properties in the Systems Applet

You will find that many of the applications you work with in Windows XP Professional make their own entries in the file system. This is especially true for applications that use a temporary or TEMP subdirectory. In addition, Windows XP looks at the options configured in Hardware and User Profiles for specific parameters on how your system needs to respond to specific requests. The System Properties options are used for defining how you want your system to perform. An example of this is in the memory usage options under Performance. You can choose to have either foreground or background tasks selected as the primary application priority.

Included in the System Properties application (or applet) are areas for adding and configuring hardware, driver signing, setting hardware profiles, user profiles, general system information, performance options, environment variables, computer name, network identification, error reports, and startup and recovery options. Throughout this section we will tour selected options on the pages of the System Properties dialog box. Figure 3.19 shows the System Properties applet.

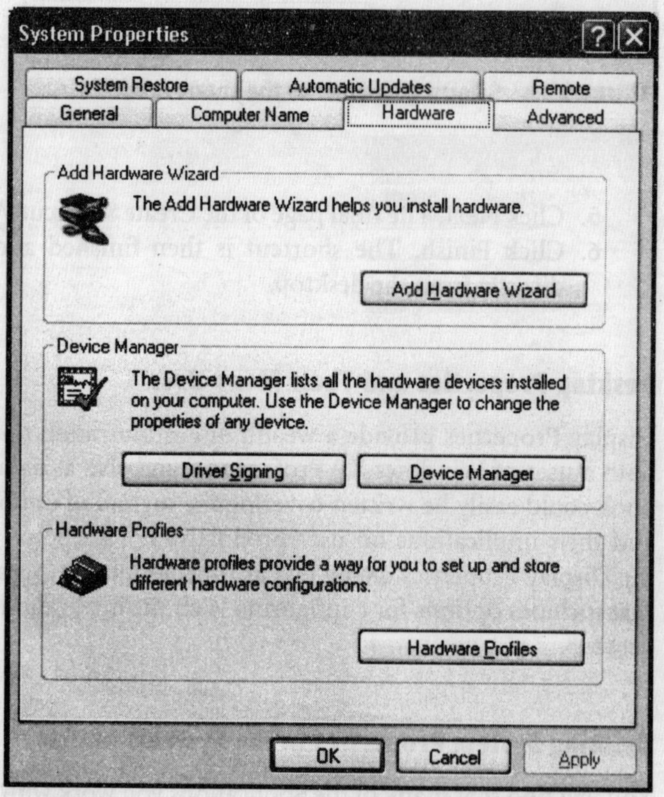

FIGURE 3.19 Touring the System Properties applet.

Touring the Performance Aspects of System Properties

Whether you are a systems administrator or a power user of Windows XP Professional, the issue of getting the most performance you possibly can from your workstation is undoubtedly a chief concern you share with associates. This is especially true if you are working in engineering or other technically challenging professions where the software performance can mean the difference between getting home before 6pm or after 10pm. Let us take a quick tour of how Windows XP uses the options set on the Performance dialog box of the System Properties applet. Using these options you will be able to tune certain aspects of your system's performance.

1. First, let us get to the System Properties dialog box. Click Control Panel on the Start menu. The entire contents of the Control Panel are now shown.
2. Double-click the System icon. The applet appears. Alternately, you can right-click My Computer on the desktop and click Properties from the menu that appears.
3. Click the Advanced tab. Figure 3.20 shows the Advanced page of the System Properties applet.

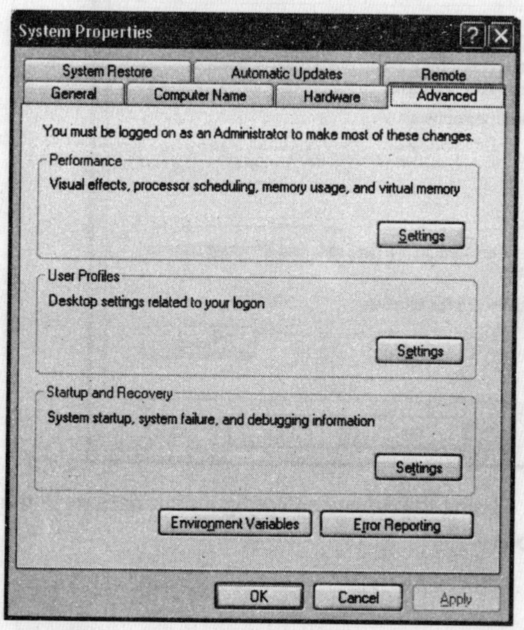

FIGURE 3.20 Modifying performance of a Windows XP workstation using the Advanced page in the System Properties dialog box.

4. Virtual memory is a method of substituting hard disk space for memory when the system runs out of physical random access memory. Memory is said to be "swapped" to the paging file, a file where virtual memory is written to when needed. When virtual memory is read it is said to be "paged" from the paging file. Virtual memory can be configured in the Performance Options dialog box of System Properties. Click the top Settings button on the Advanced page.
5. The Performance Options dialog box appears, as shown in Figure 3.21.

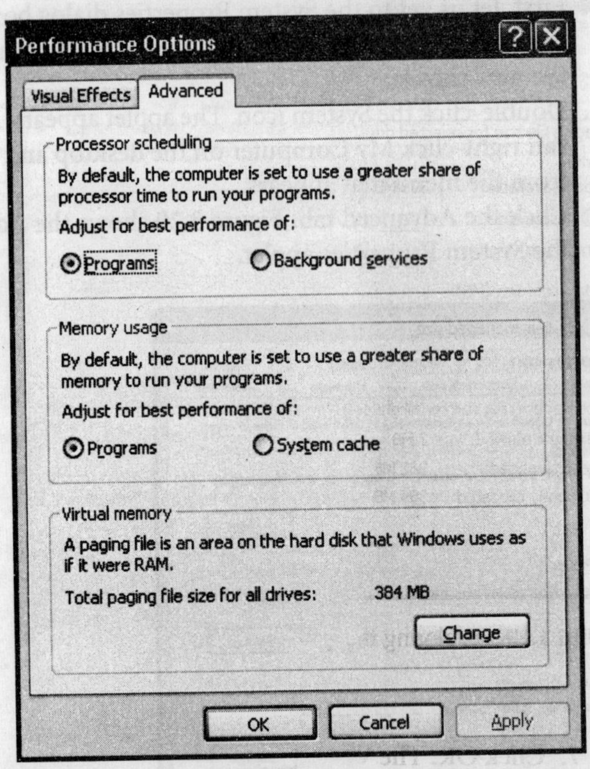

FIGURE 3.21 Using the Advanced configuration options in the Performance Options dialog box.

6. Click the Advanced tab and then the Change button within the Virtual Memory area of the Performance Options dialog

box. The Virtual Memory dialog box is shown, as illustrated in Figure 3.22.

Click the System managed size radio button in the Virtual Memory dialog box. Then click Set. This has Windows XP set the size of the paging file automatically based on the size of your hard drive and the needs of your specific installation of Windows XP.

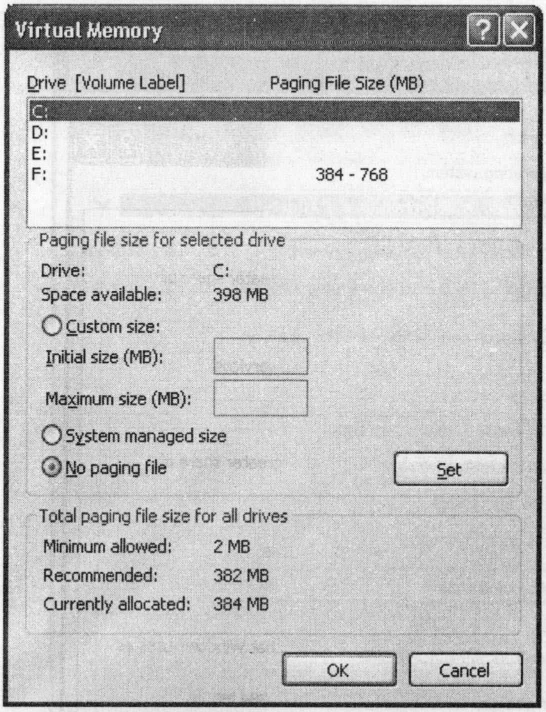

FIGURE 3.22 Exploring the Virtual Memory options.

7. Click OK. The Virtual Memory dialog box closes.
8. Click OK again to close the Performance Options dialog box. The System Properties dialog box is again shown.
9. Click OK one more time and the System Properties applet is closed. The next time you start up your system, the paging file will be created automatically by your system, and stored as *pagefile.sys*. By default Windows XP creates a paging file.

Configuring Startup and Recovery Properties

Another area within the System Properties applet you will find very useful is the Startup and Recovery page, accessed by clicking the bottom Settings button on the Advanced page. The purposes of this page are to set the operating system menu and the amount of time the FlexBoot option (menu of installed operating systems) is displayed on-screen, and various actions for the system to take when the system fails. Figure 3.23 shows the Startup and Recovery page of the System Properties applet.

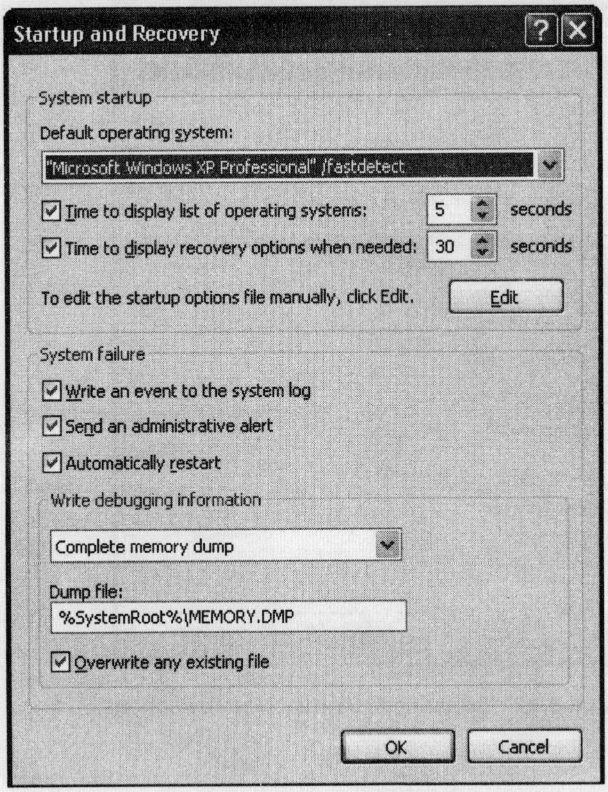

FIGURE 3.23 Configuring the System Startup and Recovery characteristics.

FlexBoot is the listing of all installed operating systems displayed on your monitor after you power on a workstation and the preliminary activities have taken place. Windows XP Professional (or Windows NT or Windows 2000) presents all operating systems that are also present on the system or workstation, giving the user the option to select the one to use. By default, the default operating system is loaded unless another system is selected within 30 seconds of the time the FlexBoot menu appears.

Let us briefly tour each of the options in this dialog box.

System Startup—The Default operating system entry lists all operating systems that are installed on the workstation. Using this option, you can configure either Windows XP Professional or another operating system to be the first one in the list during the startup sequence.

Time to display list of operating systems—This is the time period that FlexBoot will show the default operating system before booting it.

Time to display recovery options when needed—In the event your workstation has either a soft or hard error, you can configure recovery services to write an event to the system log, send an administrative alert via electronic mail (or pager if your system is configured with the proper options), write debugging information to a file, or automatically reboot. In many instances, system administrators who have many workstations to support choose the option of having the system automatically reboot itself. This makes it possible to clear any soft errors without having to physically be present at the system itself.

After selecting the options in this dialog box, click OK. Your selections are then recorded. When finished with the options in the System Properties dialog box, click OK.

CONFIGURING NETWORK PROPERTIES

Being able to share files, printers, and even processors through network connectivity is one of the most commonly cited reasons why organizations invest in network operating systems like Windows XP Professional. Networking is so integrated in Windows XP Professional that there are options found throughout for configuring it. Microsoft has also included wizards for configuring the many approaches you can take in connecting your workstation to a network. You will find the Network Connections applet in the Control Panel. Figure 3.24 shows the location of the Network Connections applet in the Control Panel.

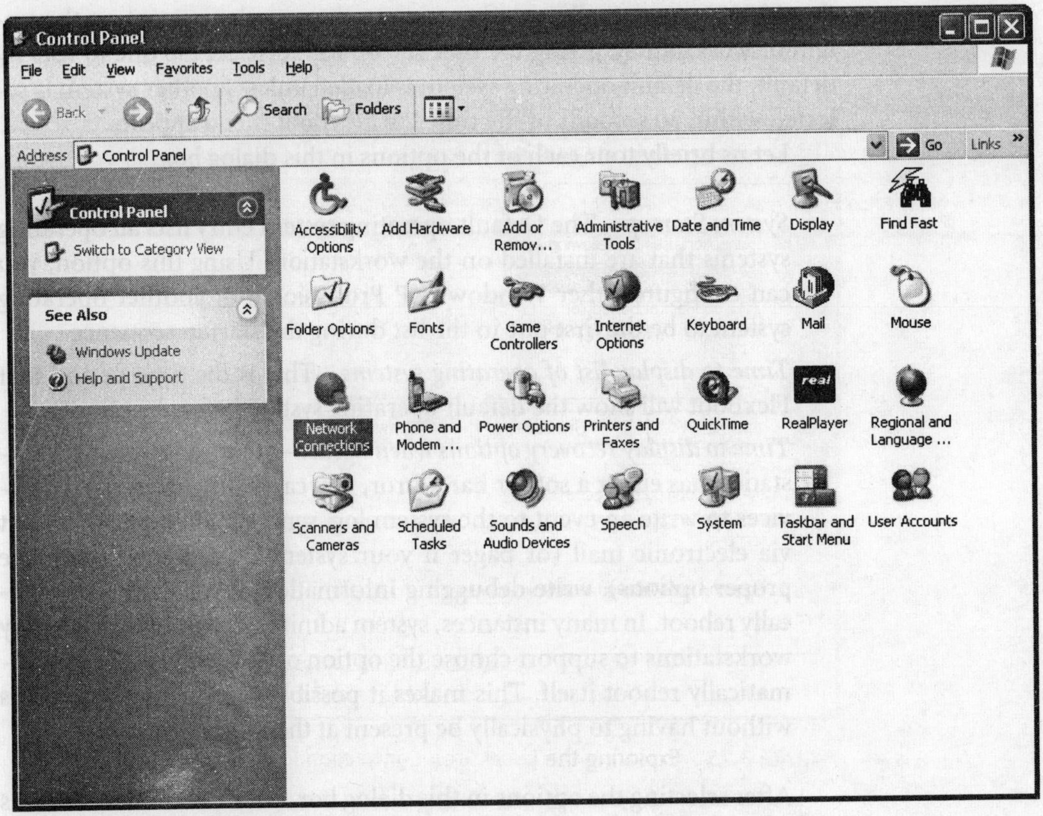

FIGURE 3.24 Finding the Network Connections applet in the Control Panel.

Opening this applet shows the default connections created during the installation of Windows XP Professional. For the purposes of this example, only a single connection is shown.

1. Right-click the Local Area Connection icon shown in the Network Connections applet's window and click Properties. The Local Area Connection Properties dialog box is shown, as shown in figure 3.25.
2. Select the Internet Protocol (TCP/IP) check box in the middle of the General page.
3. Click Properties. The Internet Protocol (TCP/IP) Properties dialog box is shown, and appears in Figure 3.26. Notice that this dialog box has two pages, the first specific to General options and the second for Alternate Configurations. Microsoft has provided this

FIGURE 3.25 Exploring the Local Area Connection Properties dialog box.

for streamlining the task of configuring two network interface cards on the same system.

4. Click Advanced. The Advanced TCP/IP Settings dialog box is next shown, and appears in Figure 3.27.
5. Notice that the Advanced TCP/IP Settings dialog box has four tabs. These include IP Settings, DNS, WINS, and Options. The WINS page is used for configuring connectivity with previous-generation Windows-based workstations, even UNIX workstations, using the LMHOSTS file as the resolver of IP addresses to find other systems throughout the network. You can also see that under the NetBIOS setting there are more options for determining the identity of workstations over the Internet using NetBIOS over TCP/IP. These options appear for the first time in Windows XP Professional.
6. Click OK. The dialog box closes and shows the Internet Protocol (TCP/IP) Properties dialog box.

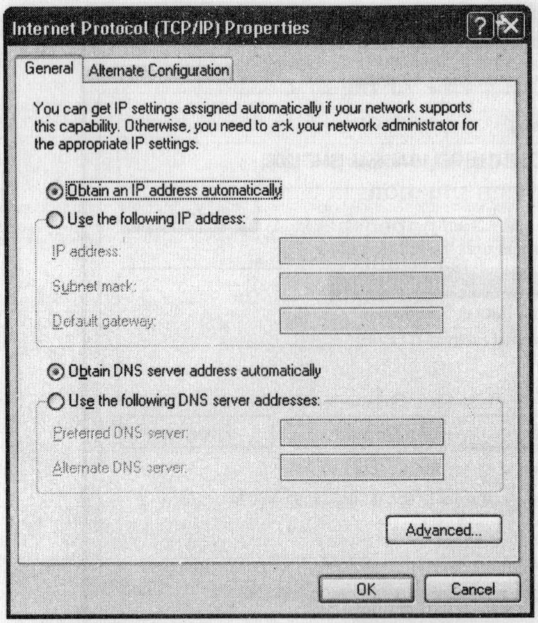

FIGURE 3.26 Exploring the Internet Protocol (TCP/IP) Properties dialog box.

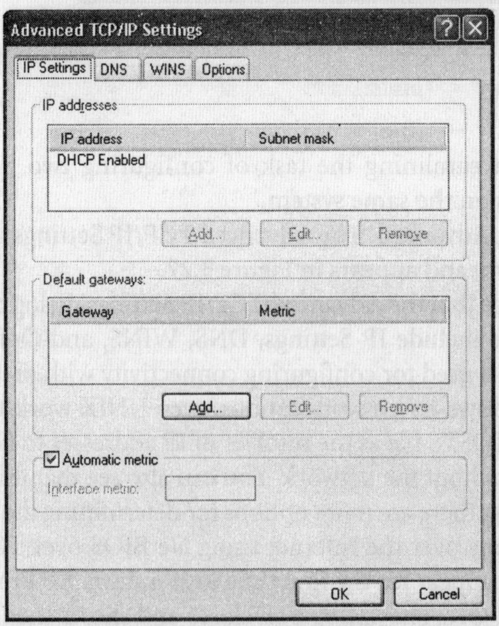

FIGURE 3.27 The Advanced TCP/IP Settings dialog box provides for configuring legacy networking support.

7. Click OK. The Local Area Connection Properties dialog box is again shown.

   One of the new features of Windows XP Professional and Home Editions is the addition of Internet Connection Firewall support. In some cases, you should enable the ICF. There are certain situations in which you should not, however:

   - Do not enable ICF on any Internet connection that is not a direct connection to the Internet.
   - Do not enable ICF on Virtual Private Networks (VPNs).
   - There is no need to enable ICF if your network already has a firewall or proxy server.

8. Click the Advanced tab of the Local Area Connection Properties page. Figure 3.28 shows this page. This page contains only a check box to enable the Internet Connection Firewall.

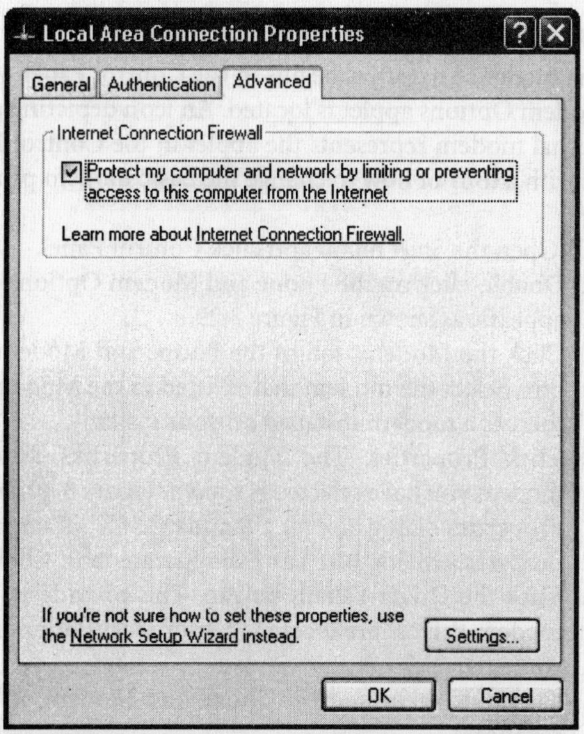

FIGURE 3.28 Configuring the Internet Connection Firewall in Windows XP Professional.

9. Select the Internet Connection Firewall check box as long as your system does not fall into any of the categories described in the previous list.
10. Click Close.

You have just toured the properties associated with network connections in Windows XP Professional.

Remote Connections and Their Properties in Windows XP Professional

As e-mail and Internet access become more and more important to people on a daily basis, and as traveling employees need more frequent access to their employers' networks, modems on laptops have become especially important. Windows XP is designed to make remote Internet and intranet access as efficient and user-friendly as possible.

Accessing and Changing Phone and Modem Properties

Touring modem properties begins in the Control Panel, where the Phone and Modem Options applet is located. An icon depicting a cell phone and an external modem represents the applet in the Control Panel. Let us get started with a tour of how to change the basic modem properties here.

1. Open the Start menu and click Control Panel.
2. Double-click on the Phone and Modem Options icon. The applet appears, as shown in Figure 3.29.
3. Click the Modems tab of the Phone and Modem Options dialog box. Select the modem that is listed in the Modem box (assuming there is a modem installed on your system).
4. Click Properties. The Modem Properties dialog box for the modem you have selected is shown. Figure 3.30 shows the Modem Properties dialog box for a Standard 56K Modem. Notice that the properties dialog box has five separate tabs. Click the Driver tab.
5. Click the Driver Details button. This provides a list of where the modem drivers are located in your workstation. After viewing its contents, click OK.
6. Click OK again and the Phone and Modem options dialog box reappears.
7. Click OK. The main dialog box closes, showing the Control Panel.

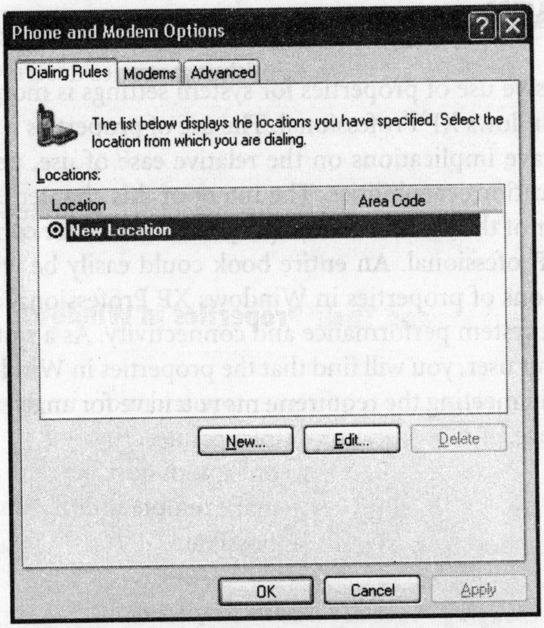

FIGURE 3.29 The Phone and Modem Options dialog box.

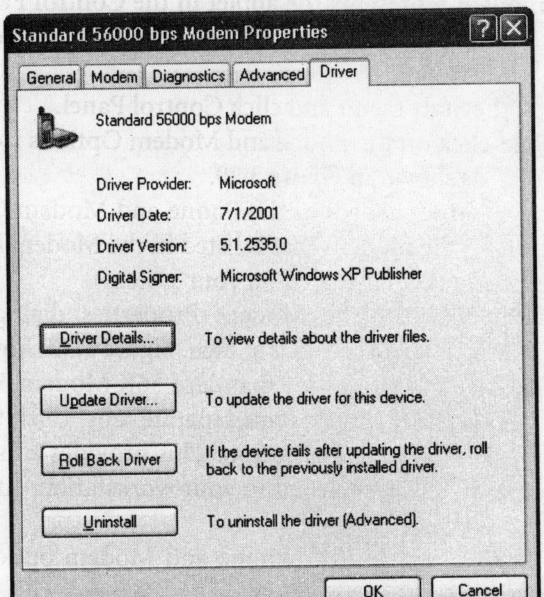

FIGURE 3.30 The Driver page of the Modem Properties dialog box.

CHAPTER SUMMARY

The extensive use of properties for system settings is more pervasive than ever in Windows XP Professional. The use of properties is comprehensive, and can have implications on the relative ease of use, performance, and communications capabilities. The intent of this chapter is to present you with a tour of the more common properties which are configured in Windows XP Professional. An entire book could easily be written on all the combinations of properties in Windows XP Professional and their implications on system performance and connectivity. As a system administrator or power user, you will find that the properties in Windows XP give you flexibility in meeting the requirements you have for analyzing system-wide performance.

4 Installing Applications in Windows XP Professional

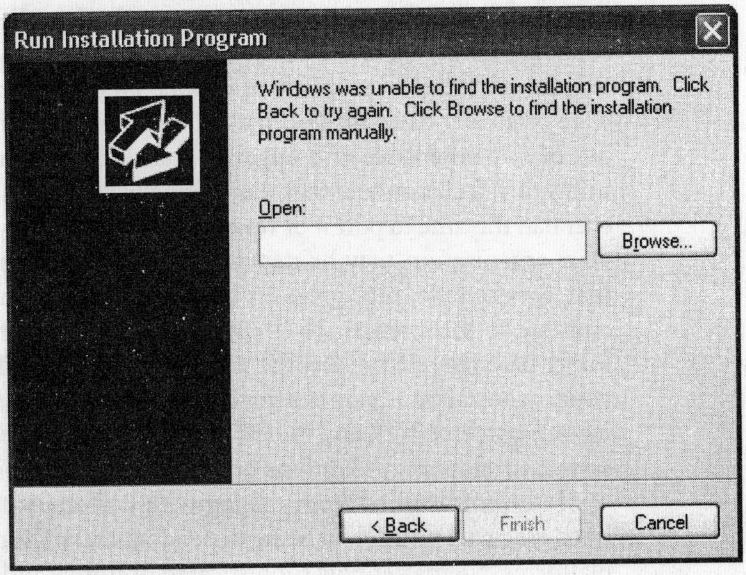

INTRODUCTION

Even before the first version of Windows NT was introduced, there were development kits available for creating 32-bit applications that would take advantage of the speed increases possible with its platform, now in its current generation in Windows XP Professional. Microsoft's efforts have been successful in the area of getting software companies to port to Windows 2000 and now Windows XP. The most interesting development for Microsoft continues to be the development of the .NET initiative. In a nutshell, .NET is a family of products from Microsoft based on XML Web services. That initiative's development efforts continue to gain mindshare, and while a few have criticized the .NET initiative, it is gaining momentum. The challenge for Microsoft is going to be to take the world-class set of applications now running on legacy APIs from many different developers and motivate that same group of companies to provide support for .NET. For additional information on Microsoft's .Net initiatives please see www.microsoft.com/net. A survey of software companies completed by International Data Corporation showed that there is over a 90% compound annual growth rate in the anticipated number of titles being ported to the Windows 2000 and XP platforms. With any luck, if your organization uses applications that do not run on Windows XP, they will be ported soon. However, there are certain applications that will not be ported to Windows XP due to a variety of factors. First, many of these applications were originally developed on the DOS platform and have long since been out of a maintenance and upgrade cycle. Your organization may have a utility or calculation tool that was originally developed for DOS and no one ever had the time to port it or rewrite it for the Windows platform. Second, your organization may be dependent on a communications application that, for example, runs great on UNIX and has a Windows client version, and due to the strength of UNIX demand in the software vendor's customer base they do not feel the need to migrate to Windows XP. Third, if your organization is part of a government agency and has made significant investments in UNIX and POSIX, there is the need for any new operating system to support applications originally developed on these platforms.

Microsoft learned from talking with customers that many organizations are in the position of being dependent on applications based on other platforms. No matter how sophisticated, intuitive and responsive an operating system becomes, there is always the need for compatibility with the previous generation of applications the customers have been using. Operating systems fulfill the role of being the foundational element of compatibility in a workstation.

In this chapter you will learn how to continue using these applications on Windows XP Professional.

USING APPLICATIONS WITH WINDOWS XP PROFESSIONAL

Windows XP Professional is a 32-bit operating system that is distinguished from Windows 3.x by the integration of multithreaded support of applications and the capability to preemptively multitask applications in and out of memory to ensure consistent performance.

Another differentiating feature of Windows XP Professional when it comes to applications is the ability it has to run each application in a memory-protected subsystem to ensure reliability. These protected memory subsystems are assigned to an application once they are launched. There are subsystems in Windows XP's kernel to support the native 32-bit applications, sometimes called Win32-compatible applications, in addition to Win16. What about DOS? Windows XP uses an emulator that is accessible from the Command Prompt application to provide compatibility for DOS-based applications (see Figure 4.1). Subsystems are included in the Windows XP operating system structure to ensure reliability with these various applications.

Win16 applications that use virtual device drivers (VxDs) will not run on Windows NT, 2000, or XP.

FIGURE 4.1 The command prompt application provides an emulator in order for Windows XP Professional to run MS-DOS programs.

Windows XP Professional supports 32-bit applications in native mode, where the applications can make calls into the Windows XP Executive for resources. When a Win16 application is launched, it is first loaded into memory then assigned to the Win16 subsystem for ongoing processing. This subsystem approach to segmenting applications ensures a high level of reliability in Windows XP Professional. In the event a 16-bit application stops functioning or freezes, the remaining applications on the workstation can continue running, unless there are multiple Win16 applications running on the same VDM. In that case, if one Win16 application crashes, all of the Win16 applications running in the same VDM will also crash, but any other applications should remain intact.

Using this subsystem approach also makes the request for hardware resources transparent to Win16 applications. When a Win16 application makes a request for hardware resources the request is taken by the Windows XP Executive and then queued up for a given hardware resource along with requests from other subsystems. Windows XP's Win16 subsystem takes the request for resources and translates it into a 32-bit request. Once the task is complete, a response is then reformatted into a 16-bit compatible response, which is in turn forwarded back to the application occupying the 16-bit subsystem. This entire process is just like going to another country and having an interpreter translate to you what a native is saying and vice-versa. As you might suspect, 16-bit applications do pay a performance penalty in Windows XP environments due to the overhead of having to translate requests for resources back and forth. The term VDM stands for Virtual DOS Machine, which is the term applied to the program threads associated with the Win16 subsystem. An essential part of the Windows XP architecture is the WOWEXEC, or Win16 on Win32 Executive. This area of Windows XP makes it possible to have Win16-compatible applications running on a Windows XP Professional workstation.

What Is WOWEXEC?

When using a computer, I like to have several applications open at the same time, typically Microsoft Outlook, a variety of text and graphics programs, and even a Web browser or two. The trouble begins on Windows 9x when one application suddenly either runs out of memory or just stops working. The entire system then locks up, and often a user loses portions of a file he has been working on. You no doubt have had the same experiences. It is frustrating, and can cause you to be cautious about using a multiple series of applications at the same time on Windows 9x. Inevitably you end up rebooting the system to clear the memory.

Windows XP Professional's integration of subsystems is aimed at solving this problem. A Win16-based application that suddenly quits working is recoverable in Windows XP Professional. Why? It is because of WOWEXECs. These are the memory segments in the Win16 subsystem which each Win16-based application uses to separate itself and its commands from other applications. The payoff of WOWEXEC is a significantly higher level of reliability in Windows XP for running 16-bit based applications. The downside is performance, as each application using WOWEXEC must go through the Win16 subsystem for resources to complete tasks. Also, since the kernel for Windows XP Professional relies on the Win16 application being launched from your workstation to detect the type of application being used, WOWEXEC does not apply to Win16-based applications launched over a network.

When you launch an application in Windows XP, the operating system checks to see if it is a 16- or 32-bit based program. If it is Win16-based, then WOWEXEC is initiated.

By default, when a Win16-based application is started it is assigned a memory space separate from that of other types of applications. However, also by default, additional Win16 applications will run in the same memory space as the first open Win16 application. You can use the Group Policy snap-in to configure the Run dialog box to have a check box allowing you to choose whether you want to have the application assigned a completely separate memory space. Here is the procedure:

1. Open the Run dialog box from the Start menu. Enter **gpedit.msc** and click OK to open the Group Policy snap-in.
2. Open the User Configuration container in the left pane (click the '+' sign), then open Administrative Templates. Then click the Start Menu and Taskbar folder icon. A list of settings appears in the right pane.
3. Locate the "Add 'Run in separate Memory Space' check box to Run dialog box" setting and double-click it. A dialog box opens.
4. In the Settings page of the dialog box, click to select the Enabled radio button and click OK.
5. Close the Group Policy snap-in. The check box now appears in the Run dialog box. However, the check box is dimmed until you enter the name of a 16-bit program in the box.

There is another way to start Win16 applications in their own, individual memory spaces. From a command prompt, navigate to the executable file for the program. Then run the command **start /separate** ***file_name.exe***.

In general, it is a very good idea to have this feature turned on if you plan on launching applications from the Run dialog box. It is important to recognize that Windows XP looks at the application being profiled in the path definition to see if it is a 16-bit application first, then makes the option of selecting separate memory space available. By default, the option is dimmed.

Windows preemptively multitasks Win16 applications with respect to 32-bit applications and with respect to other Win16 applications running in separate memory spaces.

Single-Threaded vs. Multithreaded Applications

With the increase in Win32-based applications there is increasing interest in the performance gains of single-threaded versus multithreaded applications. A single-threaded application is typically 16-bit, developed using the Win16 application programming interface (API) guidelines. For a software company to have a Windows 3.x-compatible application, they needed to write their application using the Win16 API. A development limitation of writing applications for Windows 3.x environments was the availability of single threads or requests for processor and memory resources. Each application could generate one thread or request for resources at a time. If a user running the 16-bit version of Word, for example, has several documents open at the same time, there is a single thread created for the application's resource needs. As a user opens more and more applications in Windows 3.x, the overall performance becomes very slow and the system eventually stops running as there are no more resources available.

Conversely, a Win32-based application is based on the Win32 APIs that have been so aggressively promoted by Microsoft; these applications are multithreaded. Due to the commands in the Win32 APIs, applications are capable of taking advantage of the multithreaded aspects of Windows XP. This API also provides support for the flat memory model of Windows XP, and the support of protected memory mode functioning. A 32-bit application also has the ability in a Windows XP environment to make native calls for resources in the operating system, ensuring faster performance. You will notice the difference in performance between a Win16-based and Win32-based application.

What then are the key differences between Win16- and Win32-based applications?

- Win16-based applications are native to the Windows 3.x environment. Due to the integration of the Win16 subsystem, VDMs and WOWEXEC, they are also compatible with Windows XP Professional, as long as they do not use virtual device drivers. Their performance will be influenced by the need to have resource calls translated from Win16 to Win32 and back again.
- Native applications in Windows XP are Win32 based and are structured so as to have direct access to Windows XP resources. All other things being equal, it is better to choose a Win32-based application for your work and recreational needs as it is tailored specifically to the strengths of Windows XP Professional.
- Software companies which have completed migrations of their Win16-based applications to Win32 have reported speed increases from 40 to 60% with their Win32-based programs. Just as automobile manufacturers say "your mileage may vary" there is a definite speed increase in multithreaded Win32-based applications over their Win16-based counterparts mainly due to the decrease in overhead.

Installing Applications in Windows XP Professional

While most or all native Windows XP applications are installed by inserting the CD and following the prompts, or in the case of downloaded applications, double-clicking the icon of the compressed file, there are other methods also. While the other methods can in most cases be used with Win32 applications, some of these methods are especially well-suited to 16-bit applications. They are:

- Using the Run dialog box.
- Launching Setup from Windows Explorer
- Using the Add Program Wizard

Using the Run Dialog Box

Installing applications using this approach is very similar to using an MS-DOS prompt to launch an application by entering the path of the program file, or using Windows 3.x dialog boxes (remember those?) for getting an application up and running. Let us take a quick look at how you can install an application using the Run dialog box. Be sure to have the CD of the application you want to install handy. If your application also requires a diskette, be sure to have both inserted into their respective drives before starting this process.

1. Click Run from the Start menu. It is by default just above the Log Off command.
2. Click Browse to find the application you want to install.
3. From within the Browse dialog box, click Open. The path for the application is then placed in the Run dialog box. Since this application is 16-bit based, the check box for running in a separate memory space, if enabled, is available as an option. Select this check box.
4. Click OK. The executable file that appears in the Run dialog box is initiated and the application is installed.

Launching Setup from Windows Explorer

You can use Windows Explorer to install applications in Windows XP Professional as well. To install from Windows Explorer, follow this procedure:

1. Select My Computer from the Start menu or desktop. This starts a Web-enabled interface for navigating the contents of your system. Figure 4.2 shows the Windows Explorer interface which is used to traverse the contents of your system's disk drive(s).
2. Using the functions in Windows Explorer, navigate to the installation file icon for your application, usually called install.exe or setup.exe. Then double-click the icon to start the installation.

Using the Add Program Wizard in Windows XP Professional

This last approach to installing applications centers on a series of tools which can be found in the Add or Remove Programs applet in the Control Panel and has a series of selections and corresponding paths for adding, upgrading, repairing, or removing existing programs from your workstation.

The procedure outlined here shows how to use the Add Program Wizard for installing a new application. In this instance, the application being installed will be Acrobat. Only programs written for Windows can be installed using this option.

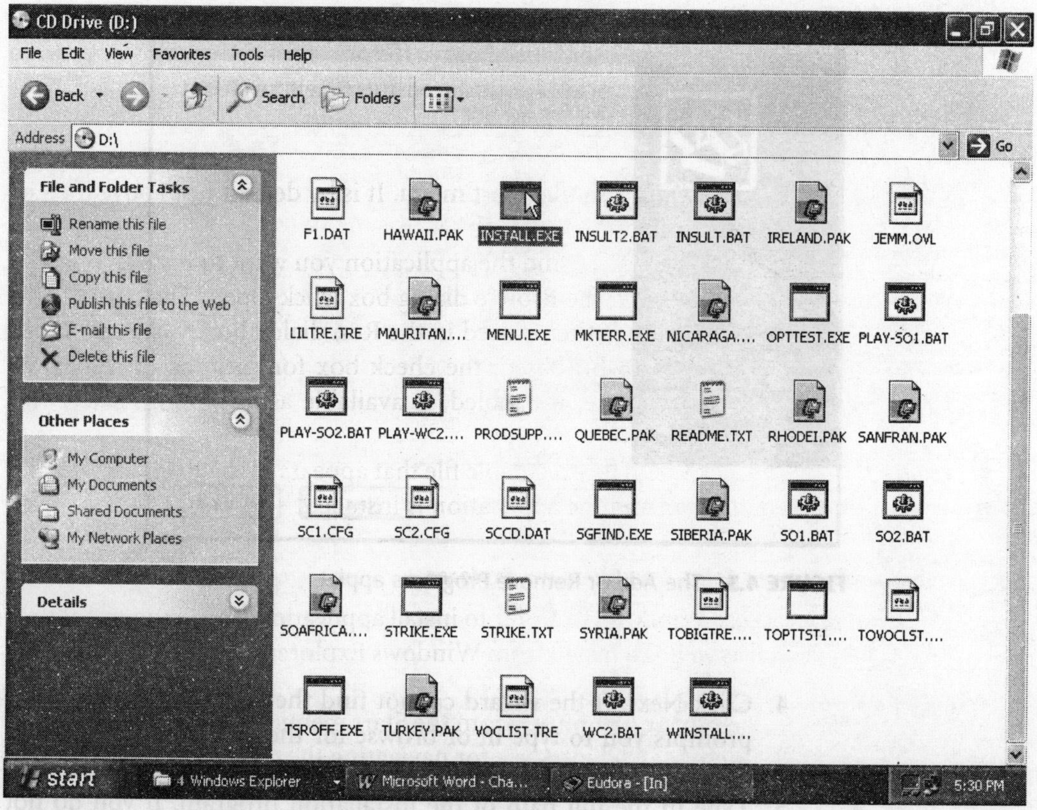

FIGURE 4.2 Using Windows Explorer to install applications.

1. Double-click the Add or Remove Programs icon in the Control Panel. The introduction page of the Add or Remove Programs applet is shown, and appears in Figure 4.3.
2. Click Add New Programs, the second icon on the introduction screen of the Add or Remove Programs applet. A new page appears containing two selections; one for adding a program from CD-ROM or floppy disk and another for getting updates from Microsoft on the latest additions and bug fixes for Windows XP Professional.
3. Click Add a program from CD-ROM or floppy disk. A wizard is launched.

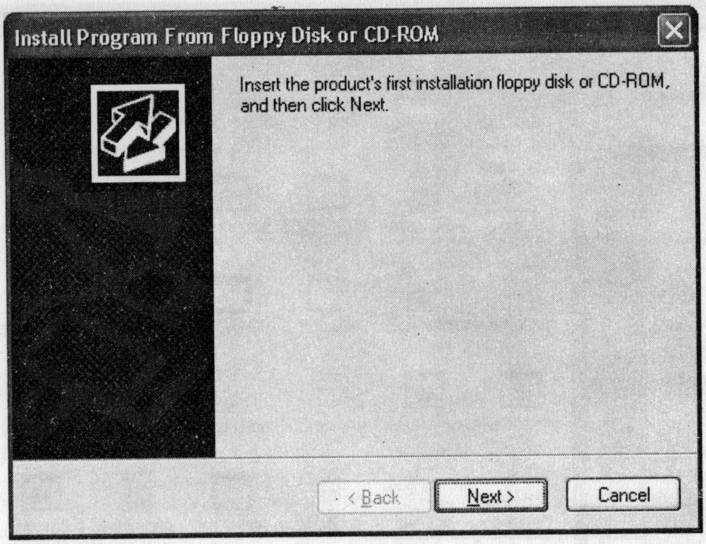

FIGURE 4.3 The Add or Remove Programs applet.

4. Click Next. If the wizard cannot find the installation program it prompts you to type in or browse for the application's location. Figure 4.4 shows this second page of the Add Program Wizard.
5. Type in the full path of the installation program. If you do not know the path, click browse and navigate to it. You will see a series of dialog boxes like the one shown in Figure 4.5. When you have found it, click Open. The wizard page returns, this time with the path of the installation program showing in the text box.
6. Click Finish. The application begins to install, showing the first of several splash screens for completing installation.

Installing and Using MS-DOS Applications

To install an MS-DOS program on Windows XP Professional, you can use the Windows Explorer method or the Run dialog box method as described in the previous section. MS-DOS applications are not really installed in the way Win32 applications are—the files are simply copied into a new folder on the main partition. The program is not registered in the Registry nor copied into the Program Files folder as are Win32 applications.

You can run your MS-DOS applications in Windows XP, and actually get more done than would have been possible using a standalone PC with

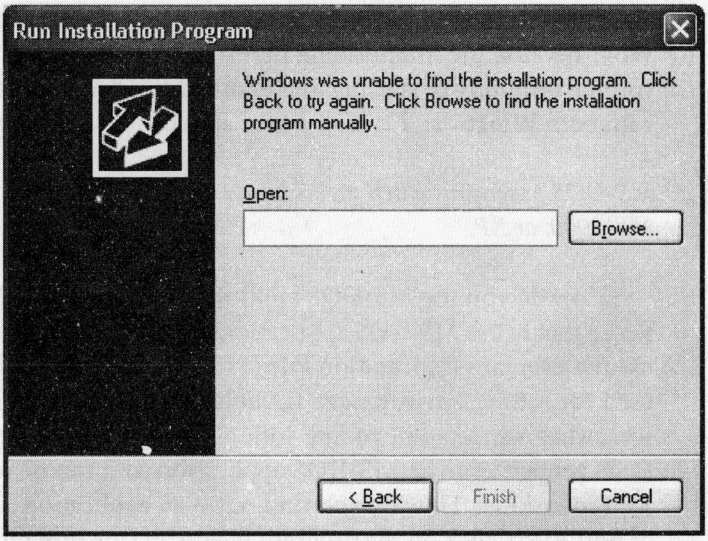

FIGURE 4.4 The wizard prompts for the location of the application's installation program.

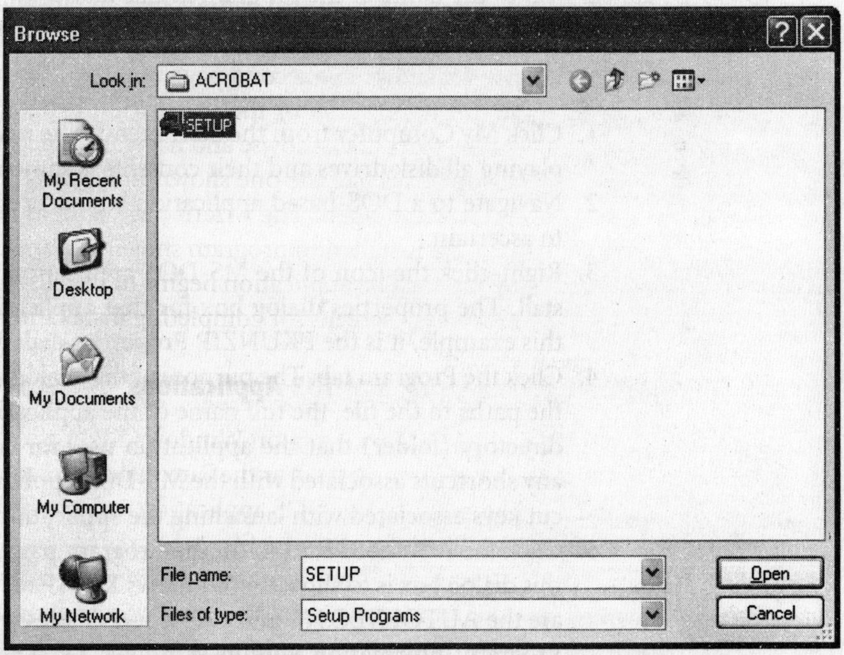

FIGURE 4.5 Using the Add Software Wizard to install a single application.

the fastest processor, highest amount of memory and best disk subsystem. Why? Because the multitasking nature of Windows XP Professional gives you the flexibility of starting and ending MS-DOS applications in parallel with both Win16- and Win32-based applications running concurrently.

MS-DOS programs which access hardware directly will not run in Windows NT, 2000, or XP.

How do you use MS-DOS applications in Windows XP Professional? Recall that to use MS-DOS applications in Windows 3.x you would have to use the Program Information File (PIF) Editor. The PIF Editor was a tool used for setting environment variables and system requirements. It was somewhat cumbersome to fine-tune. The following procedure shows how to set properties of an MS-DOS application so it can be used in Windows XP Professional. How do you find out if an application is MS-DOS based or not? Right-click on the program file's icon (the program file will almost always be called by the program's name or initials and have the .exe extension) and click Properties. Click the Program tab from the Properties dialog box that appears. If it is a DOS application, the MS-DOS icon will appear next to the name of the program in this tab.

Here is the procedure for accessing the properties of a given MS-DOS application:

1. Click My Computer from the Start menu. The new format for displaying all disk drives and their contents is shown.
2. Navigate to a DOS-based application whose properties you want to ascertain.
3. Right-click the icon of the MS-DOS application you want to install. The properties dialog box for that application is shown. In this example, it is the PKUNZIP Properties dialog box.
4. Click the Program tab. The purpose of this dialog box is to confirm the paths to the file, the full name of the application, the working directory (folder) that the application uses for completing tasks, any shortcuts associated with the MS-DOS application, and shortcut keys associated with launching the application.
5. Click the Advanced button on the Program page. The purpose of this dialog box is to show the Windows XP PIF file locations. These are the AUTOEXEC.NT and CONFIG.NT files which serve as the Program Information Files in Windows XP. These files are used

for launching DOS applications just as AUTOEXEC.BAT and CONFIG.SYS were used for running applications in MS-DOS and older versions of Windows. In the case of Windows XP launching MS-DOS applications, both the AUTOEXEC.NT and CONFIG.NT files are initialized and run with every request. You can change the options in these two files to more finely tune MS-DOS applications to run on Windows XP.

6. Click OK.
7. Click Change Icon. The Change Icon dialog box appears and gives you the option of setting a different icon to represent your application.
8. Click the icon you want to use, then click OK. Notice at the top of the Program page the icon you have just selected is shown.
9. Click the Font tab. From this page you can set the font which will be used in the Command Prompt window. You can choose between bitmapped or TrueType fonts. Many people prefer the TrueType fonts as they scale directly to the size of the screen.
10. Click Bitmap only, then TrueType only, and Bitmap only again. Notice how the Window preview area of the dialog box changes in size to reflect type of font technology chosen.
11. Click an entry in the Font size scroll box. Notice how the size of the font and the size of the window in the Window preview area changes correspondingly.
12. After experimenting with these options, select the one that best fits your preferences and then click Apply. The selections made will then be applied directly to the MS-DOS application you are setting parameters for.

Configuring Memory Options to Support DOS Applications

The most important aspect of any DOS application's performance in Windows XP is the use of memory. The Memory page is used to set the way that conventional, expanded and extended memory are used in conjunction with the DOS application.

Due to the number of possible options available on this page, each major area is defined in detail here. As you read through these options keep in mind the DOS applications you may want to run and decide how you would configure system memory.

Exploring Conventional Memory

In this area of the dialog box, you have the option of setting parameters for both Total and Initial environment memory classifications. Let us briefly look at what each of these do.

- **Total**—Refers to the total number of kilobytes that PKUNZIP needs to work. By default this is set to Auto. This will allocate just as much memory as necessary to ensure your MS-DOS application runs. If you have time to test each memory range, you can also do that by using the variety of options available. In general, it is a good idea to let this value stay at Auto.
- **Initial environment**—Sets the number of bytes (not kilobytes) reserved for the initialization files on your workstation. Files that are part of the initialization sequence include COMMAND.COM and AUTOEXEC.NT. Since this variable defines the initial amount of memory allocated to PKUNZIP's start-up process it is a good idea to have this set to Auto all the time as well.
- **Protected check box**—While by default this is not selected, it is a good idea to select this option with all DOS applications. Selecting this option creates a dedicated memory partition into which a DOS application is loaded and runs. Not selecting this option opens you up to the potential of having an errant DOS application crash other DOS applications which may be running on your computer.

Configuring Expanded (EMS) Memory

Most DOS applications do not use expanded memory. It is best to leave this option set to None. In the event a customized application your organization uses has built-in support for expanded memory, use the drop-down combo box to set the memory needed to run it.

Configuring Extended (XMS) Memory

This memory specification was created to provide DOS applications with memory above the 1024KB DOS limitation. Many relatively recent applications support extended memory, so be sure to check the DOS application's manual for compatibility with XMS. When using this option keep in mind that CONFIG.SYS is loaded into the high memory area on Windows XP, so selecting the Uses HMA check box may be irrelevant to your application. Be sure when using this option to specifically select a memory amount that is within your workstation's capacity, as a number exceeding available memory will cause the application not to load. High Memory is a historical term from the early days of DOS when applications would load themselves into memory locations above a system's standard memory locations.

Configuring DPMI Memory

This is managed extended memory that you can allocate to an application. Unlike Extended Memory, this type of memory can be set to a value higher than the amount that is physically installed in your workstation, and the application will still run. This type of memory is somewhat similar to using a protected memory structure, yet stops short of providing the dedicated memory partitions that are essential for reliable application performance.

Exploring the Screen Page

The purpose of this page is to set the appearance of the Command Prompt window when it opens and runs the DOS application. Let us take a look at the options you can use for setting screen properties using this page of the PKUNZIP Properties dialog box.

Choosing between Full-screen or Window

Keep in mind that many DOS applications were developed for CGA, EGA or even VGA screen resolutions, and will modify the size of the Command Prompt window to reflect the standard set in the software. Do not worry if you intend to run the DOS application only in a single window. As DOS applications include their own video drivers, changing the size of the window will distort their appearance on your screen. You can easily resize the window once the application is up and running. The window settings vary based on the application. Peruse these settings and adjust them to fit your needs.

Performance Attributes

You can also use the Screen page for increasing the performance of your application. Here are brief summaries of the two check boxes in the Performance box of the Screen page:

- **Fast ROM emulation**—If your video adapter supports Fast ROM emulation, select this check box to increase the speed of MS-DOS program output, especially text, on the screen.

- **Dynamic memory allocation**—If your DOS applications display the majority of their functions in text mode with a few in graphics mode, you will want to select this check box. In fact, if any portions of your DOS applications use graphics displays, be sure to select it. This feature tells Windows XP to use system memory for both text and graphics screens.

Additional Properties

There are other pages as well in DOS applications' Properties dialog boxes, and you can explore them to see how the settings they contain can further customize the appearance of your DOS applications. You may find the Misc. and General pages interesting.

Once you are finished configuring the application, click OK. The changes to the Properties dialog box are then recorded and ready for the next time you use the DOS application.

CHAPTER SUMMARY

One of the main design goals of Windows XP Professional is the capability of reliably running previous-generation applications. To this end, Microsoft has created a series of subsystems that use protected memory partitions to ensure reliability and consistent performance. This chapter explores the key concepts of how the Windows XP architecture has been created with the goal of compatibility in mind, and how the subsystems support Windows 16-bit, 32-bit, and DOS-based applications. Beginning with an overview of the organization of the Windows XP kernel and progressing through the approaches used to ensure compatibility with the industry's previous generation applications, this chapter provides a roadmap by which you can teach others.

5 Working with Printers in Windows XP Professional

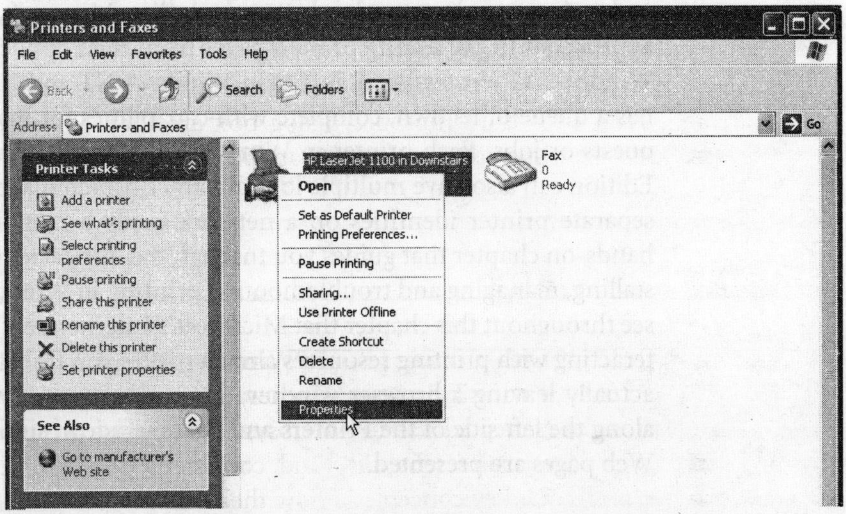

INTRODUCTION

After getting an entire network up and running, you realize that setting printers up presents a challenge. The Marketing Communications Department needs to get the latest advertisements for your company printed from their workstations on the color printer down the hall. Finance wants to get their reports by nine o'clock every Monday for the meeting with the general managers, and Development wants to use the new high-speed laser printer. In short, in almost every job in a networked environment, the work product for many people is the paper their thoughts and efforts are captured on. Printing is a big deal in any business since it is the method by which many professionals have a chance to deliver their expertise literally in black and white. Printing is here to stay, and the challenge of making this resource work for those you support or for a network you are responsible for is the topic of this chapter.

The world of printing has changed rapidly during the last five years, and with the advent of Windows-based printing architectures there has been an increasing emphasis on network printing as well. Sharing printers once meant taking a extra-long Centronics cable and passing it to your coworker; today it means sharing the printer over, in the majority of cases, a TCP/IP-based network. The decentralized aspect of printing has continued to force application developers, including Microsoft, to modify their approaches to presenting printed pages from their applications. Today in Windows XP Professional, just as in Windows NT and 2000, each printer has a queue of its own, complete with capabilities for managing print requests or jobs. Each printer in Windows XP Professional and XP Home Edition can also have multiple logical names, which makes the creation of separate printer identities on a network easily accomplished. This is a hands-on chapter that guides you through the intricacies of setting up, installing, managing and troubleshooting printing in Windows XP. You will see throughout this chapter that Microsoft's Internet-centric model for interacting with printing resources almost makes you feel as if you are never actually leaving a browser window. That is because key tasks are listed along the left side of the Printers and Faxes window, similar to how some Web pages are presented.

PRINTING FROM WINDOWS XP PROFESSIONAL

Windows XP's location for installing printers and associated output devices is called the Printers and Faxes folder. It includes an icon representing each printer and fax program installed. The approach to printing in Windows XP Professional is to focus on the customization options inherent in each output device. Printing from applications in Windows XP Professional is comparable to approaches in previous operating systems. Printing from Windows XP involves several steps. When you invoke the print command from an application, the application spools the document to the intended printer. *Spooling* is the process of writing the contents of a document to a file on disk. This file is typically called a spool file. Operating systems spool files so that the data being printed can be sent to the printer at a printable speed. Many times you will send multiple documents to the printer, and due to the imaging speed of the printer, you will need to wait from several seconds to a few minutes for the documents to be produced depending on the amount of memory dedicated to spooling documents. Documents waiting to be printed are actually stored in a *queue*. Figure 5.1 shows the selection of Printers and Faxes from the Start menu.

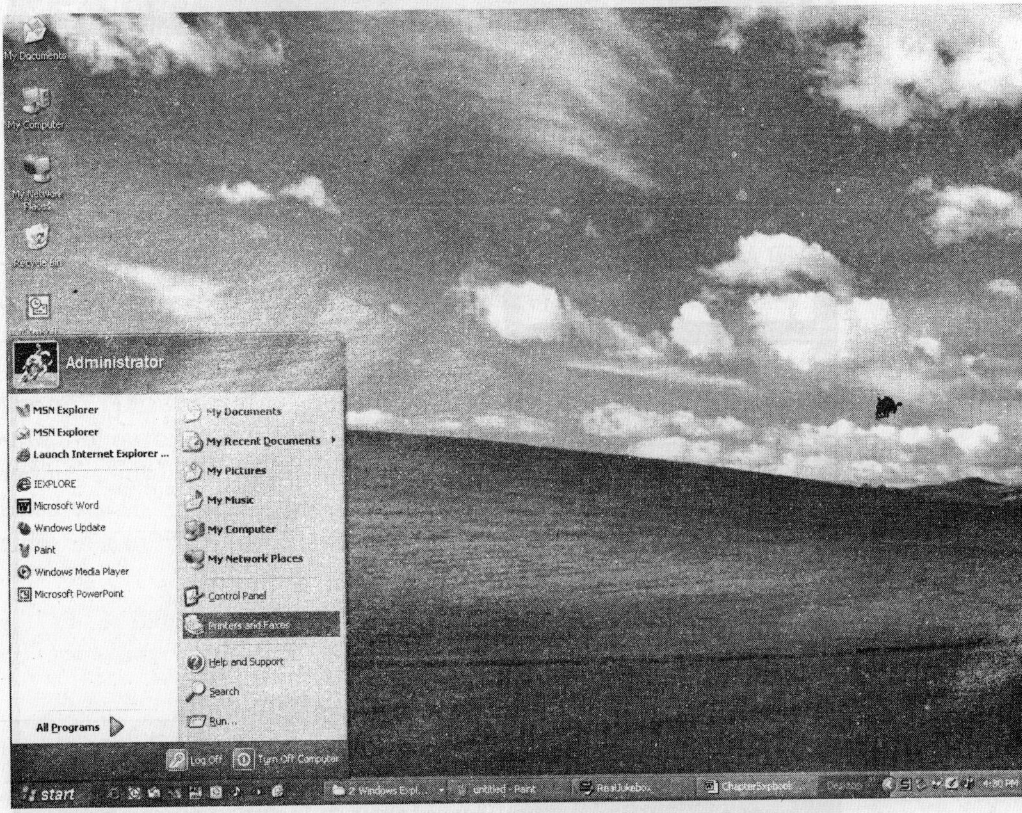

FIGURE 5.1 Touring the printing features of Windows XP begins with the Start menu.

Exploring XP's Printing Features and Their Benefits

Features of printing in Windows XP are described here:

- Windows XP has an entirely new interface that is very browser-like in its appearance. Figure 5.2 shows the interface for printing in

Windows XP. Notice that along the left column there is a menu of printer tasks. The Send a fax command is a new feature in Windows. There is also a Fax icon already included in the Printers and Fax window. Clicking that icon shows the properties you can use for sending a fax directly from Windows XP.

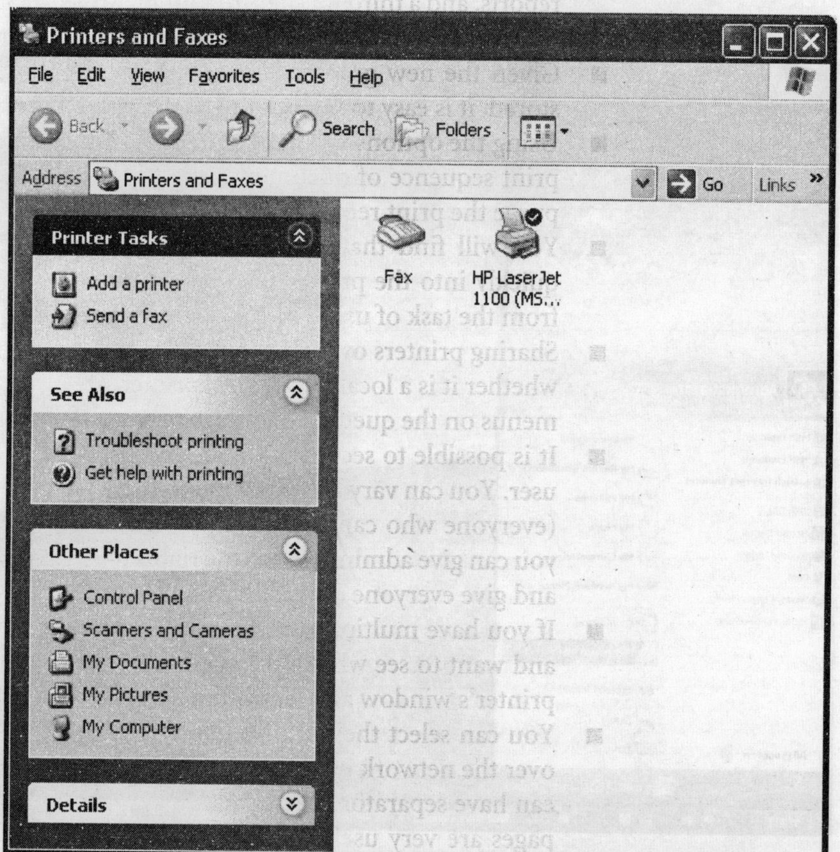

FIGURE 5.2 Introducing the new interface for the Printers and Faxes folder.

- Printer drivers supplied by Microsoft, along with those supplied by printer manufacturers continue to be improved with enhanced features. Support of additional features is more robust in Windows XP Professional than in previous versions of Windows, especially with the Hewlett-Packard printers and plotters.

- Any printer connected to a network where Windows XP is being used can have multiple logical names, meaning you can customize as many individual queues as you want for a printer, depending on the type of document you want to produce. You could, for example, have an HP Color LaserJet in your office where you create one queue specifically for transparencies, another to draft monochrome reports, and a third for high-resolution project management charts. Each queue can have settings appropriate for each purpose.
- Given the new graphical interface to how printer identities are stored, it is easy to figure out which printer to use for a given task.
- Using the options inherent with each printer, you can modify the print sequence of documents, even delete selected documents or purge the print requests of an entire printer.
- You will find that printing tasks, once requested, are spooled quickly into the printer queue, and the application is off-loaded from the task of using memory to support the print request.
- Sharing printers over a network is easy as all properties, including whether it is a local or network printer, are available directly from menus on the queue window.
- It is possible to secure a printer and define user rights by class of user. You can vary how Administrators, Power Users, or Everyone (everyone who can log on) uses the printer. Using these options you can give administrators the rights to change printer properties, and give everyone else permission to print.
- If you have multiple documents going to several printers at once and want to see when they are completed, you can open up each printer's window and watch the progress of each print request.
- You can select the option in each printer to send you a message over the network once printing has been completed, and also you can have separator sheets printed between jobs as well. Separator pages are very useful in a networked environment because they allow users who are visiting the printing room to retrieve their documents to easily determine where their document ends and the next one begins.
- Windows XP Professional can function as a print server in small network environments where there are ten or fewer users. The Windows XP Professional print architecture can operate in either a client or server role. For over 10 users, Windows 2000 Server is recommended as a print server. Windows XP Professional supports up to 10 users per Microsoft's licensing guidelines.

- Enhanced security is included in a graphical interface in Windows XP. You can, as an administrator, set the following access permissions: Print, Manage Printers, Manage Documents, and a set of more specific permissions called Special Permissions. Figure 5.3 shows the enhanced security features included in each printer's properties.

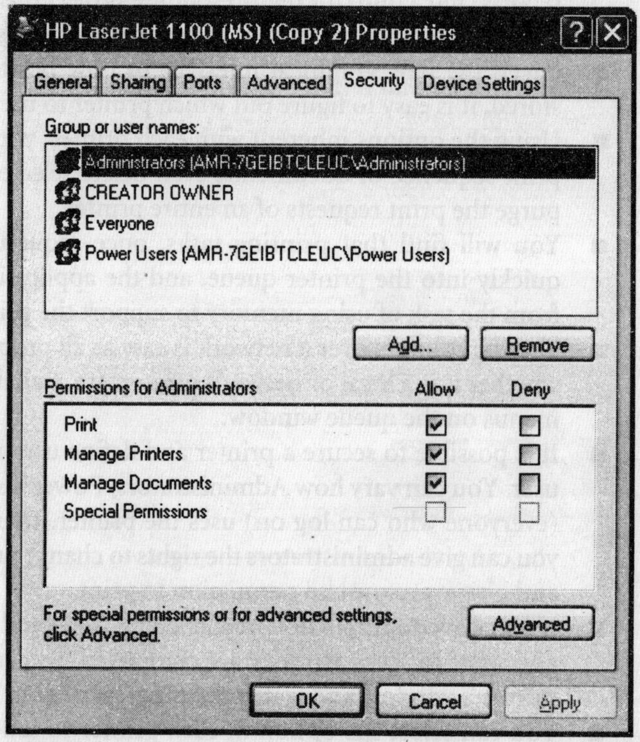

FIGURE 5.3 Exploring the Security page of a printer's properties dialog box.

Creating a New Printer

In this chapter, the term queue, *or* logical printer *refers to the software interface between the user and the physical (hardware) printer.*

Getting a printer up and running in Windows XP Professional is a matter of following the steps of the Add Printer Wizard. At the end of this process an icon is going to appear in the Printers and Faxes Folder that represents the printer queue. As mentioned earlier, different queues, or *logical printers* can be created for the same hardware. In fact, it is possible to create a logical printer for any printer model if either you or Windows has a driver for it. It does not matter if you actually have the hardware or not. This will be covered in more detail later in this chapter.

Let us start with a step-by-step guide on how to create a new printer in Windows XP Professional. Note that unless you have an HP LaserJet 1100, you will be installing a logical printer for hardware that you do not have.

If you have a printer that is connected via a USB or other hot-pluggable interface such as IEEE 1394, you do not need to use the Add Printer Wizard. If you connect and power on the printer, Windows will install it automatically. See the text on Figure 5.5 for details.

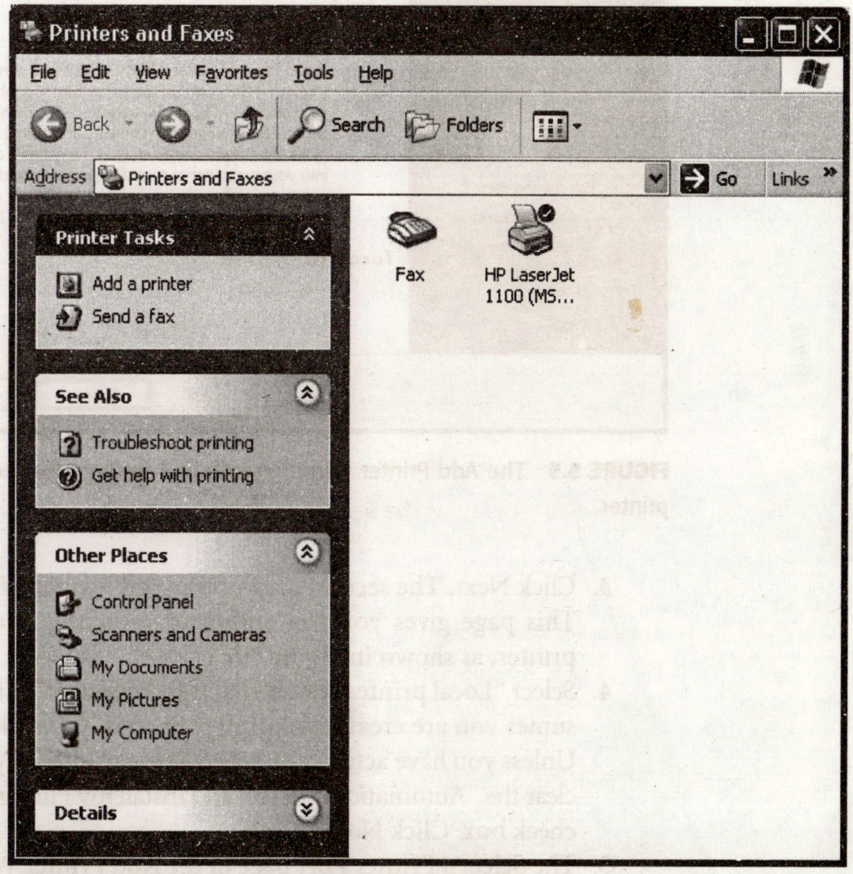

FIGURE 5.4 Using the Printers and Faxes folder.

Creating a New Local Printer

1. Click Printers and Faxes from the Start menu. Figure 5.4 shows the Printers and Faxes folder.
2. Double-click the Add a printer icon in the Printer Tasks menu on the left side of the window. The Add Printer Wizard starts. Its first page is shown in Figure 5.5.

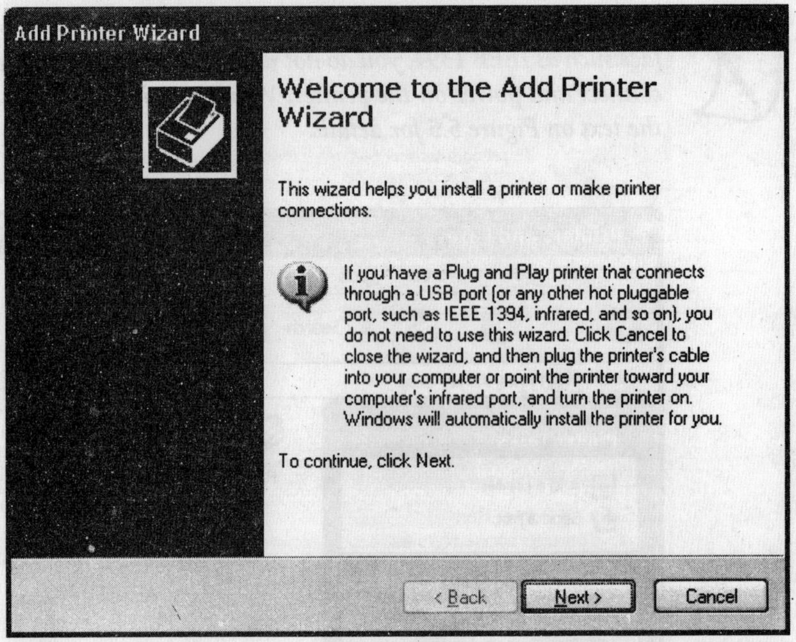

FIGURE 5.5 The Add Printer Wizard guides you through the steps of creating a printer.

3. Click Next. The second page of the Add Printer Wizard is shown. This page gives you the option of installing a local or remote printer, as shown in Figure 5.6.
4. Select "Local printer attached to this computer" as this exercise assumes you are creating a printer on your XP workstation locally. Unless you have actually attached a new printer to your computer, clear the "Automatically detect and install my Plug and Play printer" check box. Click Next.
5. The Select a Printer Port page of the Add Printer Wizard is shown next, and appears in Figure 5.7. This is the dialog box that is used

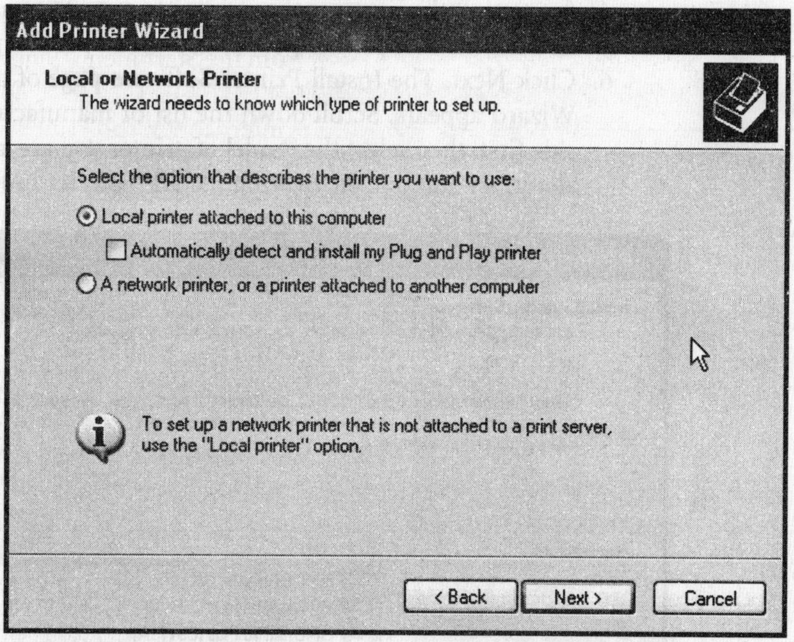

FIGURE 5.6 Selecting a local or network printer.

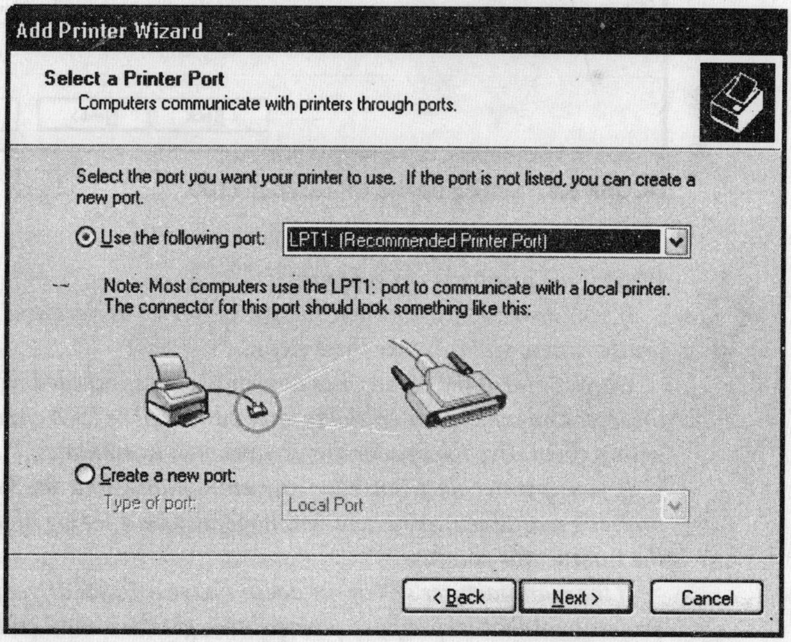

FIGURE 5.7 Setting the port to use with the newly-installed printer.

for setting the port for the printer to use. The majority of time, LPT1 is the best printer port to use with a parallel printer.

6. Click Next. The Install Printer Software page of the Add Printer Wizard appears. Scroll down the list of manufacturers to the left side first, then select the model of printer you are using. Figure 5.8 shows an example of selecting the HP LaserJet 1100.

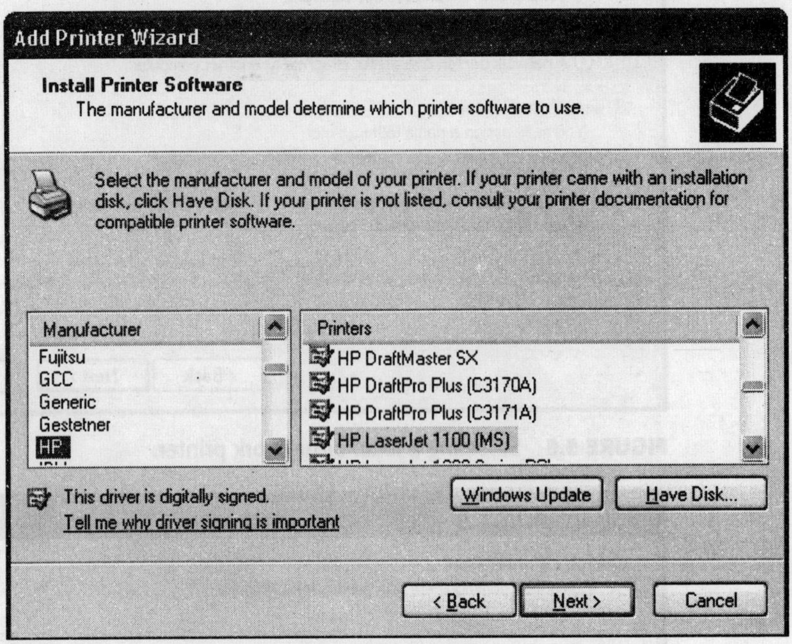

FIGURE 5.8 Setting up the HP LaserJet 1100.

What if my printer is not supported?

If you have looked through the list of device drivers and do not see your printer listed, you can take these steps:

Check to see if the printer has any emulations included within it. Many of the laser and inkjet printers today have either HP or IBM emulations included within them. Use the printer driver your printer emulates.

If your printer does not have any emulations, find the Web site for your printer's manufacturer. There will hopefully be a listing of device drivers on the Internet for your use.

If the manufacturer's Web site doesn't have a device driver for Windows XP Professional that is specific to your printer, get the e-mail address of the product manager for your printer, and write to ask that they support it.

7. Click Next. The device driver is then applied to the printer being created in the Add Printer Wizard, and the next page appears. This page takes the name of the printer's device driver and applies it to the printer's queue. You can name a printer anything you want, providing it fits within the 31-character field shown in this page of the Add Printer Wizard. Figure 5.9 shows the naming page for the printer.

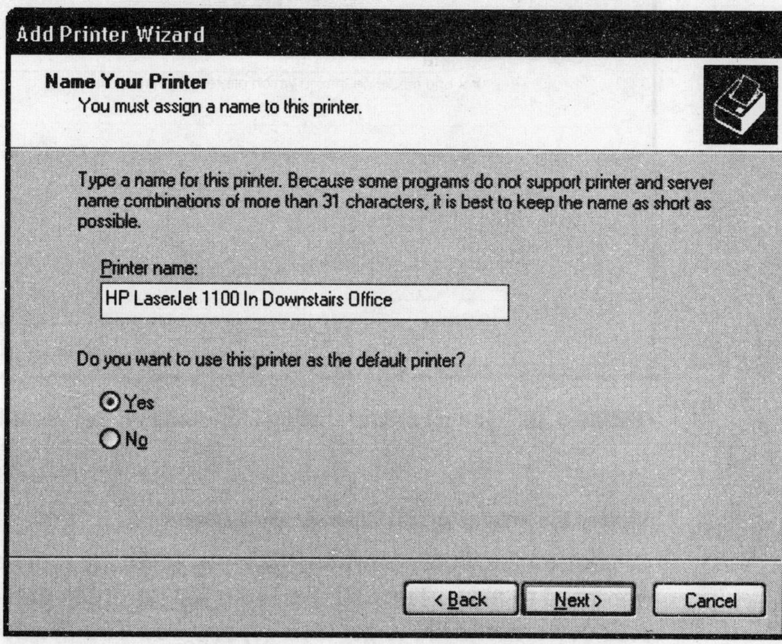

FIGURE 5.9 Naming the printer in the Add Printer Wizard.

8. Click Next. The Printer Sharing page appears. The purpose of this page is to set the printer to be shared or not, and if it is to be shared, to set the share name. Figure 5.10 shows this page of the Add Printer Wizard.
9. Click Next. The Location and Comment page of the Add Printer Wizard is shown next. While optional, this can be useful information as many networked printers are at times difficult to find for new employees and visitors to your offices.
10. Click Next. The Print Test Page of the Add Printer Wizard is shown. Click Yes to get a test print generated from your printer.
11. That's it! Your printer is up and running and ready to go!

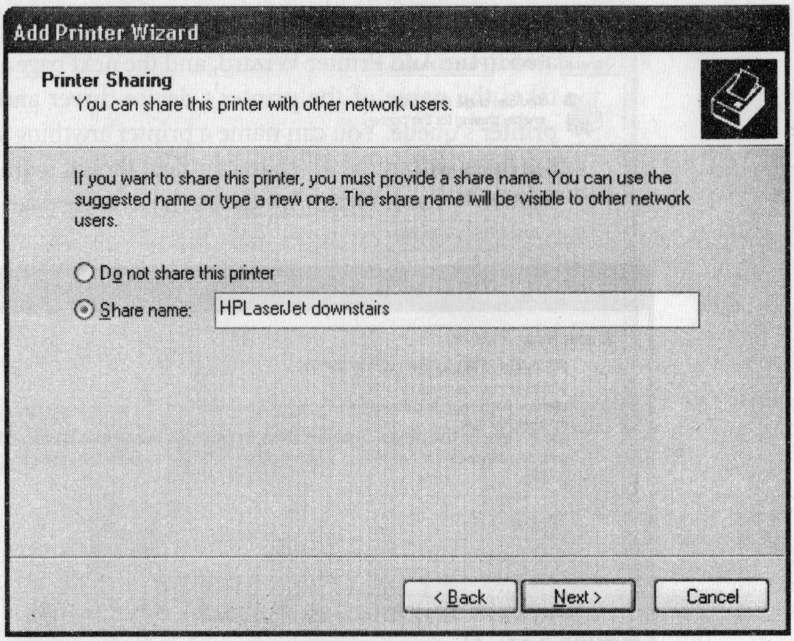

FIGURE 5.10 Setting printer sharing in the Add Printer Wizard.

Making the Printer Accessible over the Network

As your organization continues to grow, there are more and more people who need to print. The LaserJet 1100s are on order, and in the meantime your coworkers need to get their reports out. You decide that the best approach is to help them out by sharing your printer over the network. Here is the procedure for making a printer previously configured for local use available to other members of your workgroup:

1. Open up the Printers and Faxes folder from the Start menu.
2. Double-click the HP LaserJet 1100 icon.
3. Click Sharing from the Printer menu.The Sharing page of the HP LaserJet 1100 Properties dialog box appears as shown in Figure 5.11. Notice that there are six different pages to choose from.
4. Using the choices on the sharing page you can toggle between Not Shared and Shared status for your printer, and assign a share name for it as well. Figure 5.12 shows this page with the printer name filled in.
5. Click OK. The printer is now shared for others in your workgroup.

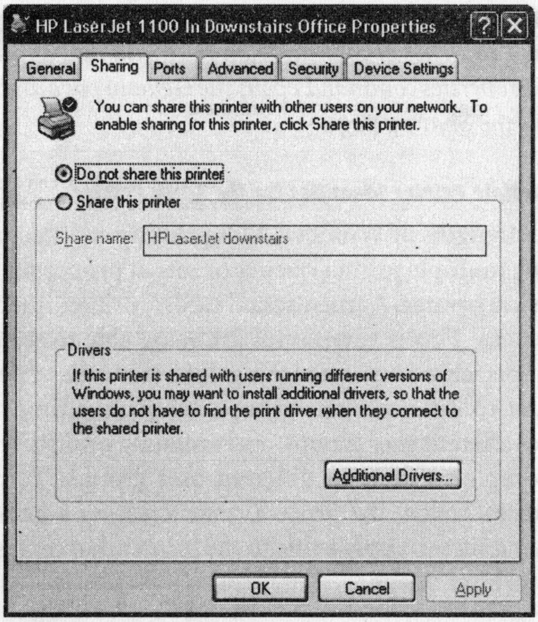

FIGURE 5.11 Sharing a printer created originally for local use.

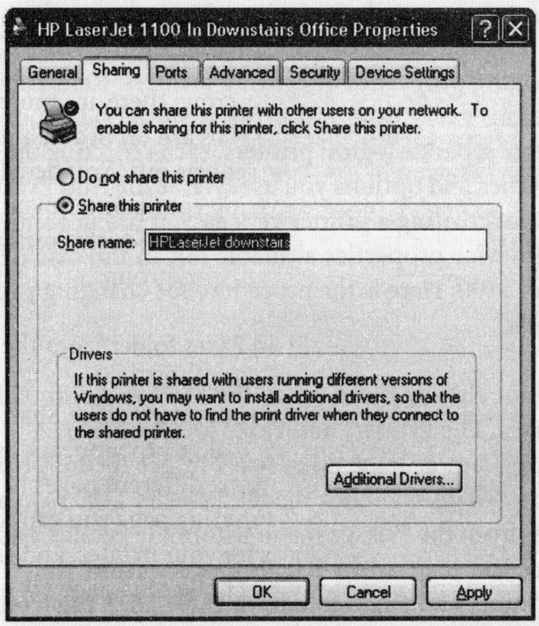

FIGURE 5.12 The printer is now shared.

You can also access the printer's properties by right-clicking the printer icon and clicking Properties or Sharing from the menu that appears. As you would expect, the Properties command opens the General page and the Sharing command opens the Sharing page.

Creating Multiple Printer Identities for the Same Printer

One of the strengths of Windows XP's printing architecture is the capability of having multiple printer queues or sets of properties associated with a single physical printer. As mentioned earlier, printer queues are also called logical printers. This is very useful for being able to select different print queues for specialized tasks, assigning different levels of permissions for the same printer to different user groups, scheduling times that a printer is available to different user groups, and assigning priority levels (whose print jobs are completed first) to different user groups. To create additional printer queues, follow the procedure for creating a printer earlier in the chapter, being sure to apply a title to the printer that represents the purpose of the new printer queue.

Exploring Printer Properties

Once a printer is created, you may want to change the properties associated with it as the needs of your organization change. This section discusses changing properties of existing printers. Remember that you don't have to do this every time you print; it would be a more efficient use of time to create separate logical printers, each reflecting the most commonly used properties and options you use. While the Add Printer Wizard made the process of creating a printer very easy, it did not show you the full extent of the device properties available for, in the case of the example, an HP LaserJet 1100. Here is the procedure for changing properties of an existing printer.

1. If not already there, go to the Start menu and click Printers and Faxes. The Printers and Faxes folder opens.
2. There are at least three ways to get to the printer's properties. You can double-click the HP LaserJet 1100 icon and click Properties from the Printer menu within the printer's queue window, select the icon and click Properties from the File menu on the Printers and Faxes folder, or right-click the icon and click Prop-

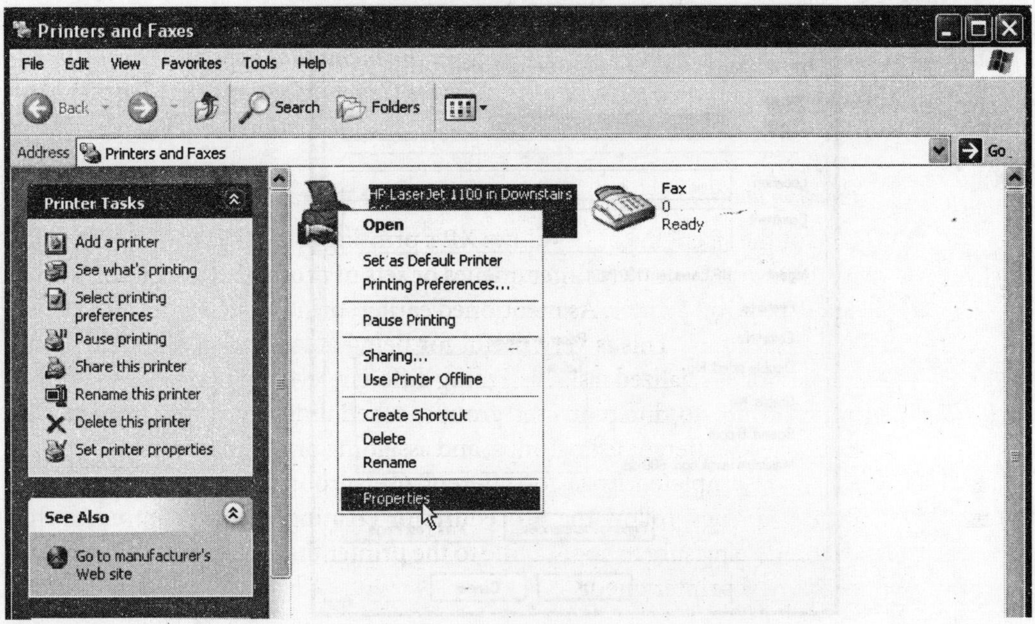

FIGURE 5.13 Accessing printer properties by right-clicking the printer's icon.

erties from the menu that appears. Figure 5.13 shows the latter approach.

3. The HP LaserJet 1100 Properties dialog box appears, and is shown in Figure 5.14. Notice that this dialog box has several pages, all tabbed at the top. This dialog box has been designed to provide access to features device drivers can control during printing.
4. Click the Device Settings tab. These are the characteristics or features of the printer that the device driver for this printer supports. You can use these settings to customize the characteristics for your specific needs.
5. If it is present, click the plus sign next to Installable Options to expand the list of options. There is an option for configuring this specific printer queue to take advantage of the memory installed in the printer. Figure 5.15 shows the Printer Memory option set to 2MB (2048 KB), which is the factory default. Click the number 2048 and the arrow to its right to open the menu of choices of memory amounts for this printer.

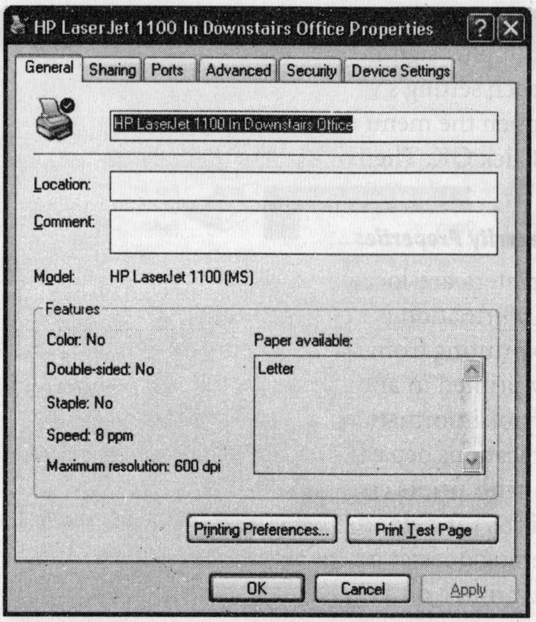

FIGURE 5.14 The Printer Properties dialog box.

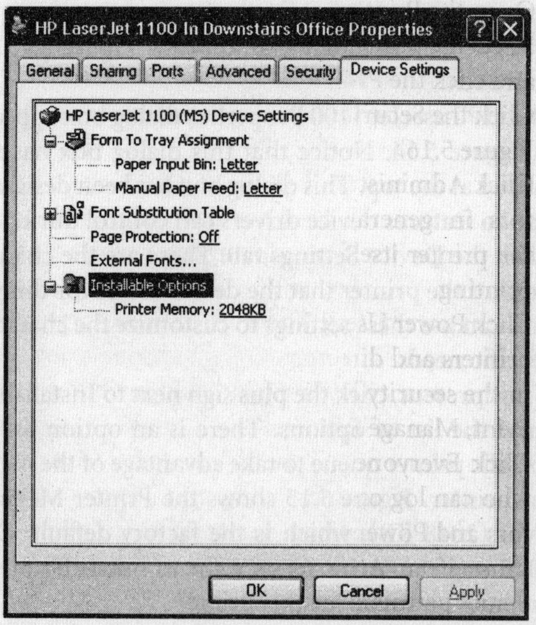

FIGURE 5.15 Exploring the Installable Options on the Device Settings page.

6. Many printers also have a Form to Tray Assignment setting. Click the plus sign next to this item to see the different settings. Click each setting's value (the default is "letter") and the down arrow to open the menu of tray settings.
7. Click OK. The HP LaserJet 1100 Properties dialog box is closed.

Setting Security Properties

Many printers are located in rooms where confidential accounting and finance information is kept, including payroll records. Being able to limit access to printing from confidential areas so that sensitive data is not inadvertently printed in another department is essential to preserve the confidentiality of information in an organization. Many times the marketing communications departments have the best color and high-resolution laser printers, with prints costing up to $4 each to produce. Limiting access to these printers is a good idea so that, for example, an invitation to a new club opening doesn't mistakenly end up in your company's catalog. If you shared a printer on your desk and find that now the entire company is using it, you can limit access to that printer to your workgroup only. Here is the procedure for setting up security on your printers.

1. Open the Printers and Faxes folder from the Start menu.
2. Select the printer you want to secure the use of. Right click the icon and click the Properties command.
3. Click the Security tab. The Security page is shown, and appears in Figure 5.16.
4. Click Administrator in the top portion of this page. Administrators in general need to have the option of managing both the printer itself and documents in case there is a problem with printing.
5. Click Power Users. These are users of the computer who can share printers and directories. They are one level below Administrators in the security levels of XP. Notice that by default this group has Print, Manage Printers, and Manage Documents permissions.
6. Click Everyone. As the title suggests, Everyone refers to anyone who can log onto the computer. (Everyone includes Administrators and Power Users—it excludes no one. This is important, because if an Administrator denies permissions to Everyone, he denies permission to Administrators as well as everyone else.). It is a good idea to select Print only for this group, unless the Everyone

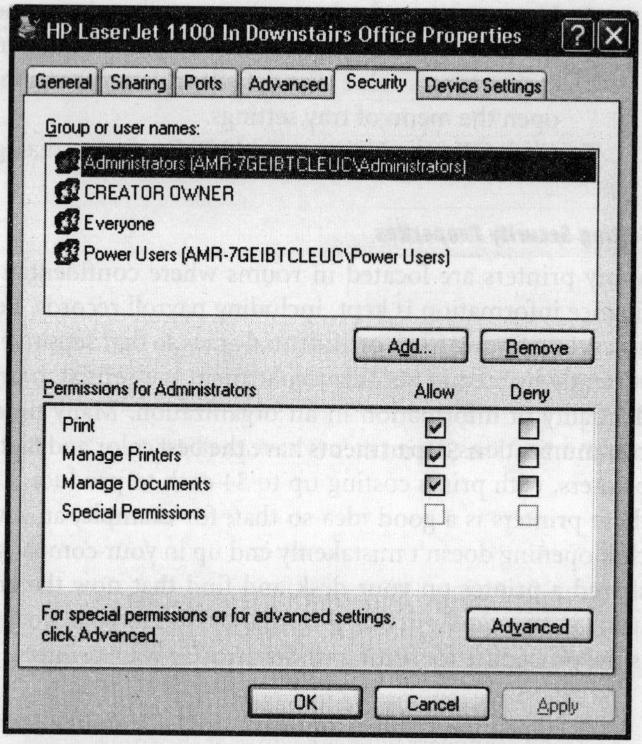

FIGURE 5.16 The Security page of the Printer Properties dialog box.

group is small and includes the members of your immediate work area.

Adding New Users and Permissions

As your organization grows you will want to add new users to the security profile for the printer they are going to use. You do not have to do this for every single user who joins your organization and uses the network. This procedure applies to an entirely new class of users, for example, guests who are logging onto your network. Let us look at the procedure for adding Guests to the Security profile for the HP LaserJet 1100 we are using for this example.

1. With the Security page of the Printer Properties dialog box showing, click Add. Figure 5.17 shows the Select Users or Groups dialog box.

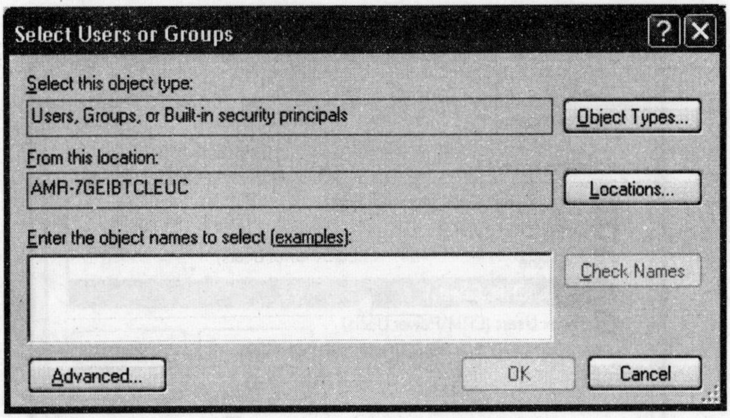

FIGURE 5.17 The Select Users or Groups dialog box.

2. Click Advanced on the Select Users or Groups dialog box. A new dialog box with the same name appears. Click Find Now. A list of all of the users and groups on the computer is displayed. Select Guests and click OK. The original Select Users or Groups dialog box reappears with the name of the computer followed by a backslash and the word "Guests" in the text box.
3. Click OK. The Security page reappears with Guests listed in the Group or user names box. Figure 5.18 shows the results of adding Guests to the security profile for this specific printer.
4. Click OK. The Guests group is now one of the groups that can access this printer, and the dialog box closes. By default, the Guests group has Print permissions only.

Scheduling Printer Availability

At certain times of the day a very popular networked printer can have a queue that resembles a freeway at rush hour with job after job queued up waiting to get to its destination (the printer). As a system administrator you can manage when a printer's queue is available to others on a network. This is accomplished using the Advanced page of the Printer Properties dialog box. Figure 5.19 shows the Advanced page of the Printer Properties dialog box. Notice that along the top of this dialog box there are selections for setting the printer on as always available, or available from one time to another.

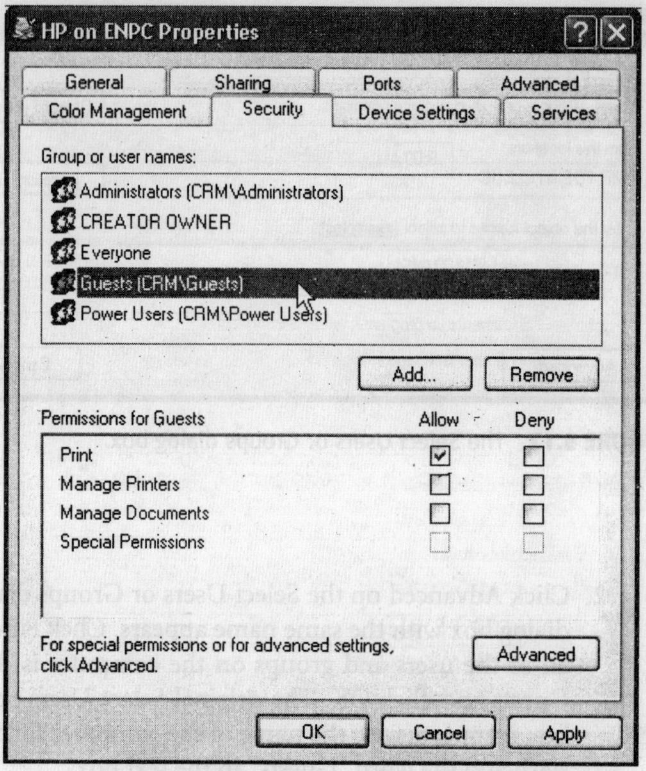

FIGURE 5.18 Adding Guests to a printer's security profile.

What happens to a print request submitted when the printer is not available? The print request stays in the printer's queue until the system becomes available. When a printer is available, all print requests are completed. The security model of Windows XP printing allows for restricting or granting access to groups or individual users. If you want to make a printer available 100% of the time for Administrators, you can create a second printer that shares that specific printer's name with the Administrators in your organization.

Setting Print Job Priorities

What if your top-of-the-line Color LaserJet is suddenly getting more print requests that a wedding invitation printer gets in April? The answer: create a shared printer queue for the high-use group with a priority of 99, and create a second queue for others that may not have as high a demand for color

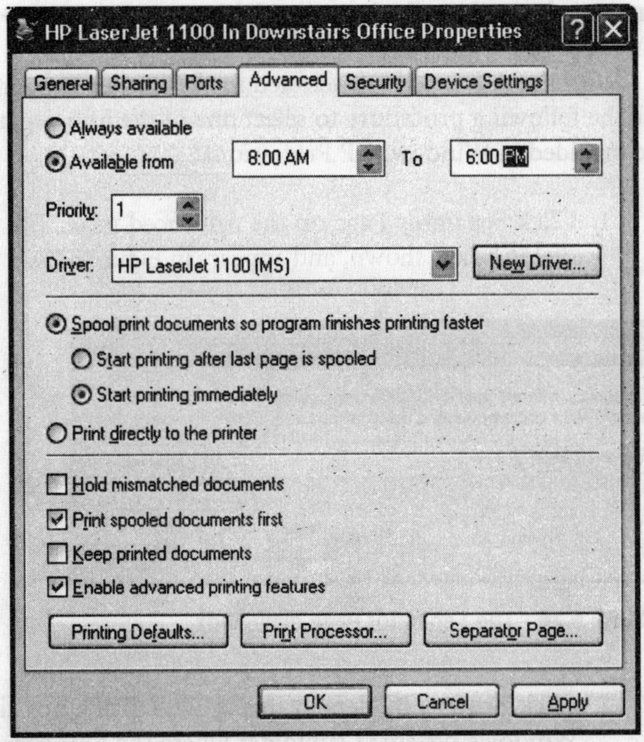

FIGURE 5.19 Options for scheduling printer availability.

printing at 1. This serves the group that requires color printing well; they can get their work done faster with the higher priority queue.

Remember that when setting priorities, the higher the number the higher the priority. The default value for the sliding scale on the Scheduling page is 1.

Configuring Separator Pages

When several people are sharing a common printer, figuring out which document is whose can be challenging, especially on busy days when each person has a project due. Separator pages have been developed specifically to solve this problem. They are used for delineating which print job is whose. You can create your own separator page using Notepad or Wordpad. To select one of the separator pages included in Windows XP, go to the Advanced tab in the printer Properties dialog box. The Separator Page button is located on the bottom of this page. Figure 5.19 shows the Advanced page.

With the Advanced tab selected in the Printer Properties dialog box, use the following procedure to select one of the four separator pages that are included in Windows XP Professional:

1. Click Separator Page on the Advanced page. The Separator Page dialog box is shown, and appears in Figure 5.20.

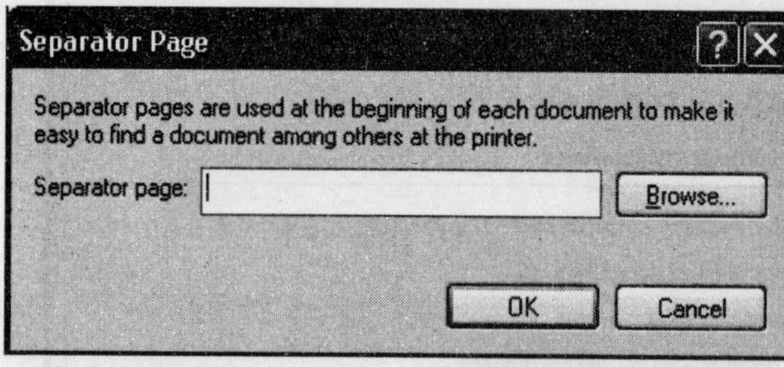

FIGURE 5.20 The Separator Page dialog box.

2. Click Browse. By default this browse dialog box takes you to the Windows\system32 subfolder where the four separator pages are located. These are pcl.sep, pscript.sep, sysprint.sep, and sysprtj.sep. The file extension .sep defines a separator page file. Since the HP LaserJet 1100 is running HP's Printing Control Language (PCL), that page is selected. Figure 5.21 shows the system32 subfolder.
3. Click OK to close Printer Properties and store the separator page information in the Registry of your workstation.

You can create your own separator page using Notepad or any other application capable of generating ASCII text files. Here's how:

After opening up Notepad, enter a control character on the first line of the file. This character is referred to by the operating system as the control character, and informs Windows XP this a file that will be used for functions, preventing it from being read as a document. You can enter any non-alphabetic character. Consider using the # sign as the control character. This character goes at the top of the file in the first position. You may also see articles describing this process using the $ sign. Either the # or $ sign is fine to use as both work. Table 5.1 shows the control codes and how they work in the creation of a customized separator page file.

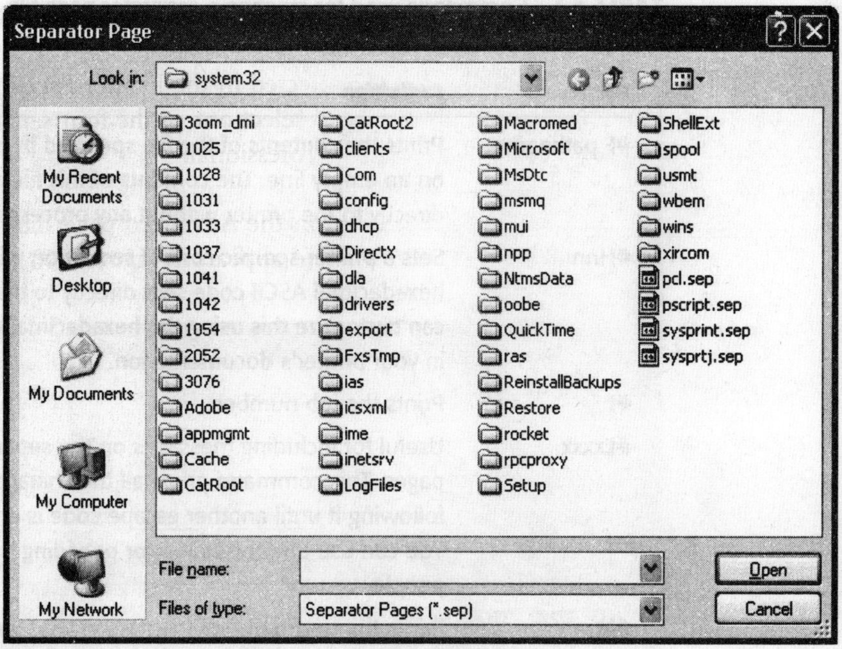

FIGURE 5.21 Browsing for separator page files.

TABLE 5.1 Commands used for creating a separator page file.

Variable	*Definition*
#B#M	The B value prints the preceding text in double-width until the #U character is read.
#B#S	Prints text in single-width block characters until #U is encountered.
#D	Prints the date the job was printed. The representation of the date is in the date format set in the Regional and Language Options applet in the Control Panel.
#E	Ejects the page from the printer. Use this code at the beginning of a new separator page or to end a separate page file. You may need to experiment with this value as it can produce an extra blank page.

(continues)

TABLE 5.1 Commands used for creating a separator page file (*continued*).

Variable	*Definition*
#F pathname	Prints the contents of the file specified by path, starting on an empty line. The contents of this file are copied directly to the printer without any processing.
#Hnn	Sets a printer-specific control sequence, where nn is a hexadecimal ASCII code sent directly to the printer. You can customize this using the hexadecimal values found in your printer's documentation.
#I	Prints the job number.
#Lxxxx...	Useful for including messages on the separator file pages. This command prints all the characters (xxxx) following it until another escape code is encountered. You can use this command for providing messages to people.
#N	Prints the user name of the person who submitted the print job.
#n	Skips the number of lines (from 0 to 9). Skipping 0 lines moves the printing to the next line.
#T	Prints the time the job was printed. The representation of the time is in the time format selected in the Regional and Language Options applet in the Control Panel.
#U	Turns off block character printing.
#Wnn	Sets the width of the separator page. The default width is 80; the maximum width is 256. Any printable characters beyond this width are ignored

In order to make sure that settings discussed so far always apply to a printer regardless of whether the printer is accessed locally or over the network, the settings must be made on the computer that the printer is physically connected to. Every computer with a local printer that is shared over the network is considered a print server. *To make configuration changes that affect all local printers, choose Server Properties from the Printers and Faxes folder's File menu. There are four pages of settings there.*

Configuring a Network-Based Printer

It should not surprise anybody that many of the higher-end monochrome and color laser printers are used primarily via networks. In addition to the benefits of being able to amortize the cost of a higher-end printer over more users when networked, the actual performance of printers has continually increased in an effort to provide more responsive performance to users. This section explores those features.

What's New in Network Printing

In addition to enhanced support for client printing (as will be shown in the hands-on tour of setting up a networked printer), Windows XP Professional includes these new features:

- **Internet Printing**—Enhancements made to the Windows XP printing architecture make printing from the Internet seamless. Client workstations can access shared printers either over a corporate intranet or over the Internet. URLs can point directly to printers. Users can query as to the status of print tasks over the Internet, and, in addition, install printers over intranet and Internet connections. Drivers are also installable directly over the Internet.
- **Simplified User Interface**—A new Web view of the Printers and Faxes folder and print queues include direct links to further information and technical support. There are enhanced printer properties in most new drivers and an enhanced command set developers can call from in the development of their own device drivers. There is also an Add Driver Wizard in the Server Properties dialog box for installing additional printer drivers for down-level clients. Driver properties are also available to Administrators for managing printing tasks at a print server level.
- Enhanced security and auditing features include the capability to add or delete classes of users to or from individual queues.

Creating and Connecting to a Network Printer

Let us get started with the procedure for connecting to and creating a network printer. You will find that these steps parallel in some respects the sequence of events in the Add Printer Wizard for creating a local printer. One of the major differences is in the selection of drivers for the client systems located on your network that have an operating system different than Windows XP Professional.

1. Click Printers and Faxes from the Start menu.
2. Click the Add a Printer command on the menu on the left side of the Printers and Faxes window. The Welcome page of this wizard is shown. Click Next. The Local or Network Printer page appears. Figure 5.22 shows this screen with the Network printer option selected.

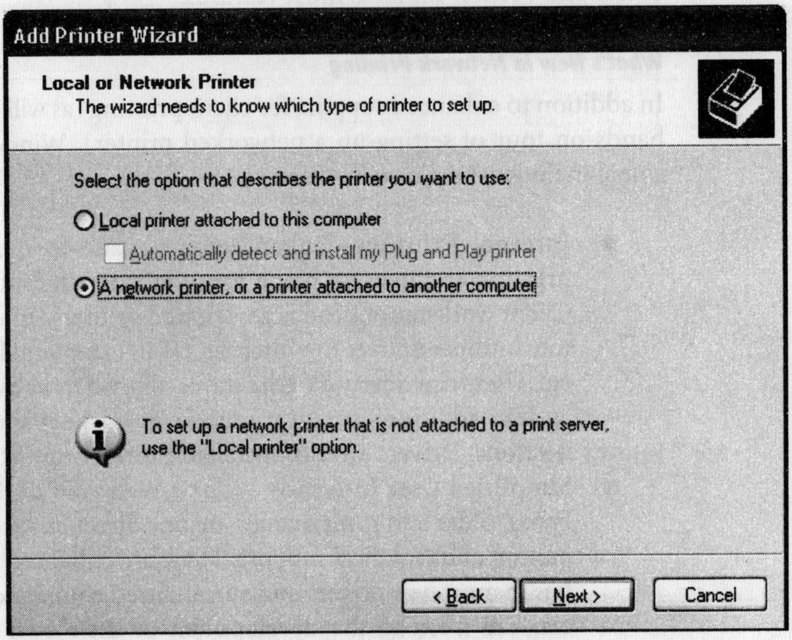

FIGURE 5.22 Using the Add Printer Wizard to connect to a networked printer.

3. Click Next. The Specify a Printer page is used for selecting the networked printer you want to connect to. You can also opt for an Internet printer on this page by entering its URL. Figure 5.23 shows this page.
4. Click the Microsoft Windows Network item in the Shared printers box to view the shared printers on your network. If there is a shared Internet printer already available on the network an entry for Windows XP Internet Printing will appear here as well.
5. If you do not see the printer you want to connect to within the Microsoft Windows Network, type in the path to the printer in the Printer text box.

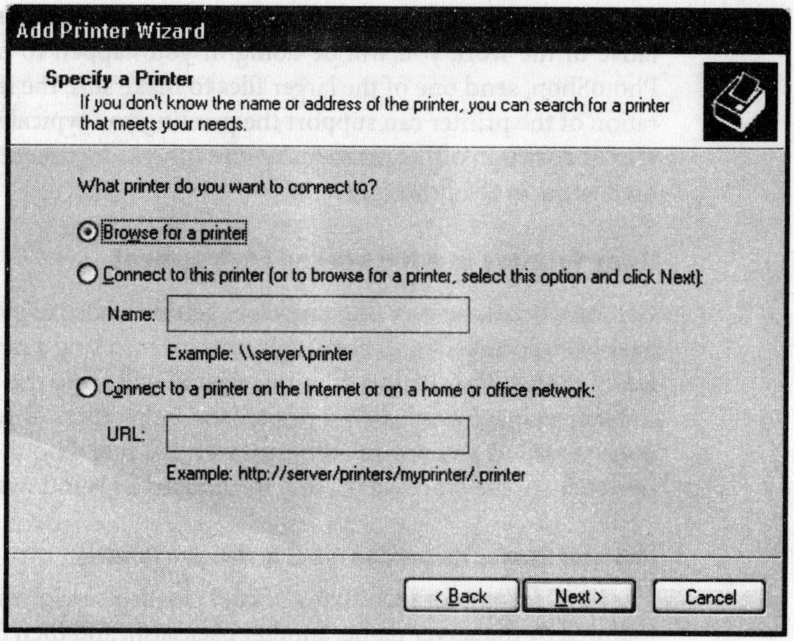

FIGURE 5.23 Locating the printer on the network.

6. Once the printer is found, the next screen of the wizard is shown. This screen prompts you to choose whether or not to designate this printer as the default printer. If this is the primary department printer, select Yes. If this printer will be used only under special circumstances, click No. Once you have made your choice, click Next.
7. Click Finish to close the wizard. The connection to the networked printer is now complete. It is represented as an icon in the Printers and Faxes folder. You can tell this icon refers to a networked printer by the depiction of a hand on the bottom. Whenever an icon has a hand on the bottom, that designates the resource as shared.

Testing the Connection

How can you be sure your workstation can now "see" and use the networked printer over the network? Simple. Open up any application, choose a sample document, and click Print from the File menu. Make sure the printer you want to test is listed in the printer name drop-down menu of the Print dialog box. Select a document or drawing that is most representative of the work you will be doing. If you happen to use AutoCAD or PhotoShop, send one of the larger files to make sure the memory configuration of the printer can support the printing you typically do. It is a good idea to do this in off-hours to make sure others' documents do not wait behind yours in the print queue.

Using Printers in a Networked Environment

Getting work done very often involves getting a hard copy of the work you have been completing. Increasingly, this means using a networked printer. Using the hands-on tutorials in this section will show you how to more effectively manage a networked printer and help others in getting their work done as well. If you are an administrator you may find these steps a quick refresher course on concepts first introduced in Windows NT 4.0.

Universal Naming Convention (UNC) in Network Printing

The UNC format for identifying printer resources involves two backslashes followed by the server name, another backslash, and then the printer name. This UNC naming convention is frequently used to identify virtually every network object. For a printer named Sparta located on a server called Colussus, the UNC name would be \\Colussus\Sparta. You would use this path in the Add Printer Wizard for selecting a printer to be shared. Figure 5.24 shows the entry of UNC name of a shared printer in the Add Printer Wizard.

How Client/Server Printing Works in Windows XP Professional

One of the core strengths of Windows XP as an operating system is its reliance on a client/server approach to printing, in addition to file and application sharing. The benefit of client/server printing is that the individual client workstations offload printing tasks to a server for completion. Why not just have each workstation process and submit the print requests? Windows XP is a powerful multitasking operating system, and as long as the hardware is sufficient, should be able to handle printing as a background task. Why not just keep printing local?

If you happen to have a color printer that takes quite a bit of memory to print a document or graphic, your workstation's applications may have slightly slower performance during print time. This is due to the fact that each thread for the applications you are running is competing for memory. A device driver handling an extensive color printing task will also generate

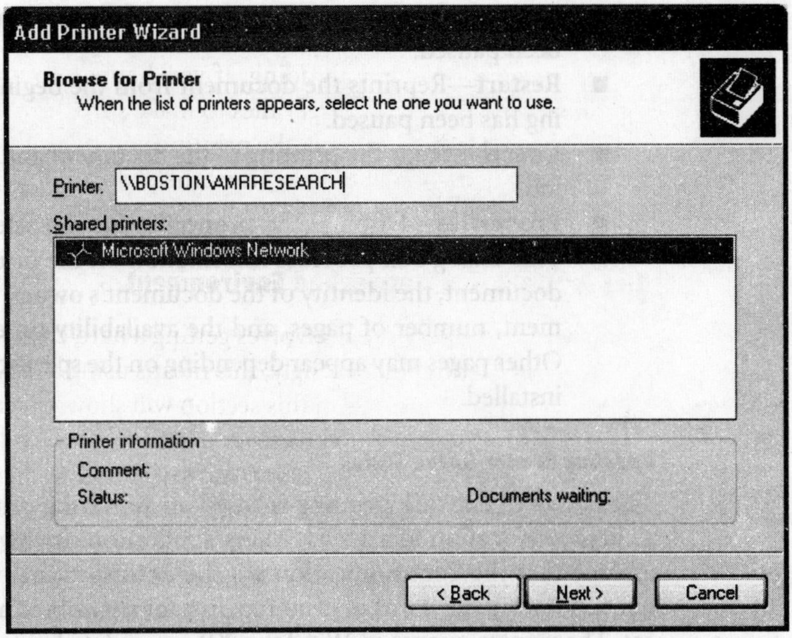

FIGURE 5.24 A shared printer name in UNC format.

a thread, in effect a request for memory and processing time, just like every other application. Taking the print task and sending it to a server for processing frees up resources on your workstation so applications can complete their tasks. This is the essence of why client/server printing is so popular.

Managing Printers in Windows XP Professional

Document Menu Commands

If you are the owner or Administrator for a printer (more on these subjects later in this section) you can actively manage the documents in a printer queue using the commands located in the Document menu. If your printer is attached directly to your workstation, you most likely have Administrator privileges. Let us take a look at each of the commands in the Document menu.

- **Pause**—Pauses the printing of a document. This is useful to pause the printer so that you can, for example, replace an ink or toner cartridge.

- **Resume**—Continues the printing of the document after it has been paused.
- **Restart**—Reprints the document from the beginning after printing has been paused.
- **Cancel**—Stops the printing of the document and deletes the print job.
- **Properties**—Displays the properties for the selected document. This dialog box provides information on the print priority of the document, the identity of the document's owner, size of the document, number of pages, and the availability times of the printer. Other pages may appear depending on the specific printer software installed.

Updating Printer Queue Status

The nature of network printing is based on delivering print requests from a client workstation to a server. Many applications involved with printing assume that the communication will be unidirectional with the printer queue showing the status of print requests for networked and shared printers. The printer queues in Windows XP are updated via network connections periodically, and depending on the network traffic, the updates can take up to a minute. If you want to get the immediate status of a printer queue, press F5 with the printer queue active. This immediately queries the status of the queue and displays the current list of jobs.

Assigning Printer Permissions

Presented here are the steps for assigning permissions:

1. From within the Printers and Faxes folder, right click the icon of the printer to which you want to assign permissions.
2. Click the Security tab of the Printer Properties dialog box. All of the groups and users who have access to the printer are shown in "Group or user names" area of this page.
3. Click Add. The Select Users or Groups dialog box is shown. The purpose of this dialog box is to add users and groups to the access list of this printer.
4. Click Replicator This is a group that is responsible for system maintenance, including replicating print and application files in a networked environment. At times during the support of a networked printer, members of the replication group may be the only staff onsite when a printing error occurs.

5. Click OK. The UNC name for the Replicator group is now added to the access list for the printer being configured.
6. Highlight the Replicator group in the top part of the Advanced page. The Replicator group's permissions to this printer are displayed in the box on the bottom portion.
7. Select or clear the check boxes in the box to grant the appropriate permissions. It is usually not necessary to deny permissions. If you deny permissions to a group, no member of that group will have that permission, even if the same permission is granted directly to the user or to another group of which the user is a member.
8. Click OK. The dialog box closes and the Replicator group now has the permissions you have set.

Ownership of a printer entitles you to change its properties, set security levels, change the priority of documents waiting to be printed, and change the times the printer will be available in a shared mode. Printers created from within an Administrator account automatically take that account as the owner. You can change the owner of a printer using the following procedure:

1. From within the Printers and Faxes folder, right-click the icon of the desired printer. Select Properties from the menu that appears.
2. The Printer Properties dialog box appears. Click the Security tab. The Security page is shown.
3. Click Advanced. The Advanced Security Settings dialog box appears.
4. Click the Owner tab. The Owner page appears. The current owner is displayed in the text box on the top of the page. Select the new desired owner from the list in the box on the bottom part of the page. Click OK. The new owner is set and the Security page reappears.
5. Click OK to close the Printer Properties dialog box.

Repositioning Print Jobs in Queues

If you are the owner of a printer or have at least Manage Documents permission, you can change the priority of a document waiting to be printed. This will, in effect, change the order of documents waiting to print. Here is the procedure for doing so:

1. Open the printer's queue.
2. Right-click the document whose priority you want to change. A menu appears.
3. Click Properties on the menu. The document's properties dialog box appears.
4. Locate the Priority slider on the General tab of the document's properties. Move the slider to the appropriate priority level—a higher number if you want to move this document up in the printing order, a lower number if you want to move it down.
5. Click OK. The document's order should change accordingly. This will not, however, be reflected in the list.

Deleting Printers

Many shared logical printers have a specific purpose, and once you have used one to complete a project, you may want to delete it. You may also find that you have several queues for the same printer, and want to trim down the number of logical printers you have created. Once a printer has been deleted the device driver and font files associated with it stay on your workstation, in the event you want to re-create it. Follow this procedure for deleting a printer from the Printers and Faxes folder:

1. Right-click the icon of the printer you want to delete.
2. From the menu that appears, click Delete.
3. A confirmation dialog box is shown next. Click OK to confirm that you want to delete the printer. The printer is then deleted.

Troubleshooting Printing Problems

This section covers troubleshooting and other printer support issues.

Supporting Printers in Windows XP Professional—Obtaining a Device Driver

Let us say you are running the Add Printer Wizard and you suddenly find that there is no printer driver for your printer. You can solve this problem using the following procedure:

1. Using the manufacturer's Web site search capabilities, see if they have a Windows XP Professional device driver for your printer. Often these Web sites have Downloads pages where you can find drivers. Make sure the device driver you download is specifically for Windows XP, as Windows 9x drivers use different system-level

resources. If there are no Windows XP drivers, Windows 2000 or NT 4.0 drivers may work.

2. Check your printer's user manual, or if you do not have one, check the printer manufacturer's Web site for the emulation that is included in your printer. Select the printer driver for the emulation supported in your printer. If you use an emulated driver, some of the advanced features of your printer may not work.
3. If your printer does not have a device driver or emulation that is supported in Windows XP, call the printer manufacturer and ask when a device driver for Windows XP will be available. Calling Tech Support may also yield a workaround that the company may have found to work with Windows XP Professional. Also, many times manufacturers will develop interest lists of customers who need device drivers. Once a device driver is complete, manufacturers will send the device drivers to the people requesting them.

How to Test Your Printer with Windows XP Professional

The best approach to testing a printer in Windows XP Professional is to try and print a test page from the Printer Properties dialog box. When a printer is first created in Windows XP a printer test page is submitted at the end of the wizard. If you have just created a printer and are not getting any printing, try going back and reinstalling the device driver. If your printer has already been installed and the printer just quits working, you can submit a print test page from the General page of the specific printer's properties dialog box. In the lower right-hand corner of the dialog box there is a Print Test Page button that sends test data to the printer.

Solving Network and Local Printing Problems

You may submit a print request over a network and have the print request show up in the print queue, but then it suddenly disappears. This could be caused by a few factors, described here:

- **Inadequate disk space on your workstation**—Check to make sure there is enough disk space on your system to print the document. Print files take up to twice the space of their corresponding document file. If you have just a little free space on your hard disk you may find it difficult to print.
- **Problems with the print server**—Is the print server up and running? Is there enough disk space and system memory on the

server? Is the disk drive running? Are there many other queues running on the server as well?

- **Shortage of memory**—If your workstation is running low on memory either due to many applications being open or having a minimal amount of memory to run Windows XP Professional, you will want to free up memory by either closing applications or adding more memory.
- **Connectivity problems**—Is your workstation talking with the network? Check another network-based resource to see if you can communicate on the network.
- **Printer problems**—Is the printer powered on and running? Check the printer's power and data connections.
- **Mis-selected driver options**—Check the printer driver options using the printer properties dialog box to make sure the options selected match the physical attributes of the printer.
- **Bad printer cable**—If the printer still does not work, try replacing the cable. Cables are prone to damage, especially parallel cables that are not IEEE 1284 compliant.
- **Corrupted print driver**—When all else fails, try reinstalling the printer driver. For some reason, printer drivers are prone to corruption.

CHAPTER SUMMARY

Printing from Windows runs the gamut between Centronics parallel or serial connections to being able to print directly on network-based peripherals. The printing architecture for Windows XP Professional includes printer-specific properties that give you the option of tailoring printer queues for individualized tasks and even creating multiple queues for the same physical printer. Security features in Windows XP Professional also make it possible to ensure users who need a given printer's resources always have them available while preventing unauthorized users from printing.

6 Networking Fundamentals in Windows XP Professional

INTRODUCTION

Consider the state of networking even five years ago and its state today. It was not so much the proclamations but the technology advances and the need users had for quickly and efficiently sharing information that drove the widespread migration of networking into the Internet, extranets, and the rapid growth of virtual private networks (VPNs), and made networking grow and become so widespread that even the language of this technology has entered the mainstream of how people communicate.

How does Microsoft continually contribute to this growth? What are the market dynamics affecting the integration of TCP/IP and other protocols into operating systems? How do these fundamental design decisions surrounding a network and its connectivity impact operating system development, and it turn, how you use it? The answers to these questions and more are included in this chapter.

If you are an administrator you will find this a useful chapter for getting others up to speed with the current state of networking technology and how it applies to Windows XP-based networking, and a glimpse into the future of how Windows will change to reflect the ongoing needs of clients. If you are an intermediate to advanced user of Windows XP Professional or networks in general, you will find this chapter useful as a tutorial to get up to speed on the latest changes in networking, thanks to both market and technology dynamics.

WHAT ARE NETWORKS COMPOSED OF?

A local area network is used the majority of the time for sharing print and file resources, with Microsoft, Novell, Sun Microsystems and other companies offering operating systems competing on the relative performance of handling these tasks. Local area networks are also extensively used for sharing applications through a client/server configuration. File and print services and application software availability are available either on a dedicated or peer-to-peer network. A dedicated network is most often found in a client/server network, where one or more servers are defined as the servers to perform no other task but share their resources. Depending on the size of the network, there can potentially be several types of servers included in the network configuration. A server that stores applications, data files, and other reference data is called a file server. A server that hosts the print resources for a network, sharing its printers with other computers in a network is called a print server. A server that shares a large database is called a database server. Servers are designed to fulfill multiple roles, and have features that make them fault tolerant and capable of handling multiple tasks simultaneously in a network environment.

A peer-to-peer network is one in which the role of each system on the network fulfills the role of a server. Any computer can act as a server on the network. The strengths of this approach include ease of integration, security (as protocols which support peer-to-peer are in many cases not routable), and availability of resources throughout the network being transparent to users. The weaknesses of this approach include the speed of the network, the lack of routability, and the limited nature of this approach in terms of the performance demands on a workstation also being used as a server. Once the demands for applications and file and print services expand past the scope of workstations, servers are typically integrated into a network. The continuing growth of an organization also drives many networks from a peer-to-peer to dedicated network architecture.

In the majority of networks being used today, there is a combination of dedicated and peer-to-peer network structures. As more and more users are added to the network, there are new applications that rely on dedicated network architecture. An example of an application that relies on this approach is Oracle's Manufacturing Modules, which run on a centralized server. Client workstations use the applications on the server. Data sets are most often housed on the server to enable other members of a design or engineering team to use them also. Client/server networks are predominantly used for sharing larger data sets where a centralized server is considered essential for the functioning of the network.

UNDERSTANDING HOW NETWORKS ARE ORGANIZED

Networks are really a group of systems gathered together by cables or wireless communications such as infrared or RF (radio frequency) communications. Each of the systems on a network is called a node, and communications among nodes uses the physical components that comprise the network itself. These components are in addition to the nodes themselves, and serve to create the infrastructure of the network. Components in this category include bridges, routers, repeaters, network interface cards, and the other hardware components. Taken together, these elements are considered the physical network. The following sections provide an overview of the key components in a physical network.

The Network Interface Card (NIC)

An essential component in every network, you will find every workstation attached to a network will have a network interface card (NIC) installed (network interface cards are also known as network adapters). The NIC is the adapter card which is physically very similar in appearance to a video adapter, disk controller, or other adapter cards in your workstation. Providing the essential link between the network and your workstation, the NIC is the intermediary which combines the software device drivers that make it recognizable by an operating system with the protocols being transmitted by a network. Increasingly, the protocol being transmitted is TCP/IP, so there has been a corresponding high level of growth in the sales of NIC cards which are TCP/IP-compatible. As you would suspect, the NIC card acts as the information intermediary or translator, receiving, processing and passing data to the network and the operating system. Its primary function is to work with data packets, or collections of data encapsulated for transmission. It is also important to note that although the use of dial-up service through modems has made it possible for thousands of workstation and laptop users to gain access to the Internet, virtual private networks (VPNs) including intranets, and Internet company networks, the high growth of NICs is not affected, as they have much higher performance than modems. Figure 6.1 shows an example of what a NIC looks like.

Each NIC has a unique network address assigned to it during production. This unique address makes it possible to enable network packets to be directed specifically to the NIC in much the way you would direct a letter to a specific business or home based on its street address or even fax number. The NIC has circuitry that monitors the packets coming from the network, and if the packet is meant for the workstation, the NIC processes the packet and transmits it up the OSI model (more on this later) to the operating system. If the packet is meant for another node, the NIC simply passes on the packet. The NIC does not perform this function by itself, however. The layers of the OSI mode serve really as the foundation of a more global operating system, enabling the NIC to perform its tasks seamlessly between the network and the operating system.

Being at the point in the network connection where the network communicates with the workstation, the NIC plays a central role in how efficient both the network performance is on a workstation, and in the performance of the network overall. Because data can be transmitted over the network faster than the NIC can process the data, packets must first be

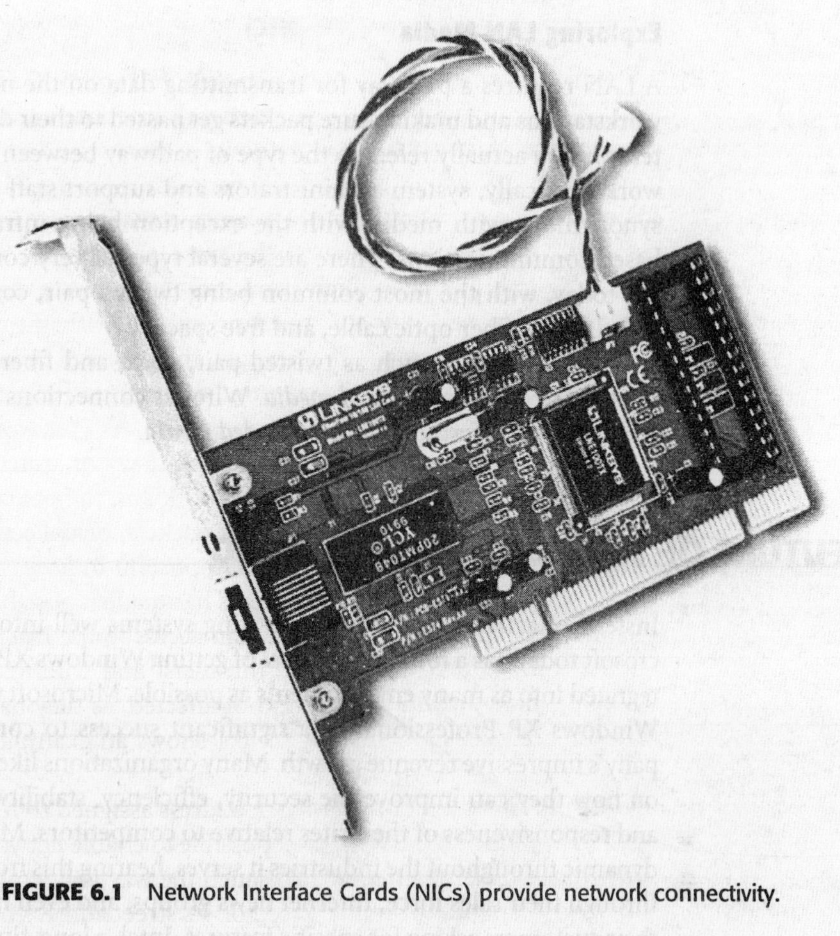

FIGURE 6.1 Network Interface Cards (NICs) provide network connectivity.

buffered until the NIC can process them. A slow NIC can eventually slow an entire network down, as the packets are queued up, waiting to be read. Conversely, newer NICs have the capability to dynamically flex between 10 and 100 megabits per second, making it possible to accommodate both dominant speed ranges of networks available today. Even newer, faster NICs are available and gaining market acceptance.

In some operating systems including Windows NT, it was necessary to make hardware settings such as IRQ and I/O address. Windows XP is a Plug and Play operating system, so it would be rare for you to have to configure these settings manually.

Exploring LAN Media

A LAN requires a pathway for transmitting data on the network between workstations and making sure packets get passed to their destinations. The term *media* actually refers to the type of pathway between nodes on a network. Typically, system administrators and support staff refer to cable as synonymous with media, with the exception being infrared and radio-based communications. There are several types of very common media in use today, with the most common being twisted pair, coaxial cable (also called coax), fiber optic cable, and free space.

Physical media such as twisted pair, coax, and fiber optic cable are often referred to as *bounded media*. Wireless connections such as infrared and radio are referred to as *unbounded media*.

FUTURE OF WINDOWS NETWORKING

Instead of actively promoting operating systems well into the future, Microsoft today has a focus on the goal of getting Windows XP Professional integrated into as many environments as possible. Microsoft will need to have Windows XP Professional be a significant success to continue the company's impressive revenue growth. Many organizations likewise are focused on how they can improve the security, efficiency, stability, manageability, and responsiveness of their sites relative to competitors. Microsoft sees this dynamic throughout the industries it serves, hearing this from existing users through their sales force, Internet news groups, and even from letters from their customers asking for specific features. Intel, a long-time strategic partner with Microsoft, is likewise enamored with the idea of being closer to their present and potential customers than anyone else. Both companies have cultures that reward aggressiveness and in-depth knowledge of customers' needs. With both Intel and Microsoft focusing on the future, the key attributes of a future operating system can be ascertained from the Intel roadmaps by division and their public announcements of entering the network hardware and electronic commerce consulting businesses. Here is a list of the key attributes that Microsoft has recently introduced in Windows 2000 and now are included as standard in Windows XP:

- Strengthening of Kerberos security and integration of Microsoft Wallet-like purchasing capabilities in client-based systems. Server-based operating system counterparts will include electronic commerce components to alleviate potential customers from having to look at secondary software providers for their tools on the Windows XP Professional platform.

- True 64-bit operating system performance is available in the 64-bit version of Windows XP Professional to complement the Intel Itanium and McKinley 64-bit processors.
- Increased intelligence in the interaction of the user interface, so that the PC can handle even more tasks for the user.
- A focus on natural user interfaces that enable the user to speak to the PC, and for the PC to be able to read aloud.
- Complete elimination of the differences in interfaces with various types of communication such as mapping drives for servers and using hypertext on the Internet.
- Automatic load balancing across large clusters.
- Self-repairing network topologies.
- Seamless integration of TCP/IP on Windows XP Professional with Sun Microsystems implementation of DNS, and integration with Novell NetWare.

UNDERSTANDING TCP/IP IN WINDOWS XP PROFESSIONAL

In creating Windows XP, Microsoft began and continued a commitment of listening to their customers, especially the ones in larger networked configurations. Clearly if there was a position in the market where Microsoft could gain a presence, it was in mid- to high-end networking in organizations. Resoundingly, these customers said that in the world of connectivity, TCP/IP is a definite requirement for any new operating system, and especially those being targeted at the Internet. TCP/IP stands for Transmission Control Protocol/Internet Protocol, and is the suite of protocols (rules or languages for network communication) used on the Internet. TCP/IP is considered the great equalizer, making it possible for network-based devices of all types to share all types of data, regardless of the operating system of a given node.

The customer feedback just mentioned was first obtained back when Microsoft started developing the Windows NT operating system. An essential part of the Microsoft culture is to thoroughly deploy its own technology internally. Such is the case with the Microsoft implementation of TCP/IP. This approach to product design makes the development teams accountable to their fellow employees for the performance of applications, and the development team's reputation is typically gauged by the level of bug-free performance their products provide. Talk about pressure! You have to face the people using your products the very next day after they are released. This is called "eating your own dog food" and is an essential part of Microsoft's culture. Realizing that it would be the best way to learn about TCP/IP, Microsoft integrated 55,000 nodes within their own company to learn more about this protocol. Managing or administering such a large network proved daunting, which led Microsoft to appreciate the need for powerful tools that would make system administration easier than before. It was through these experiences that Microsoft realized that while the first implementations of TCP/IP were robust for smaller workgroups, they definitely needed work in terms of being able to scale accurately for the thousands of users within Microsoft's headquarters and regional offices throughout the world. As a result of the thorough internal testing of these protocols, both DHCP and WINS were integrated into Windows NT 4.0 and now Windows XP. Microsoft is being very careful to not market a proprietary solution, so the RFCs for the DHCP and WINS implementations have been presented to the Internet Engineering Task Force.

Since then, the depth of TCP/IP support has undergone significant enhancements. Microsoft learned and capitalized on the fact that TCP/IP is the pavement of the information superhighway among companies and even continents. Indeed, TCP/IP is the backbone of the Internet itself. From this knowledge gained through experience, Microsoft continues to refine the TCP/IP protocol implementation.

A Brief History of TCP/IP

Originally developed to meet the needs of universities, researchers, and even defense contractors to quickly share data across broad geographic distances, TCP/IP has progressed into an ever-increasing range of protocols. ARPANET (Advanced Research Projects Agency NETwork) was originally created as an experiment in large-scale packet switching. The foundation of what is today the Internet was created due to the goals of the ARPANET project. First being created as a research endeavor, the TCP/IP protocol is not slanted to a given vendor or manufacturer. This actually made the ARPANET more ubiquitous and more nimble at responding to the needs of its users since the growth of the network could draw on the resources of multiple contributing companies and universities, and did not have to be constrained by the technology of a single provider. ARPANET, and now the Internet, are successful because it takes the best of multiple sources of technology rather that just a single source of innovation.

The earliest use of TCP/IP was as a network protocol to support research between universities and government agencies and that would enable accurate and secure transmission of data between locations. Integral to the development of the TCP/IP protocol was the evolution of *packet switching* technology. Research was begun in 1969 with the primary goal of providing a common protocol for data transmission, ensuring commonality between vendors providing products during the initial procurement process. The second design goal for TCP/IP is the creation of a networking protocol that ensures interoperability between hardware and software components. This second objective has continually generated competition in all arenas of the TCP/IP marketplace due to interoperability leveling the playing field among competitors. Having connectivity as a baseline forces the hardware vendors to compete on performance and ever more closely align themselves with the needs of the customers integrating TCP/IP into their businesses, schools, universities, and governments. Third was the need for a network that has the capability to handle a multitude of transactions and information requests transparently among thousands of users concurrently. The network protocol to orchestrate requests for what was first research information and is today used for handling transactions was originally developed to support a robust series of data transactions used in Department of Defense requests for information between network clients. The fourth design objective for TCP/IP was to develop a protocol that had an ease of configuration with the capability of having addresses assigned to each system on a network. Due to the initial customers being with the Department of Defense with an expanding series of systems needing configuration, the design objective of being able to dynamically assign IP addresses to each system was considered essential. That objective is met by DHCP, covered later in this chapter and in Chapter 7.

TCP/IP continues to gain enhancements due to the fact that it is based on standards that are available to anyone. The standards organization that manages the TCP/IP protocol is quite approachable, and actually publishes proposed additions to the standard in the form of Requests for Comments, or RFCs for short. These RFCs are actually descriptions of planned enhancements to the standard, and anyone is welcome to comment on the content of these documents. Some of these are quite technical, but many are understandable for someone with a solid understanding of the OSI model, the essentials of TCP/IP, and the patience to read through them. So TCP/IP's open standards are truly open; unlike with other highly technical standards, you do not need to be invited to comment. You can find these Requests for Comment at the following Web and ftp sites:

- http://sunsite.org.uk/rfc/
- ftp://ftp.ncren.net
- ftp://ftp.sesqui.net

Another force driving the increased adoption of TCP/IP is the inclusion of applications based on this protocol that make sharing, transferring and managing files on dissimilar systems possible. For example, you could use the ftp command to transfer files from a mainframe running TCP/IP to a Windows XP workstation, where a spreadsheet would complete analysis. After finishing the spreadsheet, you ftp the file to a UNIX system where a time series could be completed using the telnet command. All this could be accomplished from the Command Prompt window of the Windows XP workstation you are using. You can easily trade files with mainframes, Macintoshes, and UNIX workstations of any type. As long as the TCP/IP protocol suite is installed, the type of operating system is immaterial.

How TCP/IP Fits into Microsoft's Networking Strategy

The role of TCP/IP in the product strategy of Windows XP Professional is to create a foundation within each of the operating systems released from Windows NT 3.51 forward. This translates into several product generations today which have been used to translate users' needs into a TCP/IP command set robust enough for the needs of corporate users interested in ensuring connectivity among large numbers of users.

Microsoft continues to use added functionality and differentiation within the TCP/IP command set to continually add value to the Windows product family. The role of TCP/IP in the Microsoft product strategy is to accomplish a variety of tasks. First, TCP/IP provides a solid foundation on which to build a connectivity strategy and drive the development of heterogeneous (mixed) networks which include systems of many different operating systems. Secondly, TCP/IP plays the critical role of streamlining the integration of Windows XP Professional workstations and Windows 2000 servers with the Internet—and many of you as system administrators will be faced with the task of ensuring connectivity between servers and the Internet via either routers and T1 lines from your own organization or via Internet Service Provider (ISP) connections. Thirdly, the customization of the TCP/IP command set by Microsoft for Windows XP creates a differentiator that positions Microsoft effectively as a viable alternative to UNIX and NetWare.

With the latest release of TCP/IP in Windows XP Professional, Microsoft set the objectives of making their interpretation standards-complaint, and capable of being portable across platforms. Specifically, the objectives as defined by Microsoft's design teams included making TCP/IP meet the following objectives:

- Standards-compliant
- Interoperable
- Portable
- Scalable
- High performance
- Versatile
- Self-tuning
- Easy to administer
- Adaptable

Integrating Microsoft TCP/IP into a Network

Two market forces that have lead to the rapid adoption of TCP/IP into the organizational networks is the growth of the Internet and the need for integrating Windows NT, Windows 2000, and now Windows XP Professional into heterogeneous networks. TCP/IP is now very much the foundation of connectivity of the Internet, and is effectively leveling the playing field of operating system competition. Many organizations today have multiple network operating systems running at the same time. There are a multitude of scenarios which can lead to this condition, with the most common being an integration of PC network architecture and protocols with those that are mainframe-based.

Organizations today increasingly find that Novell NetWare has provided excellent file and print services, while Windows NT/2000/XP, due to the pervasive support for Win32 APIs in the application development community, has the majority of 32-bit applications. Consequently, organizations have typically integrated Windows NT/2000/XP workstations into their networks as low-end application servers.

Taken together, the needs of users for running client/server applications that use data from UNIX servers and print services from NetWare creates a challenge for system administrators in troubleshooting problems. These separate protocols all cause redundant traffic and make it difficult to troubleshoot transmission problems over a network. Many administrators use TCP/IP as the unifying protocol in these kinds of scenarios, as TCP/IP is supported on all three platforms.

UNIX and Windows NT/2000XP have TCP/IP protocol support at the kernel level. This includes the many variants of UNIX, which makes interoperability possible. Novell NetWare began native TCP/IP support in version 5 and continues it with current versions. In earlier versions of NetWare, however, TCP/IP is supported only by using the NetWare/IP product. The bottom line is that TCP/IP is a protocol that spans platforms, making the task of integrating otherwise dissimilar network operating systems possible.

Understanding the Role of Client/Server Technology

You may be surprised by how many companies continue to either have standalone personal computers completing isolated tasks, or at the other end of the spectrum, companies that are very focused on their mainframe systems. These two groups of users have a common thread: they both need to have easier access to rapidly changing data that often is difficult to deliver to the desktop.

TCP/IP Architecture Explained

The architecture of a computer system simply refers to how it is designed to work in conjunction with other parts of the system efficiently. Windows XP Professional and the Microsoft family of servers have both been designed to provide a strong foundation so that protocols already supported in each of these operating systems can be in turn forwarded on to the next generation of users. Windows XP supports Novell NetWare IPX/SPX through the use of NWLink, plus the full TCP/IP suite. One of the most important parts of TCP/IP is the Dynamic Host Configuration Protocol, or DHCP for short. What is DHCP? It is an innovative approach to assigning IP addresses. The DHCP protocol works very much like a library that checks out books. Instead of issuing books, the server actually dispenses addresses. The DHCP protocol is very popular with many electronic commerce vendors who serve multiple industries. Many Internet Service Providers (ISPs) also rely on this protocol for handling the task of getting

IP addresses allocated to each customer. Specifics on how to configure DHCP for use in your organization are explained in Chapter 7.

TCP/IP is actually a suite of protocols that perform specific network communications tasks. You as administrators have the flexibility of selecting from the suite of commands available in TCP/IP to accomplish networking goals. Chapter 7 will give you a chance to practice configuring the various components of a TCP/IP network.

Microsoft-based networks can involve multiple protocol suites, so developing a plan that clarifies the relations between the various protocols being used in a specific situation and the needs they are addressing is paramount. The conventional approach to comparing network protocols is to use the OSI reference model as the backdrop or conceptual framework, which is an excellent approach to handling the understanding of the layering of network protocols. The OSI Reference Model is an excellent place to begin learning how networks are created, and is covered next.

INTRODUCING THE OSI MODEL

In learning about network protocols and how they compare, it is useful to have a frame of reference or a structure to apply to the myriad of terms and concepts. The Open Systems Interconnect (OSI) model provides this framework for illustrating the components of the TCP/IP networking protocol. While the OSI Model is used mainly for showing the differences among network commands and protocols, it is important to realize that there are just as many variations in how protocols are structured as there are protocols. So the OSI Model is a good foundation on which to learn. In this section you will first get an overview of the OSI Model followed by an explanation of how the TCP/IP protocol fits into this structure. You will also see how the OSI Model is organized to provide for data packets or datagrams to traverse the levels of the model to ensure communication and data reliability.

The OSI Model is organized into a vertical hierarchy in which data travels from the bottom to the top in the case of incoming communication, with each layer stripping away data elements needed for handling the data transaction, or in the case of an outgoing message, top to bottom, adding data at each layer to ensure the targeted system receives the complete message. Figure 6.2 shows a diagram of the OSI Model.

The first two layers, Physical and Data Link, define the way data is physically transferred on the network. The Network layer deals with

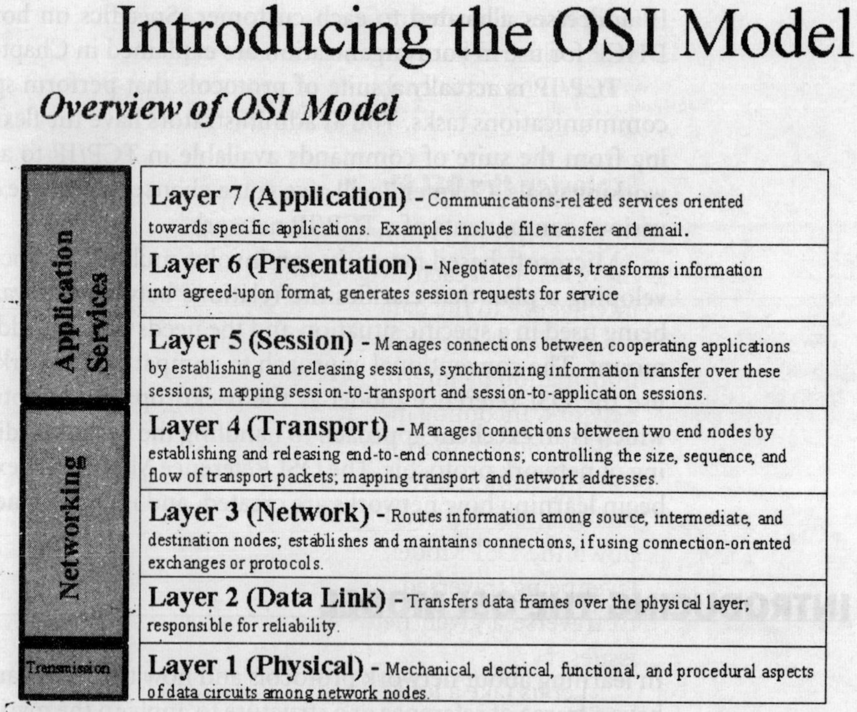

FIGURE 6.2 The OSI Model provides a useful framework for comparing network protocols.

addressing issues on larger networks. The Transport layer is chiefly concerned with establishing connections and error and flow control, while the Session layer manages dialogs between computers. The Presentation layer is responsible for converting machine-specific data into data that can be shared on any system and vice-versa, and the Application layer is the interface between Applications and the network. Above the Application layer are the user interface and general applications that use network resources.

By breaking the network model into different layers, it is much easier to see how computers communicate on a network. For example, the network protocols (TCP/IP, NetBEUI and so on) are not dependent on the network interface card (NIC) or cabling, but instead work on any hardware because the intervening layers translate and process the network traffic into the format these protocols can understand. Layering components of the OSI Model also helps make the network functionality transparent to the user interface and applications. Because the layers hide the protocols and physical hardware from the interface and applications, you can change protocols and hardware without making any changes to the interface or your programs to enable them to access network resources.

Exploring the OSI Model Layers

Just as bricks in a building, the layers of the OSI Model build one on top of the other, with each layer relying on the previous one to provide additional intelligence to the data as it travels from layer to layer.

Notice that each of the layers has a predefined task and actually adds information by interpreting the messages being sent between systems on a network. Incoming messages over a network filter upward through the OSI Model and are then interpreted and acted upon by the computer user at the Application layer. Once a command, query, request or action is completed at the top level of the OSI Model, the message then flows back to down the OSI Model, with increased intelligence being added with every layer being traversed. As you can see this layering approach makes it easier to traverse a given network topology and even troubleshoot networking issues.

Let us take a look in more detail at each layer of the OSI Model. These are descriptions of each layer, beginning with the bottom-most layer and moving upward.

The Physical Layer

This is the lowest layer, and is focused on two key tasks: sending and receiving bits over the network. Network interface cards (NICs) are predominantly found at this level of the OSI Model, as are peripheral devices such as repeaters. Ensuing levels above this one in the OSI model are responsible for collecting bits into a single message. As you would suspect, this layer gets very elementary in its representation of data to the point of seeing data in the pattern of state transitions in the bits being received over the network.

A wide variety of media are used for communicating bits to the Physical layer. These include electric cable, fiber optics, light waves, and radio, even microwave transmissions. The medium used can vary yet the logic behind the Physical layer does not change. The upper layers are completely independent from the particular process used to deliver bits through the network medium.

An important distinction is that the OSI Physical layer does not, strictly speaking, define the media attached to it. The Physical layer describes the bit patterns to be used, but does not define the medium; it defines how data are encoded into signals and the characteristics of the media attachment interface. In actual practice, many Physical layer standards cover characteristics of the OSI Physical layer as well as characteristics of the medium.

The function of the Data Link layer is to provide system-to-system communication on a single local network. Many times you will also hear the term node-to-node communication pertaining to the Data Link layer. A node is actually a computer system. This layer of the OSI model focuses on enabling communication between nodes on a network. To provide this functionality, the Data Link layer needs to provide an address mechanism that enables messages to be delivered to the correct nodes, and must also translate messages from the upper layers into bits that the Physical layer can transmit.

What happens when the Data Link layer receives a message to transmit? It first formats the message into a *data frame*. A data frame is also known as a *packet*. Figure 6.3 shows an example of how a data frame is constructed.

Individual sections of a data frame are called fields. The fields that comprise a data frame vary by network protocol, but the ones listed below have a high level of commonality among all protocols:

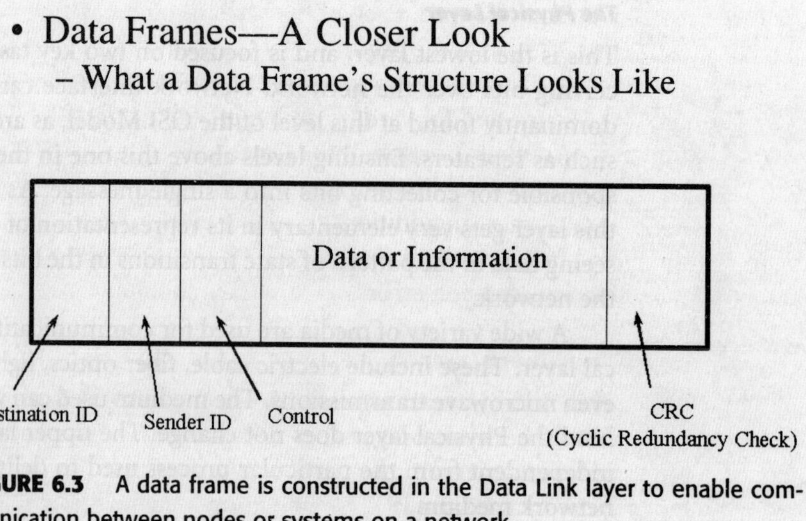

FIGURE 6.3 A data frame is constructed in the Data Link layer to enable communication between nodes or systems on a network.

- **Start Indicator**—A specific bit pattern which indicates the start of a data frame.
- **Source Address**—The address of the sending node is also included so that replies to messages can be addressed properly.
- **Destination Address**—Each node is identified by an address. The Data Link layer of the sending node adds the destination address to the frame. The Data Link layer of the receiver looks at the destination address to identify messages that it should receive.
- **Control**—In many cases, additional control information must be included. This is the task of the control bit and provides specific data depending on the network protocol being used.
- **Data**—This field contains all the data that was forwarded to the Data Link layer from the protocol layers located in the upper layers of the OSI model.
- **Error Control**—This field contains information that enables the receiving node to determine whether an error occurred during transmission. A common approach to ensuring accuracy is to use cyclic redundancy checking (CRC), which is a calculated value that sums all of the data in the frame. The sending node calculates a checksum and stores it in the frame. The receiving system recalculates the checksum, and if the receiver's calculated CRC matches the CRC value in the frame, it can be assumed that the frame was submitted over the network without error.

In the case of TCP/IP-based networks, the transmission of a data frame is straightforward. Each of the systems on the network checks the destination address at the beginning of the frame. If the destination address in the frame matches the node's address, the Data Link layer at the node receives the frame and forwards it up the protocol stack.

Another function of the Data Link layer is to convert outgoing frames into individual bits for transmission, and reassemble incoming bits back into frames. In addition, this layer establishes node-to-node connections and manages the transmission of data between nodes, as well as checking for transmission errors.

The Network Layer

The Network layer is primarily responsible for routing data packets efficiently between one system and another on the network. Two network protocols that are most commonly used in networks where routing is required are IP and IPX. The IP protocol, which is part of the TCP/IP suite, is responsible for routing at the Network layer. IPX, which is typically used in Novell NetWare environments, serves the same purpose.

In addition to TCP/IP, Windows XP also includes NWLink, Microsoft's version of Novell NetWare's IPX/SPX protocol suite. In the first versions of Windows NT (3.1 & 3.51), NetBEUI was the default network protocol. Starting in Windows NT 4.0, TCP/IP became the default protocol and that continues with Windows XP Professional. Windows XP no longer supports NetBEUI. The reason for this change is that NetBEUI was originally designed to provide efficient transport in small networks. NetBEUI cannot be routed, however, which eliminates its use in large, complex networks where routing is often necessary. If you are going to route data from one location to another, you will find TCP/IP the best choice for linking dissimilar systems or IPX/SPX if your entire network or the majority of it is Novell NetWare-based.

If you are involved in the world of electronic commerce, there is rarely a situation in which your Web site will be seen only on a single network. Most probably the Web sites and revenue-generating applications you are creating will be accessed from several different networks. This is where the Network layer becomes a valuable asset. In the case of a series of distributed networks, called an internetwork, the Network layer provides network addressing for each network being communicated with. This does not apply to the Internet itself; rather in terms of speaking of the Network layer and internetworking, the discussion revolves around sending and receiving a packet that has source and destination network addresses. The process the Network layer completes to get a data packet to the correct location on the network is called routing. You may have heard the term router, and this is the device used for getting a data frame from one location to another on a network. There are two types of nodes on internetworks. These nodes are the targets for data frames coming from the originating nodes on a network:

- *End nodes* use the network layer to add network address information to packets, but they do not perform routing. End nodes are sometimes called end systems or hosts. In the case of TCP/IP implementations the latter name is most typically used.
- *Routers* use a special mechanism that checks the data frames and then sends them to the target destination. Routers are actually standalone systems in their own right, and are called intermediate systems in the OSI Model, or in the world of TCP/IP they are also called gateways.

The Network layer relies on the Data Link layer to organize incoming bits into an assemblage that is usable. Since routers are Network layer devices, they are used to forward packets between physically different networks. A router can join an Ethernet or token ring network. Routers also are often used to connect systems to local area networks, whether they be Ethernet, token ring, or others.

The Transport Layer

The Transport layer is primarily focused on taking messages and in effect creating smaller packets for ease of transmission and accuracy of received messages. At the originating workstation each message is broken into a series of fragments, with the Transport layer at the destination system being responsible for re-creating the messages that have been packetized.

Although the Network layer is responsible for routing, its protocols do not perform error checking; they simply pass the packets back and forth. There is no guarantee that a packet will arrive with all its components, or if there are contiguous packets, if they will all arrive in the proper order. Some level of error checking is required, and the Transport layer sometimes provides this reliability. Transport layer protocols check for errors and cause the packets to be retransmitted when an error in sending or receiving occurs. In essence, the Transport layer acts as the main point of quality assurance in the path of a transaction over the network although both the Data Link and Session layers are responsible for some error-checking and correction also.

Two Transport layer protocols that are pervasively used due to their routing characteristics are TCP and SPX. These two protocols also provide reliable transmission due to their inclusion of additional features at the Transport layer. TCP is the protocol that is responsible for error checking and placing packets in the correct order. SPX performs the comparable function in the IPX/SPX protocol. Another Transport layer protocol is UDP. Part of the TCP/IP suite, UDP performs the same function as TCP, except without error checking. It is preferred when network overhead is at a premium.

Almost every protocol or network architecture defines a size for the packets being sent from one location to another on a network. Ethernet, for example, sets the size of the data field at 1,500 bytes. Limiting the size of the packets is essential due to the following two reasons:

- Smaller frames tend to improve network efficiency when many devices share the network. This is comparable to partitioning messages into smaller segments so they can be successfully sent over a network.

- Smaller frames lead to less translation during the process of being sent from the network carrier to the destination system.

The Session Layer

Controlling the dialog between two systems and making sure nodes on a network agree to exchange data through the network is the responsibility of the Session layer. This layer of the OSI Model is one of the most critical, with a series of communications, otherwise known as dialogs, being completed. A dialog is the term used by LAN engineers to define the communication between two systems on a network. The Session layer's purpose is to enable the dialog between multiple systems. These dialogs can take place in three dialog modes, listed here:

- **Simplex**—A dialog between systems where one node transmits exclusively, while another exclusively receives.
- **Half duplex**—Only one node may send at a given time, and the nodes take turns transmitting.
- **Full duplex**—Nodes may transmit and receive simultaneously. Full-duplex communication requires some form of flow control to ensure that neither device sends data faster that the other device can receive it.

Regardless of the type of communication being completed, each type of dialog consists of the following three phases:

1. **Creating a connection**—This is the introductory phase where one node initiates and holds communication with another system. During this phase the two systems negotiate for rules of communication, including the types of communication rules or parameters to be used for communication.
2. **Data transfer**—This is the second step in the process in which the actual communication between each of the systems on the network takes place.
3. **Connection release**—When the communication between network nodes has been completed, the connection between systems is completed and each system completes a series of steps to stop communication.

You can see that looking at these three steps from the standpoint of commercially-based transactions flowing through the OSI Model, the need for efficiency on both the connection establishment and connection release are critical. This layer also involves security authentication that defines which resources will be available to specific users of the network.

The Presentation Layer

The function of this layer is to be an intermediary between the Session layer and the Application layer. Presentation layer protocols gather the frames of data and create a cohesive grouping or set of data for use at the Application Layer. The Presentation layer translates the data from one format to another if required for the Session and Application layers to communicate. The Presentation layer can also perform such tasks as data compression and encryption.

Let us look at an example of how the Presentation layer works: a Web site composed of several types of systems. In the case of UNIX-based workstations running Sun's Solaris operating system, some systems running Windows NT, and a mainframe computer, the Presentation layer completes the role of gateway in this specific network topology, translating communications to each of the different types of systems. The Presentation layer is then actually responsible for acting as the gateway in distributed, and often in the world of electronic commerce, heterogeneous environments.

The Application Layer

This layer provides the interface between the network and user interface and applications. In general, the Application layer provides a layer of abstraction between the user and the network, making the network essentially transparent. Because of the Application layer, a program you are using to open a file can do so as easily across the network as it does locally.

This is the most prevalently used layer of the OSI Model, as applications' interfaces reside at this topmost position of the OSI Model. From an electronic commerce perspective, this is the layer of the OSI Model where the majority of programming of electronic tools is located. Specifically, tools for completing auctions on the Internet, setting up and maintaining electronic storefronts, and the creation of interactive purchasing sites that store the preferences and tastes of shoppers as they peruse an online mall all are created and reside at this layer of the OSI Model.

Let us take a look at the more common applications found at the Application layer of the OSI Model and their implications on the future of Windows XP, and their role in electronic commerce:

- **Electronic mail transport**—Inherent in the Application layer are protocols that enable electronic mail between networked systems.
- **Remote file access**—There continues to be a dominant trend in operating system design of enabling both applications within operating systems and applications themselves to support network connectivity. Inherent in seamless interoperability is the need for electronic commerce applications and sites to provide users with access to any location on a Web site or intranet. The need for remote file access that is platform independent is critical for the success of an electronic commerce application.
- **Remote job execution**—Long the stronghold of the UNIX power user as a reason not to migrate to Windows NT, remote job execution is supported in Windows NT/2000/XP and other network-based operating systems from within the Application layer. In the context of electronic commerce, remote job execution is not used very often, as many applications and their resulting transactions are meant to be transparent to the user.
- **Directories**—Central to the ongoing debate over directories is the role Active Directories in Windows 2000 domains will have relative to the NetWare Directory Services (NDS) loyal customer base. An integral part of the Application layer, many companies creating electronic commerce Web sites use NetWare for file and print services, and use Windows 2000 servers for their adeptness at application server capabilities. The point of this ongoing debate revolves around the dilemma facing the Novell NetWare-based companies and the opportunity to continue using Novell Directory Services (NDS) or migrate to Windows 2000's Active Directory. This decision is anything less than black-and-white; rather, many companies are comparing each of the directory architectures to see which is better suited for their specific needs. Which is the best for electronic commerce? There is no right answer, but rather you need to ask yourself what the best architecture is for serving your customers.
- Electronic commerce is streamlining the flow of data up and down the layers of the OSI Model. This is particularly seen in the development of Internet applications that span the entire range of OSI

layers. The implication for companies building Web sites is that vendors selected for software development, service providers, and even the hardware selected need their products to provide upward compatibility and connectivity with the latest additions to the TCP/IP command set.

- Driving the adoption of TCP/IP in electronic marketplace is the security inherent in its structure and the development of Internet standards using the OSI Model. By the very nature of the OSI Model, the various levels are protected from the others, with the lower levels passing data to the upper levels, with each successive layer adding more information to the message.
- Electronic commerce specifically and the Internet in general are flattening the OSI Model by making increased functionality available more efficiently than ever before. The HTTP protocol is now the standard for sharing data and handling transactions globally over the Internet. Due to the emerging growth of electronic commerce, the OSI Model is being reinvented in real-world terms with each succeeding product generation that addresses electronic commerce as an objective for companies participating in this market segment.

The Internet Model Explained

Applying the Internet to the OSI Model brings about a different picture than the one shown in the classical seven-step model shown in this chapter. What does the Internet do to the OSI Model? How does this impact your decisions on electronic commerce over the Internet? In simple terms, the Internet is shrinking the OSI Model into a frame of reference where the combination of HTTP, SET and SST technologies has actually flattened the OSI Model. The impact of the Internet on the OSI Model has been to actually traverse it, making networking available to more customers than ever before.

What then are the implications for you as you set up your Web site? What does this mean for you? Simply put, the OSI Model gives you a great cross-reference for explaining your plans and accomplishments with regard to electronic commerce. The OSI Model is also useful from the standpoint of pointing out how networking has progressed over time. In the mid-1980s the OSI Model showed a more disjointed approach to networking, while today the OSI Model is maturing at a rapid rate. This translates into a customer base with little or no barriers to purchasing electronically over time.

UNDERSTANDING HOW TCP/IP ENABLES COMMUNICATION IN WINDOWS XP PROFESSIONAL

Three processes are critical for having datagrams, which are the containers the network uses for sharing data between nodes routed from the source computer to the destination host via the intended or destination network. These three processes are:

- **Addressing**—With an IP address, every network and every workstation have a unique identity, and can be reached using their specific address.
- **Routing**—The process by which messages pass through routers to reach the destination workstation or network. A gateway or router routes messages based on logical network addresses, rather than physical addresses burned into network adapter cards.
- **Multiplexing**—The process by which data is forwarded to a compatible protocol and port, out of the many running on a network.

IP Addressing

This attribute gives a network, workstation or even an intranet its own identity within a large extranet or even from the Internet. It has been called the biggest single differentiator in the entire TCP/IP protocol suite. Many organizations prefer to have each workstation always have its own IP address. This is typically called static IP addressing, which makes a lot of sense, especially when the workstations will be staying in the same locations. Dynamic Host Configuration Protocol (DHCP), in contrast, is a network protocol specifically developed for assigning IP addresses just as a library dispenses books—on demand. Both the static IP addressing approach and DHCP use the same values for the IP address. An IP address consists of 32 bits, notated as four decimal values representing one octet each, separated by periods. An octet consists of eight bits and can have any value from 0 (all zeroes) to 255 (all ones), although certain address values are not available, having been reserved for other uses. Using this approach, it makes it possible for an IP address to be applied to an individual workstation or an entire network.

If you are running TCP/IP on a network which is not linked to the Internet, you can assign any valid IP address values you want on your networks and hosts. Any computers that you will be connecting to the

Internet must be on a network with an address that has been registered with InterNIC, the Internet Network Information Center. InterNIC is a clearinghouse for all Internet IP addresses, ensuring host addresses are all unique.

InterNIC, however, does not register individual workstations, only networks. As a system administrator, use the range(s) of IP addresses specific to your organization for providing a unique one for each workstation. The network address is part of the 32-bit IP address. The address class and the subnet mask determine which part of the address represents the network and which part represents the host.

IP Address Classes

InterNIC uses three classes of IP addresses, designating the specific class by the first three bits of the address. These classes vary depending on needs of the organizations receiving them. The classes of IP addresses are as follows:

- Class A—The first bit of a class A address is always 0, meaning that the first octet of the address can have a value between 1 and 126. Only the first octet is used to represent the network, leaving the final three octets to identify 16,777,214 possible hosts (individual computers).
- Class B—The first two bits of a class B network are always 1 and 0, meaning that the first octet can have a value between 128 and 191. The first two octets are used to identify 16,384 possible networks, leaving the final two octets to identify 65,534 possible hosts.
- Class C—The first three bits of class C network are always 1, 1, and 0, meaning that the first octet can have a value between 192 and 223. The first three octets are used to identify 2,097,151 possible networks, leaving the final octet to identify 254 possible hosts.

IP Routing

The other side of getting messages delivered over a network is having the IP routing in place to ensure datagrams are delivered to the correct workstation or network. When the source and destination workstations are not on the same network, then one or more routers are needed to route packets to the correct network.

"Gateway" and "router" are terms often used interchangeably. Technically, however, gateways are routers with additional features allowing translation of one protocol or even one type of network architecture to another. When configuring TCP/IP on Microsoft operating systems, you will see the term "default gateway." This refers to a router. We will use the terms interchangeably unless otherwise noted.

Every TCP/IP system maintains an internal routing table that helps it to make routing decisions. For the average host computer, located on a network segment with only a single router, the routing decisions are simple; either a packet is sent to a destination host on the same network or it is sent to the router. As stated earlier, IP is aware only of the computers on the networks to which it is directly connected. It is up to each individual router to route packets on its next leg of the journey to the destination.

It may be the case that a host computer is located on a network segment with more than one router. Initially, packets addressed to other networks are all sent to the default gateway (router) that is set as part of the host configuration. However, the default gateway may be privy to routing information that is unavailable to the host, and send a redirect packet instructing the host to use another gateway when sending to a particular IP address. This information is stored in the host's routing table. Whenever the host attempts to send packets to that same IP address again, it consults its routing table first and sends the packets to the alternate gateway.

How can you be sure the routing table contains the correct values? Using the command NETSTAT -R or the ROUTE PRINT command, you can view the table. Both commands list the IP addresses found in the table, the gateway that should be used when sending to each, and other information about the nature and source of the routing information.

Depending on the destination host (which can be either a network or an individual workstation or server) the routing implications can become elaborate. There are several TCP/IP protocols designed for use only by gateways to exchange routing information that allows them to ensure the most accurate and efficient routing possible, such as the Gateway to Gateway Protocol (GGP) and the Exterior Gateway Protocol (EGP). This prevents the traffic for each individual host from flooding the entire Internet in search of a single network. As you can see from this example, the majority of TCP/IP routing is based on tables. Hosts and gateways each maintain their own routing tables and perform lookups of the destination address found in incoming packets. While the Internet at one time relied on a collection of central core gateways as the ultimate source of routing information for the entire network, this become impractical due to the tremendous growth of the Internet. Routing is now based on collections of autonomous systems called routing domains that share information with each other using the Border Gateway Protocol (BGP). As a user of the Internet, much of this is hidden to the users, yet there are Web sites for showing the number of connections datagrams make as they traverse from the targeted host to your workstations and back again.

Getting to Know IP Multiplexing

After IP datagrams have been received by the host computer, they must be delivered to the Transport layer protocol for interpretation and use by the targeted application service. On the sending workstation, the process of combining the requests made by several different applications into traffic for a few Transport protocols, and then combining the Transport protocol traffic into a single IP data stream, is called multiplexing. Multiplexing is really the process of taking several messages and sending them using a single signal. At the receiving computer the process is reversed, in effect creating a demultiplexing routine of steps for inbound messages.

The numeric values assigned to specific protocols and application services are defined on the host computer in text files named Protocol and Services, respectively. These are located in the <system_root>/System32/drivers/etc folder on a Windows XP Professional computer. Many of the values assigned to particular services are standardized numbers found in the Assigned Services RFC. FTP (File Transfer Protocol), for example, traditionally uses a port number of 20 on all types of host systems. Port numbers are individually defined for each Transport protocol. In other words, TCP and UDP (User Datagram Protocol) both have different assignments for the same port number. The combination of an IP address and a port number is known as a socket. Be sure not to confuse the TCP/IP term "socket" with the term "Windows Sockets," which are a development standard created by Microsoft, even though the Windows NT TCP/IP utilities were developed using this standard.

CHAPTER SUMMARY

The future of Windows XP Professional is clearly in the direction of enabling electronic commerce through the many enhancements to the networking functionality included in this latest version. The OSI Model is used throughout this chapter as a reference point to how the Internet, and with it, electronic commerce are changing how systems will communicate in the future. The role of the Internet-based protocols on the future direction of Windows XP Professional is unmistakable. Continually changing the direction of networking connectivity is in the process of taking HTTP over TCP/IP into the new standard for operating system connectivity. S-HTTP and secured protocols are increasingly important and will also begin to be included as standard within the next generation of operating systems, with the intent of bringing down the barriers of completing electronically-enabled transactions.

7 Configuring TCP/IP in Windows XP Professional

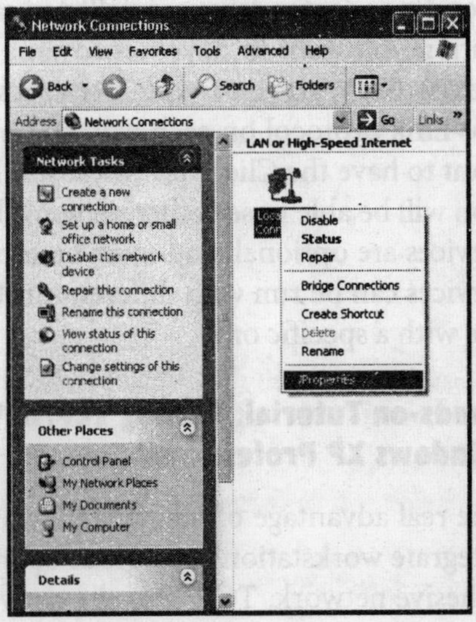

INTRODUCTION

TCP/IP is more than just a networking protocol. It contains important programs that make large-scale networking and the Internet possible. These include DHCP for automating TCP/IP configuration, APIPA to allow network connectivity in case there is no DHCP server available, and DNS, WINS, and static HOSTS files for various types of name-to-address and address-to-name resolution. Also in TCP/IP are several command line utilities. The installation and use of these programs and utilities are covered in this chapter.

Due to the extensive graphical interface of Windows XP Professional, configuring TCP/IP is relatively easy. You will find that there is greater control over the configuration of options due to the extensive use of tabs within the Network dialog box. Having these tabs gives you an easier approach to configuring network options.

As in previous versions of Windows, the networking components of Windows XP are broken down into three types: adapters, protocols, and services. These types form a stack corresponding to the overall network architecture; the services run on top, passing application data through the protocols, which code it for transmission via adapter.

At a minimum, you will need to have network adapters and corresponding adapter drivers installed in each Windows XP Professional workstation you want to have joined on a network. In the case of integrating Novell NetWare into your networks, you will also want to install the NWLink protocol on each workstation. On the workstation you will also want to have the Client for Microsoft Networks installed so each workstation will be able to see other network-based systems. Many of the network services are optional, and must be explicitly installed. Some Windows XP services can be run with different protocols, while others are designed for use with a specific one.

Hands-on Tutorial: Getting TCP/IP Working in Windows XP Professional

The real advantage of having a network operating system is the ability to integrate workstations of various operating systems together into a single, cohesive network. TCP/IP is the network protocol of choice for ensuring the communication of workstation, servers, and in short, any computer that needs to reside on a network and share resources. Throughout this section of the chapter we will explore how to configure Windows XP Professional for use in a TCP/IP-based environment.

Installing TCP/IP

If you have an existing network when you first install Windows XP or upgrade a previous version of Windows to Windows XP, the appropriate networking wizards will guide you through network configuration, doing most of the work automatically. Because TCP/IP is the default network protocol suite, and one of only two supplied by Windows XP, it is very likely that TCP/IP is already installed on your system. Due to Windows XP Professional using a browser-like shell for many of the properties and attributes, which are configurable, the entire process of installing and customizing TCP/IP is relatively simple. Windows XP employs wizards that are used for creating connections to the various networks that users connect to. Like many other connection-centered functions in Windows XP, network connections also has its own folder. Along the left side of the window are commands to run wizards that can be used for creating network connections. Figure 7.1 shows the Network Connections folder with the Network Tasks listed along the left side of the screen.

The procedures in this chapter, however, do not make use of wizards. Because the possibility exists that you will need to "manually" install a

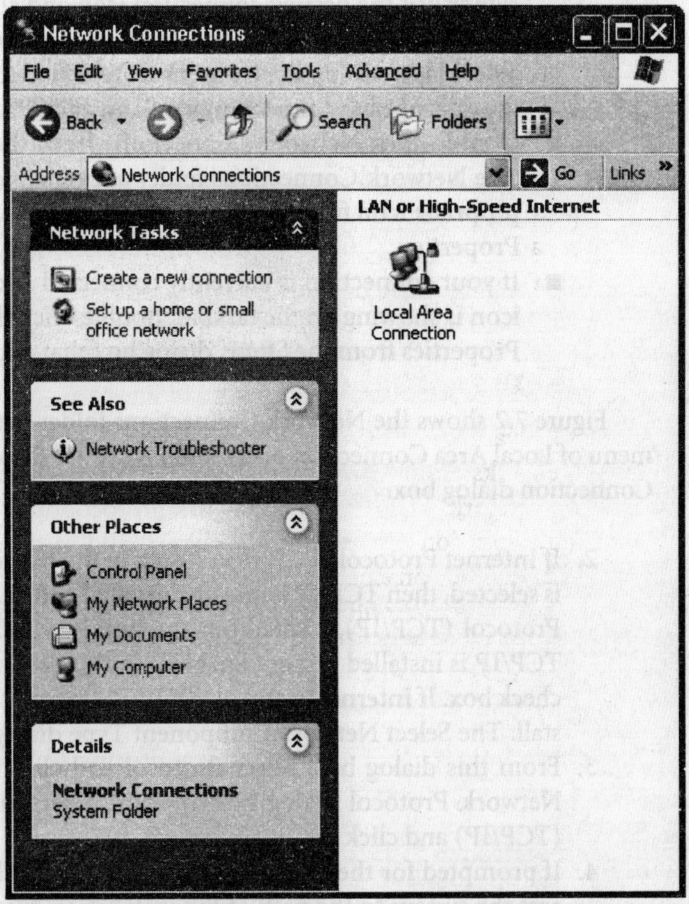

FIGURE 7.1 Exploring the Network Connections Folder in Windows XP Professional.

network protocol or perform another configuration, it is important to be familiar with the dialog boxes used for installing, configuring and removing network protocols, adapters, and services. These dialog boxes, while not as easy to use as wizards, are fairly user friendly, at least for administrators.

The following procedure describes the steps for installing TCP/IP, but you can use this procedure to install any network client, protocol, or service supported by Windows XP Professional.

1. Access the Properties dialog box for the connection you want to configure by using any of the following methods:
   - From the Start menu, select Connect To (if available), then right-click the desired connection icon and click Properties.
   - From the Start menu, Click Network Connections (if available). This calls up the Network Connection folder. Right-click the appropriate connection icon and click Properties.
   - Double-click Network Connections from the Control Panel. The Network Connections folder appears. Right-click the appropriate icon from the network Connections folder and select Properties.
   - If your connection is currently connected and the connection icon is showing on the taskbar, double-click the icon and click Properties from the Status dialog box that appears.

Figure 7.2 shows the Network Connections folder with the right-click menu of Local Area Connection open, and Figure 7.3 shows the Local Area Connection dialog box.

2. If Internet Protocol (TCP/IP) is listed in the box and its check box is selected, then TCP/IP is already installed and enabled. If Internet Protocol (TCP/IP) is listed but the box is not checked off, then TCP/IP is installed but not enabled. In this case, simply select the check box. If Internet Protocol (TCP/IP) does not appear, click Install. The Select Network Component Type dialog box appears.
3. From this dialog box, select Protocol and click Add. The Select Network Protocol dialog box appears. Select Internet Protocol (TCP/IP) and click OK.
4. If prompted for the Windows XP installation disk, insert it or direct the system to the path of the installation files. Click OK. You may be prompted to restart the computer. Save any open files and do so. Once the computer reboots, TCP/IP is installed.

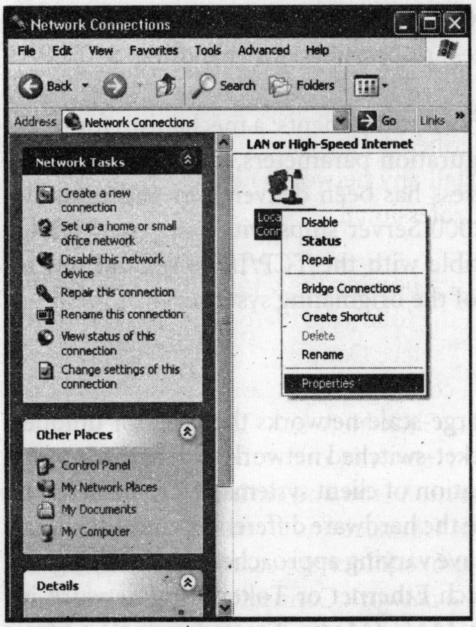

FIGURE 7.2 Using the menu associated with the Local Area Connection.

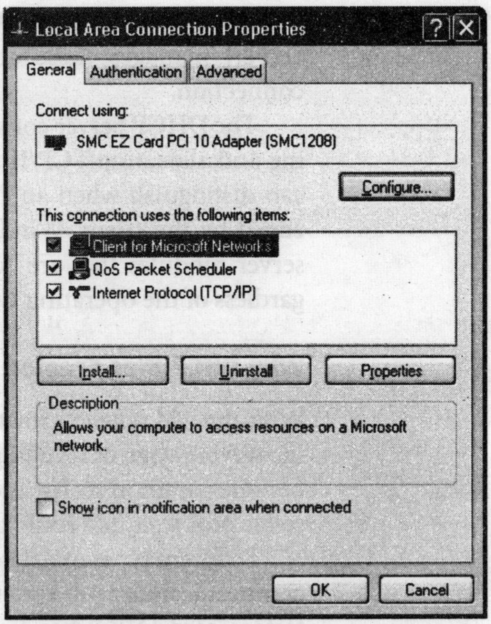

FIGURE 7.3 The Local Area Connection Properties dialog box provides access to network configuration pages.

What Is DHCP?

Let us say you are responsible for supporting fifty to one hundred laptop users who travel extensively and then come back into the office to check e-mail and download files for use at customer sites. How can you create a network that makes it possible for members of this group to get full TCP/IP access while in the office or even using Remote Access Service (RAS) from elsewhere? This can be done through the use of the Dynamic Host Configuration Protocol (DHCP) originally developed by Microsoft. This protocol truly functions just as a library checks books in and out—only this protocol checks IP addresses in and out. Best of all, this IP address mechanism is for the most part administered at the server level, alleviating ongoing configuration at the client level. This means that once a laptop is configured with the ability to accept an IP address, the user at the remote location does not need to configure any other parameters.

DHCP is an element of the TCP/IP protocol suite that enables you as a system administrator to automatically configure parameters such as IP addresses, subnet masks, and default gateways for any clients on a

TCP/IP-based network. A DHCP server, running on Windows 2000 Server, manages these attributes responsible for handling a TCP/IP connection.

The DHCP Server consists of two components: a mechanism for tracking and allocating TCP/IP configuration parameters, and a protocol that can distinguish when an IP address has been delivered to and acknowledged by the client. Windows 2000 Server ships with integrated DHCP server modules that are compatible with the TCP/IP command set, regardless of the operating system of the originating system.

Why DHCP Was Created

With the widespread growth of large-scale networks the need for uniquely identifying systems on a large, packet-switched network such as the Internet became paramount. The identification of client systems had to be based on stable protocols that could traverse the hardware differences among systems.

Different types of networks have varying approaches to identifying and communicating with systems. Each Ethernet or Token Ring network interface card (NIC) has a unique MAC (Media Access Control) address hard-coded into it by the NIC's manufacturer. Because each manufacturer numbers its card sequentially, and because part of that MAC address consists of a code identifying the manufacturer itself, the device's address is unique not only on the local network where it is used, but on all networks everywhere. No other adapter exists that uses the same address.

For the majority of home Internet users today, there are simply no NIC cards installed in their systems, and they are using modems to dial up to ISPs and gain access to the Internet. This approach to connectivity to the outside world necessitated a network protocol which could effectively assign IP addresses dynamically from a "pool," or inventory of addresses, ensuring that each client on the dial-up system has a unique identity.

Understanding How DHCP Works

When a client is configured to use the DHCP protocol, it will attempt to communicate with the DHCP servers available on the local network each time it is rebooted, or when the TCP/IP stack is reinitialized. Windows XP's DHCP communications are defined through the use of Remote Procedure Calls (RPCs). An RPC is a system that allows applications to use services from different computers on the network. All DHCP communications use the same packet format.

DHCP's assignment of IP addresses is called *leasing*. When a DHCP server assigns an address to a DHCP client, it is said to lease the address. Just like real estate leases, DHCP leases expire after a given amount of time. After the expiration, the client requests a renewal of the lease, although each time the address could be different.

Let us walk through the major steps of how DHCP works. First, a DHCP client broadcasts to all DHCP servers on the network. It is the responsibility of the routers and computers functioning as DHCP relay agents on the local network to propagate or forward the traffic generated by a client to other networks where additional DHCP Servers may be located.

Installing DHCP Client Services

DHCP is designed to alleviate the complexities of configuring TCP/IP addresses, and giving client workstations the flexibility of having addresses assigned to them dynamically. This is particularly valuable when a laptop is running Windows XP Professional and needs access to either an intranet within a company or to the Internet via an ISP. Every time a DHCP-enabled computer is rebooted, the TCP/IP protocol stack is reinitialized and the communication between DHCP clients and servers restarts.

Configuring TCP/IP for DHCP Support

This procedure describes how to configure DHCP in Windows XP Professional:

1. Open the Internet Protocol (TCP/IP) Properties dialog box by using one of the methods listed in step 1 of the procedure earlier in this chapter for installing TCP/IP.
2. Click the Internet Protocol (TCP/IP) entry.
3. Click the Properties button.
4. The Internet Protocol (TCP/IP) Properties dialog box is shown. Click the "Obtain an IP address automatically" radio button.
5. Click the "Obtain DNS server address automatically" radio button.
6. Click Advanced. The Advanced TCP/IP Settings dialog box is next shown. Once DHCP is enabled it will be shown under the IP address heading.
7. Click OK to close the Advanced TCP/IP Settings dialog box.
8. Click OK. The Local Area Connection Properties dialog box is again shown.

9. Click OK to close this last dialog box and get back to the Network Connections folder.

Your workstation will now attempt to receive its IP configuration from a DHCP server whenever a connection is started.

As an administrator it is important to realize the circumstances that can leave a DHCP client in an unconfigured state. Here are the ways that a Windows XP Professional computer configured as a DHCP client can be in an unconfigured state:

- The DHCP lease has expired and not been renewed.
- The workstation has just been configured and has not yet entered into a lease.
- The workstation has moved from its existing subnet to a new subnet which is unrecognized by the DHCP server which originally assigned the IP lease.

What happens if a DHCP client attempts to contact a DHCP server for IP address configuration but no DHCP server is available? In the past, it was likely that the client could not connect to the network. Microsoft remedied that situation starting with Windows 2000 by providing two alternatives to this problem. One is Automatic Private IP Addressing (APIPA), and the other is Alternate Configuration. APIPA is the default setting. It automatically assigns an IP address in the range of 169.254.0.1 through 169.254.255.254 and the default subnet mask of 255.255.0.0. These IP addresses are not in use on the Internet. The DHCP Client service continues to attempt to contact a DHCP server. Once that communication has been completed and a lease is offered, the DHCP configuration replaces the APIPA configuration.

The other solution to this problem is Alternate Configuration. This allows static IP configuration information to be used in case of the inability to get a lease from a DHCP server. The following procedure explains how to configure APIPA or Alternate Configuration:

1. Open the Internet Protocol (TCP/IP) Properties dialog box by using one of the methods listed in step 1 of the procedure earlier in this chapter for installing TCP/IP.
2. Click the Alternate Configuration tab. Unless someone has changed it, the Automatic Private IP address radio button is selected. To use Alternate Configuration, click the "User configured" radio button. Then enter the required information.

UNDERSTANDING DOMAIN NAME SYSTEM/SERVICE

When you access the Internet you can enter the domain name, such as *www.charlesriver.com*, or its IP address. This system of every server on the Internet having both a domain name and an IP address is called *Domain Name System (DNS)*. Because most people have an easier time remembering domain names as opposed to long numbers, the *Domain Name Service* (also called *DNS*) is used. So any time you enter a domain name in your Web browser, your browser consults a DNS server in order to provide the IP address of the server you are trying to reach.

The Domain Name System works by having the domain name start out with the specific server and progress to a top-level domain. In its full form, the host name comes first, followed by the organization name and then the top-level domain such as *com*. For example, the combination of the host name (such as columlou) and the domain name (such as gateway.com) forms a fully qualified domain name (FQDN) which is in this example columlou.gateway.com.

In addition to the Internet, DNS is used for resolution on Windows 2000/XP networks also. Each computer with Windows 2000 or XP has its own domain name.

It is easy to get confused between the term "domain" when used in conjunction with the Internet, and the term applied to a Windows NT/2000 domain. Although both represent groups of computers, an Internet domain is registered with InterNIC to identify computers belonging to a particular company or organization. A Windows NT/2000 domain is a collection of computers located on a single internetwork that have been grouped for administrative efficiency of management. Windows XP Professional is able to integrate with Windows NT and Windows 2000 domains.

A Brief History of DNS

Created during the 1980s to handle the increasingly growing set of name resolution needs on the Internet, DNS was originally run on only a small set of computers. The network where DNS was first tested was the now-famous ARPANET network of systems that linked many of the nation's campuses together. The earliest versions of DNS relied on a host table to resolve computer names into IP addresses. At the time, it was possible for every connected computer to have a complete listing of all computers on the internetwork. Changes were e-mailed to the Network Information

Center at the Stanford Research Institute, which maintained the list and made it available to all users. Each user of the APRANET system had only to download the latest version every few weeks to stay current with all the names and associated IP addresses on the entire network.

As more and more computers were included on the ARPANET network, the entries to DNS tables matching all members to their associated addresses grew quickly. As the beginnings of what would eventually turn into the Internet, with millions of users across the world, the volume of entries would quickly create a file that would take too much time to parse for address definition. DNS was created based on the logic of the first computers having an exhaustive list of every other system on the network. DNS has grown from the simple files used for handling name resolution in ARPANET to a distributed name service and database system that was designed to spread the administration tasks around the network, dividing it into domains. Now, only domains are registered within the central repositories of the Internet, with InterNIC being the corporation which in effect rents unique domain addresses throughout the world. Unlike the first days of when DNS was being created where each individual system was listed in a DNS file, today only domain names are tracked centrally. The network administrator performs the assignment of a host name to each workstation.

How DNS Naming Resolution Happens

DNS servers actually are centrally located computers on which the names of individual workstations are compared and then cross-referenced for the originating system, making it possible to communicate with a targeted server. Requests for the identity of a workstation or node are sent to a DNS server which then looks into the DNS database and, if it is available, returns the IP address corresponding to the targeted workstation.

In the distributed architecture of DNS, there is no single listing or database that contains all the computers using the Internet. There is instead a collection of computers known as root servers that contain a complete listing of the domain names registered to individual networks. The entire DNS architecture is heavily based on a tree-like structure, emanating out of the root servers. The listings of root servers for each domain includes the IP addresses of the DNS machines that have been designed as the defining servers for DNS-based traffic.

The Role of the HOSTS File

In the context of DNS, the HOSTS file is the "deliverable" or the item where the host or workstation name and IP address are recorded. Since the inception of the TCP/IP protocol, the HOSTS file has actually been the clearinghouse or common place where name and IP address resolution is completed. The HOSTS file was challenged in its performance by the rapid adoption of TCP/IP networking and with it, the triple-digit compound annual growth rates of systems of all types needing an IP address identity. In small networks, however, the HOSTS file does provide an efficient name resolution approach because it is consulted before communication begins. Keep in mind that performance is maximized when there are up to fifteen Web site addresses in the HOSTS file. After that point, performance tends to get bogged down. The most commonly used IP addresses need to be placed at the top of the file for best performance.

Configuring DNS on Windows XP Professional

In most cases, DNS is easy to configure on a client system. If DHCP is configured for the workstation, the DHCP server most probably supplies the IP addresses of the preferred and alternate DNS servers. If not, this can be entered manually. The procedure for configuring DNS is as follows:

1. Open the Internet Protocol (TCP/IP) Properties dialog box by using one of the methods listed in step 1 of the procedure earlier in this chapter for installing TCP/IP.
2. On the bottom part of the General tab there are two radio buttons. If the addresses of the DNS servers will be supplied by a DHCP server, select "Obtain DNS server address automatically." If not, select Use the following DNS server addresses. Enter the IP addresses of the servers in the appropriate boxes.
3. Click OK twice to close the dialog boxes.

WINS IN WINDOWS XP PROFESSIONAL

Up until Windows 2000, Microsoft computers all relied on NetBIOS names. A significant limitation of the NetBIOS naming convention is that the names do not propagate across routers, and NetBIOS names are disseminated using broadcast datagrams, which IP routers do not forward. The NetBIOS names on one network, therefore, are invisible to computers on networks connected via routers.

In a routed Microsoft network using TCP/IP, if you searched for a computer by its NetBIOS name, a mechanism was needed to resolve NetBIOS names to IP addresses. There were two ways this resolution could happen. An *LMHOSTS* file could be used. An LMHOSTS file contains lists of NetBIOS names and IP addresses of computers on the network. An easier way to achieve resolution was with the *Windows Internet Name Service (WINS)* server. Unlike a static LMHOSTS file, a WINS server keeps track of changes to its database so it should always be up to date.

Windows 2000-based networks rely on domain names, so in a network in which all computers run Windows 2000 and XP, there is no use for a WINS server. Windows 2000 has the WINS server service available for routed networks in which some computers run earlier Microsoft operating systems. If you are running Windows XP on a routed network along with versions of Windows earlier than Windows 2000, there may be a WINS server you can connect to or an LMHOSTS file to use for resolution. The following procedure tells you how to connect to the WINS server:

1. Open the Internet Protocol (TCP/IP) Properties dialog box by using one of the methods listed in step 1 of the procedure earlier in this chapter for installing TCP/IP.
2. On the General tab of the Internet Protocol (TCP/IP) Properties dialog box, click the Advanced button.
3. The Advanced TCP/IP settings dialog box appears.
4. Click the WINS tab to open the WINS page.
5. To add a WINS server IP address, click Add and enter the address into the box that appears. You can add several—add them in the order of use. You can use the arrow buttons to change the order of multiple addresses. You can correct mistakes using the Remove or Edit buttons.
6. If you need to use an LMHOSTS file, select the Enable LMHOSTS lookup button. Note that to use this file, it must reside on your computer. Click the "Import LMHOSTS" button to locate the file and place it in the correct location.
7. Click OK and close all open dialog boxes.

Note that WINS is used only on Microsoft networks.

TCP/IP CONNECTIVITY UTILITIES

In using TCP/IP as the unifying protocol in a network of heterogeneous operating systems, a series of connectivity and diagnostic utilities are always useful to have for checking connections and ensuring reliability of the network. Microsoft develops its own versions of TCP/IP utilities that are found on other platforms supporting this protocol.

Finger

Finger is a command line utility that displays information about user(s) logged onto a remote system (see Table 7.1). The remote system must be running the finger service for this command to function, and the output of this command varies depending on the remote system being addressed. While the finger *utility* is available on Windows 2000 and XP, the finger *service* is not. Therefore, the remote system that is being queried by the finger utility cannot be running Windows 2000 or XP.

Syntax: finger [-l] [username] @hostname

TABLE 7.1 Finger options and parameters.

Option/Parameter	Description
-l	Displays information in long list (verbose) format.
Username	When this is not defined, all users on the remote system are listed. Use this option to check the status of an individual user.
@hostname	Use this option for defining the IP address or host name of the system you are querying.

FTP

Many times FTP is seen as a command, yet it is in fact a protocol that uses the TCP/IP connection to transfer files to and from remote computers regardless of the file systems being used at either end. FTP stands for File Transfer Protocol (FTP). Predominantly used for moving larger files between locations quickly and mostly transparently to users, FTP is the "glue" that holds together client/server applications that use UNIX as a server component with Windows NT, 2000, and XP clients. Also, with Windows servers serving UNIX clients, FTP really embodies as a command the goal of hardware interoperability between platforms.

You can use FTP both within shell scripts, and interactively for moving files around a network, or even the Internet. You can, in fact, use a Web browser (Microsoft's Internet Explorer, for instance) to access FTP sites anywhere in the world, providing they are either public domain or you have the user name and password to log in.

To connect from a workstation to another system via FTP, the destination system needs to be running an FTP server component. Microsoft includes FTP as standard within Windows XP Professional. FTP Service for Windows XP Professional is included in Internet Information Services, a Windows component. You can configure a Windows XP Professional-based workstation as an FTP server using Internet Information Services, making it possible to quickly post files and images for others to gather and use via the FTP command.

FTP is also delivered as part of Microsoft's Internet Information Server, and ships with the Windows XP operating system. In the instance of configuring IIS for FTP use, FTP actually runs as a network service, allowing multiple users to connect with and use the server simultaneously. Nearly all UNIX operating systems run an FTP server daemon by default; FTP is often used for file transfers between UNIX and Windows NT/2000/XP systems. A daemon is the UNIX equivalent of a service in Windows. It is a program or utility than runs all of the time, and provides resources that are available to any process that requests them.

Using the FTP command to connect with another system, you will use the syntax provided in Table 7.2. When logging into an FTP site, you may be prompted to enter your user name and password.

After logging into the remote system you can traverse the directories that have been made available. If you are a system administrator, you will find that Windows XP's FTP Service can be used to quickly configure an anonymous FTP site.

When you want to download files from an FTP server using commands rather than a Web browser, you use the command GET. Conversely, loading files onto a server requires the PUT command. Some servers have restrictions on where files can be loaded, so be sure to check with the permissions set on the login and password you have before trying to load files to an FTP server. Keep in mind that the file names and commands themselves are case sensitive, which makes sense given the fact that the commands included in this protocol bridge both Windows (not case sensitive in its file structure) and UNIX (whose file names are case sensitive).

Providing the organization you want files from has an FTP site, you

TABLE 7.2 FTP options and parameters.

Option/Parameter	***Description***
-v	Prevents the display of remote server responses to client commands
-n	Prevents autologin upon connection
-i	Prevents individual file verifications during mass file transfers
-d	Displays debugging messages
-g	Allows wildcard characters to be used in file and directory names
Hostname	Defines the host name or IP address of the remote system to be accessed
-s:filename	Allows you to specify a test file containing a series of FTP commands to be executed in sequence. This parameter in effect launches a shell script of FTP commands to be executed on the remote system.

can get 2MB or greater files in a matter of seconds. Microsoft maintains a comprehensive FTP site at ftp.microsoft.com, which can be accessed through any Internet browser. Simply type in the FTP location in the place of a Web address, and the FTP site will be displayed. While the standard interface for the FTP command line is quickly becoming outdated due to the pervasiveness of using browsers for traversing FTP sites, there are also utilities, both public domain and offered for sale that streamline the FTP process. Once FTP has been installed on Windows XP Professional on your system you can use the command line below for accessing and downloading or updating files to selected FTP sites. If you are using a public domain or purchased program for FTP functions, these commands are the basis for activities in those programs.

Syntax: ftp [-v] [-n] [-i] [-d] *[hostname] [-s:filename]*

What about using the commands in the FTP protocol? Table 7.3 shows the most commonly used commands during FTP sessions.

TABLE 7.3 FTP commands and parameters.

Command/Parameter	***Description***
open hostname	Initiates a command session with a remote FTP host
close	Terminates the current session (without closing the FTP command window or program)
quit	Closes the FTP program, returning you to the command prompt
ls	Lists some of the files and subfolders in the current directory
ls –l	Lists full information for the files in the current directory
cd *dirname*	Changes to the specified directory
cd ..	Moves up one level in the directory tree
pwd	Prints the current folder on the remote computer
binary	Sets the file transfer mode on FTP to binary or bit-by-bit mode. It is a good idea to use this command by default, especially on image-based files.
ascii	Specifies that the file to be transferred is an ASCII file
get *filename*	Transfers the specified file to the local system
recv *filename*	Functions in the same manner as get; transfers the specified file to the local system
mget *filename*	Used in conjunction with wildcards in the command statement, this command transfers multiple files to the local system.
put *filename*	Transfers the specified file to the remote system
send *filename*	Functions in the same manner as put; transfers specified files to the remote system
mput *filename*	Transfers multiple files to the remote systems. This command is typically used in conjunction with wildcards.
hash	Toggles the # character printing for each block of data transferred.
prompt	Toggles the use of prompts for each individual file during multiple transfers
help	Provides the FTP command summary

TFTP

This protocol is based on using UDP as the transport protocol, and as a consequence is less secure and less reliable than its FTP counterpart, which uses TCP as its transport protocol (see Chapter 6 for more information on UDP and TCP). There are no user authentication services in TFTP. Further, TFTP does not provide for browsing of directories, as the UDP protocol is not connection-oriented. If you plan to use this command you will need to know the exact file name and location of what you need to retrieve.

Syntax: tftp [- i] *host* [get] [put] source *{destination}*

TABLE 7.4 TFTP options and parameters.

Option/Parameter	***Description***
- i	Defines the file to be transferred in binary mode
Host	Replaces the hostname or IP address of the remote system
Get	Command for transferring a file or files from the remote system to the local system
Put	Command for sending a file from the local system to the remote system
Source	Defines the name of the file to be transferred
Destination	Defines the location where the file is to be transferred

Telnet

This is a terminal emulation program, which makes it possible to log into and use a remote workstation or server running Telnet server services. Many UNIX servers do have telnet server capabilities, and this command can be used from the Command Prompt window of Windows XP Professional as it is built in as a common feature. Using the options associated with the Command Prompt window, you can set the terminal and display preferences for the telnet sessions you plan to initiate from a Windows XP Professional computer.

Syntax: telnet [*host*] [*port*]

TABLE 7.5 Telnet parameters.

Parameter	Description
Host	Specifies the host name or IP address of the remote system you want to log into.
Port	Defines the port number in the remote system to which you will connect. When omitted, the value specified in the remote system's services file is used. If no value is entered in services, then port 23 is automatically used.

Note that Windows XP also has a telnet server service available.

RCP

The purpose of this utility is to provide you with a command for copying files between a local system and a UNIX remote system which is running a remote shell server, rshd. Alternatively, you can direct two remote UNIX systems running rshd to exchange files between themselves using this protocol. It is important to note that neither Windows XP nor Windows 2000 have rshd service. RCP can be used on an XP system to copy files with a UNIX system or to direct 2 UNIX systems to copy between each other.

A text file on the remote system, called .rhosts, contains the host and user names of the local system so it is identified before the file transfers take place.

Syntax: rcp [-a] [-b] [-h] [-r] source1 source2 ... sourceN destination

TABLE 7.6 RCP options and parameters.

Option/Parameter	Description
-a	Specifies that the file(s) be transferred in ASCII mode
-b	Specifies that the file(s) be transferred in binary mode
-h	Allows hidden files on a Windows XP system to be transferred

(continues)

TABLE 7.6 RCP options and parameters. (*Continued*)

Option/Parameter	***Description***
-r	Copies the contents of all of the source's subdirectories to the destination (when both source and destination are directories)
source	Specifies the files to be transferred (and optionally its host and user names, in the format *host.user:filename*)
destination	Specifies the file name to be created at the destination (and optionally its host and user names, in the format host.user:filename)

REXEC

This utility provides for batched, or noninteractive commands which are executed on a remote system. This command needs to have rexec service running on the remote system to be available to Windows XP clients. Redirection symbols can be used to refer output to files on the local system (using normal redirection syntax) or on the remote system (by enclosing the redirection symbols in quotation marks, for example, ">>").

Syntax: rexec hostname [-l user] [-n] command

TABLE 7.7 REXEC options and parameters.

Option/Parameter	***Description***
hostname	Specifies the host name of the system on which the command is to be run
-l user	Specifies a user name under whose account the command is to be executed on the remote system (a prompt for a user password will be generated at the local machine)
-n	Redirects rexec input to NUL (NUL is a virtual output device that takes input and discards it.)
command	Specifies the command to be executed at the remote system

RSH

This command is used for executing commands and options on remote systems. This command requires the remote system to have the rsh service running on it to be useable; Windows XP does not provide RSH service itself. It has the same redirection capabilities as REXEC and the same .rhosts requirement as RCP.

Syntax: rsh hostname [-l user] [-n] command

TABLE 7.8 RSH options and parameters.

Option/Parameter	*Description*
hostname	Specifies the host name of the system on which the command is to be run
-l user	Specifies a user name under whose account the command is to be executed on the remote system (a prompt for a user password will be generated at the local machine)
-n	Redirects rsh input to NUL
command	Specifies the command to be executed at the remote system

LPR

This utility provides the flexibility of printing a file to a printer connected to a remote BSD type printer subsystem that is running an LPD server.

Syntax: lpr -S*server* -P*printer* [-J*jobname*] [-ol] *filename*

TABLE 7.9 LPR parameters and options.

Option/Parameter	*Description*
-Sserver	Specifies the host name of the system to which the printer is connected
-Pprinter	Specifies the name of the printer to be used

(continues)

TABLE 7.9 LPR parameters and options. (*Continued*)

Option/Parameter	Description
Jjobname	Specifies the name of the print job
-ol	Used when printing a non-text (PostScript) file from a Windows XP system to a UNIX printer
-l	Used when printing a non-text (PostScript) file from a UNIX system to a Windows NT printer
Filename	Specifies the name of the file to be printed

CHAPTER SUMMARY

Over the years, TCP/IP configuration has gotten easier, as systems like DNS, DHCP, and WINS have been developed. In Windows XP Professional, network configuration is handled mostly by wizards, reducing even further the need for network administration. Still, there are times that configuration needs to be done, and the primary procedures were covered in this chapter.

DHCP alleviates the need for an administrator to keep track of every IP address on the network. Configuring Windows XP Professional to be a DHCP client is very easy; the most important work is done at the DHCP servers.

DNS is the name-to-address resolution system that makes the Internet possible. Now that Windows 2000 and XP no longer rely on NetBIOS names, DNS can handle all the internal name resolution for these systems. WINS is used only for compatibility with previous versions of Windows.

Despite their age, command line utilities and protocols such as FTP, Telnet, and REXEC still serve many useful functions in Windows XP Professional.

8 Exploring E-Mail Capabilities in Windows XP with Outlook Express 6

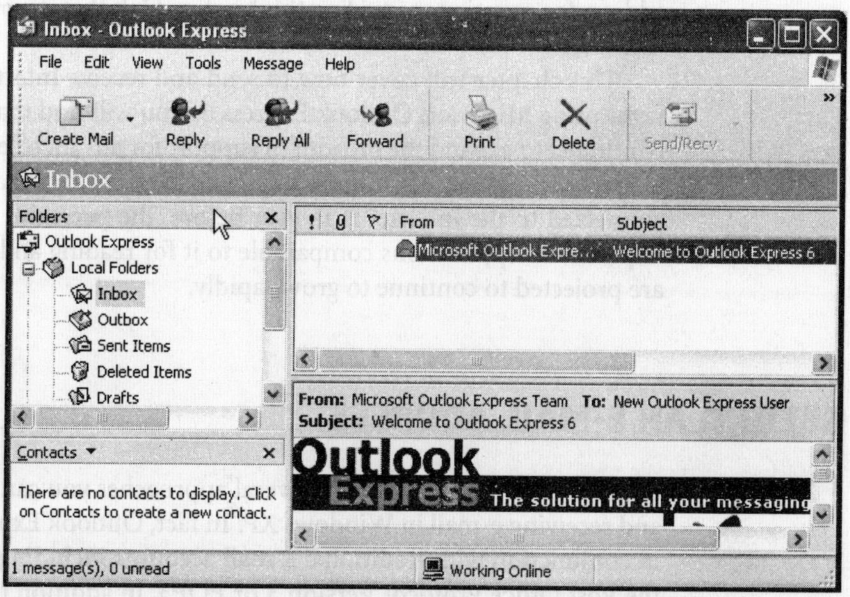

INTRODUCTION

If there is one area where you are likely to be spending the majority of your time in Windows XP Professional or XP Home Edition, it is in e-mail. Today, many research companies including International Data Corporation point out that there is more e-mail sent in some companies than regular mail. Given the heightened security issues around conventional mail, e-mail looks to continue growing exponentially throughout the coming years. Windows XP Professional's extensive support of Internet-based e-mail starts in Outlook Express, a "lite" version of the full Outlook application that is included in the Office XP Professional application suite. It is the intent of this chapter to provide you with the necessary instructions and techniques for getting the most out of using Outlook Express.

To start, first realize what an e-mail address is. Just as people have unique phone numbers, e-mail addresses are also unique. You can create them to reflect your specific interests, or the purpose of the communication you are initiating. The format is typically *yournameoridentity@location.com*. For example, I selected *xpbookadvice@yahoo.com* as my e-mail address for questions regarding this book as I felt that it would be easily remembered.

This chapter will cover how to send and receive Internet e-mail messages using Microsoft Outlook Express 6. You will find that Microsoft has continued to expand the breadth of support for advanced e-mail functions in the latest edition of Outlook Express. Given the fact that more PCs are connected to the Internet than ever before, the pervasive use of Outlook Express and applications comparable to it for reading and sending e-mail are projected to continue to grow rapidly.

GETTING AN E-MAIL ADDRESS

Outlook Express is just one of several approaches you can take to sending and receiving e-mail in Windows XP. In fact, Outlook Express is best used in conjunction with traditional e-mail accounts including those based on the Post Office Protocol Version 3 or POP3, in addition to Internet Message Access Protocol (IMAP) and Hypertext Transfer Protocol (HTTP). If you already have one e-mail address at work or with an ISP, you can configure Outlook Express to support an existing e-mail account through the steps detailed in this chapter.

You do not necessarily have to have an e-mail account from an ISP before starting to use Outlook Express. You can get free e-mail accounts from probably thousands of Web sites, most notably Yahoo at *www.yahoo.com* and Microsoft's HotMail at www.hotmail.com. However, you can also sign up for a Hotmail account directly from your workstation by following this procedure (you will need to have an open Internet connection):

1. Click Control Panel from the Start menu.
2. Double-click the User Accounts icon and click on your account name or picture.
3. Click Set up my account to use a .NET Passport and follow the instructions presented by the wizard to create a new Hotmail account. If you do set up a Hotmail account, you will have two options for managing your e-mail:
   - Open Internet Explorer and use the options in *www.msn.com* to read your e-mail.
   - Configure Outlook Express to handle your Hotmail account using instructions provided later in this chapter.

If you have an e-mail account through your work or through an ISP, you will need to have the following information to configure Outlook Express in Windows XP Professional:

- Outgoing (SMTP) mail server name
- Incoming mail server type (POP3, IMAP, or HTTP)
- Incoming mail server name
- Your e-mail address
- Your e-mail account name
- Your e-mail password

You also need to know whether or not your ISP or employer's network has a requirement to log on using Secure Password Authentication (SPA). Contact your ISP or the system administrator at your employer if you need any of this information.

GETTING STARTED WITH OUTLOOK EXPRESS

As with many of the developments in Windows 2000 and now XP, there are several different approaches to starting applications including Outlook Express. Here are six different ways to get Outlook Express up and running:

- Click Outlook Express from the top left portion of the Start menu.
- Double-click the Outlook Express icon (an envelope with a blue arrow around it) on your desktop.
- Click the Start button and choose Outlook Express from the All Programs menu. Start Internet Explorer and click the Mail button

on the Standard Buttons toolbar, and then click Read Mail from the menu that appears.

- Start Internet Explorer and click "Mail and News" from the Tools menu, then click Read Mail from the extended menu.
- Click the Outlook Express icon in the Quick Launch toolbar.

When you start Outlook Express for the first time, a wizard starts to guide you through the process of configuring the application for use with a new or existing e-mail account. Following the steps in the wizard configures Outlook Express so that your e-mail account(s) can be accessed from the Windows XP system you are working on. Figure 8.1 shows a page of the Internet Connection Wizard, which guides you through the setting of the POP3 and SMTP account values for your e-mail accounts.

Be sure to accurately enter all of the information requested by the wizard. The information is specific to your account and is used by Outlook Express to determine which of the accounts at an ISP are yours. The following

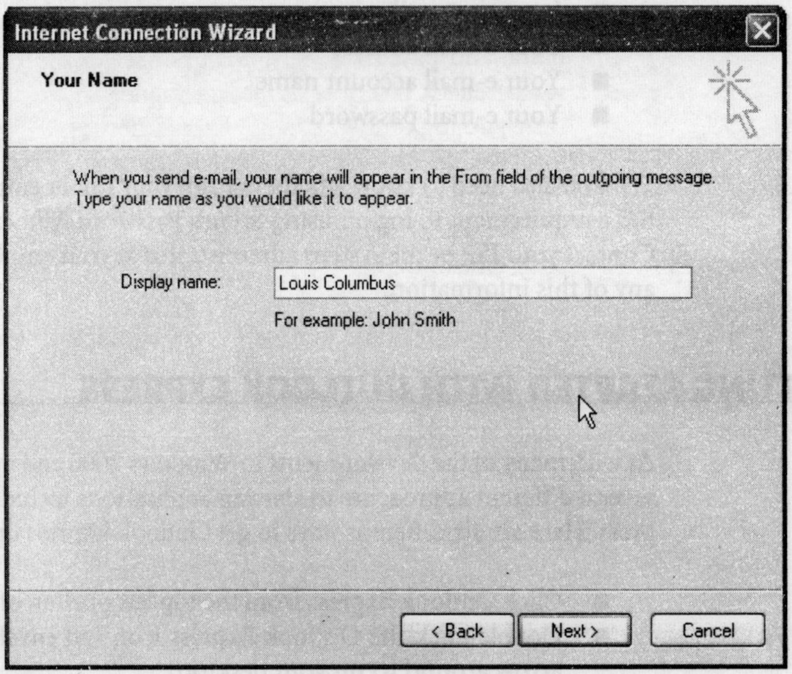

FIGURE 8.1 The Internet Connection Wizard guides you through the configuration of your e-mail account.

procedure provides instructions on how to answer all the prompts in the e-mail portion of the Internet Connection Wizard. Note that the pages you see can vary based on your selections.

1. Start Outlook Express using one of the previously listed methods. If this is the first time you have opened Outlook Express, the Internet Connection Wizard starts. The first page asks if you will be creating a new or existing account. Click the Use an existing Internet Mail account option, then click Next.
2. The Your Name page appears with your user name showing in the Display name text box. Accept your user name or enter a new one. This is the name that will appear in the from field on all outgoing mail. Click Next. The Internet E-mail address page appears.
3. Enter your e-mail address and click Next. The E-mail Server Name page is shown.
4. Select whether your incoming mail server is an IMAP, POP3, or HTTP server, then enter the server's name. Enter the outgoing mail (SMTP) server's name in the appropriate box. Click Next
5. On the Internet Mail Logon page that appears, enter your account name and password. If you do not select the "Remember password" check box, you will be prompted for your password every time you log onto Outlook Express. If your ISP requires it, select the "Log on using Secure Password Authentication (SPA)" check box. Click Next.
6. The final page appears, congratulating you and instructing you to click Finish. Do so.

If you are configuring Outlook Express on a system that you had upgraded from a previous version of Windows with Outlook Express or even a previous release candidate of Windows XP Professional or Home Edition, the new Outlook Express will automatically pick up these account settings. In this case, when you start Outlook Express for the first time, you will be prompted for the password on your existing e-mail accounts. After that, the Outlook Express application launches and you are ready to begin sending and receiving e-mail.

Once the steps of the Internet Connection Wizard are complete, Outlook Express launches. Any of the existing messages are shown in the Inbox of the Outlook Express screen. Figure 8.2 shows the Outlook Express screen.

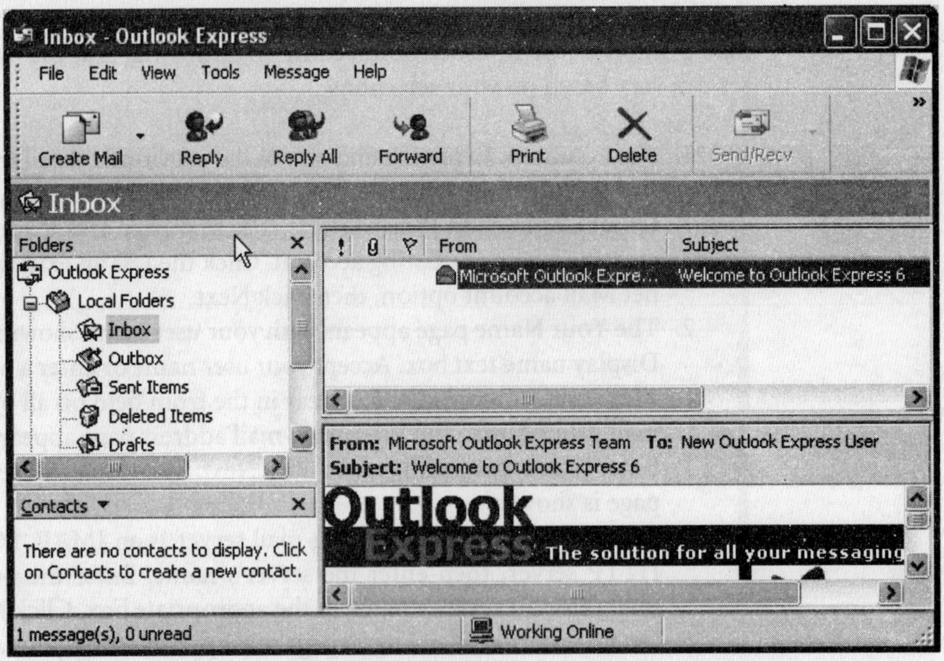

FIGURE 8.2 The main Outlook Express screen.

COMPOSING MESSAGES IN OUTLOOK EXPRESS

Typing and sending a message is easier than writing a letter and putting it into the mail. Here are three approaches you can take to creating messages in Outlook Express:

- Click the Create Mail button on the far left side of the Outlook Express toolbar.
- Select New Message from the Message menu.
- Type Ctrl+N at the same time when Outlook Express is open.

All three approaches open the New Message window. Think of this area as an open sheet of paper you can compose your messages on. Figure 8.3 shows the New Message window.

Notice the To, CC, and Subject boxes in the window. For an e-mail to be delivered all you really need to enter is the address in the To box, as this

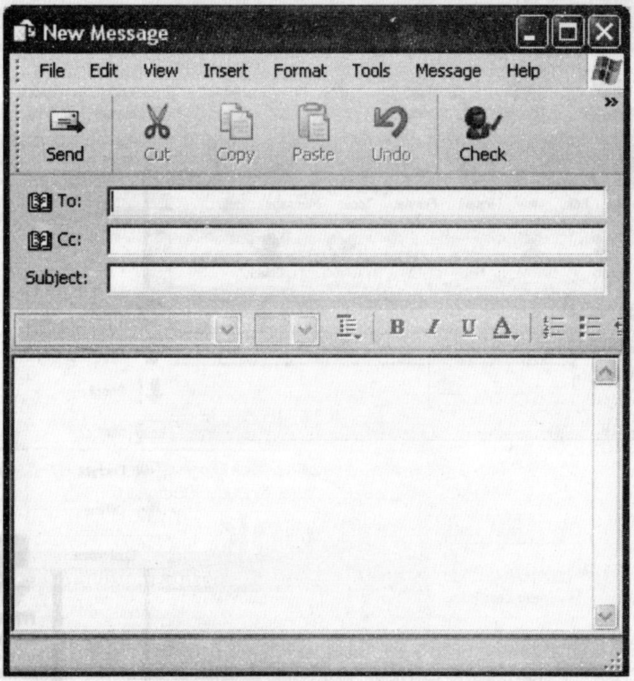

FIGURE 8.3 The New Message window.

is comparable to writing the address on a letter. The procedure for creating a message in Outlook Express follows:

1. In the To box enter the mailing address of whomever you want to send a message to. Entering *xpbookadvice@yahoo.com* causes the message to be sent to me, for example. If you are going to send this same message to multiple recipients, you can type a semicolon between each e-mail address to have it reach each person.
2. Although entering an address in the CC (carbon copy) box is not required in order to send a message, it is useful to send others copies of the message.
3. You may want to enter the subject of the message in the Subject line. You can type anything you want, but if you leave this field blank Outlook Express will prompt you to confirm you do not want to include a subject line before it sends the message.
4. Next, select the priority of your message. By default, messages are sent at normal priority. To reach the priority icon, either maximize

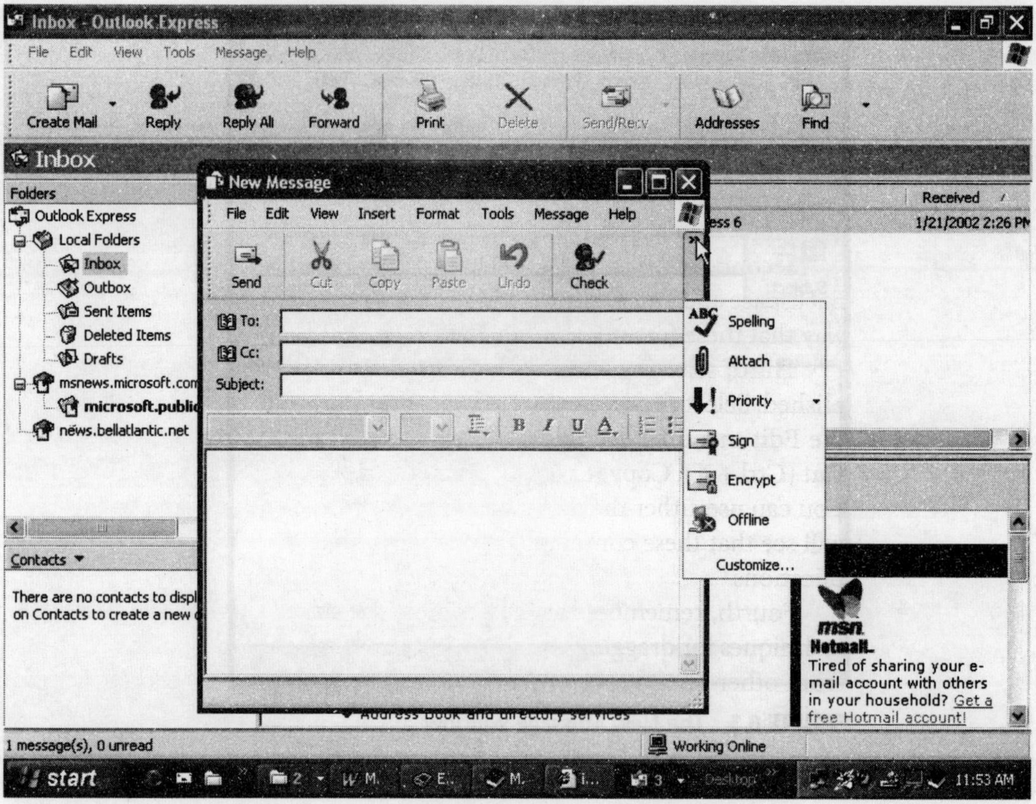

FIGURE 8.4 Click the arrow to access additional buttons.

the New Message window or click the small arrow on the upper right corner of the window as shown in Figure 8.4.

Clicking this icon takes the message through three states of High, Normal, or Low Priority. Notice that when an e-mail message is sent with High Priority a red exclamation point is placed next to the listing of the inbound message in the recipient's e-mail inbox.

5. Now you are ready to begin composing your e-mail message in work space below the formatting toolbar.

EDITING E-MAIL 101

Now that you have created an e-mail message you may need to edit it before sending it. If you have worked with many of the other Microsoft products including Word, WordPad or other word processing tools included in applications, then this is going to be easy. In case you have not had a chance to get up to speed with the basics of word processing on Microsoft products, here are a few points to keep in mind when editing e-mail in Outlook Express:

First, text in the work space area of a New Message window will wrap line to line. Just continue typing from sentence to sentence. Creating a new paragraph is easy; just press Enter and a new paragraph begins.

Second, you can highlight any text you want to change. Using the Backspace and Delete keys in the middle of text also works exactly the same way that these features work in Word.

Third, selecting, cutting, replacing and copying text is easily accomplished. Select the area of text you want to move and use the commands in the Edit menu of the New Message window. Note the main commands: Cut (Ctrl + X), Copy (Ctrl + C), Paste (Ctrl + V), and Select All, (Ctrl + A). You can use either the menu commands or the keyboard commands. You will see that these commands are nearly universal in Windows and in applications.

Fourth, remember that you can use the standard Windows Clipboard techniques for dragging and dropping text throughout a document, to and from other documents, and even to and from documents on other applications.

Fifth, remember that just as with Microsoft Word, there are plenty of tools included in Outlook Express for editing documents and adding in emphasis and graphics. Those features are extensively covered throughout the latter parts of this chapter.

SENDING E-MAIL

When you have completed the e-mail message, you are ready to send it to the recipients entered in the To box of the New Message window. There are three approaches to sending a message once it has been composed. These are:

- Click the Send button in the New Message window toolbar.
- Press the Alt and S keys at the same time.
- Click Send message from the File menu.

As the message is sent the New Message window will close. By default, all messages are sent immediately. However, if you do not have a permanent connection to the Internet and want to have Outlook Express hold the messages until you are again connected to the Internet, you can click Options from the Tools menu and clear the "Send Messages Immediately" check box. The messages will then stay in your Outbox until the computer is connected to the Internet.

FORMATTING E-MAIL MESSAGES

Just as with Microsoft Word and many other word processing applications, the text management features in Outlook Express give you a wide latitude in how you choose to compose e-mail messages. You can make your messages appear as Web pages complete with headings, images, fancy fonts, hyperlinks, background colors and more. When you first log onto Outlook Express you can also see how Microsoft has created the Web page look for the Microsoft Outlook Express welcome message.

Just as with Microsoft Word, the formatting to your message happens in the work space in the New Message window. You can select any type of formatting approach you wish. The following sections discuss the features that give you this flexibility in greater detail.

Working with the Formatting Toolbar

Microsoft has positioned the formatting toolbar in Outlook Express similarly to the toolbar in Word. The formatting toolbar is located between the area of the New Message window where you type in the recipients and the subject, and the message box. Let us go through the following procedure to see how to use the formatting toolbar:

1. Maximize the New Message window in order to view all of the buttons and options on the formatting toolbar.
2. In the New Message window select any block of text you want to modify.
3. Click any of the formatting options in the toolbar. The text is changed to reflect that attribute. You can also move your mouse directly above each of the tools in the formatting toolbar and a pop-up message will tell you what each one does.
4. Open the first drop-down menu on the formatting toolbar. This is the font menu. Notice that when you click one of the many items in this menu the selected text in your e-mail message changes.

5. Open the next drop-down menu on the toolbar. This is the font size menu. Click a new size.
6. Type in new text and notice how the size of it changes in the workspace area. You can easily change the entire message back to a common font size by selecting the entire message and then clicking a font size from the pull-down menu.
7. Click the B, then the I, then the U. These are the Bold, Italic, and Underline buttons and are called toggles as they allow you to toggle these font style changes on and off.
8. Now look to the right of the font menus past the numbering, bulleting, and indentation icons to the text alignment icons. You probably will find the majority of the e-mails you receive are left-justified, or left-aligned. You can easily center, right-justify, left-justify or even left and right justify a new paragraph. Notice the four icons for handling the alignment of text. Make sure there are several lines of text selected in the message and click through these icons to view each one's effect.
9. Clean up the message and then send it on to the recipient(s) appearing in your To field of the New Message window.

Creating Lists in E-mail Messages

If you are creating an e-mail that has many points in it, try not to build them all together into a single paragraph. It is tough to read and is sometimes glossed over by others with not enough time to read it in detail. Using the tools in the formatting toolbar you can create bulleted or numbered lists very easily. Following the procedure here you can get a bulleted or numbered list together in no time!

1. Select the first line of text to which you want to add bullets or numbers and then click either the Bullet icon or the Numbered List icon. These options and more are available in the Format menu, which works just the same as in Word or any other Microsoft product.
2. Type each point of your list, pressing Enter at the end of each list to build a separate point for each.
3. Finish the list by clicking outside of the highlighted area.

INSERTING PICTURES IN E-MAIL MESSAGES

If you have an existing e-mail account you have most likely received e-mail messages with pictures included in them. While in certain older versions of Outlook Express this could have been difficult, you will find that embedding pictures into your e-mail messages is easy using the tools in Outlook Express 6. Follow this procedure to insert a picture into a new e-mail message:

1. Click in the workspace area where you want the image to appear.
2. Click the Insert Picture button on the formatting toolbar, or click Picture from the Insert menu.
3. Click Browse to find the image you want to include. You can also set various layout and spacing parameters using options in the Insert Picture dialog box.
4. Click OK. The selected picture is now embedded in the message.

Supported Image File Formats

Microsoft's work on Outlook Express has been outstanding from the standpoint of streamlining the task of embedding images into e-mails and having them "stay put" in the inline viewing area. One of the more useful aspects of working with Outlook Express in composing e-mails is getting files in a graphics format that can be imported and used by this application. The industry-standard graphics formats (JPEG, BMP and GIF) have always been supported. In this version, Microsoft includes support for GIF (.gif), JPEG (.jpg), bitmap (.bmp), Windows Metafile (.wmf), XBM (.xbm), and ART (.art) formats. The default formats continue to be JPEG and GIF.

Attaching Files to Your E-mail Messages

The most common approach to distributing files to many people at the same time is using the attachments feature nearly all e-mail programs have today. Attachments can be any file—from a document to motion video. Attaching files to mass mailings is a very common practice in marketing organizations, for example, where the data on new products needs to reach as many people as possible, and e-mail is typically the best vehicle for getting this accomplished.

When you receive a message with an attachment, there will be a paperclip icon to the left of the listing in the inbox, and also on the right of the preview header visible once the message is opened. Some attachments will appear within the body of the message and others will appear only as a file name. Despite the appearances of the paperclip icons, it is a good idea to point out in the message the presence of the attachment so the recipient(s) will be alert for it, especially if the attachment is not displayed within the body of the message. You can attach files to your e-mail message using either of the following two approaches:

- The first approach to attaching a file is to click the Attach icon in the toolbar near the top of the New Message window (by default, this icon appears only if the New Message window is maximized or if you click the small expansion arrow on the right of the toolbar). This icon opens the Insert Attachment dialog box, which is shown in Figure 8.5.

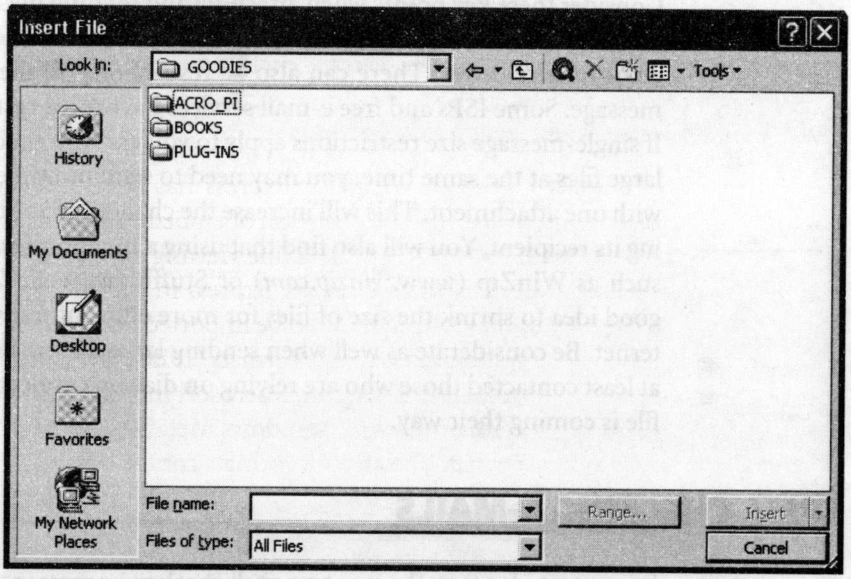

Figure 8.5 Attaching files to an e-mail message.

By stepping through the options in this dialog box you can attach as many files as you want to your message.

- The second approach is to go to the Insert menu and click File Attachment.

Opening Attachments

When you receive an attachment in Outlook Express, there are two operations you can perform, view and save. If the attachment appears in the body of the message, you can view it there. If not, click the paperclip icon on the right side of the preview pane header (the wide bar on top of the message). A small menu appears with two choices. The first choice contains the name and size of the file. If you click this one, Windows XP will open it immediately, as long as there is a program installed on the computer which can open that type of file. The other command is Save attachments. Clicking this opens the Save Attachments dialog box, which allows you to select a folder in which to copy the file.

Points to Ponder on Attachments

Consider these key points when attaching and sending files to others. First, it is becoming increasingly common to see companies restrict the size of employees' inboxes. There can also be restrictions on the size of a single message. Some ISPs and free e-mail services have these restrictions as well. If single-message size restrictions apply to you and you need to send several large files at the same time, you may need to send multiple messages, each with one attachment. This will increase the chances of your message reaching its recipient. You will also find that using a file compression application such as WinZip (*www.winzip.com*) or Stuffit (*www.aladdinsys.com*) is a good idea to shrink the size of files for more efficient transfer over the Internet. Be considerate as well when sending large files; make sure you have at least contacted those who are relying on dial-up connections that a large file is coming their way.

SPELL CHECKING E-MAILS

It is a great idea to make sure you spell check your messages before they are sent. That way you look good and the people getting your e-mails have a greater understanding of what you are talking about. Having spell checking completed for an e-mail also shows you care about how you are communicating. There is a definite difference between e-mails correctly spelled and clear versus ones that have misspelled words and unclear meanings.

It is strongly suggested that you enable spell checking for your e-mail messages. Outlook Express uses the spell checker that comes with Microsoft Office. If you do not have Microsoft Office installed, spell checking will not be available in Outlook Express.

Just as with many other features in Windows XP, you can access the spell checking function in two different ways. Either of these methods needs to be repeated for every message. In the following section we will look at how to enable spell checking for every message sent. You can manually check the spelling of each message by:

- Pressing F7 after typing each message
- Clicking Spelling from the Tools menu after typing each message

You can configure spell check to run automatically by using the procedure in the following section.

Making Sure Spell Checking Is On All the Time

Ideally, every e-mail message you send should be checked for accuracy. After all, when you get an e-mail that is unclear you inevitably have to either call the sender or write him back. Here is how to make sure you have spell checking turned on all the time:

1. Go to the Outlook Express main window.
2. Click Options from the Tools menu. The Options dialog box for Outlook Express is shown. Notice that this dialog box has ten pages associated with it.
3. Click the Spelling tab of the Options dialog box. You can see that by default, the spell checker is not turned on. Select the "Always check spelling before sending" check box.
4. Click Apply and/or OK. Spell check is now enabled for every e-mail message you write.

Further Spell Checking Points to Consider

The approach to spell checking by any application is not foolproof. Be vigilant and read over your e-mails even after the spell checker is done with them just to make sure the meaning is what you want it to be. As the spell checker continues through your message and an error is encountered, the Spelling dialog box is shown.

The buttons in the dialog box are as follows:

- **Ignore**—Ignores the unrecognized word and continues with the spell check.
- **Ignore All**—Ignores each instance of the unrecognized word throughout the entire message.

- **Change**—Changes the word with the recommended replacement in the Suggestions list, or with the changed spelling that you have entered. You will find that the spell checker will display a list of words that are similar to the one highlighted.
- **Change All**—Changes all instances of the unrecognized word in the entire message to the one that is selected in the Change To box.
- **Add**—Adds the highlighted word or phrase to the dictionary for the spell check.
- **Suggest**—Suggests a series of words when prompted that are similar to the one chosen.
- **Options**—Displays the Spelling Options dialog box which enables you to customize the current spelling options.
- **Undo Last**—Undoes the most recent change to the text being spell checked.
- **Cancel (or Close)**—Closes the spell checker.

Once your e-mail message has been spell checked you will see a confirmation dialog box asking you if it is OK to send the message. If you are satisfied the message is clear in its meaning, then click OK and the message is sent.

REPLYING TO MESSAGES

Once you get your e-mail address out to a dozen people or so you will probably start receiving e-mail as well.

You can reply to any e-mail by either clicking the Reply button on the toolbar or by pressing the Ctrl+R keys at the same time. When you do this the To box in the reply message will contain the e-mail address or display name of the original sender, depending on configuration.

The procedure for replying to messages is basically the same as that for forwarding of e-mail messages. In this latter case, you will enter the recipient's address in the To box of the New Message window.

IMPORTING AND EXPORTING MESSAGES

This is one of the areas in which Microsoft is distancing itself from competitors; it is getting much easier to get e-mails imported into and exported out from Outlook Express than was the case in previous versions of this application. Built to support the migration of users who are switching from Eudora Pro, Eudora Lite, Microsoft Exchange, Microsoft Internet Mail For Windows 3.1, Microsoft Outlook, Microsoft Windows Messaging, Netscape Communicator, Netscape Mail, and previous and even identical versions of Outlook Express, there are typically many messages left behind when importing from some of these other e-mail programs. When you first start Outlook Express the program may prompt you to import messages, settings, and address book data from previous applications. The wizard will prompt for these e-mail files if you have another e-mail program present; the wizard will be checking the Registry and subdirectory structure for the specifics on another e-mail program.

Procedure for Importing E-Mail Messages

Here is the procedure to get e-mail messages imported from another program to Outlook Express:

1. From Outlook Express click Import from the File menu. From the next menu that appears, click Messages.
2. Select the program you had been using for e-mail.
3. Click Next. You are prompted for the location of the messages. Using the Browse button you can search for the e-mail files that you want to transfer into Outlook Express.
4. Click Next. The wizard continues, and imports the e-mail messages from the previous application.
5. When all importing is complete, the messages will appear in the Outlook Express folders labeled just as they were in the previous e-mail program. The Outlook Express Import functions retain the same structure as was used before.
6. All the imported messages can now be used in Outlook Express.

Steps for Exporting Messages from Outlook Express

If you are moving from Outlook Express to Microsoft Outlook or Microsoft Exchange, follow the procedure shown here:

1. Open Outlook Express and click Export from the File menu. Click Messages from the next menu to appear.
2. Click OK to confirm that Outlook Express files will be exported to Outlook or Exchange.

3. When the Choose Profile dialog box appears, choose a Microsoft Outlook or Microsoft Exchange profile from the Profile Name drop-down list and then click OK. The profile is a collection of personal information about a user including address, work information, family information, etc.
4. When prompted to select the folders to export, choose All Folders or Selected Folders, and then select the folders to export.
5. Click OK to export the messages.

PERSONALIZING OUTLOOK EXPRESS

In this section you will learn how to personalize the components that make up Outlook Express including the appearance of the window, among other items.

Customizing the Outlook Express Windows

You can use the commands on the View menu of the main Outlook Express window to choose which features appear on-screen and which are left off. The options are controlled by the Window Layout Properties dialog box. To get to this dialog box click Layout from the View menu.

Notice that throughout this dialog box there are options for toggling which components are shown on screen. It is a great idea to make sure the preview page is shown as it gives you the chance to see the specifics on incoming messages when the Inbox folder is selected in the main window of Outlook Express.

The Preview Pane is useful for seeing the content of your e-mails without opening each one. Here are four potential approaches to customizing the Preview Pane:

- To display the preview pane, select the Show Preview Pane check box; to hide the preview pane, clear the check box.
- To split the windows so the preview pane appears next to the messages, with the Show Preview Pane check box selected, click the Beside messages radio button.
- To split the window so the preview pane appears below the messages, with the Show Preview Pane check box selected, click the "Below messages" radio button.

- To display or hide the preview pane header, with the Show Preview Pane check box selected, select or clear the Show Preview Pane Header check box.
- When you are finished with the changes, click OK.

Configuring Columns

This is very useful as it gives you the chance to view the desired data on the incoming messages you receive. To set these options follow this procedure:

1. Click Columns from the View menu. The Columns dialog box appears.
2. To add a column to the message list, select the check boxes for the columns you want to add, and clear the check boxes for the columns you want to remove. You can do this either by clicking in the check boxes or using the Show and Hide buttons. The Move up and Move down buttons can be used to change the order of the columns.
3. You can also click on the column headers to re-sort messages. For example, if you want to sort messages by whom they are from rather than by date, click the From bar and the messages will be re-sorted instantly. Click the Date bar to restore date sorting.
4. When you are through making the changes, click OK. The new list of columns will appear in the Outlook Express message list.

Customizing Default Mail Options

From working with spell checking earlier in this chapter you have had a chance to see the Options dialog box. It is full of potential for customizing Outlook Express to work to your liking. To get started, open up the Options dialog box by clicking Options from the Tools menu.

General Page

The page by default that is active when this dialog box is open, the General page has toggles for the send/receive commands and default messaging programs. One of the more valuable settings on this page is the interval between checks for new messages. You may want to set this interval to 1 minute to make sure you get your messages without delay.

Send Page

The purpose of this page is to set the format used for sending messages. Setting outgoing messages to be sent in HTML format (the default) enables the text formatting options discussed earlier in this chapter, and also the addition of graphics to messages. Because of this, most people will want to enable HTML.

Read Page

The settings on the Read tab of the Options dialog box control what happens when Outlook Express receives new messages. You can choose whether to mark previewed messages as read and how long to wait before marking them. You also can choose the font used to display your messages.

Connections Page

The Connection tab of the Options dialog box makes life much easier for people using dial-up phone lines to access the Internet. From this dialog box you can set which connection to use. You can also choose whether you want Outlook Express to hang up automatically after sending and/or downloading messages.

Creating an Automatic Signature

This is one of the distinguishing characteristics of peoples' e-mails that you receive. A signature is a brief block of text placed at the end of messages used to give an identity to messages, or at the very least, save the sender from typing his name on every message. Using the options in Outlook Express you can embed a signature in your e-mail messages automatically. Using the Signatures tab of the Options dialog box, you can create your own signature file, as described in the following procedure:

1. Click New on the Signatures page of the Options dialog box. You will notice that "Signature #1" appears in the list of signatures in the middle of the dialog box.
2. If it is not already selected, click the Text radio button in the Edit Signature portion of the dialog box.
3. Place the cursor in the Text Box next to the Text radio button, and type in the text you want to be included in your signature.
4. Select the "Add signatures to all outgoing messages" check box to make sure your signature appears on every e-mail you send.
5. Click OK. The Options dialog box closes.

6. Open a new message. Your signature file is now at the bottom of the e-mail! You can even get more daring and use the File options back in the Signatures dialog box to create your own customized graphics as well.

CHAPTER SUMMARY

There is much more that could be discussed on the subject of e-mail in the Outlook Express 6 application that ships with Windows XP Professional and Home Editions. Having just scratched the surface, you should really get adventurous and go through the entire Options dialog box and experiment with creating a very customized experience in your e-mail management. At a bare minimum, be sure to get a signature file set up so you can include your e-mail address, name, and favorite saying, and if you work for a company and have a title and business phone, include that as well. Let us just go over the major points that were covered in this chapter:

- Outlook Express 6 is automatically installed on your system when you install Windows XP or when you install Internet Explorer 6.0 on another version of Windows.
- Using the Options dialog box you can configure Outlook Express to match your specific tastes for an e-mail program.
- It is possible to attach a wide variety of files to your e-mail messages using the techniques provided in this chapter. You can also embed images into your messages.
- You can easily start a new message in Outlook Express by pressing Ctrl+N or by clicking New Message from the Toolbar.
- It is easy to migrate from most other e-mail programs to Outlook Express.
- You can create signatures that will appear on all or selected messages.
- Outlook Express gives you a wide variety of options for formatting your messages.

9 Strengthening Security in Windows XP Professional

INTRODUCTION

The single biggest challenge for Microsoft and every operating system developer is the increasingly complex task of making their operating systems secure. Just as new technologies are emerging that thwart existing security threats, new security concerns arise. It is a continual challenge to stay on top of Internet-based security, as there seems to be just as much creativity going on relative to how to break into systems as to how to keep unauthorized users out. There are steps you can take in Windows XP to ensure both you and the users you support are more secure than if nothing had been done. The intent of this chapter is to provide you with steps you can take to strengthen the security of your systems when they are running Windows XP Professional.

ENABLING AN INTERNET FIREWALL

Given the fact that Microsoft projects that virtually everyone running Windows XP Professional will be connected to the Internet, the need for protecting systems from unwanted access over the Internet is critical. For the first time, Microsoft has included a software firewall in an operating system. Windows XP Professional and Home Edition both have software-configurable firewalls. Called an Internet Connection Firewall (ICF), this is a software application that blocks others from accessing your system while you are on the Internet. The firewall actually foils attempts by hackers to gain access to your system, and then logs their efforts. Firewalls have been around quite a while, and can be either in hardware or software form. Most companies use both approaches to make sure their data and accounts are kept safe. Keep in mind that there are degrees of security in any operating system; no one operating system can be considered completely safe from hackers or intrusion. It is more of a matter of making your system impenetrable by the majority of hackers out on the Internet. Figure 9.1 shows a diagram of a firewall.

FIGURE 9.1 A firewall's place in an Internet connection path.

Microsoft has created the ICF so that it can be enabled regardless of the type of direct network connection to the Internet. All connections share common properties, and the ICF is one of them. It is very easy to toggle on the ICF for a connection. Presented here is the procedure for enabling the ICF for connections:

1. Click Network Connections in the Start menu.
2. Right-click the icon that represents your Internet connection and click Properties on the menu that appears.
3. Click the Advanced tab that is shown in Figure 9.2.
4. Click the "Protect my computer and network by limiting or preventing access to this computer from the Internet" check box.
5. Click OK, and the ICF is now in place. You will have to reboot to enable the ICF.

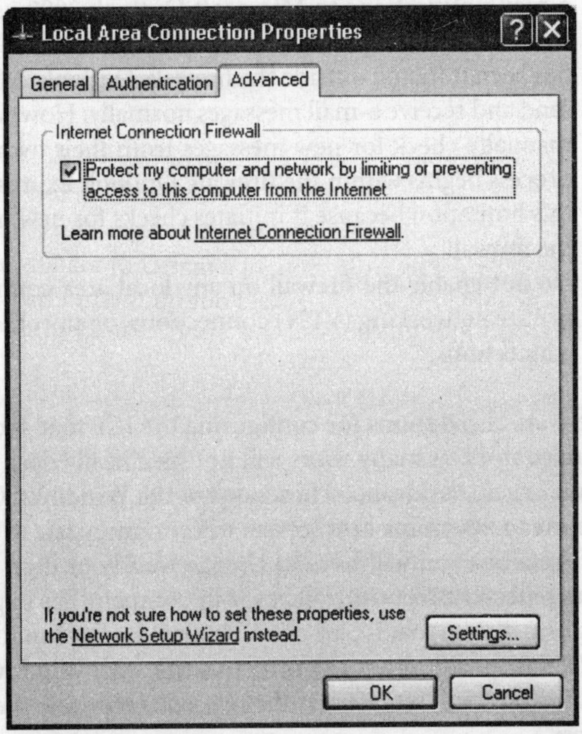

FIGURE 9.2 Configuring the ICF through the Connection Properties dialog box.

Administering the ICF and Touring Its Advanced Options

There are several points to keep in mind when you are working with an Internet Connection Firewall. These are key points specifically for those of you who will be administering them in organizations. Keep these tips in mind to troubleshoot ICF functions as well.

- If your company or organization currently runs a VPN there is a good chance that the server that is hosting the connection already has a firewall. If so, the ICF on Windows XP systems and the firewall(s) on the VPN hosting servers may conflict. If you have Windows XP-based systems suddenly not communicating on the network, check to make sure there is not a conflict at the firewall level.
- Keep in mind that if your network uses Microsoft Exchange server to handle e-mail, the firewall will prevent the server from sending e-mail notifications to Microsoft Outlook 2000 users. That is because the remote procedure call (RPC) that sends the notification has been initiated outside the firewall. Outlook 2000 users can still send and receive e-mail messages normally. However, they need to manually check for new messages from their own systems so the process begins within the firewall. Outlook Express does not have this limitation because it initiates checks for new mail from inside the firewall.
- Do not enable the firewall on any local area connections, virtual private networking (VPN) connections, or any other non-Internet connections.

There are also options for configuring the ICF that should be set only by administrators, as many users will not specifically deal with these configuration issues. As advanced functions of the Windows XP ICF, they are meant more to determine how servers will communicate to clients; so these are not functions you will have to change weekly or even monthly. They will more reflect the security policies your company has in place. If you are working on a system that is part of a VPN then do not modify these settings as the VPN is specifically configured to work with Windows XP in a predetermined protocol set. Here is the procedure to view the advanced ICF functions:

1. Right click on the network connection of interest. Click Properties from the menu that appears.
2. Click the Advanced tab.
3. Click the Settings button located at the bottom of the Advanced page. The Settings page appears and is shown in Figure 9.3.
4. It is a good idea to check with your system administrator before changing any of these elements, as each permits access from the Internet to your system and servers. If you are a system administra-

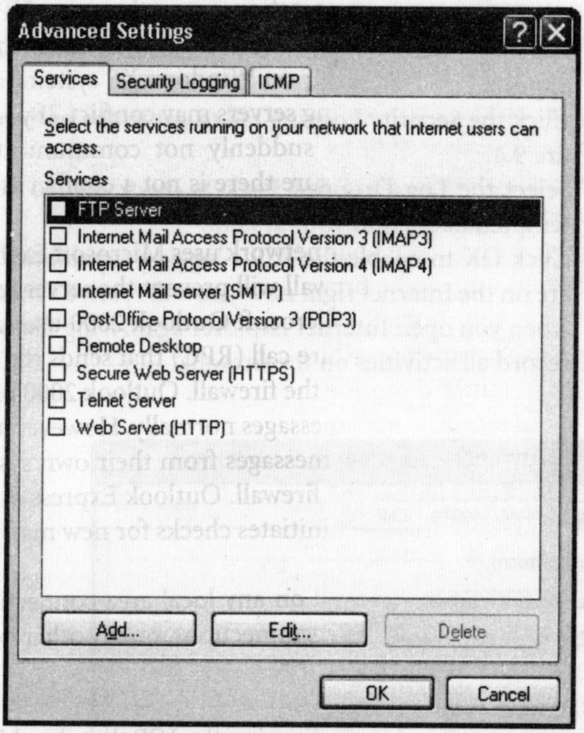

FIGURE 9.3 Advanced ICF settings.

tor, you can toggle the levels of support you want to provide to allow others to get through your firewall for specific purposes.

5. Click OK to close the dialog box.
6. Click OK again to close the Properties dialog box.

Tracking Your Firewall's Activity

All firewalls have the ability to report activity, with the most advanced firewalls even providing statistics by IP address as to who is trying to get into your company's networks. Microsoft has provided a logging capability to track the activity of the Windows XP ICF. Here is the procedure for activating event logging with the Windows XP ICF:

1. Open your default Internet connection.
2. Right-click on the Internet Connection's icon and click Properties from the menu.

3. Click the Advanced tab.
4. Click the Settings button. The Advanced Settings dialog box appears.
5. Click the Security Logging tab to get to the options shown in Figure 9.4.
6. Select the Log Dropped Packets check box to keep track of attempted hacks into your system.
7. Click OK to enable the ICF's logging capabilities. Assuming you are on the Internet right now you will receive a message saying that when you open Internet Explorer again a log file will be created to record all activities on the firewall.

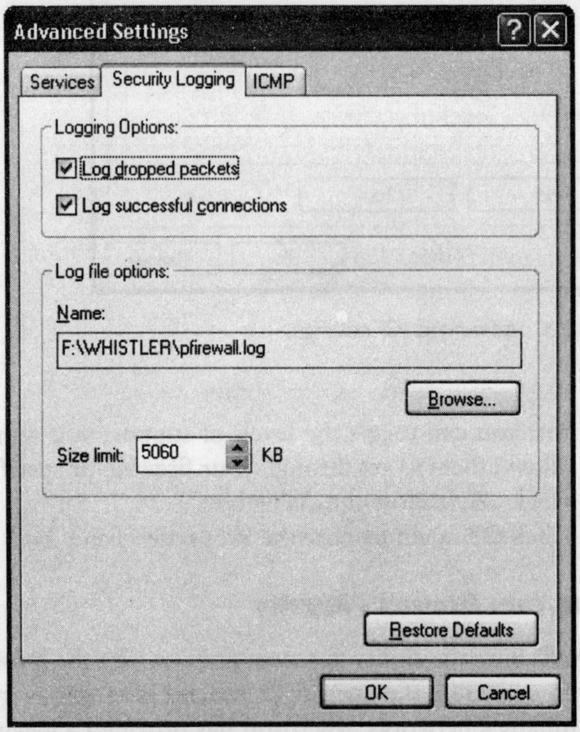

FIGURE 9.4 Using the Security Logging capabilities of Windows XP to track events on the ICF.

MAKING YOUR BROWSER SECURE

The first steps of Internet security in Windows XP have to do with the connections you make to check e-mail, send and receive messages, and visit Web sites. The underlying connectivity in Windows XP has the added element of security that is possible with the ICF explained in the previous section. The ICF is a foundational element in an overall security strategy. Configuring your browser for the highest level of security you want is explained here. Keep in mind there is a tradeoff between the level of security your browser provides and the relative ease of navigating and using the Internet. If you want the most robust security in your browser possible, your navigation of the Internet will be slowed down due to many checks and preventative measures. It is best to look for a balance leaning towards greater security for best results. Any highly confidential files and data should be hidden behind a firewall and inaccessible via browser at all for the highest level of security.

Microsoft includes the option of installing Internet Explorer 6.0 during the Windows XP Professional installation. IE 6.0 appears to be faster and more reliable than previous browser versions and actually is better at handling e-mails than Netscape Communicator. The fact is that IE 6.0 does have some strong security features that when coupled with the security options in Windows XP make for a strong combination in maintaining privacy.

Follow this procedure for setting the level of security you want in Internet Explorer 6.0:

1. Open Internet Explorer 6.0. It is installed with Windows XP if you toggle the install screen for it during the operating system's setup process.
2. Click Internet Options from the Tools menu.
3. Click the Security tab. Figure 9.5 shows an example of the Security page of the Internet Options dialog box in IE 6.0.
4. Notice that there are four zones shown in the dialog box. The higher the level of security set for each of these zones, the more restrictions are placed on how you navigate around the Internet. For comparison purposes, here are the default settings for each zone:
   - **Internet**—All new Web sites that you have never visited before are placed in this zone. Default security level for this zone is Medium.

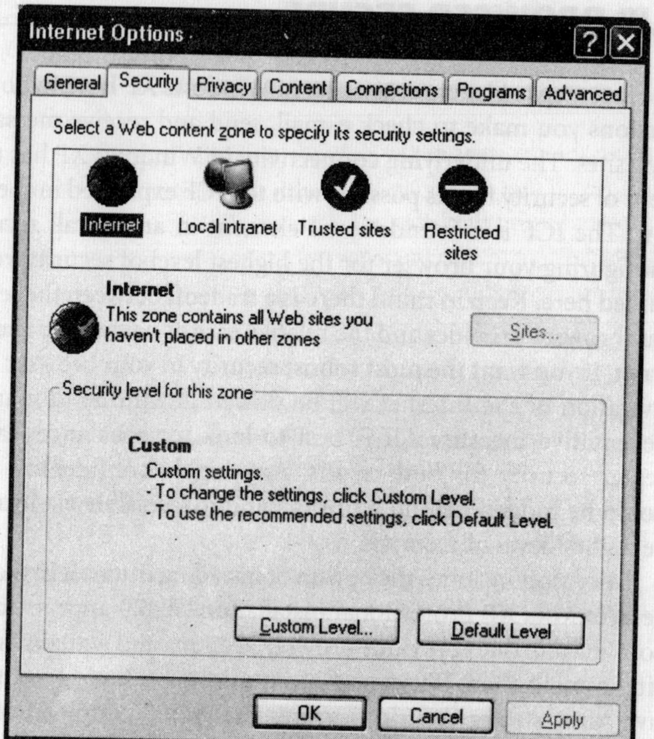

FIGURE 9.5 The Security page of the Internet Options dialog box is used for configuring the relative level of security you want while browsing the Web.

- **Local intranet**—Includes Web sites available for your company's own intranet, as opposed to sites on the public Internet. Default security level is Medium Low.
- **Trusted sites**—Initially empty, you can place Web sites that you trust into this category to maximize their access to your system. Default security level is Low.
- **Restricted sites**—Initially empty, this category works the same as the Trusted sites domain. Using this category you can record sites you visit but do not trust. The default level for this domain is High.

5. Here is an example of how you can go about changing the security level for any of the four zones. Click Internet, for example, then select any level along the slider bar underneath the Security level for this zone area of the dialog box.

6. Once the security level has been set, click Apply. The security level you have chosen is then recorded for the Internet.
7. Click OK to close the Internet Options dialog box.

You can use the steps in the example to set the security level for any of the four zones. Recall that the higher the level of security per zone, the more restrictive accessing and using the Internet will be. A good idea is to add the trusted sites as soon as possible to maximize performance when visiting those sites. Others not trusted but needed should be entered into the Restricted Sites zone.

Stopping an E-Mail Virus

In the midst of a flurry of e-mail viruses that happened coincidentally with the development schedule of Windows XP, Microsoft created options for stopping e-mail viruses. The majority of viruses are transmitted as attachments in e-mail, and the approach Microsoft has taken in IE 6.0 is to try and alleviate as much of the transmitting and further broadcasting of viruses as possible. Be aware that just opening an attachment can unleash a virus on your PC, so if you don't know the person sending you an attachment, or cannot recall having someone tell you he is sending you an attachment, do not open it. In any case, there is no need to get paranoid about every attachment, just be careful about ones you open as they can launch a virus on your PC. A favorite technique of the people who create viruses is to program them to e-mail the attachment to everyone on your contact list in Outlook Express. If you do get a virus and it does get sent to everyone, be sure to e-mail everyone on your contact list telling them that your system has been impacted by a virus and to delete the e-mail with the attachment.

The good news is that the version of Outlook Express that ships with Windows XP has security features you can configure in the Options dialog box discussed in the previous chapter. While this feature of stopping e-mail viruses is not all-encompassing, it does slow down the ones Microsoft was aware of when Outlook Express was created. Following this procedure here will turn on virus protection in Outlook Express:

1. Open Outlook Express.
2. Select Options from the Tools menu.
3. Click the Security tab.
4. Click the Restricted Sites zone (more secure) option and the "Warn me when other applications try to send mail as me" and

"Do not allow attachments to be saved or opened that could potentially be a virus" check boxes.

5. Click OK. Keep in mind that these steps will cause Windows to notify you when any attachment arrives that could potentially have a virus associated with it.

Of course, the most important step you can take against viruses is to use a good antivirus program. One mistake many people make is to buy an antivirus program and forget it. Make certain to follow the developer's instructions to update the program and virus pattern files every time an update is available and to run scans as recommended. Most of these programs have automatic updating, but this must usually be configured. Also, every so often you may need to upgrade the program to a newer version.

MANAGING USER ACCOUNTS

Admittedly, the managing of user accounts in Windows XP could fill a book by itself. The level of authentication and security is to a large extent configurable from within Windows XP. From a security standpoint, there are two huge differences between hard drives formatted with NTFS and those formatted with FAT16 or FAT32. The first difference is that anyone who can log onto a computer can access any folder or file on a FAT-formatted hard drive, while there are many options for local security on NTFS drives. The other is the capability of NTFS drives for users to set security on individual files, as opposed to the folder-only limitation on FAT-based hard drives. That has been one of the shortcomings of having a system configured with FAT file systems in Windows 9x as well. If you are sharing your Windows XP computer with others it is a good idea to convert the file system to NTFS as quickly as possible.

In addition to converting the file system to NTFS, you also need to make sure you include passwords on every account, and be sure to use another word besides PASSWORD which is often the first choice of anyone trying to access your system illegally. You definitely will want to set passwords for each user account on the systems you support as well.

Creating Passwords on User Accounts

With Windows XP, any user can set her password and change it whenever she wants unless "User cannot change password" is selected in the user configuration. If part of a Windows NT 4.0 or Windows 2000 domain, there are many more settings that an administrator can make that affect whether or not a user can change her password. However, it is critical for the overall security of each system that each user create her own password. Follow this procedure to set a password:

1. Open the Control Panel from the Start menu.
2. Click the User Accounts icon.
3. Click Change an account.
4. Click on the account name you want to password-protect.
5. Click "Create a password."
6. Type the desired password in each password field and then enter a hint to remember your password.
7. When asked if you would like to make your personal folders private, click Yes, Make Private. If you do not see this option you will need to convert your file system to NTFS from FAT32.
8. Click OK. The passwords are now set and you have set your documents as private.

Recovering Passwords

Many times an administrator will be asked to reset passwords or to recover passwords that have been forgotten. Windows XP supports the creation of a password reset disk, specifically developed for the needs of administrators. If you are an administrator and get called on to reset passwords, be sure to create a password reset disk. You will need to have a blank floppy disk to complete this procedure:

1. While logged on as an Administrator, go to User Accounts in Control Panel.
2. Click on your account name and picture.
3. Click "Prevent a forgotten password" in the Related Tasks menu on the left side of the window.
4. The Forgotten Password Wizard begins and guides you through creating the floppy that will contain the password for your account.
5. Follow the steps in the wizard to create the floppy disk.

There are a couple of key points to keep in mind about these floppies. First, lock it up, as it gives anyone with it the ability to get into your account at any time. Second, you need to have users create these and lock them up so you can recover their user names and passwords quickly. The recovery process that uses these floppies is just as easy to follow as the wizard to create them, so it is a breeze to get your password restored and your system up and running again.

CHAPTER SUMMARY

There are steps you can take to safeguard your Windows XP system and those that you are responsible for. Chapters later in this book will include additional administrator-level steps you can take to safeguard your systems. To recap, here are the major lessons learned in this chapter:

- Be sure to set the file system on your hard drives to NTFS rather than FAT32.
- Install an antivirus program and keep it up to date.
- Password-protect all user accounts.
- Make sure to enable the Internet Connection Firewall (ICF) if your computer has a direct connection to the Internet.
- Install Internet Explorer 6.0 with Windows XP and configure the four zones with appropriate levels of security.
- Configure Outlook Express to check for attachments that may be virus infected.
- Make password reset disks and keep them locked up.

10 Exploring Network and Remote Access Connections in Windows XP Professional

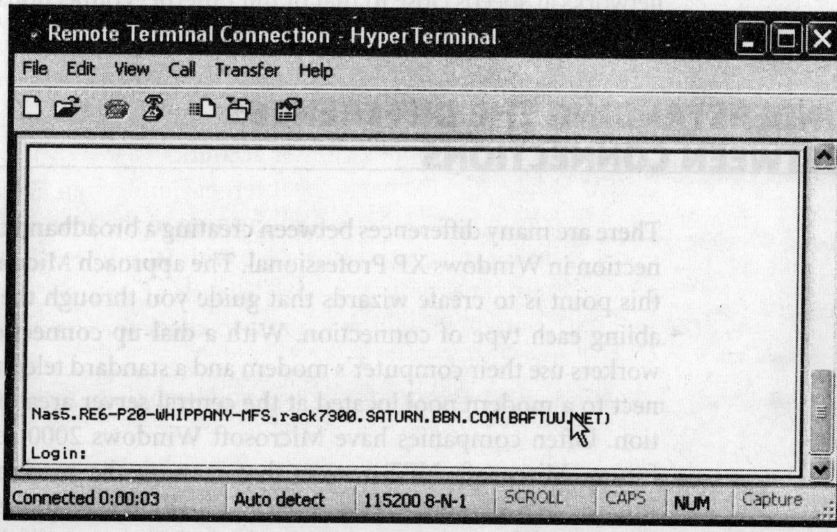

INTRODUCTION

Microsoft projects that virtually every user of Windows XP Professional will be connected to the Internet. Additionally, most users of this operating system will be connected to at least one network. As a result, Windows XP Professional has been designed to make it easier than ever to connect to all different types of networks, from two-computer local area networks (LANs) to the Internet, and even to workplace networks through the

Internet. The key to this ease of connection is through the use of wizards which are more streamlined than their Windows 2000 predecessors. This chapter covers connections through modems and network adapters to these different types of networks.

You may find that with the power management and remote networking capabilities of Windows XP Professional there are going to be more mobile users in your organization than ever before. Dial-up networking and VPNs are making it easier to access the home network from almost anywhere in the world. This is transforming how companies deploy laptops, and how they build applications as well. Offsite computers most often connect to the main systems in a company through dial-up or broadband connections. There is also a growing trend of companies creating Virtual Private Networks (VPNs) so that their employees will be able to get online and access their workplace networks at speeds close to that of full Ethernet connections.

UNDERSTANDING THE DIFFERENCES BETWEEN CONNECTIONS

There are many differences between creating a broadband or a dial-up connection in Windows XP Professional. The approach Microsoft has taken to this point is to create wizards that guide you through the process for enabling each type of connection. With a dial-up connection for example, workers use their computer's modem and a standard telephone line to connect to a modem pool located at the central server area of your organization. Often companies have Microsoft Windows 2000 servers, or in the future, Microsoft .NET servers that manage the modem pool and run Routing and Remote Access Service (RRAS). RRAS allows users to be authenticated from a remote location in the same way as if they were logging directly onto a network computer. If authenticated, remote users have the same access to all resources that they would if they were logged on from a dedicated connection. The authentication approach that Windows XP Professional uses is the same as on Windows 2000.

NETWORKING WIZARDS IN WINDOWS XP PROFESSIONAL

Microsoft has decided to automate the tasks involved with making connections on a network by providing wizards. There are two different wizards in Windows XP Professional for creating network connections. A wizard is a graphical program that eases users through the process of creating and/or configuring aspects of parts of operating systems and programs. Today you can use Visual Basic, Java, JavaScript or even C++ to create your own wizards. Given the fact that Microsoft has made such a strong push towards wizards in Windows XP, it is likely that the next major revision of the operating system will have a wizard to create wizards. For purposes of creating connections for remote access it is important to get to know the following two wizards:

New Connection Wizard—The New Connection Wizard allows you to connect to the Internet, connect to a workplace network either by dial-up or VPN connection, set up a direct connection with another computer via a serial, parallel, or infrared connection, or set up Windows XP to accept incoming connections via modem. Another selection, "Set up a home or small office network" causes the wizard to close and opens up the Network Setup Wizard. The Connect to the Internet option allows you to create new ISP accounts, and create dial-up or broadband connections to existing ISP accounts. This wizard can be accessed from several locations:

- **Network Connections**—Available from the Control Panel. It is also available from the Start menu by clicking Network Connections if your Start menu is so configured. If your Start menu is configured to say "Connect To," point to it and then click Show All Connections. The Network Connections folder will open. To start the wizard, click "Create a new connection" in the Network Tasks menu on the upper left side of the window.
- **Internet Options**—Available from Internet Explorer by clicking Internet Options from the Tools menu, or from Control Panel. Go to the Connections tab and click the Setup button.
- **Communications folder**—Go to All Programs in the Start menu and click Accessories, Communications, and then New Connection Wizard.

Figure 10.1 shows the main menu page of the New Connection Wizard.

- *Network Setup Wizard*—This wizard allows you to share your Internet connection, set up the Internet Connection Firewall (ICF), and share files, folders and printers. You can access this wizard from at least three locations:

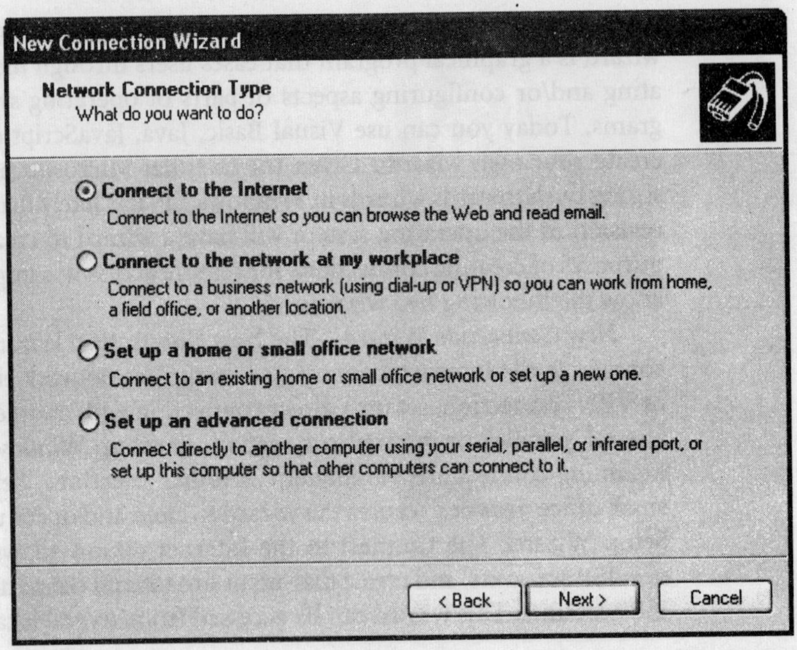

FIGURE 10.1 The New Connection Wizard is used to create various types of connections.

- Run the New Connection Wizard, click the "Set up a home or small office network" option, and follow the steps as the New Connection Wizard closes and the Network Setup Wizard opens.
- From the Network Connections folder, click the "Set up a home or small office network" command in the Network Tasks menu on the upper left side of the Network Connections window.
- From the Communications folder, go to All Programs in the Start menu and click Accessories, Communications, and then Network Setup Wizard.

Figure 10.2 shows the Network Setup Wizard.

Creating a Dial-Up Connection Using the New Connection Wizard

There are two different kinds of dial-up connections that can be made from Windows XP. You can create a dial-up connection to an ISP or to a remote network (referred to as the workplace). The purpose of these steps is to create an applet that will handle getting you connected. While

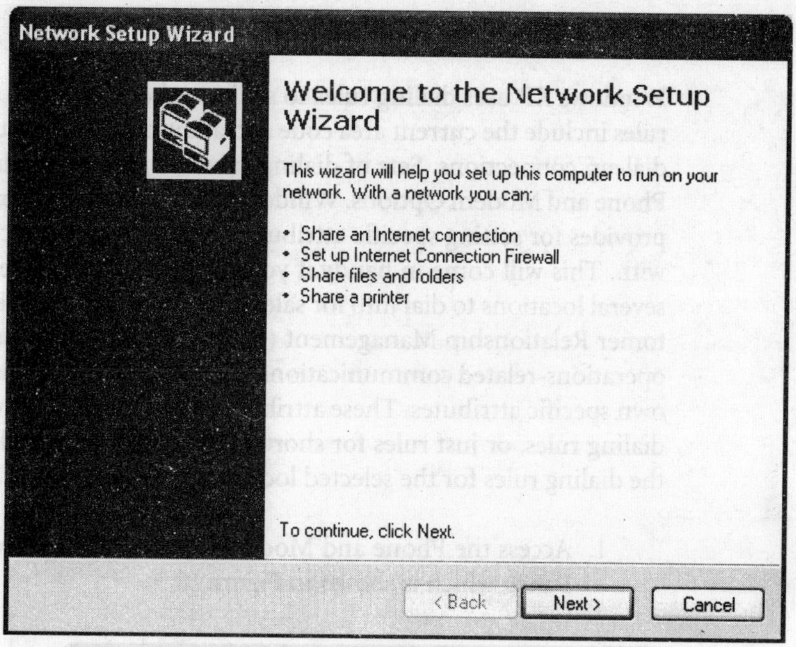

FIGURE 10.2 The Network Setup Wizard.

the connections are very similar, there are a few exceptions, which include:

- A dial-up connection to an ISP does not use the Client for Microsoft Networks component. By default, this connection redials if the line is dropped.
- A dial-up connection to the workplace does use the Client for Microsoft Networks component and by default does not redial if the line is dropped.

The Client for Microsoft Networks allows Windows XP systems to communicate on a Windows domain or workgroup. Because most of the workplaces use Windows domains but most ISPs do not, the component is configured for workplace environments and not for ISPs.

Creating dial-up connections is a two-part process. Before creating a dial-up connection be sure to check the current telephone number and modem options to make sure the connection will be successful. Once the dialing rules are configured, you can create the dial-up connection.

Setting Dialing Rules and Locations

Windows XP uses dialing rules to set how phone lines are accessed. These rules include the current area code and additional features used for making dial-up connections. Sets of dialing rules are saved as dialing locations in Phone and Modem Options. Windows XP's communications software also provides for setting specific attributes for every dialing location you work with. This will come in handy if you are supporting a sales force that has several locations to dial into for sales order tracking, another for their Customer Relationship Management (CRM) system, and possibly a third for operations-related communications. You can create dial-ins that have their own specific attributes. These attributes in Windows XP are actually called dialing rules, or just rules for short. Following this procedure will modify the dialing rules for the selected location:

1. Access the Phone and Modem Options dialog box in the Control Panel, which is shown in Figure 10.3.

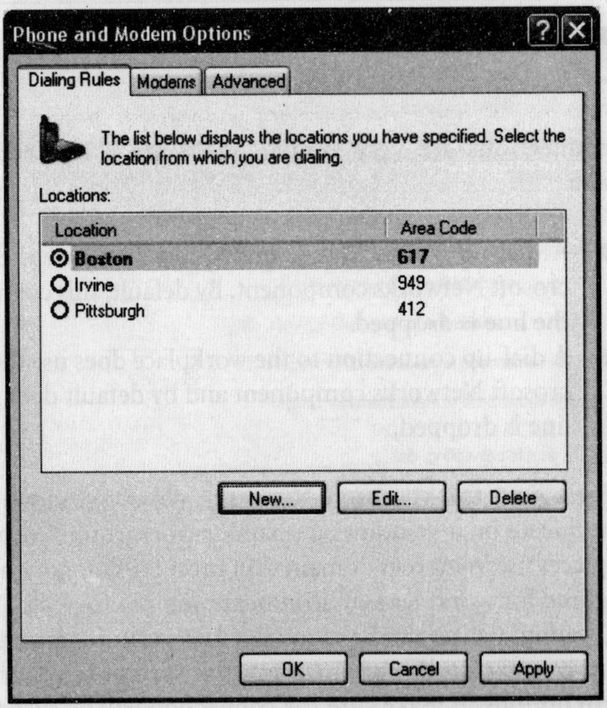

FIGURE 10.3 Using the Phone and Modem Options dialog box.

2. Click the Dialing Rules tab of the Phone and Modem Options dialog box if a different page appears. Locations configured for the computer are shown in the Locations list by name and area code. The location from which you are currently dialing is selected and highlighted in bold.
3. If there is more than one location in the list you can select a different location to make this the current or default location.
4. Select the desired location, and then click Edit to see the configuration of the location's dialing rules. The Edit Location dialog box appears as shown in Figure 10.4. (If you click New, the New Location dialog box appears. Except for their names, both dialog boxes are identical.)
5. Notice that this dialog box has three tabs. These include General, Area Code Rules, and Calling Card. Each of these contributes to

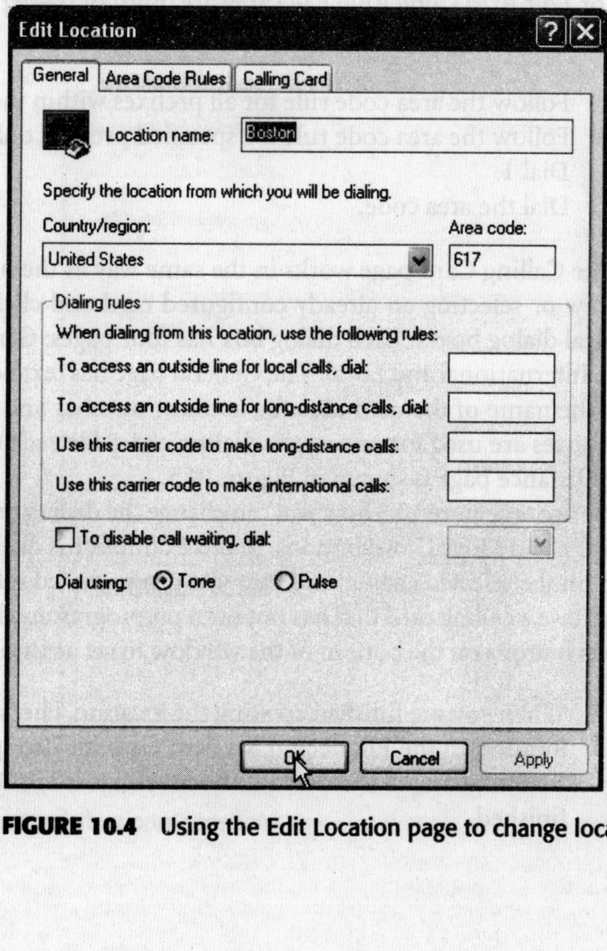

FIGURE 10.4 Using the Edit Location page to change location properties.

the overall configuration of dialing properties by location and is briefly described here:

The General tab contains:

- Country/region
- Area code
- Number to dial to access outside line for local calls
- Number to dial to access outside line for long distance calls
- Carrier code for long distance calls
- Carrier code for international calls
- Code to disable call waiting
- Tone/pulse dialing selection

The Area Code Rules page allows you to select a rule for editing or to create a new rule. After you click New or Edit, the New Area Code Rule page or Edit Area Code Rule Page appears. Both of these pages are identical and include the following:

- Follow the area code rule for all prefixes within the area code.
- Follow the area code rule for specified prefixes only.
- Dial 1.
- Dial the area code.

The Calling Card page works in the same way as the other two. Clicking New or selecting an already configured card and clicking Edit opens identical dialog boxes. Each dialog box has four pages: General, Long Distance, International and Local. The General page has text boxes in which to enter the name of the card plus the account number and PIN. The other three boxes are used for setting the dialing order for each type of call. The Long Distance page is shown in Figure 10.5.

Notice on Figure 10.5 how you can change the dialing order by using the Move Up and Move Down buttons. In this example, the dialing order was set based on the selected calling card that was programmed into Windows XP. If you have a calling card that has not been preprogrammed you can use the various buttons on the bottom of the window to set a custom dialing order.

6. When you are finished creating the location, check that the default location in the Phone and Modem Options dialog box is correct. You might need to select a different entry. Click OK when you are finished.

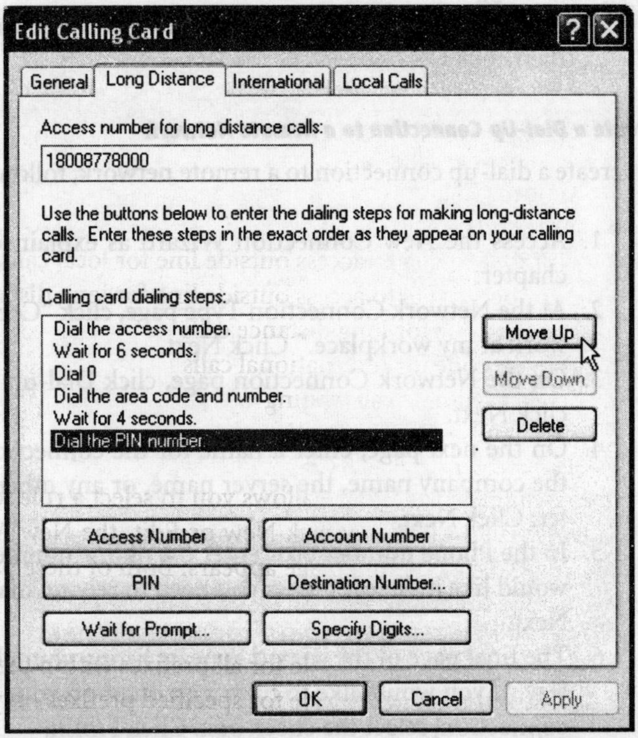

FIGURE 10.5 Changing the dialing order in order to use a calling card.

Unfortunately, these dialing rules are not particularly reliable and may take quite a bit of trial and error before you get them to work as desired. You should test your settings thoroughly at the home office before traveling. If Windows ignores your calling card settings from a hotel room you could end up dialing direct, incurring possibly astronomical telephone charges.

Deleting Dialing Locations

To delete a dialing location, follow these steps:

1. Access Phone and Modem Options in the Control Panel.
2. In the Phone and Modem Options dialog box, select the location you want to permanently remove and then click Delete. If prompted to confirm the action, click Yes.

3. Select the dialing location that you want to use as the default and then click OK.

Create a Dial-Up Connection to a Remote Network

To create a dial-up connection to a remote network, follow this procedure:

1. Access the New Connection Wizard as explained earlier in this chapter.
2. At the Network Connection Type page, click "Connect to the network at my workplace." Click Next.
3. On the Network Connection page, click Dial-up connection and click Next.
4. On the next page, enter a name for the connection. You can use the company name, the server name, or any other name you prefer. Click Next.
5. In the Phone number box, enter the phone number exactly as you would like it dialed, unless you need to rely on dialing rules. Click Next.
6. The final page of the wizard appears listing your choices along the way. If you would like to have a shortcut on your desktop for this connection, select the check box. Click Finish.
7. The Connect dialog box for your new Internet connection appears, with user name and password fields. If you want to have Windows remember your user name and password, select the "Save this user name and password for the following users" check box. If you select it, you will have two options: "Me only" or "Anyone who uses this computer." If all users use the same user name and password for this connection, select the latter. Otherwise, select "Me only."
8. Click Properties on the Connect dialog box. If you are relying on dialing rules, on the General tab, select the Use Dialing Rules check box, and click OK. If you are not relying on dialing rules, leave this box cleared.

EXPLORING INTERNET CONNECTIONS WITH WINDOWS XP PROFESSIONAL

Approaches to connecting to the Internet vary in terms of speed of connection, relative level of automation, and the level of reliability of connection. Throughout this section we will look at the various approaches you can use for connecting to the Internet. Going back to Windows 3.1, HyperTerminal is by far the longest-running solution in the Windows family, yet does not provide the throughput users have come to expect with the widespread availability of high-speed connections. At the opposite end of the spectrum is accessing the Internet through a Network Interface Card (NIC) and also through connection with a USB cable/DSL router. The NIC Card in a workstation is connected to a local area network that is in turn routed to the Internet. The most common form of Internet connectivity is to use a dial-up connection for connecting to an ISP.

Establishing Service with an ISP

Different ISPs provide different levels of service. Many, especially the larger ISPs, provide you with software, usually on CD-ROMs or via downloads from the Internet (obviously, you cannot download software from the Internet without having a connection to start with). All you do is insert the CD or execute the downloaded file and follow the instructions on your screen. Often, all you need to establish an account is a credit card number. You choose your user name and password during the process of establishing an account.

Before signing up to an ISP to gain dial-up access to the Internet, be sure to check and see if the provider has a local access number, so you will not get billed for toll calls.

One way to find an ISP is by running the New Connection Wizard as described earlier in this chapter. If you select "Connect to the Internet" on the Network Connection Type page, and "Choose from a list of Internet Service Providers" on the next page, you will be redirected to the Online Services folder, which gives you a selection of larger ISPs. Follow the instructions on your screen to choose one and connect.

Other ISPs do not provide software—they provide you with operating system-specific instructions to connect to their service. You set up an account with them over the phone, on their Web site, or in the case of some very small companies, especially in small towns, in person. If you are establishing a dial-up connection to the ISP, in their instructions, they will give you a telephone number—in many cases it will be a toll-free number that you use to download all of the available numbers that access their Internet servers. In Windows 9x and NT you would use the Control Panel's Dial-up Networking applet to configure a connection for this type of ISP. In Windows XP you use the New Connection Wizard. You can follow the instructions provided by the ISP, or the instructions in the following procedure:

1. Make sure your dialing rules are set appropriately, especially if the connection will be used away from your home base.
2. Start the New Connection Wizard as described earlier in this chapter.
3. Click Next to display the Network Connection Type page. Click Connect to the Internet, click Next, then click Set Up My Connection Manually. Click Next.
4. In the next window, select "Connect using a dial-up modem" and then click Next. In the ISP Name field, enter the name for the connection, usually the name of the ISP you are using. Click Next.
5. You can now set the phone number to dial for this connection using the Phone Number text box. Click Next.
6. The next window is the Internet Account Information page. Enter your ISP user name and password, and confirm your password. By default, the three check boxes on the bottom of this page are selected. Accepting the default makes this the default Internet connection on the computer, sets your user name and password as the only user name and password for this ISP, and enables the Internet Connection Firewall. Configure these settings as necessary. With connections to ISPs, you will want to turn on the Internet Connection Firewall to guard from attacks. Select or clear these check boxes as necessary. Click Next.
7. The Completing the New Connection Wizard page appears, listing all the choices you made along the way. To add a desktop shortcut, a feature that makes it quick and easy to establish connections, select "Add a shortcut to this connection to my desktop."
8. Click Finish to complete the connection creation process. The Connect page for your connection appears.
9. On the Connect page, enter your user name and password for the remote network. Other options are the same as in step 7 of the previous procedure.

Normally, with an ISP you will have one account with one user name and one password, so you would click the "Anyone who uses this computer" option. You can now connect to your ISP. However, you will find by clicking Properties that there are five more pages of configuration options. You can peruse these at your convenience but there is one crucial setting on the General page—the "Use dialing rules" check box. If unchecked, the connection will definitely ignore any dialing rules you may have set up.

Additional Considerations

There are a few more points to consider when creating a dial-up connection to a remote location:

- If users are dialing up through an Internet Service Provider that has point of presence (POP) locations throughout the U.S. and/or the world, you will usually want to configure dialing rules and connections for specific locations. You could create individual dial-up locations called Pittsburgh, Irvine, and Boston. In this configuration you would set the area code for Boston as well as any special dialing rules and then configure the connection to use the ISP's access numbers in Boston. You will also need to show users how to change their current location when they travel from location to location, so that the connection can be completed and unnecessary phone costs can be saved—dialing direct from hotel rooms can be exorbitantly expensive.
- If users are dialing a toll-free (800, 888, 877, 866 as of this writing) or direct long distance number to access the office modem pool, you will usually want to configure separate connections rather than separate locations. Here, you will want to create a connection that dials long distance to establish the connection and a connection that is used when the user is in the local area. Simply enter the entire number including any digits required to get an outside line, an example of which is shown in Figure 10.6. You would need only one dialing location.

Connecting by Dial-Up

Dial-up connections are established between two modems using a telephone line. To connect, follow these steps:

1. You can access dial-up connections you have created in several different ways. From the XP Start menu, click Start, point to Connect To or Network Connections, depending on your configuration, and then select the connection you want to use. With Classic Start Menu, click Start, point to Settings, point to Network Connections, and finally select the connection you want to use.

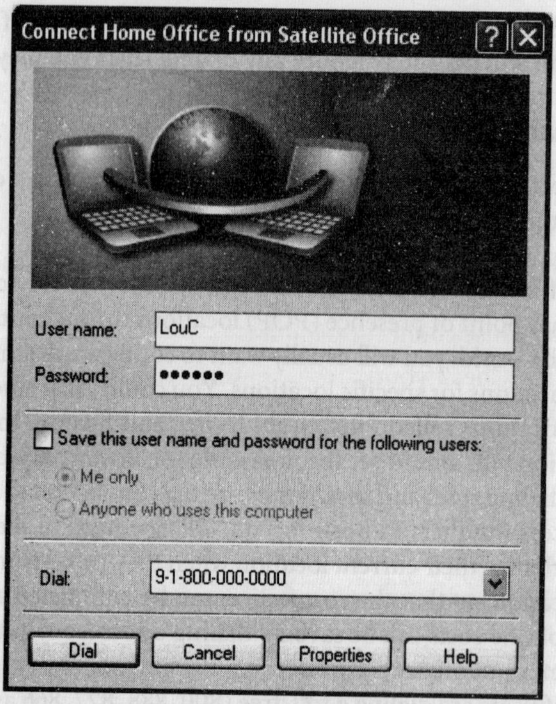

FIGURE 10.6 A direct-dialed connection.

2. Confirm that the user name is correct and enter the password for the account if it does not already appear.
3. To use the user name and password when any user attempts to establish this connection, select "Save this user name and password for the following users" and then click "Any user."
4. The Dial drop-down list shows the number that will be dialed. The primary number is selected by default. To choose an alternate number, click the drop-down list and then select the number you want to use or type in a new number.
5. Click Dial. When the modem connects to the ISP or office network, a connection speed will be displayed. The connection speed is negotiated on a per-call basis and depends on the maximum speed of the calling modem and the modem being called, the compression being used, and the condition of the telephone lines.

Troubleshooting Tips for Dial-Up Connections

Given the fact that there are so many variables involved with getting a modem connection up and running, there is a good chance you will need to troubleshoot one of these connections. Here is a summary of problems and their solutions for this connection type:

Problem: Modem dials and reaches another modem but cannot connect. It continues to make connection noises until you cancel the operation. The phone lines are usually the problem. Static or noise on the line can cause connection failures.

Solution: Check your connection between the modem and the wall first. You may also want to check with the phone company to see if they can test the line and resolve the noise problems.

Problem: Modem dials and seems to connect, then the connection is dropped. The connection does not complete successfully.

Solution: Check your networking protocols and components. If these seem to be configured appropriately, make sure your user name and password are correct for the ISP or network and that Caps Lock is not activated and causing your password to be incorrect.

Problem: Cannot access resources in the Windows domain.

Solution: The Client for Microsoft Networks might be required to be installed in order to access resources on the office network. Enable this component and ensure that the logon information is correct for this network.

Problem: User can never get through. The modem seems to be dialing the number incorrectly. You can hear it dialing too many or too few numbers.

Solution: Check the dialing rules for the connection as well as the currently selected dialing location. Make sure these are configured properly for the user's current location. Make sure that the General page of the connections properties dialog box has the "Use dialing rules" check box selected. Also note that the Dialing Rules applet is rather unreliable and difficult to configure so that the rules are actually applied.

Problem: A No dial tone message is displayed but the modem is installed correctly and seems to be okay.

Solution: Check the phone line and ensure that it is connected properly. Most modems have two jacks, one labeled Phone and one labeled Line (often they are labeled with icons). The phone line should be plugged into the Line jack. Some jacks are configured for data only, indicating a jack for a high-speed line rather than a phone or modem.

Problem: Some services freeze and do not work.

Solution: Check the proxy and firewall settings. These settings can restrict services that are available, for example accessibility to the Internet for any group of employees.

Creating a Broadband Connection

Compared to dial-up connections, broadband connections are much easier to set up and more reliable as signals rarely get dropped. When you work with broadband, you do not need to set up dialing rules or locations. You do not need to worry about calling cards, ISP access numbers, redialing preferences, area codes, or even if there is a phone in the room. All you need is a broadband connection to the network.

Most broadband providers give users a router or modem, which users need to connect to the service provider. Users must also install network adapters on their computers (unless they use USB routers) connected to the back of the DSL or cable modem that provides the essential link to the Internet. In this configuration, the necessary connection is established over the local area rather than directly to the ISP. Therefore it is the local area connection that must be properly configured to gain access to the Internet. You will not need to create a broadband connection from your computer, but instead from the router.

You can, however, create a direct broadband connection if needed. In some cases, you need to do this to set specific configuration options required by the ISP, such as secure authentication and access to network drives, or you might want to use this technique to set the user name and password required by the broadband provider. You create a broadband connection by following these steps:

1. Start the New Connection Wizard.
2. Click Next to display the Network Connection Type page. Select "Connect to the Internet," click Next, click "Set up my connection manually," and finally click Next again.

3. If you are creating a connection that is always active and does not require you to sign on, click "Connect using a broadband connection that is always on." Afterward, click Next and then click Finish. Skip the remaining steps.
4. If you are creating a broadband connection that requires authentication, select "Connect using a broadband connection that requires a user name and password."
5. Click Next and then enter a name for the connection, such as Broadband. Keep in mind that the name should be shorter than 50 characters, but very descriptive.
6. Follow steps 6 through 8 of the procedure given earlier for creating a dial-up connection to the Internet to complete the configuration.

Keep in mind that you will need to have a DSL modem/router or cable modem to test the connection. Be sure to configure any special settings required by the ISP.

Connecting with Broadband

Broadband connections are established using a cable modem and a cable line or a DSL modem or router and a telephone line. To establish a broadband connection, follow these steps:

1. Click Connect To or Network Connections from the Start menu and click the appropriate connection (if it is not there, that means it is already connected).
2. Confirm that the user name is correct and enter the password for the account if it is not already displayed.
3. To use the user name and password whenever you attempt to establish this connection, select "Save this user name and password for the following users" and then click "Me only." To use the user name and password when any user attempts to establish this connection, select "Save this user name and password for the following users" and then click "Any user."
4. Click Connect.

Troubleshooting Tips for Broadband Connections

While modem-based communications are plagued more by connectivity problems, broadband connections can also be troublesome. In general, however, broadband is much more efficient to set up and use. Here is a summary of problems and solutions for this type of connection:

Problem: Cannot connect, connection does not seem to work at all.

Solution: Check your network connections and ensure that the cables are properly connected to the router or modem and the system is plugged in correctly.

Problem: Connections are dropped unexpectedly. The connection does not seem to complete successfully.

Solution: Check your networking protocols and components as discussed in this and previous chapters. If these components are working and configured correctly, make sure your user name and password are correct for this connection. Make sure Caps Lock is not on and changing your password.

Problem: Some services freeze and do not work.

Solution: Check the proxy and firewall settings. These settings can restrict services that are available, for example accessibility to the Internet for any group of employees.

Creating a VPN Connection

VPNs are used to establish secure communication channels over an existing dial-up or broadband connection. The term VPN stands for Virtual Private Network, and is increasingly what companies are using to protect their information and users from being hacked. A VPN provides access over a broad geographic region, and is most often used by companies that have offices throughout multiple regions of countries and continents. To create a connection to a VPN, you need to know the IP address or host name of the Routing and Remote Access Server to which you are connecting. If you know the necessary connection is available and you know the host information, you can create the connection by following these steps:

1. Start the New Connection Wizard.
2. Click Next and then select "Connect to the network at my workplace." Click Next.
3. Select "Virtual Private Network connection" and then click Next.
4. Type a name for the connection in the Company Name field and then click Next.

5. To specify that an existing connection should always be used to establish the tunnel, select "Do not dial the initial connection." In this configuration, the user will need to establish a connection—either dial-up or broadband—before attempting to use the VPN.
6. To have the computer automatically initialize the connection over dial-up or broadband prior to using the VPN, select "Automatically dial this initial connection" and then select the default connection you want to use.
7. Next, type the IP address or fully qualified domain name of the computer to which you are connecting, such as 172.16.14.107 or external.marketdynamics.com. In most cases this is the Routing and Remote Access Server you have configured for the office network.
9. Click Next. To add a desktop shortcut, a feature that makes it quick and easy to establish connections, select "Add a shortcut to this connection to my desktop."
10. Click Finish to complete the connection creation process. Just as with the other types of connections, the connect page appears and you are ready to connect, unless you want to configure the connection further in the Properties dialog box accessible by clicking Properties.

Connecting through a VPN

VPN connections are made over existing connections. These connections can be a local area connection, a dial-up connection, or a broadband connection. To establish a VPN connection, follow these steps:

1. Point to Connect To or Network Connections from the Start menu and select the desired VPN connection.
2. If the connection is configured to first dial another type of connection, Windows XP tries to establish this connection before attempting the VPN connection. If prompted to establish this connection, click Yes.
3. Once the necessary connection is established, you will see the Connect dialog box. After you confirm the user name is correct and enter the password for the account if it does not already appear, click Connect.

Troubleshooting Tips for VPN Connections

The basic technologies behind VPN connections resemble broadband connections from the use of TCP/IP technology. The following are problem/solution scenarios to help you troubleshoot any VPN connections.

Problem: Cannot connect, the connection does not seem to work at all.
Solution: Check your network connections and ensure that all the cables are connected to the DSL router or cable modem, and the modem and computer are plugged in properly.

Problem: Returns error message regarding the host name.
Solution: The host name might be incorrectly specified. Check the settings to ensure the host name is fully expressed, such as research.boston. DNS resolutions are most likely not working properly either. If this is the case, enter the IP address for the host rather than the host name.

Problem: Returns error message regarding a bad IP address.
Solution: Check or reenter the IP address. If the IP address was correct, TCP/IP networking might be improperly configured. You might need to set a static IP address and a default gateway for the connection.

Problem: Cannot map network drives or access network printers.
Solution: File and Printer Sharing for Microsoft Networks is required to map drives and printers. You can enable this service by using the configuration options within the TCP/IP Properties dialog box.

CONFIGURING CONNECTION PROPERTIES IN WINDOWS XP

Whether you are working with dial-up, broadband, or VPNs, you will often need to set additional properties after creating a connection. The key properties that you may work with are explained in this section.

Establishing Connections

As has been mentioned throughout this chapter, you can configure Windows XP to either complete an Internet connection automatically when a browser starts, or start Internet connections manually. The manual method lets users choose when to connect, while the automatic method connects when users start a program that requires network access.

Configuring Connections

Windows XP can be configured to automatically select a connection method with the launching of Internet Explorer, for example. It is your choice: you can either dial up manually or have your connection to the Internet start up right after you launch your browser. Automating connections works in ways that depend on settings in the Internet Options tool. The options include the following:

- **Never dial a connection**—Users must manually establish a connection.
- **Dial whenever a network connection is not present**—The connection is established automatically when needed but only when the local area connection is not working.
- **Always dial my default connection**—The default connection is always established when an Internet connection is needed.

The approach you take to configuring automatic connections really depends on the way your company works. Contrary to what most administrators think, laptop users are much happier when their computers are set to never dial a connection. This is because laptop users might not have access to a dial-up connection while out of the office and having the computer attempt to dial a connection when visiting customers or giving a presentation is disruptive.

To configure XP-based laptops to connect manually, follow these steps:

1. Double-click the Internet Options tool in the Control Panel and then, in the Internet Properties dialog box, click the Connections tab.
2. Click Never dial a connection and then click OK.

You can also configure automatic connections by following these steps. It is a good idea to give your laptop users the ability to enable or disable automatic connections themselves:

1. Double-click the Internet Options tool in the Control Panel and then, in the Internet Properties dialog box, click the Connections tab.
2. Click "Dial whenever a network connection is not present" to establish connections automatically if a local area connection is not working. Click "Always dial my default connection" to always attempt to establish connections.
3. The Dial-up and Virtual Private Network settings list shows the dial-up and VPN connections that are currently configured. Select the connection you want to use as the default when establishing connections and then click Set default.
4. Click OK.

AT THE FOUNDATION: REMOTE TERMINAL EMULATION IN WINDOWS XP PROFESSIONAL

Remote Terminal Emulation is really synonymous with having your system act like a remote terminal to a host mainframe. You would think that so much time has passed since the use of mainframes that having remote terminal emulation would be only sporadically used, if at all. After all, this approach has the lowest level of performance of them all. The fact is that some organizations are relying on their terminal emulation sessions just as much as before. It is partly because larger companies are resistant to change in the world of network connectivity, as it takes much time and effort to change configurations once they are proven to work. Second, larger organizations may have grown reliant on their mainframes over time and need to have the specific applications available through terminal emulation as well.

Beginning at the most basic type of connection, Figure 10.7 shows an example of a remote terminal connection. As the most fundamental of communications approaches for ensuring connections between remote systems and Windows XP Professional-based PCs, this one relies on creating a serial link from one system to another. This approach is based on using terminal emulation features within communications programs to enable the connection. Unless the host system is located in the same building, you will use a modem to dial up and connect with another system through a phone line.

As with any connection method, there are strengths and weaknesses to this approach. You will still need to have a modem. Using a remote

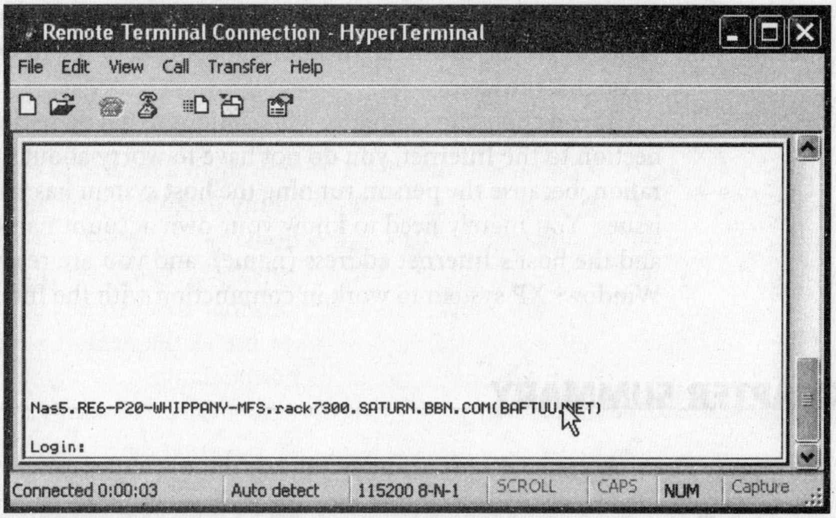

FIGURE 10.7 At its most basic level, Windows XP can connect to the Internet via remote terminal connection.

terminal connection also puts very little strain on a workstation, allowing it to support a large number of simultaneous remote terminal sessions. That is because the most demanding tasks can be completed on the server, and the data or information required on the client system can be quickly transferred via modem.

The level of functionality and performance associated with terminal emulation is limited to what the host system provides during the communications session. When workstation users opt for this approach, the applications being accessed are nearly all character-based rather than graphical. In order to connect to an ISP the ISP needs to provide instructions on configuring the connection for browser use.

The most common remote terminal access programs are both on the UNIX platforms, and between UNIX and Windows NT systems. In a UNIX command session, the UNIX-like commands such as telnet, FTP, ping, and grep are often used.

When working with a UNIX workstation, the shell account replicates exactly what the Command Prompt window shows on a Windows XP system. Alphanumeric characters are displayed on the screen, enabling binary transfer of files through a modem from one location to another. All the TCP/IP commands are being interpreted and completed on the host. As commands are completed on the client workstation, the representation is displayed locally yet the command is completed on the host system. This is increasingly the case as applications are ported to the Internet for use only through a browser.

If you choose to configure workstations to have a remote terminal connection to the Internet, you do not have to worry about network configuration, because the person running the host system has taken care of these issues. You merely need to know your own account name and password, and the host's Internet address (name), and you are ready to configure a Windows XP system to work in conjunction with the Internet.

CHAPTER SUMMARY

Companies are increasingly relying on a mobile, geographically distributed workforce to do the same or even more work than was done in the past. The concept of virtual teams pervades world business, and the need for being able to connect and gain, share and transmit messages and content is critical to the success of these virtual teams. Windows XP's approach to handling the connections to the Internet and remote networks includes dial-up, broadband, and VPN, and the use of wizards makes administration of these easier than ever. The intent of this chapter is to provide a roadmap for you as an administrator to guide and support users who are working with each of the three connection technologies. You will find that modem-based connections are the most challenging and require the most work to keep running. It is no surprise that many companies are moving away from dial-up to tunneling technologies that provide their associates the flexibility of using a broadband connection to access network resources.

Although the direct cost of travel is lower since September 11, the increased inconveniences add significantly to travel time, making the need for creating virtual teams that have the ability to work on a 24/7 basis essential. The role of networking in Windows XP is quickly becoming the backbone of many companies today. The growth of broadband and VPN will continue to accelerate this trend.

11 Learning to Use Windows XP Professional's Administrative Tools

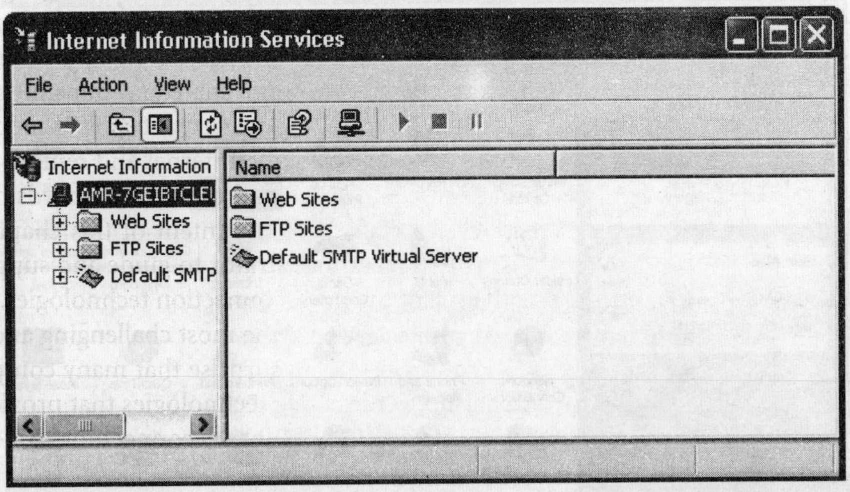

INTRODUCTION

Windows XP Home Edition is the first home version of Windows to have the same selection of Administrative Tools as Microsoft's business desktop version. These tools go beyond the other configuration options in the Control Panel to provide a much higher level of fine-tuning capability than in the Windows 9x. Administrative Tools give you control over disk resources, user and group configuration, security, database programs, services, computer performance, event logging, troubleshooting, and much more, even down to the level of whether certain check boxes appear in certain dialog boxes. This chapter covers some of the most used functions of Administrative Tools.

ADMINISTRATIVE TOOLS OVERVIEW

Administrative Tools are available in the Start menu, if so configured, and the Control Panel. Figure 11.1 shows the location of Administrative Tools in the Control Panel.

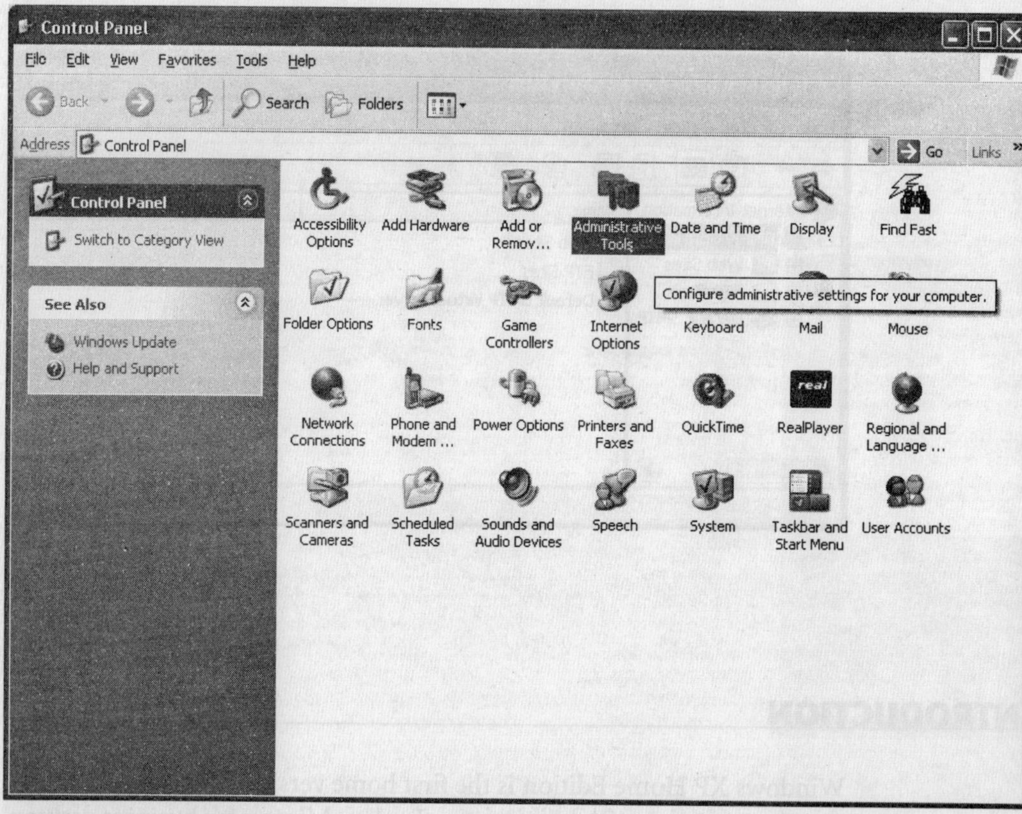

FIGURE 11.1 Administrative Tools can be accessed from the Windows XP Professional Control Panel.

The individual tools include Component Services, Computer Management, Data Sources (ODBC), Event Viewer, Internet Information Services, Local Security Policy, Performance, Server Extensions Administrator, and Services. (If your Administrative Tools folder does not contain all of these applications, you may want to install Internet Information Services or other Windows components using the Windows Component Wizard in order to add them. See Chapter 2 for details.) Of these, the System Monitor component of the Performance tool has been in continuous use the longest as a Windows NT (in which it was called Performance Monitor), then Windows 2000 and now a Windows XP application. Figure 11.2 shows the contents of the Administrative Tools folder in Windows XP Professional.

If you have used any of these tools in Windows NT Workstation or Server, you will find that the core functionality is the same. The graphical

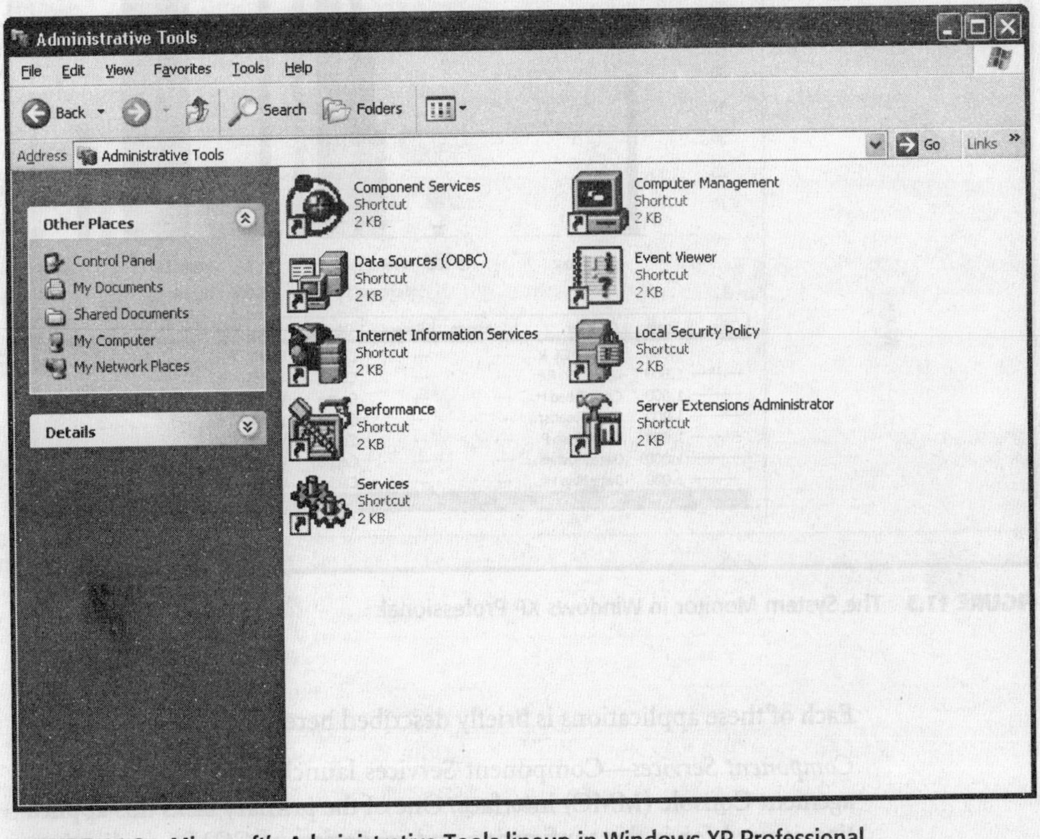

FIGURE 11.2 Microsoft's Administrative Tools lineup in Windows XP Professional.

interface has become much more Web-like, using the Microsoft Management Console (MMC) interface for organizing the Performance tool relative to other applications. The structure of the MMC may remind you of a Web browser interface, making the navigation fairly intuitive. Figure 11.3 shows an example of the Microsoft Management Console interface with the Performance tool's System Monitor running.

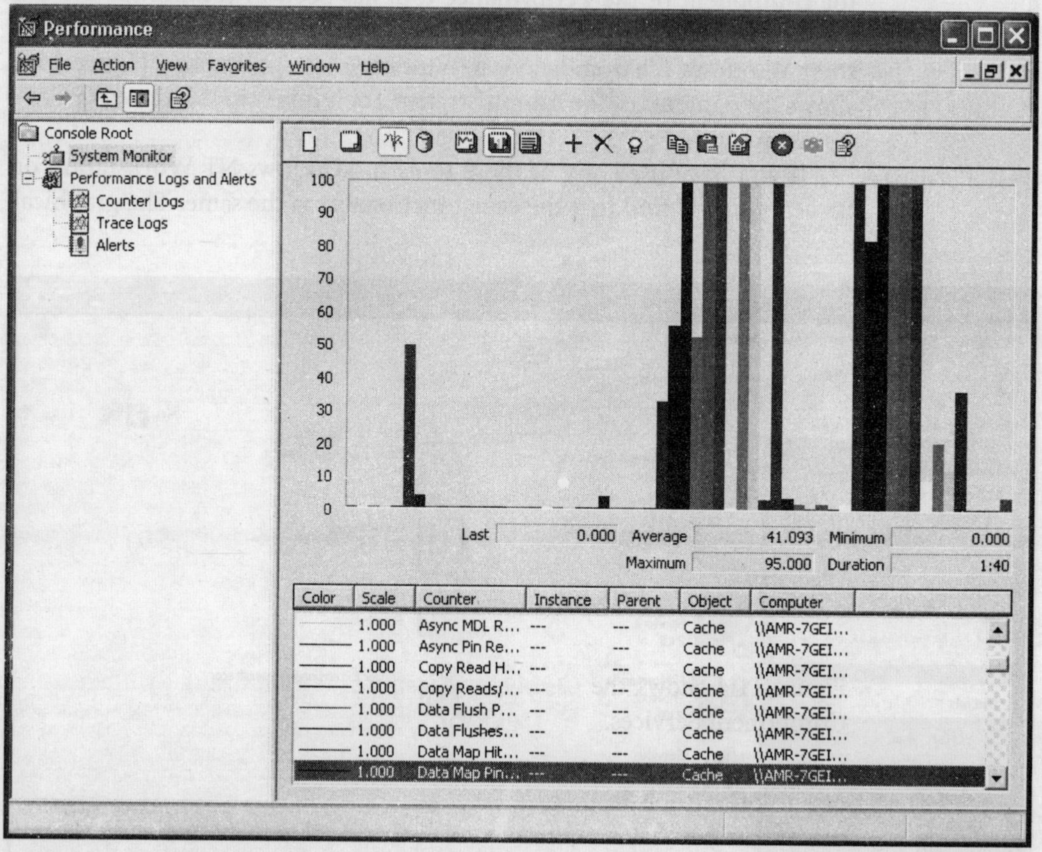

FIGURE 11.3 The System Monitor in Windows XP Professional.

Each of these applications is briefly described here:

Component Services—Component Services launches the Microsoft Management Console (MMC) interface. One of the primary tasks this application is used for is the configuring and managing of COM+ applications.

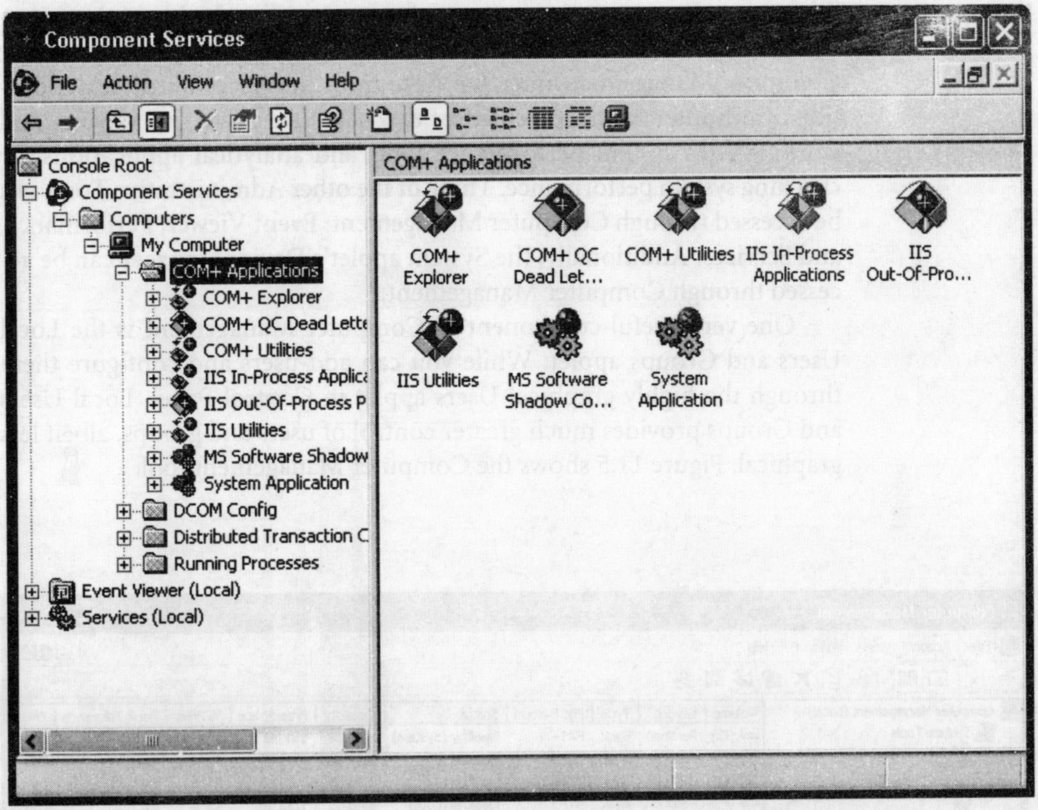

FIGURE 11.4 Tracking COM+ application performance using Component Services.

Figure 11.4 shows the COM+ applications that are being profiled using Component Services.

Computer Management—This application manages disks and provides access to other tools to manage local and remote computers. The extensive use of navigational tools in this application, coupled with its access to system monitoring and system performance metrics makes this application one of the most useful of those included in the Administrative Tools set. Using the MMC interface, it is possible to check the status of all major performance metrics. You can also use the Computer Management application for inquiring as to the file system that is being used by disk volume on a workstation. This is particularly useful if as an administrator you inherit a series of workstations from another department, and want to see how the file systems have been configured on each hard disk drive. The Explorer-like approach to managing system information is invaluable in that many of the system attributes and characteristics are available from the single Computer Management interface. Like most interfaces on these applications Computer Management uses the MMC interface for viewing and working with system performance tools and analytical applications for checking system performance. Three of the other Administrative Tools can be accessed through Computer Management: Event Viewer, Performance, and Services. Additionally, the System applet's Device Manager can be accessed through Computer Management.

One very useful component of Computer Management is the Local Users and Groups applet. While you can add users and configure them through the highly graphical Users applet in Control Panel, Local Users and Groups provides much greater control of users and groups, albeit less graphical. Figure 11.5 shows the Computer Management tool.

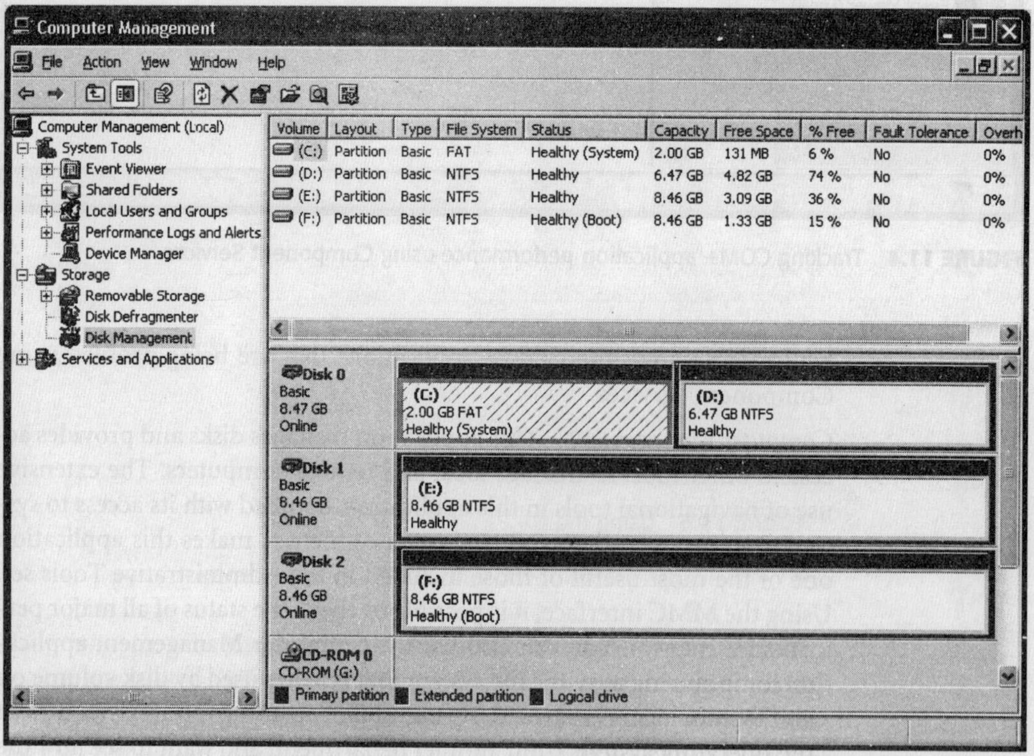

FIGURE 11.5 Using the Disk Management snap-in of the Computer Management tool.

Data Sources (ODBC)—The Data Sources (ODBC) tool is used to help configure Open Database Connectivity (ODBC)-compliant database programs to access different ODBC-compliant databases. This is done by adding and configuring Open Database Connectivity (ODBC) drivers for databases on workstations relative to servers. This tool also provides the administrator the ability to set ODBC drivers for tracking in System Monitor, and options for setting Data Source Name (DSN) values that enable communication between databases. This application is particularly useful for defining the relationships between databases and the applications that build queries to use the data included in them. The role of the ODBC drivers is to provide the connections between databases and the applications you will be using them for.

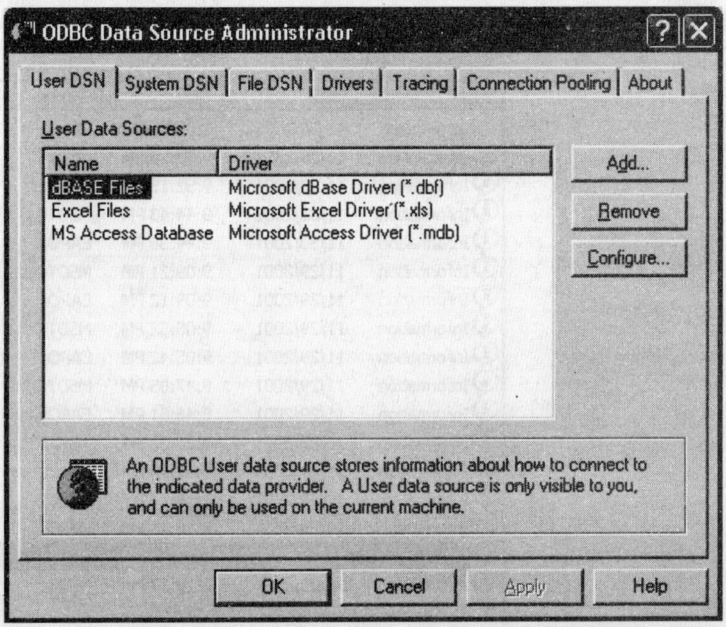

FIGURE 11.6 Using the Data Sources (ODBC) application for creating database links.

Event Viewer—Event Viewer is one of the most valuable applications for tracking system activity. The Event Viewer includes Application, Security, and System logs. Windows XP Professional observes each discrete event as the operating system boots up and runs, recording events of interest into one of the three categories of log files. The analysis of log files is one of the most valuable analytical tools for checking the performance of Windows XP Professional. The Security log is also invaluable for checking to see if there have been security breaches to the workstations and servers you are responsible for. There is also the opportunity to save log files in tab delimited text (.txt), comma delimited text (.csv), or event log (.evt) format. If you plan to use these files in Microsoft Excel, be sure to export them in comma delimited format for ease of importing. Figure 11.7 shows the Event Viewer being used to check the Application log of a workstation running Windows XP Professional.

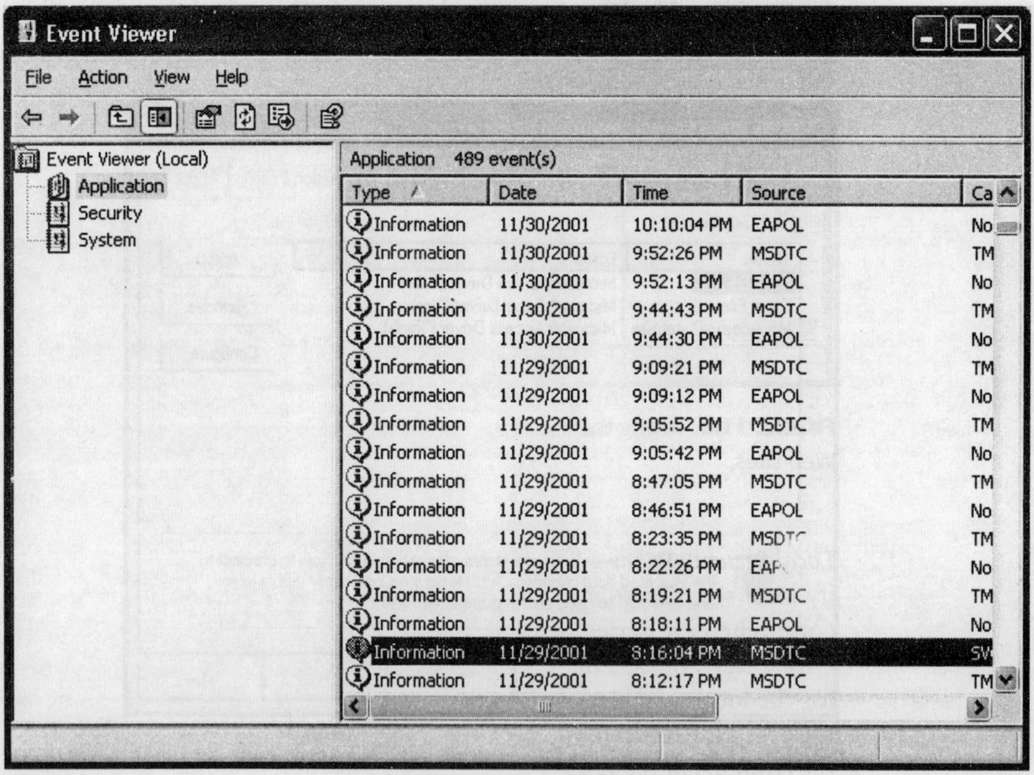

FIGURE 11.7 Using the Event Viewer for checking on application events.

Internet Information Services—Internet Information Services handles the task of managing the Internet Information Server, the Web server for Internet and intranet sites. The interface for this application is intuitive and easy to navigate. Within the Internet Information Services interface, the default FTP Site, Default Web Site, and Default SMTP Virtual Server are all shown along the left side of the page. Using this application it is possible, for example, to check on the ASP scripts for your Web site as the subdirectory structure of your site is shown on screen. Using the Explorer-like interface for navigating the FTP site, Web site, or SMTP Virtual Server makes it possible to quickly edit files regardless of their location in the hierarchy. Figure 11.8 shows an example of the Internet Information Services tool.

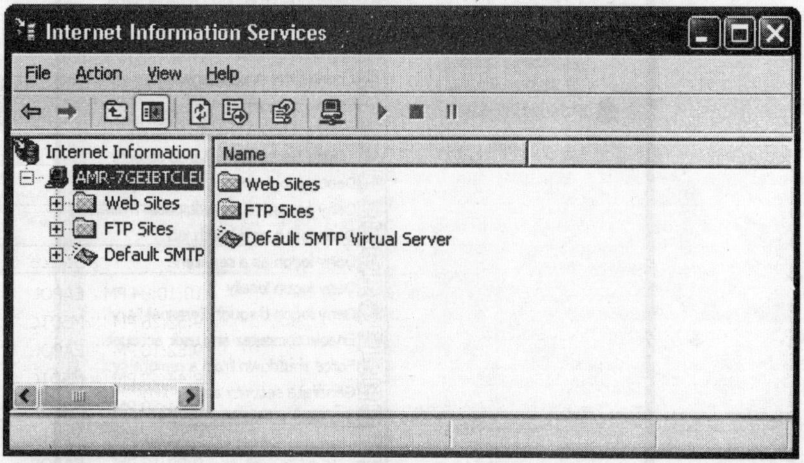

FIGURE 11.8 Using the Internet Information Services tool for managing FTP and Web sites.

Local Security Policy—The purpose of this application is to view and modify local security policy, such as user rights and audit policies. There is a comprehensive series of tools available for managing account policies, Public Key Policies, IP Security Policies, and a myriad of security options for the local workstation. You can also set logging of both successful and unsuccessful events to be viewed using the Event Viewer. Figure 11.9 shows the contents of the Local Security Policy tool.

Performance—Containing the System Monitor applet and Performance Logs and Alerts, the Performance tool has consistently been one of the most used applications for tracking system performance and analyzing the behavior of workstations and servers as modifications are made to them. There is a great deal of depth in the Performance tool as the object counter relationships are used for quantifying overall system performance by functional area. Interpreting the results that System Monitor provides is one of

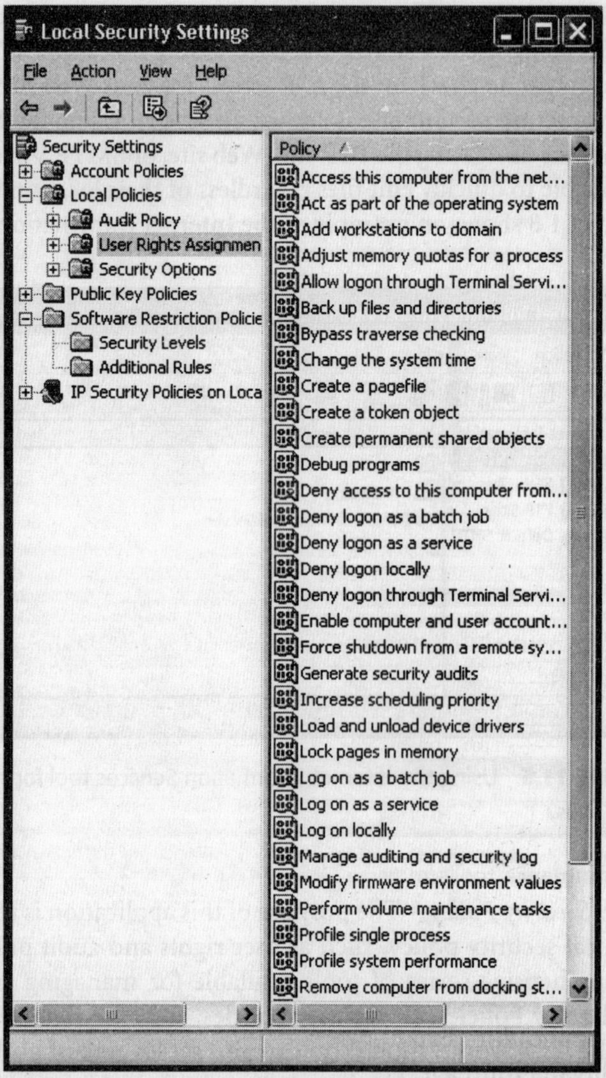

FIGURE 11.9 The Local Security Policy tool contains settings essential to ensure the security of your systems.

the most useful methods for troubleshooting in Windows XP Professional. Figure 11.10 shows the System Monitor in use.

Server Extensions Administrator—This is used for handling the FrontPage extensions for your Web site. FrontPage is Microsoft's Web site develop-

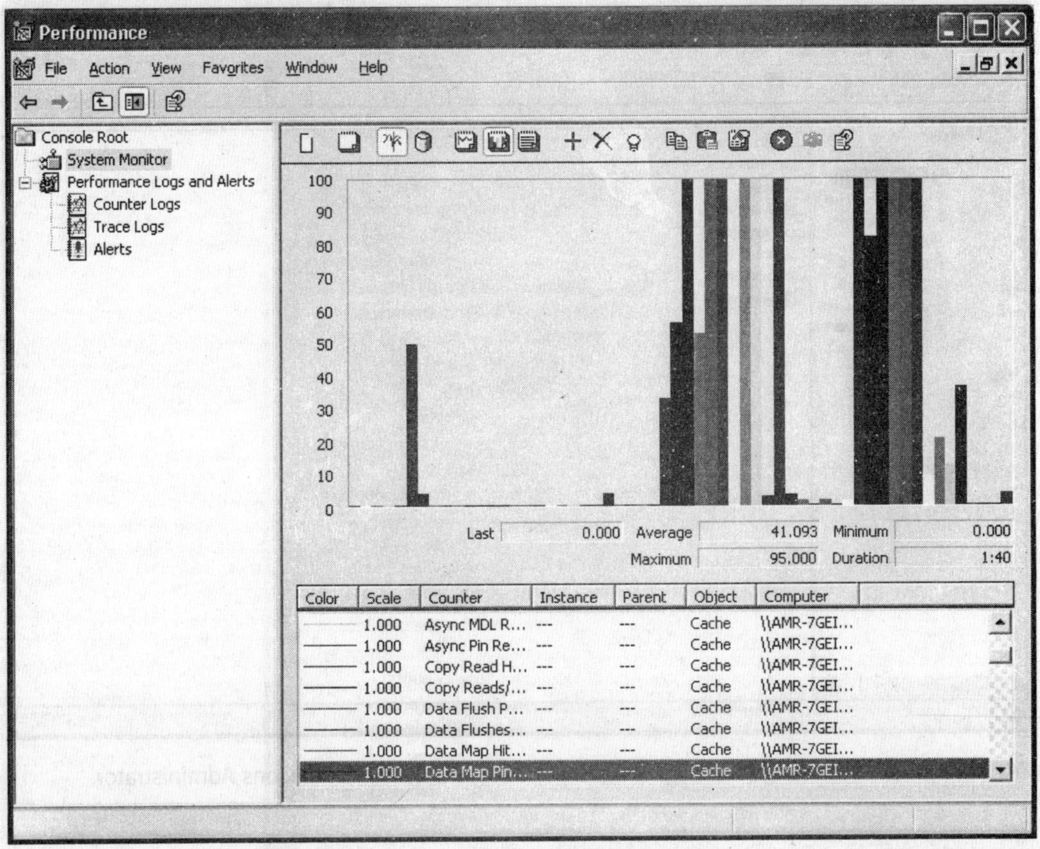

FIGURE 11.10 The Performance tool's many features make this one of the most useful tools in Windows XP.

ment application. Extensions are programs that provide additional functionality to FrontPage. FrontPage is also integral to Microsoft's Commerce Server and Content Management Server. Figure 11.11 shows an example of the Server Extensions Administrator application.

Services—The Services tool contains a list of all of the services that can run on the computer. An example of a service is the DNS client service. The list has columns which indicate the service name, description, status, startup type, and what account the service logs on under (almost always a machine account, not a user account). A service's status is an indication of whether

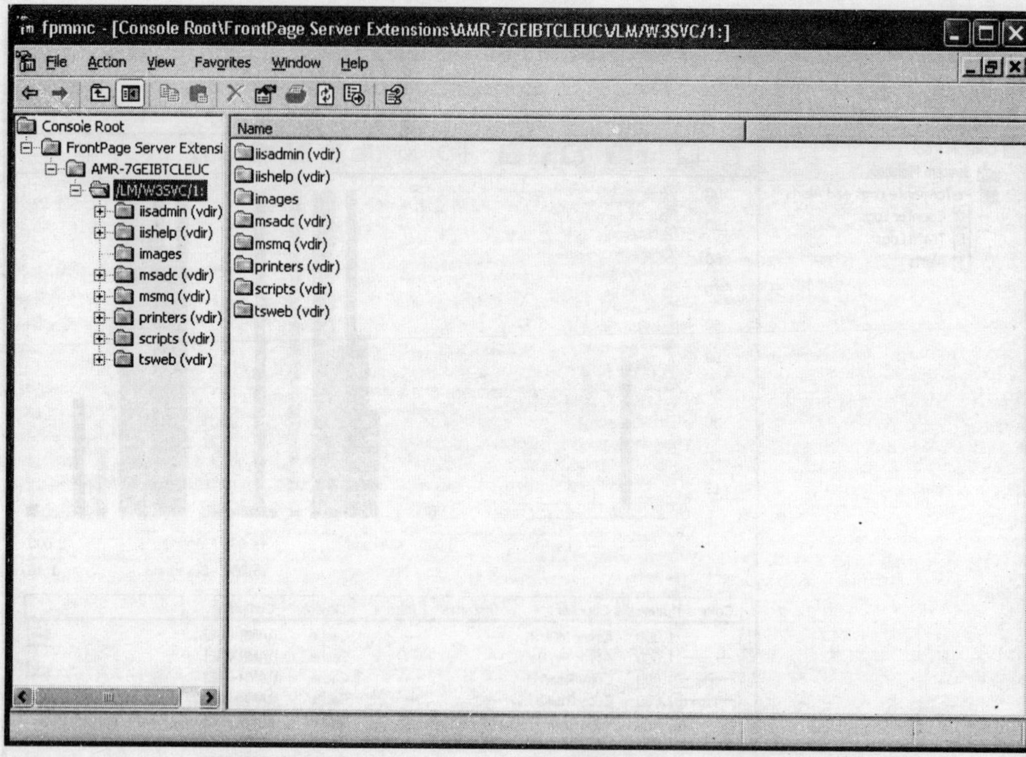

FIGURE 11.11 Managing FrontPage extensions using the Server Extensions Administrator.

the service is started, stopped, paused, or disabled. Startup type is either automatic (starts with the system) or manual (a user has to start the service). Each service has a properties sheet with four tabs allowing for manual starting and stopping, change of startup type, changing the account the service logs on with (this rarely needs to be changed), and specifying the action the computer should take if the service fails. The Dependencies page shows the services that are dependent on the service and the services that this service depends on. Figure 11.12 shows an example of services viewed through the MMC interface.

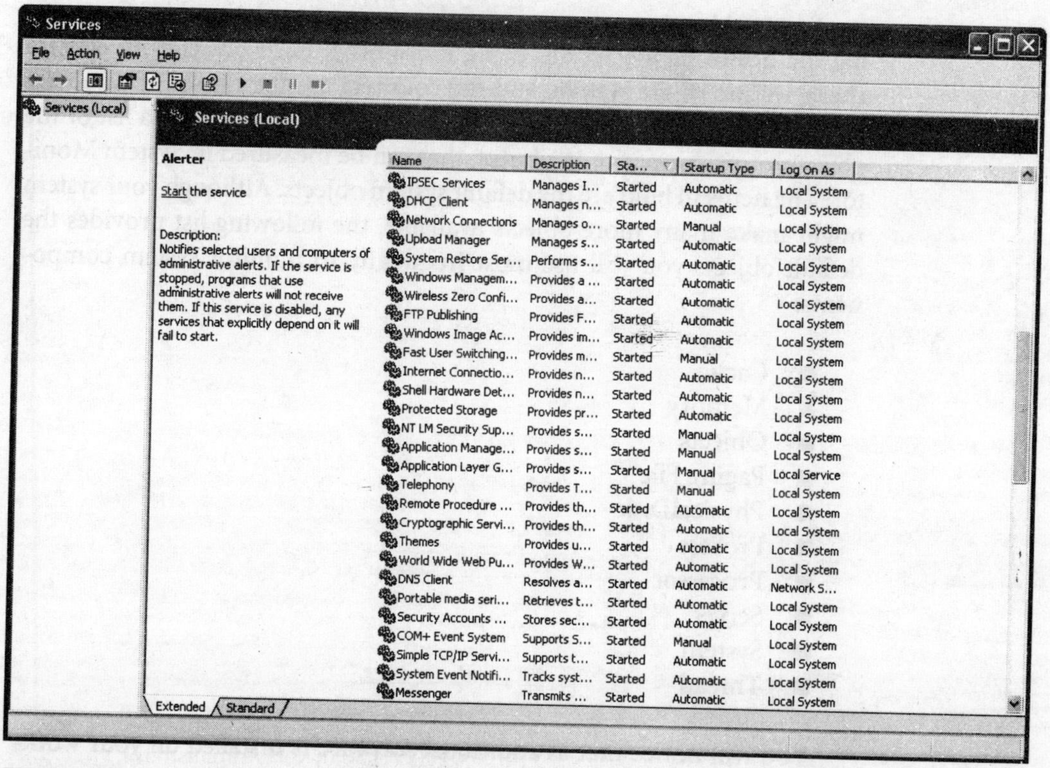

FIGURE 11.12 Services is a tool for specifying how services are run in Windows XP Professional.

WHAT IS SYSTEM MONITOR?

The most widely used tool for managing a Windows XP Professional workstation's performance is System Monitor. What is truly significant about System Monitor is the analytical insight it can provide as to systems' performance. System Monitor enables you to track a variety of items and display information on their relative performance in different ways. System Monitor is designed to provide feedback on the relative level of performance on systems. It is capable of monitoring performance of systems throughout a network as well, using the UNC naming convention to access another computer on the network. Many companies that have standardized on Windows NT/2000/XP find System Monitor to be a very useful, capable tool for troubleshooting performance issues and alleviating system bottlenecks.

System Monitor uses a series of object-counter relationships for tracking the health of the system being monitored. Each object is in effect a characteristic of the system, and the counters are the classes of values by which the object's performance is measured. The following is a list of the objects, or performance attributes, that can be measured in System Monitor. The items in bold are the default system objects. Although your system might make many more objects available, the following list provides the default objects you will use most frequently to monitor system components:

- Cache
- Memory
- Objects
- Paging File
- PhysicalDisk
- Process
- Processor
- Server
- System
- Thread

You will notice that as additional software is installed on your workstations and servers, new objects will be appearing in the System Monitor. That is because applications and components such as network protocols install their own objects in System Monitor.

System Monitor can show three different views on systems' performance. These three views are:

- **Graph**—The Graph view is the default view in System Monitor. Graph view enables objects to be graphically displayed. This view enables you to view the monitored items over a short period of time (as short as every second) by choosing the options from within the dialog boxes available in this view. This view is best for actively watching the performance of a Windows XP Professional workstation, and is illustrated in Figure 11.13.
- **Histogram View**—Also know as a bar graph, a histogram contains moving vertical bars to illustrate performance measurements. Each counter has its own bar. Figure 11.14 shows the Histogram view.

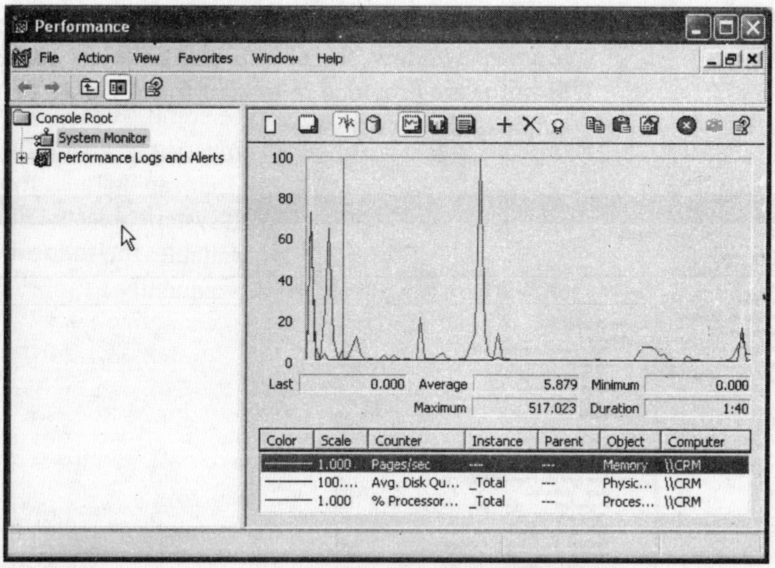

FIGURE 11.13 Using the Graph view of System Monitor.

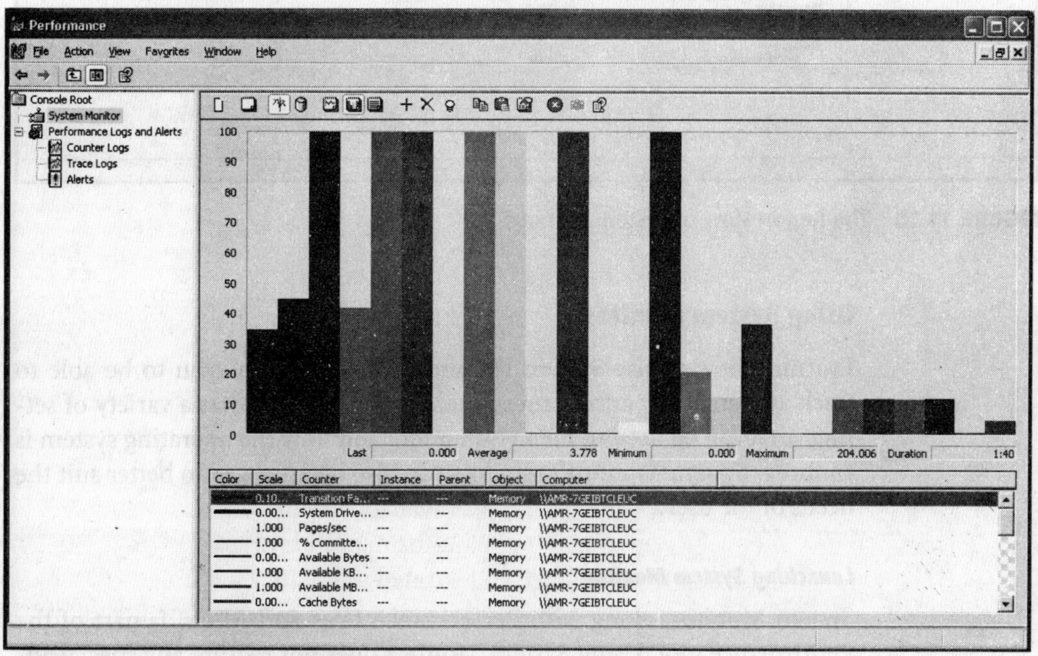

FIGURE 11.14 The Histogram view can be easier to read than the graph view, especially with many counters being tracked.

- **Report View**—Using the View Report icon in the main System Monitor window, the objects and counters added to the System Monitor are provided in tabular form. Figure 11.15 shows an example of the report view.

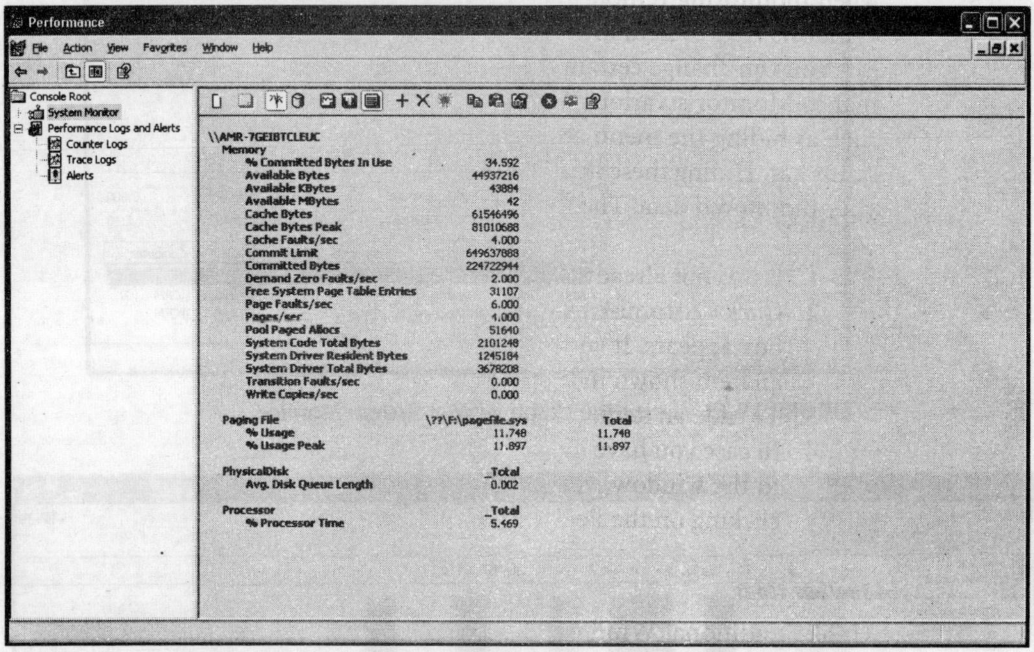

FIGURE 11.15 The Report view of System Monitor.

Using System Monitor

Learning how to use System Monitor definitely helps you to be able to track and analyze performance data. System Monitor has a variety of settings that can be used to help you understand how the operating system is running. System Monitor's window can also be arranged to better suit the needs of the user.

Launching System Monitor

System Monitor, along with Performance Logs and Alerts, is part of the Performance tool. Using System Monitor does not require any special administrative passwords or privileges and is accessible to members of any of the built-in user groups.

In Windows NT, and to some extent in Windows 2000 you had to activate disk counters by running the diskperf –y command from a command prompt and then rebooting the computer. In Windows XP Professional, disk counters are automatically activated when they are added to System Monitor. You may still need to use this command, however, when monitoring remote Windows NT or Windows 2000 systems using Windows XP's System Monitor.

You can change certain display options to better organize the Performance Monitor's various graphical interfaces. You can perform actions such as hiding the menu and title bar, hiding the toolbar, and hiding the status bar. Hiding these items enables you to have a larger viewing area for your monitored data. The following procedure shows you how:

1. If it is not already started, start System Monitor.
2. Click Customize from the View menu. The Customize View dialog box appears. It contains a series of check boxes, each representing an item shown in the System Monitor window.
3. To hide an item, clear the check box.
4. In case you have hidden the View menu and want to restore items to the window, you can open the Customize View dialog box by clicking on the Performance icon *next to the File menu.*

Toolbar Icons

Unlike traditional Windows tools and applets, most functions of System Monitor can be accessed only through toolbar icons or keystroke combinations. To see what each icon does, move the mouse pointer across the toolbar, stopping at each icon to read the popup message. Figure 11.15 shows each icon and its function.

Using & Monitoring Counters

As you can see from the series of counters included in Windows XP Professional, System Monitor can actively track the performance of many aspects of a system's performance. These object types relate to actual devices, sections of memory, or processes. Objects contain items known as counters. These counters are the specific items to be measured using System Monitor. For example, under the Processor object, a counter called % Processor Time is used to monitor the percentage of total processor time that is being used by the system.

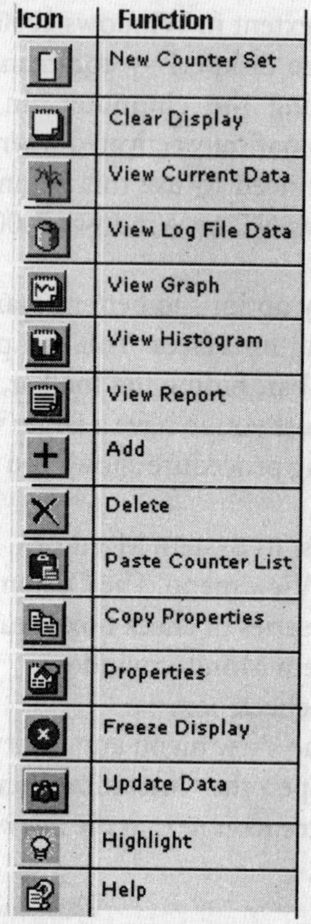

FIGURE 11.16 Icons are used to access different functions in System Monitor.

Object types also can have several instances. Instances do not appear as objects per se, but object types such as the Processor object have an instance for each processor in a workstation or server. Instances represent an individual object out of multiple objects of the same type. Other object types, for example, the memory object type, do not have any instances.

To begin monitoring performance on a Windows XP-based system you need to add counters. You will see that the process of adding counters is identical no matter which of the three views in System Monitor are being used. To add counters, do the following:

1. Launch System Monitor.
2. Select the view you want to display by clicking one of the three view buttons on the toolbar.

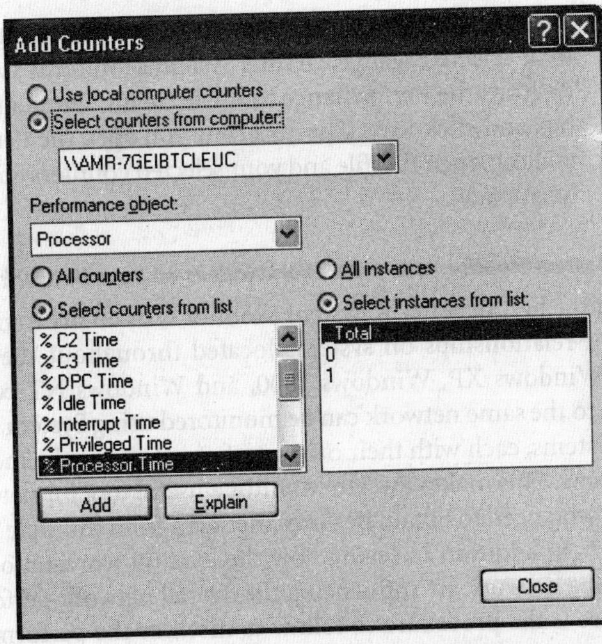

FIGURE 11.17 Using the Add Counters dialog box.

3. Click the "+" sign to open the Add Counters dialog box. Figure 11.17 shows an example of the Add Counters dialog box.
4. The Computer box displays the computer that System Monitor is tracking. The Object item in the dialog box is a drop-down list displaying the entire series of object types currently available on the system. Select the object type for which you want to see counters.
5. In the Counter list, select a counter you want to track. If you are unsure of what a counter does and you would like more information on the specific object-counter relationship, select the counter and click the Explain button. The Explain button displays a definition of the purpose of the counter. The Explain dialog box is also detached from the main dialog box as well, which makes it possible to move and copy the definition for use by other members of your team in learning how object-counter relationships work.
6. If multiple objects exist in the Instance list, select the instance of the object you want to monitor.
7. Click Close after you have added all of the counters you want to monitor. This will close the Add Counters dialog box.

8. To save these settings in an MMC file so the counters do not have to be selected again each time System Monitor is started, click Save As from the Performance tool File menu. Enter a file name in the box and click Save. The next time you open the Performance tool, you can open this file and your selected counters and instances will be in place.

Using System Monitor with Other Workstations on Your Network

One of the best benefits of System Monitor is its ability to monitor object-counter relationships on systems located throughout the network. Any other Windows XP, Windows 2000, and Windows NT computers connected to the same network can be monitored using System Monitor. Multiple systems, each with their own set of counters, can be monitored in the same view. This makes System Monitor a useful tool for network administrators who need to obtain performance data from multiple systems on the network, in addition to seeing how the load on workstations and servers across the network are influencing the overall network performance.

Here is the procedure to follow to monitor the performance of a system across a network using System Monitor:

1. Launch the Performance tool if it is not already up and running.
2. Select the view you want to use.
3. Click the "+" button on the toolbar to open the Add Counters dialog box.
4. Make sure the "Select counters from computer" option is selected. Type the Universal Naming Convention (UNC) path of the computer to monitor in the "Select counters on computer" box.
5. Select the objects and counters you want to monitor for that computer. Also, select the options for those counters. Click Add to add those counters to the current view.
6. You can select additional computers on the network and choose counters for those systems to be monitored.
7. When finished selecting counters, click Close to close the Add Counters dialog box.

Try to keep network use of the System Monitor as streamlined as possible to ensure the network traffic for other tasks enterprise-wide are not impacted. Having too many computers trying to send performance information over the network has an impact on the computers running System Monitor and on the overall capacity of the network to be able to route traffic. Do not try to monitor too many network computers or counters at once. Also, consider modifying the update intervals or use manual updates for counter information. This helps reduce the amount of data being transmitted across the network and to the machine running System Monitor.

EXPLORING EVENT VIEWER

Windows XP's System Monitor measures the magnitude of individual events, while Event Viewer creates a catalog of events that can be referenced. The Event Viewer then interprets commands as individual events, recording them in the log types as discussed earlier in this chapter. What is significant about this is that these events—seemingly unrelated and even trivial when a workstation or server is running well—can often in the case of a problem provide clues to a solution. Event Viewer is the operating system's way of telling you about events. It functions like a report card and status report by storing lists of events in log files that you can review, archive, or transfer to a database or spreadsheet for analysis.

Windows XP recognizes three broad categories of events: system events, security events, and application events. Events of each type are recorded in log files.

System events are generated by Windows XP itself and by installed components, such as services and devices. They are recorded in a file called a system log. Windows XP classifies system events according to their severity as either errors, warnings, or information events as follows:

- **Errors**—System events that represent possible loss of data or functionality. Examples of errors include events related to network contention or a malfunctioning network card, and loss of functionality caused by a device or service that does not load at startup.
- **Warnings**—System events that represent less significant or less immediate problems than errors. Examples of warning events include a nearly full disk, a timeout by the network redirector, and data errors on a backup tape.
- **Information events**—All other system events that Windows XP logs. Examples of information events include someone using a printer connected to your computer, or the successful loading of a database program.

Security events are generated by Windows XP when an activity you choose to audit succeeds (a success audit) or fails (a failure audit). Security events are recorded in a file called a security log. These include file-related events, such as attempts to access files or change permissions (NTFS volumes only), and other security-related events, such as logon/logoff events and changes to security policies. By default, Windows XP auditing is turned off, so you will likely see no events in the security log. To enable event auditing, open Local Security Policy from Administrative Tools in Control Panel. In the left pane, open Local Policies and select Audit Policy. In the right pane, right click each event type you want to audit, and then click Properties. The Audit *event_type* Properties dialog box opens. Select Success, Failure, or both Success and Failure, then click OK.

Application events are generated by applications and are recorded in a file called the application log. The application developer determines which events to monitor, and how those events will be recorded in the application log. Windows XP Backup, for example, records an application event whenever you erase a tape or run a backup.

The importance of Windows XP logs depend on your situation. If you work in a security-sensitive environment or one in which users freely access resources on other users' workstations, you will find the event logs useful in helping you keep track of who used a system, what they did, and when they did it. If you do not care about details of usage on workstations and servers, then the security log will probably be of little interest to you, but the system log can still be helpful in diagnosing performance problems and hardware errors, and the application log can give you insight into how certain applications are working. Only applications designed to record their "events or thoughts" in the application log will appear there, but those that are so designed provide an obvious benefit to you, your technical support person, and even the developer working on applications for identifying and resolving problems that may arise.

If your workstation or servers are set up to share files or a printer with other users, checking tne system log for print jobs and the security logon/logoff access will give you a feel for how and when your computer's resources are being used. Although the information might simply make you feel more in control of your system, you might also find patterns that help you determine better ways to manage it.

Viewing a Log File

You can easily see what a log looks like even if you never before thought of monitoring your system. To view a log, open Event Viewer.

1. Open the Start menu and click Administrative Tools. If Administrative Tools does not appear in the Start menu, click Programs or All programs and access Administrative Tools from there.
2. In Administrative Tools, open Event Viewer.
4. Select a log to view. The system log is shown in Figure 11.18.

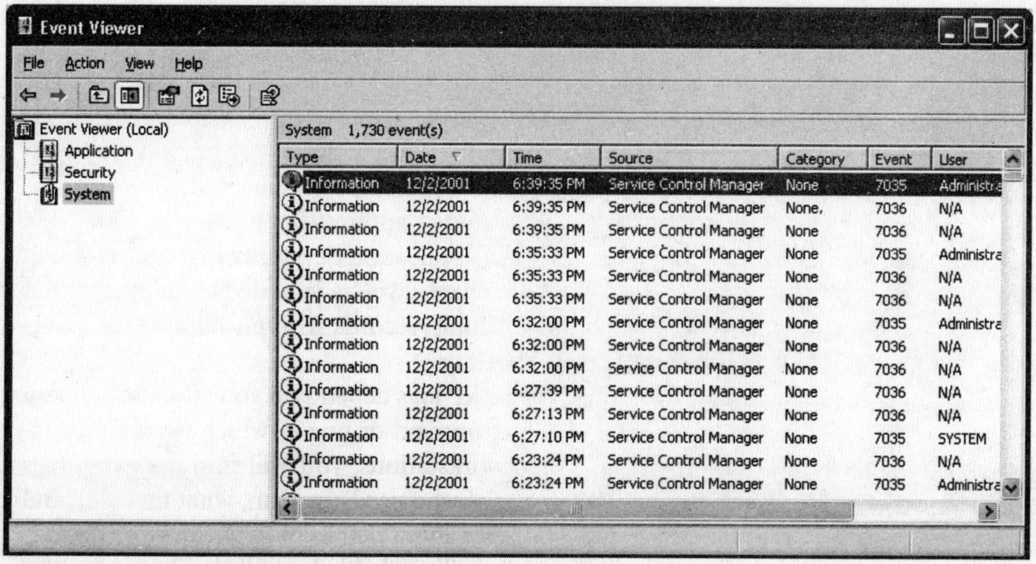

FIGURE 11.18 Using the Event Viewer to analyze an event log.

CHAPTER SUMMARY

The intent of this chapter is to provide an overview of the administrative tools available in Windows XP Professional. Using the System Monitor for tracking system performance is one of the most useful tools in Windows XP Professional as the object-counter relationships are useful for troubleshooting system-level issues. As a system administrator, trying to uncover sporadic problems is one of the more challenging aspects of that role. Taking the historical perspective on objects and their associated counters is invaluable in spotting performance-limiting aspects of overall system variable interactions.

12 Exploring Additional Features in Windows XP Professional

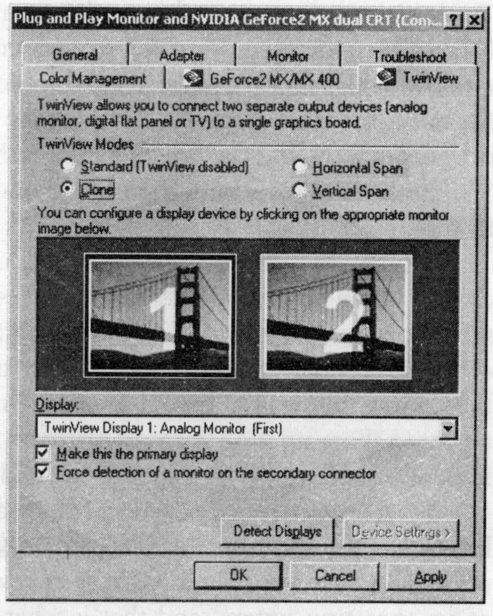

INTRODUCTION

Windows XP Professional has additional features that can be extraordinarily helpful to administrators. For the most part, these features are unique to the Professional version. As an administrator, it is critical that you have an overview of how these features work. The key features that are found only in the Professional version are support for remote desktop connections, enhanced file encryption, and additional tools for system administrators. Support for multiple monitors is new in all versions of Windows XP.

Much of the product innovation that is included in Windows XP Professional comes from technical professionals who were the early adopters of the first versions of Windows NT and then Windows 2000. The roles that these engineering-oriented companies played are best seen in the development of software-based multi-monitor support, which is critical in most design efforts. The fact that UNIX-based workstations had multi-monitor configurations working flawlessly ten years before Windows NT was introduced was an area of constant frustration for technical professionals as they worked to bring in a Microsoft-based operating system over one from Sun, Intergraph, or any other UNIX-based workstation. The initial efforts to get multi-monitor configurations to work in Windows NT required many customized drivers and even customized configurations with the most expensive of graphics adapters. Now Windows XP has multi-monitor support included at the software level. It took five product generations, but the voices of the technically-savvy early adopters of Windows NT have finally been heard and acted upon with this product feature.

Comparable stories for each of the other features described in this chapter could be told. Specifically, the roles of early adopters drive much of the innovation present in Windows XP Professional, and even forced some of the differentiation between XP Professional and Home Edition. The fact that Home Edition is aimed more at the multimedia and video aspects is meant to shore up the Microsoft platform relative to Apple's recent significant announcements in video editing and mixing.

If you are interested in giving Microsoft feedback on what you would like to see, use the e-mail address *feedback@microsoft.com*. Just as citizens elect politicians, your e-mails can elect new features to the next generation of an operating system, and that is what this chapter is based on—customers driving innovation.

MAKING THE CASE FOR MULTIPLE MONITORS

Windows XP Professional supports a dual-monitor technique called *Dualview*, a feature that enables you to connect multiple monitors to a single XP system. Each monitor becomes an extension of your desktop. Each monitor can support 800 × 600 resolution, and if you place them side by side, you can stretch applications and the desktop across the two monitors. The mouse and the keyboard act as if they are one monitor.

Installing Multiple Monitors

There are a few ways to install multiple monitors. One way is to add a PCI graphics card for each monitor in addition to the one connected to the AGP graphics card. Windows XP Professional can drive several separate video graphics adapters at the same time. If the computer already has on-board video, it needs to be set to VGA mode for Dualview to work. The mode is set through the computer's BIOS setup program, which you can usually get to by pressing Delete or F2 as the computer is starting up.

Another approach is to use a dual-head or multi-head graphics card. Graphics adapters in this class of devices typically are between 50% and 60% more expensive than the single-head graphics adapters, yet they are in high demand in many professions that require this type of configuration, including software development, graphic arts, and CAD/CAM work. And most laptop computers come with a connector for an additional monitor. Whichever approach you use, make sure you shut down your workstation first and unplug the power card and networking cables before changing or installing new cards. Do not use the following very generalized procedure as a substitute for completing the installation with the manufacturer's instructions:

With the cards installed, plug in the power cable and networking cable and turn the system back on. Windows XP Professional will detect new hardware, and then you can use the Add Hardware Wizard in the Control Panel to finish the installation. Do not be worried if both monitors do not switch on immediately when you boot up Windows XP after installing them; you will need to get the device drivers installed first.

To activate additional monitors, in addition to controlling color depth, desktop area, and all other attributes with each monitor, use the Settings tab in the Display Properties dialog box. The quickest path to this dialog box is to right-click on the Desktop and select Properties. You can also go to the Control Panel from the Start menu and double-click the Display icon. Either approach gets you to the same properties dialog box. Click the Advanced Button. Figure 12.1 shows the advanced display properties.

This dialog box shows two boxes, each representing a monitor. To activate each monitor, click on its box and select the "Extend my Windows desktop to this monitor" check box. To see which monitor is which, click the Identify button, or point to either monitor box and hold down the primary (left) mouse button. You can arrange the monitors in the box to match the arrangement of the monitors on your system. You can now set the screen resolution and color depth for each monitor by first clicking the

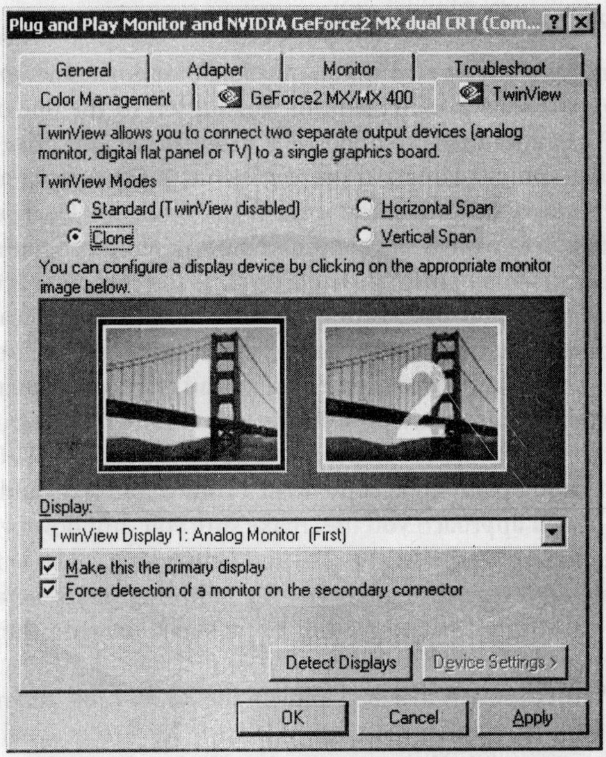

FIGURE 12.1 Exploring the advanced display properties.

monitor's box or choosing a monitor from the Display drop-down list. The resolution and color depth you choose affects only the current monitor.

One monitor will act as the primary monitor that displays the logon screen and taskbar. You can make either monitor the primary monitor by selecting it and then choosing the "Use this device as the primary monitor" check box. If you have any problems getting multiple monitors to work, try using the troubleshooter. Click the Troubleshoot button on the Settings tab in the Display Properties dialog box to get started.

Points to Think About When Configuring Multiple Monitors

Be sure to go through this list of recommendations before configuring a workstation for multiple monitors using Windows XP Professional:

1. Check to see if the graphics adapters you are using and/or considering purchasing are compatible with Windows XP Professional by looking for their names on the Windows XP Hardware Compatibil-

ity List found at *www.microsoft.com/hcl*. This step alone can save you hours of effort in making your configuration work flawlessly. Matrox and nVidia are two vendors to look at seriously; both are leaders in the area of graphics device driver development for the 32-bit Windows XP operating systems. Matrox has the distinction of being the first graphics adapter company to have all currently shipping products compatible with Windows XP through Microsoft's driver certification program. Other manufacturers, including Appian Graphics, have dual-head adapters on the XP HCL also.

2. Use a dual-head monitor if at all possible, as the configuration of a single card with multiple outputs, each for one monitor, is the best approach. It is possible to have two monitors running from separate graphics adapter cards, but dual-head is much easier to configure.
3. Use the same resolutions and settings for each monitor to keep documents and graphical elements at the same sizes and image quality.

TECH TIP: Advice has been passed around that says to place video adapter cards in the first PCI or AGP slot on a motherboard in order to maximize the level of current a video card receives thus maximizing its performance. There is no validity to this. The following list explains why:

- *If there are any motherboards with more than one AGP slot, they are extraordinarily obscure.*
- *The only reason to use the first PCI slot for the video adapter is because in many motherboards it is the only slot that does not use IRQ sharing.*
- *There are standards that motherboard manufacturers adhere to including minimum current and voltage levels that a PCI slot must make available to a peripheral, regardless of the location of the PCI slot. As long as the motherboard and power supply are working within those standards, the peripheral should work as designed.*
- *Every electronic device draws the amount of current it needs. A device will not run better with more current; it will run as designed as long as the power supply and voltage regulator provide at least as much current as the unit will ever draw, and it probably will not run as designed if the available current is less than the amount of current the unit will draw. If a device requires no more than 750 milliamps (mA) at 5 volts (v), it does not matter if the power supply puts out 750mA or 50 amperes (A), the unit will work just as well. If a peripheral manufacturer were to put out a PCI card that draws more than the PCI standard, that product would not be on the market for long as it would probably not work correctly and could damage the card, the motherboard, or both.*

WORKING WITH WINDOWS XP PROFESSIONAL'S REMOTE DESKTOP CONNECTION

The function of the Remote Desktop Connection is to allow you to access a Windows session from a remote computer. Very similar to the functionality of the Remote Office Connectivity products from Citrix (*www.citrix.com/solutions/remote_connectivity.asp*) and Symantec PC Anywhere (*www.symantec.com/pcanyware*), Remote Desktop Connections are useful for handling remote troubleshooting of systems throughout your network. Many people at Microsoft actually use this feature to get caught up on work at home by enabling the Remote Desktop Connection from work and then logging on from home later the evening to get more work done.

As an administrator, you can use Remote Desktop in a variety of scenarios, such as accessing office computers from your laptop. To get Remote Desktop to work, you will need the following:

- Your office computer needs to be running Windows XP Professional with the Remote Desktop feature enabled. The computer must also provide a network or Internet connection to which outside users can connect. As the company system administrator you need to set up the accounts and privileges to allow access as well.
- A home PC or laptop with Remote Desktop capability (Windows 9x, NT 4.0, 2000, or XP). The home computer needs to have access to the office computer through a modem, VPN, or other network connection.

If you need to connect from a Windows for Workgroups 3.11 or Windows NT 3.51 computer, use Terminal Service Client.

Enabling Remote Desktop on an Office System

To set up the office computer in this scenario for remote access, you will need to complete the following steps:

1. Access the System Applet through Control Panel or by right-clicking My Computer and clicking Properties from the menu that appears.
2. On the Remote tab, select the "Allow users to connect remotely to this computer" check box.
3. Click the "Select Remote Users" button and add existing user names to the list of allowed users.

Users are added to the group named Remote Desktop Users, which can also be managed from Local Users and Groups in Computer Management.

Enabling Remote Desktop on a Home System

After the office computer has been configured to allow Remote Desktop users and you have created accounts, you need to do the following on your office computer before leaving work.

- Make sure you know your user name and password for logging onto the computer.
- If not already known, write down the name of your computer at work. If you are not sure what the name of your computer is, follow these steps:
  1. Access the System applet from the Control Panel or by right-clicking My Computer and clicking Properties.
  2. Click the Computer Name tab. The name of the computer appears to the right of "Full computer name."
  3. Click OK or Cancel to close the dialog box.
  4. Finally, leave the office computer running. You can log off if you want, leaving the Welcome page visible on-screen.

If your home computer runs any version of Windows XP you can connect without further configuration. If it is running Windows 9x (including Windows Millennium), Windows NT 4.0, or Windows 2000, you will need a Windows XP installation CD. Follow this procedure to install Remote Desktop Connection:

1. Insert the Windows XP CD in your home computer's CD drive.
2. Click Perform additional tasks from the menu that appears.
3. Click Setup Remote Desktop Connection and follow the prompts. You may need to reboot the computer when finished.

Follow these steps to log onto the Remote Desktop:

1. Start up your computer normally and connect to the office network through your modem or Virtual Private Network.
2. From the Start menu click All Programs, Accessories, Communications, and Remote Desktop Connection.

3. In the dialog box that appears, enter the name of the computer to which you are connecting, or click Options for five pages of configuration options.
4. Click the Connect button.
5. In the next dialog box, enter your user name and password and then click OK.

The desktop you see is actually the desktop on the office computer. You now have an online session enabled with your PC at the office and can complete any task, launch any application, or work with any files, even send and receive e-mails and print documents at your printer in the office. When you are finished, you can click the "X" in the upper right corner of the Remote Desktop window to close the session.

When Remote Desktop is used in conjunction with a VPN, many companies are finding this technology gives workers the opportunity to work offsite one day a week and get more accomplished due to a lack of interruptions and saving the lost time of commuting.

WORKING WITH WINDOWS XP PROFESSIONAL'S SYNCHRONIZATION MANAGER

One of the innovations that users have driven Microsoft to create is Synchronization Manager, which enables network users to keep documents they work with offline in sync with documents stored on a network. This feature is in Windows XP Professional only, and is related to the Briefcase function in Windows 9x and Offline Files in Windows 2000.

Synchronization Manager is a tool that helps you work with shared resources on a LAN even when you are not connected to the network itself. If you have a notebook computer running Windows XP Professional and you often use it on the road, you can use Synchronization Manager to synchronize the files on your notebook with the files on the LAN each time you reconnect to the LAN.

A few buzzwords go with the synchronization process in Windows XP Professional. A computer that is occasionally disconnected from the network is called a *standalone* computer, whether it is a desktop PC or a notebook. The shared files that the standalone computer can access are called *offline files*. The process of working with those offline files is called *working offline*, appropriately enough. After you make changes to the offline files, and then reconnect to the network, the process of bringing the original files up-to-date with the changes you made offline is called *synchronization*.

A *shared resource* or *share* on a LAN is some file or folder that other users on the LAN can access. Offline files need to be shared, or stored within a shared folder. The Shared Documents folder on a Windows XP Professional computer is shared across the LAN automatically. So that folder, or any subfolder within it, is a good candidate for working offline.

The First Step in Working Offline

Working offline requires that the Fast User Switching feature of user accounts be disabled. To do that, click the Start button, open Control Panel, and open the User Accounts applet. Choose "Change the way users log on or off" and clear the "Use Fast User Switching" check box. Click the Apply button. You can then close the User Accounts window but leave Control Panel open.

Next you need to enable synchronization on the standalone computer and choose some related options. Suppose, for instance, that your standalone computer is named Boston. To enable working offline on that computer, follow these steps:

1. Double-click Folder Options from Control Panel.
2. On the Offline Files tab, make sure Enable Offline Files is selected.
3. Choose any other options that are needed for your configuration.
4. Click OK.

The Second Step Is to Map Network Drives

Let us take an example of someone who works for a company with servers located in London, Boston and California, each of the servers having files he needs to work with regularly. His work habits would require him to redefine connections every time he turns on his system. The concept of mapping network drives is to define a drive letter for each of the remote servers so they appear on his system as a local drive. This saves him significant time each day as the servers in Boston and Europe appear on his desktop as local drives.

Let us assume that you access network drives the majority of the time when working in your office. Follow the procedure here to map network drives:

1. Open My Computer and click Map Network Drive from the Tools menu.

2. Choose an available drive letter.
3. Click the Browse button and navigate to the folder you want to make available offline. Click the folder's name and then click the OK button.
4. To make sure you are automatically reconnected to the shared resource whenever you go online, make sure Reconnect at logon is selected.

In the Map Network Drive dialog box, the folder that the network drive icon will present is shown in UNC format, \\COMPUTERNAME\sharename. For example, the Shared Documents folder on the computer named Boston appears as \\Boston\Shared Documents. Click the Finish button. An icon for the shared resource appears under the drive letter you selected.

The Third Step Is to Make the Folder Available Offline

For each network drive you create, you then need to follow these steps to make the shared resource available for working offline:

1. In My Computer, select the network drive icon(s) that you want to be able to access offline. Optionally, if you want just to make certain items within the shared folder accessible offline, you can open the network drive icon and select those specific files and folders.
2. Choose Make Available Offline from the File menu. The Offline Files Wizard opens.
3. The purpose of the wizard is to explain how synchronization works and also give you the option of synchronizing files automatically when you log on or log off. Just follow along, make your selections, and click the Finish button when you are done.

The Final Step Is the Actual Synchronization

As you complete work offline and begin to amass many new files and e-mails, you will want to get back to your servers at your organization or company and sync up. Upon logging onto the network, files on your system will be synchronized and transferred back and forth, thanks mainly to the option you selected of automatically synchronizing the content between the systems. You will also see a dialog box that gives you the option by item of synchronizing content. Click the Synchronize button to get the files to sync up with one another.

UNDERSTANDING WINDOWS XP PROFESSIONAL'S ENCRYPTION

Encrypting File System (EFS) with Multi-user Support can be used to protect files stored in NTFS volumes. It is especially useful on laptops that can be stolen or frequently accessed by unauthorized people. Once encryption is enabled, the process of encrypting and decrypting files is transparent. That is to say, any encrypted file is automatically decrypted when opened and encrypted when saved.

You can encrypt individual files and folders, as well as the files and subfolders within a folder. The procedure is simple. Follow these steps:

1. Browse for the folder or files you want to encrypt.
2. Right-click the folder or file icon and choose Properties.
3. On the General tab, click the Advanced button.
4. Choose Encrypt contents to secure data.
5. Click the OK button.
6. If you encrypted a folder, choose whether you want to encrypt just the current folder or the contents of the folder as well.
7. Click OK.

It might take a while to initially encrypt all the files selected. When encryption is in place however, you can open and save documents normally and they will automatically be encrypted and decrypted as needed.

DISCOVERING TOOLS FOR ADMINISTRATORS ON THE WINDOWS XP PROFESSIONAL CD

Microsoft has also included additional tools on the Windows XP Professional CD-ROM for experienced system and network administrators. You will find documents in the DOCS folder that provide useful references to the steps required for Windows Activation. These are the type of textual document that system administrators find very useful in educating users. You will also want to get to the SUPPORT\TOOLS subfolder as there are eleven utilities there for streamlining file and network settings transfers, in addition to testing system compatibility. You will find exploring this subfolder worth your time. You will also want to spend time looking at the VALUEADD folder as it has useful tools for viewing files and the contents of the CD. Read the Readme files in the folders and subfolders for more information.

CHAPTER SUMMARY

Microsoft's introduction of these new business-oriented features is based completely on customers' requests. The dual-monitor feature, called Dualview, is a huge improvement over the first efforts in Windows NT to support multiple monitors. Synchronization is more advanced than Windows 98's more rudimentary Briefcase, and the security from encrypting files serves to differentiate Windows XP Professional from the Home Edition. Windows XP also includes support for Remote Desktop Connections, which makes it possible to work from home, and collaborate with others in your company. Remote Desktop requires one computer running Windows XP Professional while a second system has a network connection via modem or Virtual Private Network (VPN) connection. The second system must have Remote Desktop Connection installed for this to work. So here is the bottom line: Microsoft is moving closer to fixing long-standing problems of supporting multiple monitors and remote connections. Both of these features deliver the basic functions needed yet there is more work to be done to perfect these technologies.

Appendix

A Troubleshooting TCP/IP Configurations

When troubleshooting any problem, it is helpful to use a logical approach. Some questions to ask are:

- What can be done reliably?
- At what point do the TCP/IP connections stop working?
- What are the characteristics of the problem?

IPConfig

IPConfig is a very valuable utility to troubleshoot networking connections. Using this utility you can release and refresh an IP address, which is a useful step in troubleshooting TCP/IP connections. It can also give a report of TCP/IP configuration. The following is an example of the output of the IPConfig command run from a command prompt with the /all switch:

```
C:\>ipconfig /all

Windows XP  IP Configuration

      Host Name . . . . . . . . . . . . : HERCULES
      Primary DNS Suffix  . . . . . . . : test.emarkets.com
      Node Type . . . . . . . . . . . . : Hybrid
      IP Routing Enabled. . . . . . . . : No
      WINS Proxy Enabled. . . . . . . . : No

Ethernet adapter Local Area Connection 2:

      Connection-specific DNS Suffix  . :
      Description . . . . . . . . . . . : Intel EtherExpress
      Physical Address. . . . . . . . . : 00-20-AF-1D-2B-91
```

```
        DHCP Enabled. . . . . . . . . . . : No
        IP Address. . . . . . . . . . . . : 10.57.8.190
        Subnet Mask . . . . . . . . . . . : 255.255.255.0
        Default Gateway . . . . . . . . . :
        DNS Servers . . . . . . . . . . . : 10.57.9.254
        Primary WINS Server . . . . . . . : 10.57.9.254

Ethernet adapter Local Area Connection:

        Connection-specific DNS Suffix  . :
        Description . . . . . . . . . . . : AMD PCNET Family PCI
Ethernet Adapter
        Physical Address. . . . . . . . . : 00-80-5F-88-60-9A
        DHCP Enabled. . . . . . . . . . . : No
        IP Address. . . . . . . . . . . . : 199.199.40.22
        Subnet Mask . . . . . . . . . . . : 255.255.255.0
        Default Gateway . . . . . . . . . : 199.199.40.1
        DNS Servers . . . . . . . . . . . : 199.199.40.254
        Primary WINS Server . . . . . . . : 199.199.40.254
```

Ping

Ping is a command that verifies if a node on a network is working, and uses a series of requests sent in the form of data packets to see if a specific node or system is reachable or not. Typically, system administrators use this command to see if the network node or system they are trying to connect to is recognizable from the system being troubleshooted.

If you are a system administrator using Windows 95, 98, Me, NT, 2000 or XP, go to the Command Prompt application and use the ping command from there. You can also type `Ping /?` to get full details on the use of the Ping command.

Arp

This is a useful command to use for checking to see which system on a network has an identical MAC address as another, thereby causing a conflict. This is a command typically used after the ipconfig command has run. The arp command's –a switch will reflect which systems have duplicate IP and MAC addresses.

Route

This command displays the routing tables used throughout a network. The command Route print shows all routes on a network with route add and route delete predictably adding or deleting routes from the routing table itself. Typically, routers exchange IP datagrams to establish connections with each other.

Netstat

Defines the current TCP/IP connections' performance statistics. Using the Netstat –r command gives a listing of the existing routes in the network. And the –e switch shows the statistics on the Ethernet connections. You can also combine syntax options of this command to get greater insights into how a specific command is used.

Appendix

B Essentials of Broadband Technology

NETWORKING TECHNOLOGIES OVERVIEW

Since Ethernet was first developed during the 1970s it has quickly become the basis for the Internet and growth of local area networks (LANs). This is in addition to enterprise-wide networks spanning an entire geographic area, called wide area networks or WANs. These networks have in turn lead to the growth of the Internet as a global exchange capable of handling communication and commerce on a 24/7 basis. Clearly the growth of the Internet is directly attributable to the continued price/performance gains occurring today in network connectivity products from manufacturers. Committed to bringing the most proven networking technologies to market at the best possible price/performance is the hallmark of companies who will be able to capitalize on the high growth the networking marketplace provides.

Ethernet, specifically broadband technologies, work through the use of a standard referred to as the Carrier Sense Multiple Access/Collision Detection (CSMA/CD) approach to arbitrating for control of a network. How this technology works is that each workstation on a network waits until the network has no packets being sent, and then sends an initial data stream to the intended system on the network. The reason this is called the Collision Detection approach is that when multiple workstations or systems sense an opening on the network and begin sending packets at the same time, a collision of packets or data streams occurs on the network. To alleviate these potential conflicts, each system on the network stops transmitting and waits a random length of time before resubmitting a new data stream so that collisions will be alleviated on the network.

A network experiencing 30% collisions is still operable and the performance is acceptable for the majority of the applications. However, when a network reaches 50 – 60%, the performance begins to lag and the applications, even file and printer sharing, become sluggish. With the increasingly complex applications and need for Internet access, more and more networks are facing capacity limitations. The need for continually increasing performance of networks and managing the available bandwidth is driving the development of improved network products to higher levels than ever before.

Ethernet's standard bandwidth is 10 megabits per second (Mbps), a speed at which many companies today who have networks are currently working. With the continued growth of the Internet and the fact that the majority of network traffic is now graphically-intensive, the need for a faster and more robust bandwidth standard became quickly apparent. Fast Ethernet works just like Ethernet, including the standardized use of the CSMA/CD for arbitrating control of the network. The biggest difference is that Fast Ethernet operates at 100 Mbps, or 10 times the speed of Ethernet. There are many companies who provide network interface cards (NICs) that can support both 10 and 100 Mbps, even switching between the two speeds during use. The ubiquity of 10 Mbps Ethernet connections today serves as a strong foundation for companies to adopt 100 Mbps, and the newer 1 Gbps, 2 Gbps, and even 10 Gbps speeds in their networks. As organizations focus on the need for communicating their uniqueness through graphically-intensive Web sites, the need for having such a high bandwidth network throughout an organization becomes a given. Like capacities in disk drives, speed in network connectivity products and specifically NICs is expected to continue to increase.

Fundamentals of Network Transmission Media

Electrical signals are generated as electromagnetic waves (analog signaling) or as a sequence of voltage pulses (digital signaling), each representing a specific series of data elements in a data stream. To be sent from one location to another, a signal must travel along a physical path. The physical path that is used to carry a signal between a signal transmitter and a signal receiver is called the transmission medium.

There are two types of transmission media: guided media and unguided media. Guided media are manufactured so that signals will be confined to a narrow path and include twisted-pair wiring, similar to common telephone wiring; coaxial cable (which is being phased out), similar to that used for cable TV, and fiber optic cable. Figure B.1 provides a comparison of the various types of cabling used in networking.

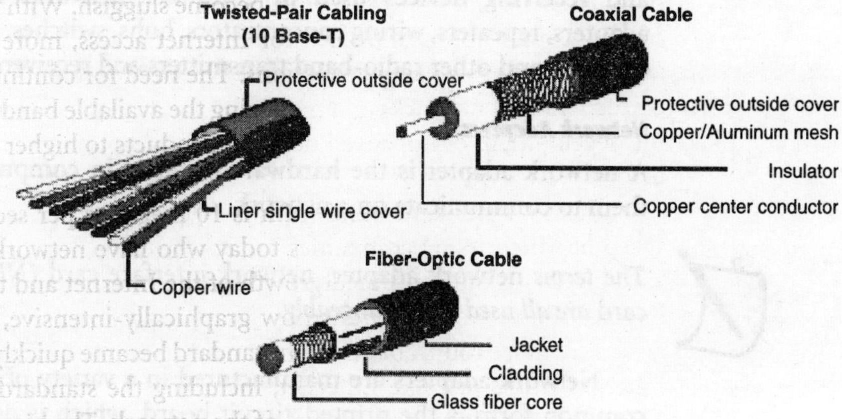

FIGURE B.1 Common guided transmission media.

When planning a computer network, many designers choose a combination of media, based on the physical circumstances involved in building the network and the reliability and data-handling performance required of the network. The objective is to keep costs to a minimum yet provide all parts of the network with the required reliability and performance.

For example, if you needed to build a network consisting of two subnetworks located in separate buildings several miles apart, you might use two or more types of transmission media. If you did not require the same level of performance on both subnetworks, you might use a different type of wire or cable as the transmission medium on each.

To connect the two subnetworks across a municipal area and ensure a reliable connection even in rain and fog, you might use a third medium, Earth's atmosphere, and connect the subnetworks through a microwave link. Alternatively, you might use a T1 or T3 connection. T1 and T3 are dedicated lines (basically special telephone lines) that support high-speed communications. They can be leased from private companies that specialize in providing communication services.

Network Devices and Their Role on a Network

Once the network transmission media are chosen, devices need to be selected for sending and receiving the signals throughout the network. These network connectivity products are designed to propagate a particular type of signal across a particular type of transmission medium. Transmitting and receiving devices used in computer networks include network adapters, repeaters, wiring concentrators, hubs, switches, and infrared, microwave, and other radio-band transmitters and receivers.

Network Adapters

A network adapter is the hardware installed in computers that enables them to communicate on a network.

The terms network adapter, network interface card *(NIC), and* network card *are all used interchangeably.*

Network adapters are manufactured in a variety of forms. The most common form is the printed circuit board, which is designed to be installed directly into a standard expansion slot inside a PC. Other network adapters are designed for mobile computing. They are small and lightweight and are designed to be inserted into PCMCIA, (also known as PC Card) slots on portable (laptop and notebook) computers so that the computer can be easily transported from network to network. Network adapters are now being built into many computers, especially portable computers.

Network adapters are manufactured for connection to virtually any type of guided medium, including twisted-pair cable and fiber-optic cable. They are also manufactured for connection to devices that transmit and receive infrared light, and radio microwaves, to enable wireless networking across the unguided media of Earth's atmosphere and outer space.

Repeaters

Repeaters are used to increase the distance over which a network signal can be propagated. As a signal travels through a transmission medium, it encounters resistance and gradually becomes weak and distorted. The technical term for this signal weakening is *attenuation*. All signals attenuate, and at some point they become too weak and distorted to be reliably received. Repeaters are used to overcome this problem.

A simple, dedicated repeater is a device that receives the network signal and retransmits it at the original transmission strength. Repeaters are placed between other transmitting and receiving devices on the transmission medium, at a point where the signal will not have attenuated too much to be reliably received.

In today's networks, dedicated repeaters are seldom used. Repeating capabilities are built into other, more complex networking devices. For example, virtually all modern network adapters, hubs, and switches incorporate repeating capabilities.

Wiring Concentrators, Hubs, and Switches

Wiring concentrators, hubs, and switches provide a common physical connection point for computing devices. Most hubs and all wiring concentrators and switches have built-in signal repeating capability and thus perform signal repair and retransmission.

In most cases, hubs, wiring concentrators, and switches are proprietary, standalone hardware devices. There are a number of companies that manufacture such equipment. Occasionally, hub technology consists of hub cards and software that work together in a standard computer.

Figure B.2 shows two common hardware-based connection devices: a token-ring switch and an Ethernet 10Base-T concentrator.

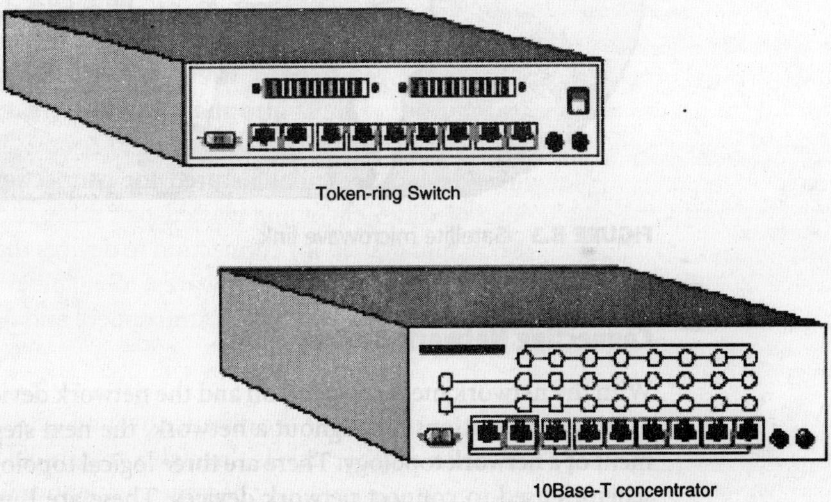

FIGURE B.2 Token-ring switch and Ethernet 10Base-T concentrator.

Microwave Transmitters

Microwave transmitters and receivers, especially satellite systems, are commonly used to transmit network signals over great distances. A microwave transmitter uses the atmosphere or outer space as the transmission medium to send the signal to a microwave receiver. The microwave receiver either relays the signal to another microwave transmitter, which sends it to another microwave receiver, or the receiving station translates the signal to some other form, such as digital impulses, and sends it along on some other suitable medium. Figure B.3 shows a satellite microwave link.

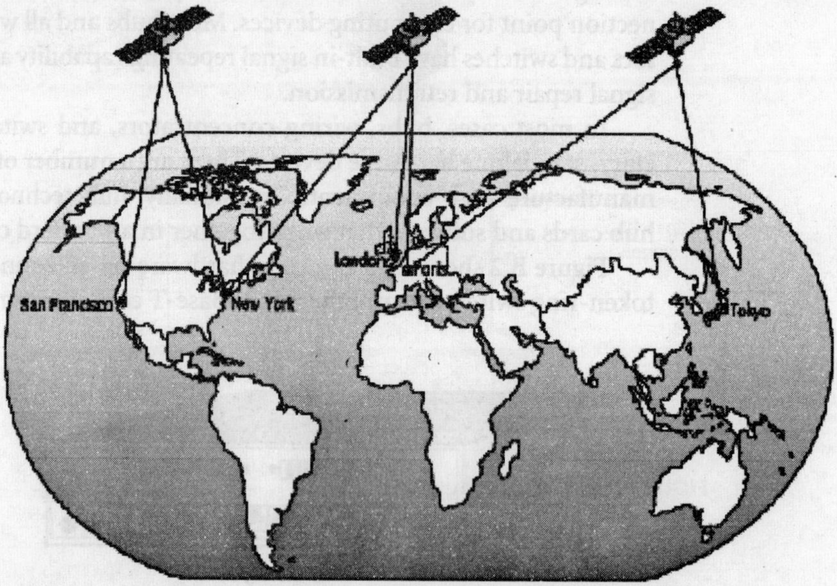

FIGURE B.3 Satellite microwave link.

Connecting Network Devices

With the network media decided on and the network devices used for connecting workstations throughout a network, the next step is the development of a network topology. There are three logical topologies or electronic schemes used to connect network devices. These are Bus, Star, and Star-Wired Ring. Physical topology is the physical layout of the guided transmission media.

Physical Bus

The simplest form of a physical bus topology consists of a trunk (main) cable with only two end points. When the trunk cable is installed, it is run from area to area and device to device—close enough to each device so that all devices can be connected to it with short drop cables and T-connectors. This simple "one wire, two ends" physical bus topology is illustrated in Figure B.4. This topology uses coax cable, which is not being used in new network installations.

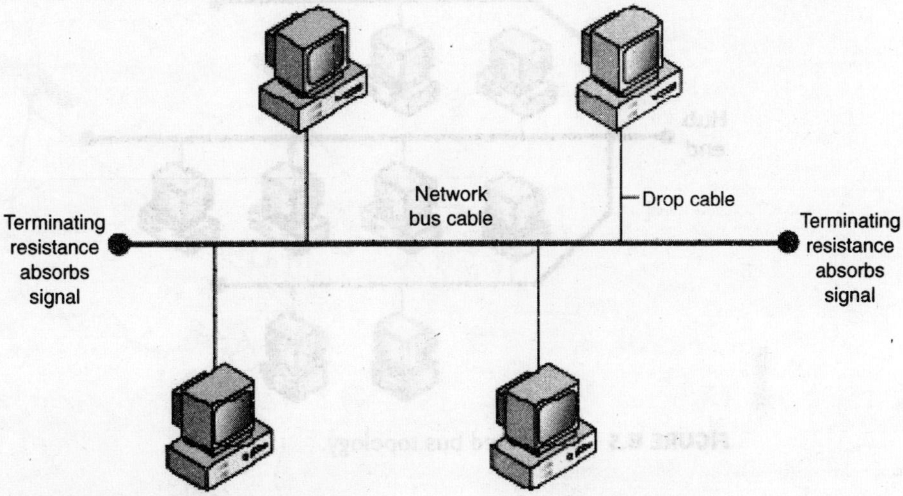

FIGURE B.4 Physical bus topology.

A more complex form of the physical bus topology is the distributed bus (also called the tree topology). In the distributed bus, the trunk cable starts at what is called a "root," or "head end," and branches at various points along the way. (Thus, unlike the simple bus topology, this variation uses a trunk cable with more than two end points.) Where the trunk cable branches, the division is made by means of a simple connector (as opposed to the star physical topology discussed later, where connections are made to a central, somewhat sophisticated connection device). The distributed bus topology is illustrated in Figure B.5.

Physical Star

The simplest form of the physical star topology consists of multiple cables—one for each network device—attached to a single, central connection device. For example, 10Base-T Ethernet networks are based on a physical star topology—each network device is attached to a 10Base-T hub by means of twisted-pair cable.

In a real-life implementation of even a simple physical star topology, the actual layout of the transmission media need not form a recognizable

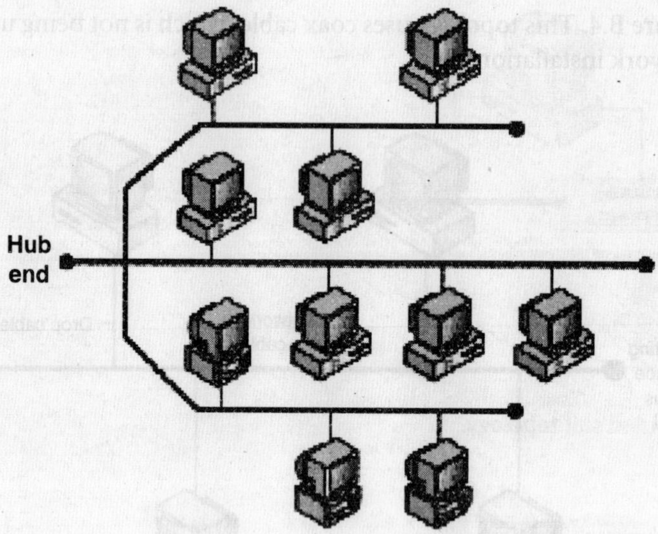

FIGURE B.5 Distributed bus topology.

star pattern; the only required physical characteristic is that each network device be connected by its own cable to the central connection point.

The simplest form of the physical star topology is illustrated in Figure B.6. A more complex form of the physical star topology is the distributed star. In this topology, there are multiple central connection points, which are all connected to form a string of stars. This topology is illustrated in Figure B.7.

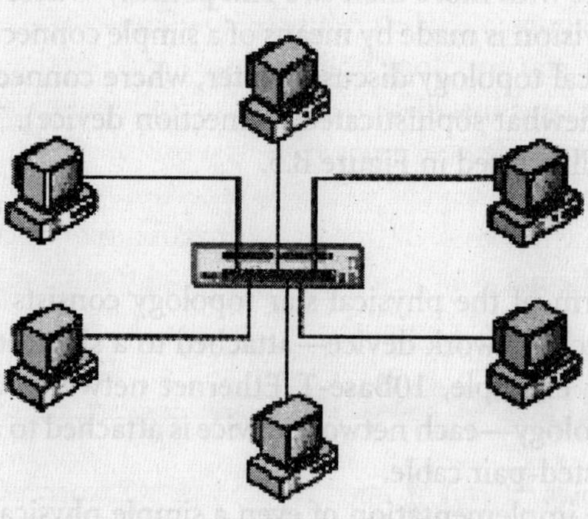

FIGURE B.6 Physical star topology.

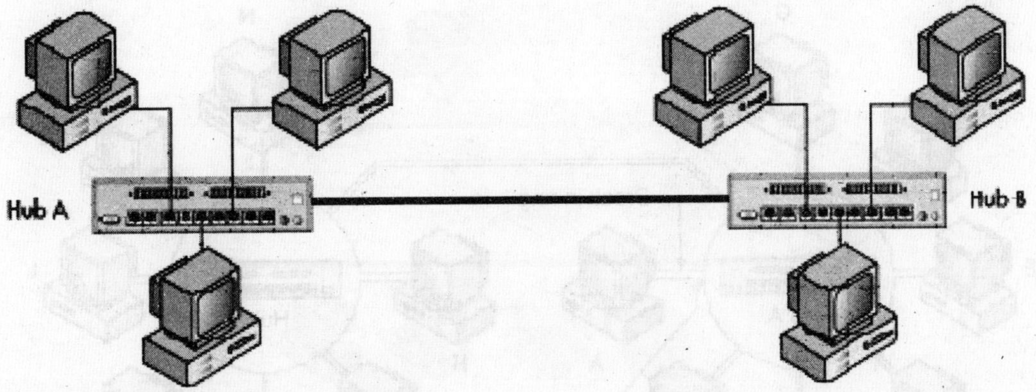

FIGURE B.7 Distributed star topology.

Physical Star-Wired Ring

In the star-wired ring physical topology, individual devices are connected to a central hub, as they are in a star or distributed star network. However, within each hub the physical connections form a ring. Where multiple hubs are used, the ring in each hub is opened, leaving two ends. Each open end is connected to an open end in some other hub (each to a different hub) so that the entire network cable forms one physical ring. This physical topology, which is used in IBM's Token-Ring network, is illustrated in Figure B.8.

In the star-wired ring physical topology, the hubs are "intelligent." If the physical ring is somehow broken, each hub is able to close the physical circuit at any point in its internal ring so that the ring is restored. Refer to details shown in Figure B.8, Hub A, to see how this works.

Currently, the star topology and its derivatives are most preferred by network designers and installers because using these topologies makes it simple to add network devices anywhere. In most cases, you can simply install one new cable between the central connection point and the desired location of the new network device without moving or adding to a trunk cable or making the network unavailable for use by other stations.

FUNDAMENTALS OF INTERNETWORKING

As a business grows, it might need to split its network. Alternatively, a business might need to connect two separate networks so that users on

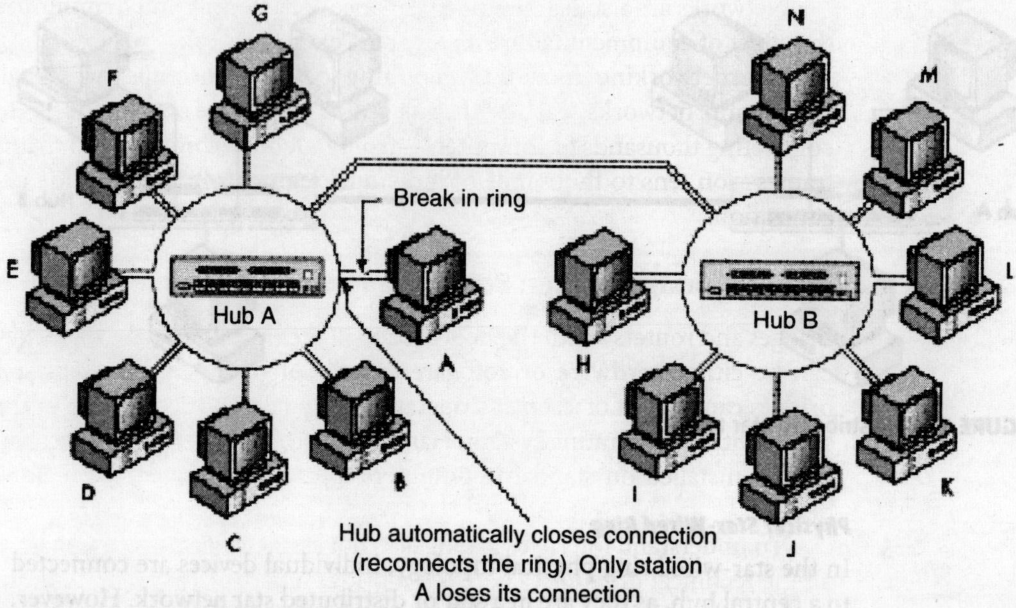

FIGURE B.8 Physical star-wired ring topology.

each can use resources on either. When a network is split (or when two networks with different addresses are connected), this results in an internetwork. An internetwork has subnetworks (network segments) that have different network addresses. Even a modest-sized business often has several subnetworks operating, each serving a specific portion of the organization.

The most common reason for segmenting a network is to increase network performance. On even the fastest and most efficient network, if the network has too many active nodes, the transmission media can become so busy that devices have to wait an unacceptable time to transmit. When this happens, users begin to notice delays when they try to save or open files or perform other operations.

When you segment a network, you give each subnetwork its own network address. This results in two separate transmission media segments which can be used simultaneously. Each of the two segments will have only half the users of the original network. Thus, you double network performance (on some networks, performance can more than double because on an overloaded network, the overhead required to manage transmission collisions takes a much larger percentage of bandwidth than on a modestly busy network).

Networks are also segmented to enhance data security and to minimize the effect of equipment failure on any part of the network.

Internetworking includes everything from connecting two small workgroup networks, each with perhaps two or three workstations, to connecting thousands of computers—from notebook computers to mainframes—on tens to thousands of individual segments in a worldwide organization.

Internetworking Devices: Bridges and Routers

Bridges and routers are the devices used to interconnect subnetworks. They can be either hardware or software based. Software-based routers and bridges can be part of a server's operating system or can at least run in the server with the operating system. Hardware-based bridges and routers can also be installed on standard computers to create dedicated, standalone devices.

To understand internetworking, it is not essential that you understand all the technical differences between a bridge and router. In fact, without some study, this can be a confusing area. For example, if you read about multiprotocol routers, you will find that these routers also perform what is called source-route bridging.

However, without a basic understanding of bridging and routing technology, you will find it difficult to understand the capabilities of some products and the reasons such capabilities are useful or important. Keep in mind that bridges and routers have one important thing in common: They both allow the transfer of data packets (frames) between subnetworks with different addresses on the network.

Bridges

A bridge operates at the Data Link layer (layer two) of the OSI model. A bridge acts as an address filter; it relays data between subnetworks (with different addresses) based on information contained at the media access control sublayer of the Data Link layer of the OSI model.

Simple bridges are used to connect networks that use the same Physical layer protocol and the same MAC and logical link control (LLC) protocols (MAC and LLC are sublayers of the Data Link layer). Simple bridges are not capable of translating between different protocols.

Other types of bridges, such as translational bridges, can connect networks that use different Physical layer and MAC-level protocols; they are capable of translating, then relaying frames.

After a physical connection is made (at the OSI Physical layer), a bridge receives all frames from each of the subnetworks it connects and checks the network address of each received frame. The network address is contained in the MAC header. When a bridge receives a frame from one subnetwork that is addressed to a workstation on another subnetwork, it passes the frame to the intended subnetwork. Figure B.9 shows how a bridge works.

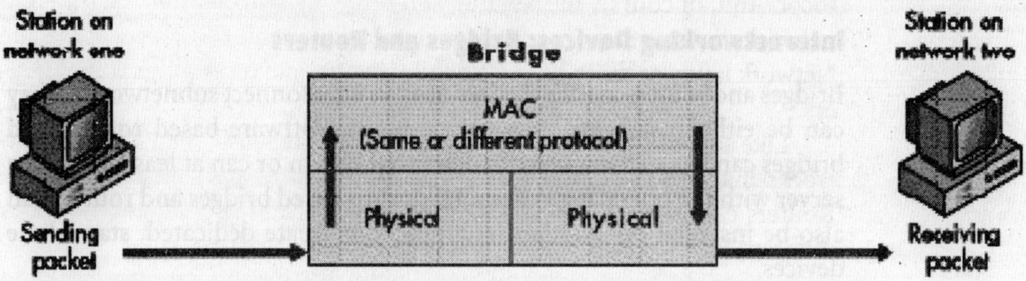

FIGURE B.9 Internetworking through a bridge.

Spanning Tree Algorithms and Source-Route Bridging

There are two terms connected with bridging that will be useful to understand: spanning tree algorithms and source-route bridging.

Spanning tree algorithms prevent problems resulting from the interconnection of multiple networks by means of parallel transmission paths. In various bridging circumstances, it is possible to have multiple transmission routes between computers on different networks. If multiple transmission routes exist, unless there is an efficient method for specifying only one route, it is possible to have an endless duplication and expansion of routing errors that will saturate the network with useless transmissions, quickly disabling it. Spanning tree algorithms are the method used to specify one, and only one, transmission route.

Source-route bridging is a means of determining the path used to transfer data from one workstation to another. Workstations that use source routing participate in route discovery and specify the route to be used for each transmitted packet. Source-route bridges merely carry out the routing instructions placed into each data packet when the packet is assembled by the sending workstation—hence the name "source routing." In discussions of bridging and routing, do not be confused by the term "source routing." Though it includes the term "routing," it is a part of bridging technology. Source-route bridging is important because it is a bridge-routing method used on IBM Token-Ring networks.

Routers

Routers function at the Network layer of the OSI model (one layer above bridges). To communicate, routers must use the same Network-layer protocol. And, of course, the sending and receiving workstations on different networks must either share identical protocols at all OSI layers above the Network layer, or there must be necessary protocol translation at these layers.

Like some bridges, routers can allow the transfer of data between networks that use different protocols at the Physical and Data Link layers. Routers can receive, reformat, and retransmit data packets assembled by different Physical and Data Link layer protocols. Different routers are built to manage different protocol sets. Figure B.10 illustrates how a router transfers data packets.

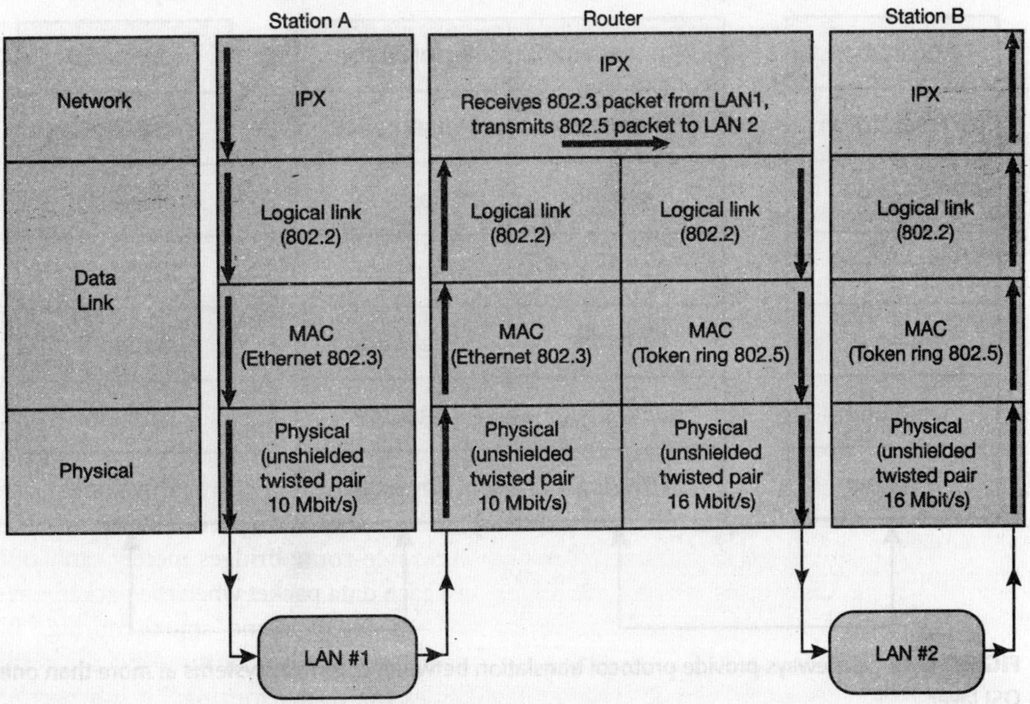

FIGURE B.10 Internetworking through a router.

Gateways

In contrast to bridges and routers which function at only one layer of the OSI model, a gateway translates protocols at more than one OSI layer. Therefore, a gateway is used to interconnect computer systems that have different architectures and that therefore use different communication protocols at several OSI layers.

A gateway may connect dissimilar systems on the same network or on different networks (thus, using a gateway does not necessarily involve internetworking). For example, a gateway might translate protocols at several different OSI layers to allow transparent communications between IPX-based systems and systems based on TCP/IP, System Network Architecture (SNA), or AppleTalk. Figure B.11 illustrates how a gateway is used to translate protocols to enable communications between two heterogeneous systems.

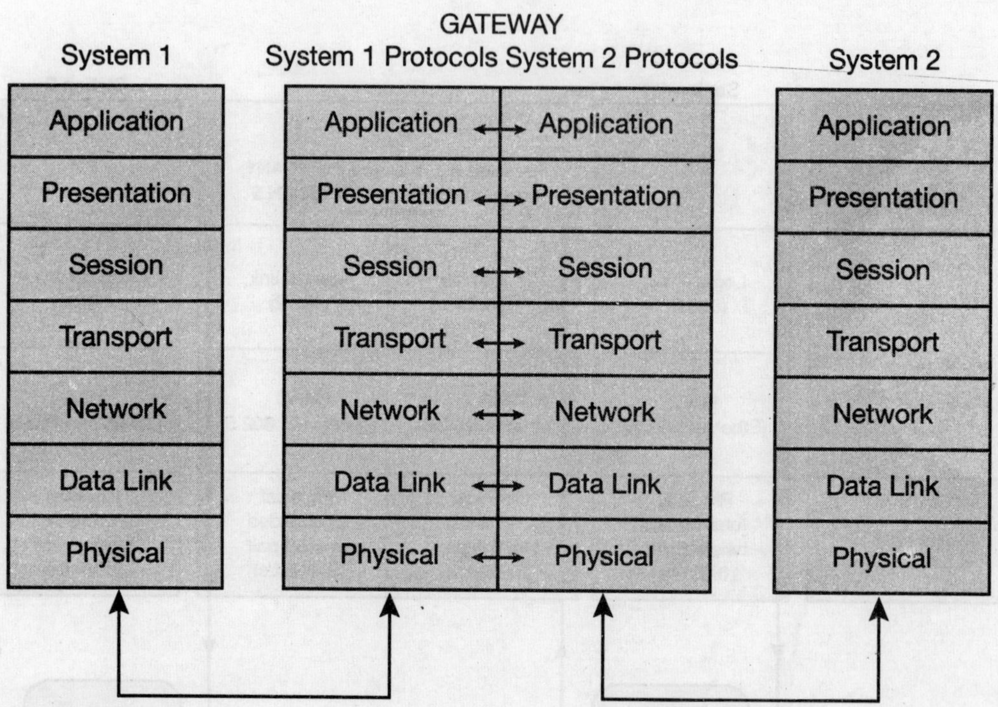

FIGURE B.11 Gateways provide protocol translation between dissimilar systems at more than one OSI layer.

A gateway may consist of hardware, software, or a combination of the two, and it may provide translation at all or at only some of the different OSI layers, depending on the types of systems it connects.

Appendix

C Security Strategies in Windows XP Professional

(Including Universal Plug and Play Security Patch)

SECURITY VULNERABILITIES IN WINDOWS XP PROFESSIONAL

Microsoft's strategy of making one of the most Internet-capable operating systems ever has come to fruition, yet there is a price associated with such a wide variety of approaches to connecting with other systems and the Internet with this operating system: security. With many approaches to getting connected to the Internet, Windows XP Professional and Home Edition have just about any method you want to use to get online, connecting to an existing VPN, or even tunneling over the Internet to a LAN that is behind a firewall. With this wealth of connectivity options also comes the need for greater levels of security. It has been very apparent that during the production of this book, which required many hours using the many networking options in Windows XP Professional, that mistakes that can open up an entire network of XP systems to being compromised over the Internet are easily made. While Microsoft does do an excellent job on many of the aspects of operating systems, security has been an elusive design goal. The responsibility of security cannot be trusted to just a single vendor for both the operating system and applications; there need to be phased levels of security within your Windows XP Professional and Home installations. The intent of this appendix is to provide you with multiple options for designing your security strategy as it relates to Microsoft's Windows XP Professional and Home Editions.

Strategies for Making Windows XP Professional More Secure

Recommendations on how to minimize your potential for security risk on the Internet and over networks span the spectrum of common sense to enterprise-wide security applications and state-of-the-art firewalls. Starting at the most basic and progressing to the most complex, the steps you need to take vary depending on the level of financial risk associated with having data exposed.

At its most basic level, security on the Internet includes these common sense steps:

1. Purchase only from Web sites owned by companies you are familiar with and that have encrypted shopping carts. Do not use your credit card with an unfamiliar site or one that does not have encrypted commerce applications. If you choose to purchase over the Internet frequently, consider getting a separate credit card for just those transactions completed online.
2. Do not visit sites that require many opt-in dialog boxes for e-mail and promptings for your approval to make them your home page. These sites also track IP addresses that are used as the basis of hacking later on.
3. Opt-in only for newsletters and materials from sites you know are reputable.

For the next level of security, consider getting a personal firewall for your PC or workstation, especially if it is connected directly to the Internet. Symantec, McAfee and others develop firewalls specifically to support Windows XP Professional. You can even test-drive these personal firewalls by downloading demo copies of them from www.zdnet.com/downloads or www.downloads.com which takes you directly to the CNET downloads site. Both of these include the greatest number of potential firewall products to evaluate for your personal use.

Personal firewalls vary in terms of their capability to monitor the level of traffic by network port and provide protection from hackers and viruses. *BlackIce Defender* by Network Ice (www.networkice.com) established itself with many cable modem users as one of the better personal firewall products. The automatic updates from Symantec for their personal firewall counter the problem of having to track the latest developments in security relating to Windows XP as well. You can download their evaluation software at www.symantec.com/downloads/.

Why use Network Ice's or Symantec's personal firewall products when Microsoft includes a personal firewall in both Windows XP Professional and Home Editions? Because Microsoft does not provide an interactive approach to managing the firewall and has only a log file to view. The entire process of using the personal firewall in both XP Editions is very user unfriendly and you have to make a leap of faith that the firewall is working. I prefer to get feedback on the status of network traffic and if there is something suspicious I would rather know immediately. The firewall in XP appears to the user as a mere check box; there is no interaction with the user. You are better off getting a personal firewall product for your system especially if you are connected directly to the Internet via DSL or cable modem.

At the highest level of security for individuals are proxy servers that are simulated through the use of routers. A router is a hardware device that enables connection to the Internet and in turn allows multiple systems to be connected. The concept of the router was first introduced by Cisco Systems (www.cisco.com) as has the concept of differentiating routers by the firmware included within them. The firmware or electronics in the router also provides for more robust security than is possible with software firewalls. The concept of a proxy server is one of providing an interim server where traffic from the Internet is first assembled and tested to ensure its accuracy and security. Routers serve many purposes in companies, including the capability to emulate proxy servers, distribute IP addresses within a company so many people will be able to log onto the Internet, and also provide protection through the fine-tuning of firewalls. D-Link (www.Dlink.com) was the first of router companies that proactively took on the task of ensuring all their router and firewall products had the capability of stopping hackers from using the UPnP (Universal Plug and Play) shortcomings in Windows XP Professional. Specifically, D-Link made sure port numbers 1900 and 5000 are blocked and monitored for unauthorized use.

If you are connecting your Windows XP-based system directly to the Internet, consider at the very least installing a personal firewall, and if you are going to be sharing an Internet connection with at least one other system, get a router. The added benefit of the security options included in the router just accentuate the fact that using one makes the most sense when you are sharing multiple systems either in your home or office.

Plug and Play Security Vulnerabilities in Windows XP Professional

When the FBI says that a security patch for an operating system is not enough, you know the potential for abuse is high. The UPnP deficiency in Windows XP Professional, first discovered by eEye Digital Security (www.eeye.com), centers on the unchecked buffers for the Universal Plug and Play Interface of Windows XP Professional and Home Edition, Windows Me, Windows 98 and Windows 98SE. Specifically, ports 1900 and

5000 are exposed to hackers who can use these ports to gain control over your systems and use your system's identity to impersonate you and launch attacks on other systems. The two unprotected ports also make it possible for hackers to destroy anything and everything they choose on your system. Your peripherals and other systems on your network are threatened as well. Given the fact the FBI is getting involved with the warnings of the magnitude of this security liability, it is a good idea to stay current on the latest developments from the U.S. government's perspective. You can find valuable information on this security issue and others at the National Infrastructure Protection Center's Web site at (www.nipc.gov). Follow the series of links to the warnings on the Universal Plug and Play vulnerabilities in Windows XP, Windows Me, and Windows 98/98SE.

The details of the Universal Plug and Play problems are actually threefold. The first is a buffer overflow in the Universal Plug and Play service that could lead to a system's root directory being compromised. The second issue regards the Simple Service Discovery Protocol (SSDP) that makes it possible for hackers to falsify their identities in order to launch Denial of Service (DoS) attacks. The third vulnerability is where hackers use your system for resources on other tasks including random character and e-mail distributions.

Using the port monitoring tools you have, be sure to have all Windows XP, Windows Me, and Windows 98/98SE systems on your network actively track ports 1900 and 5000 to see if any hackers are trying to gain access to your company's resources through the Universal Plug and Play vulnerabilities in these operating systems.

Next steps for anyone working with Windows XP Professional include the following:

1. Get to www.microsoft.com/security and download the security patch for Universal Plug and Play. You can also find the patch at www.microsoft.com/windowsxp, www.microsoft.com/downloads/, or by going to Windows Update from the programs list in the Start menu.
2. If you do not already have a firewall installed for each system in your home or office directly connected to the Internet, get one. The download sites earlier in this appendix provide locations for free trials.
3. Get a router that also has a firewall included in if you are sharing multiple systems that are connected to the Internet. The sharing features of a router enable the router to quickly pay for itself, and

the security advantage it provides alone is worth the investment. However, built-in firewalls are just the beginning of a comprehensive security strategy. Consider the levels of security that worldwide PC products distributor Ingram Micro has on their site. Included are proxy servers, hardware firewalls, and VPNs based on point-to-point tunneling to allow for authorized remote access. Enterprise-level security strategies are commonplace today.

4. Configure your system to look for security and other updates on Windows XP by having it periodically check www.windowsupdate.microsoft.com/. Do this from the Automatic Updates tab in the Control Panel's System applet.

Index

FIREWALL MEDIA

(An imprint of Laxmi Publications Pvt. Ltd.)

Computer Books *for School, BCA, MCA, IGNOU, DOEACC and Engineering Students and Professionals*

ISBN	TITLE	AUTHOR	PRICE	PAGES
	.NET			
8170087155	**Building Business Intelligence Applications with .Net**	Robert Ericsson	Rs. 295.00	404
8170083567	**Learning VB.Net Through Applications**	Clayton Crooks	Rs. 295.00	450
8131800865	**Magic of C# with .Net Frame Work**	Shibi Panikkar, Kumar Sanjeev	Rs. 495.00	950
8170082471	**Magic of ASP.Net with C#**	Shibi Panikkar, Kumar Sanjeev	Rs. 395.00	828
8170089662	**ASP.Net Interview Questions and Answers**	J. Rajaram	Rs. 95.00	175
	A TO Z SERIES			
8170083214	**Access 2002 from A to Z**	Julia Kelly, Stephen L. Nelson	Rs. 75.00	185
8170083222	**Excel 2002 from A to Z**	Stephen L. Nelson	Rs. 75.00	193
8170083230	**Front Page 2002 from A to Z**	Heather Williamson	Rs. 85.00	219
8170083249	**Outlook 2002 from A to Z**	Stephen L. Nelson	Rs. 75.00	202
8170083257	**Page Maker 7 from A to Z**	Marc Campbell	Rs. 75.00	202
8170083265	**PowerPoint 2002 from A to Z**	Stephen L. Nelson	Rs. 75.00	202
8170083273	**Windows XP from A to Z**	Pat Coleman	Rs. 95.00	249
8170083281	**Word 2002 from A to Z**	Stephen L. Nelson	Rs. 75.00	199
817008329X	**XML from A to Z**	Heather Williamson	Rs. 75.00	200
8170083303	**Dreamweaver 4 from A to Z**	Heather Williamson	Rs. 85.00	215
	BEGINNERS & GENERAL INTEREST			
817008248X	**Shortcuts to Success in Computing**	Dheeraj Mehrotra	Rs. 55.00	110
8170083311	**Pictorial Computer Dictionary**	Dheeraj Mehrotra	Rs. 45.00	156
8170083486	**Pocket Net Browser**	Dheeraj Mehrotra	Rs. 95.00	302
8170084261	**1000 IT Quizzes**	Dheeraj Mehrotra	Rs. 75.00	120
8131800679	**Information Technology Bible**	Remesh Bangia	Rs. 295.00	567
8131800377	**Fundamentals of Information Technology Including MS Office**	Dinesh Maidasani, Jai Narayan Yadav	Rs. 175.00	356
813180089X	**Fundamentals of Information Technology Including MS Office (Hindi Medium)**	Dinesh Maidasani, Jai Narayan Yadav	Rs. 175.00	425
8170089719	**Foundations of Computer Science**	Ashok Arora	Rs. 250.00	386

Please write for a free color Firewall Media Catalog for details on the above books.

ISBN	TITLE	AUTHOR	PRICE	PAGES
	CALL CENTERS			
8170082196	**Call Centers Made Easy**	Stephen Medcroft	Rs. 195.00	310
	CISCO			
8170087481	**Enabling IP Routing with Cisco Routers**	R. Das, K. Chakrabarty	Rs. 295.00	486
817008749X	**Designing Networks with Cisco**	H. Pasricha, D. Jagu	Rs. 195.00	316
8170087503	**Cisco IP Routing Protocols: Troubleshooting Techniques**	V. Anand, K. Chakrabarty	Rs. 295.00	409
	DATABASES			
8170089530	**DBMS—Complete Practical Approach**	Sharad Maheshwari, Ruchin Jain	Rs. 350.00	656
8170082404	**Learn to Program Visual Basic-Examples**	John Smiley	Rs. 295.00	482
8170082412	**Learn to Program Visual Basic-Databases**	John Smiley	Rs. 325.00	653
8170082420	**Learn to Program Visual Basic-Objects**	John Smiley	Rs. 325.00	670
817008475X	**IT Resources-Access 2002 VBA Programming Access**	Michele Amelot	Rs. 195.00	424
8170084512	**The Power of Oracle 9i**	Rajiv Parida, Vinod Sharma	Rs. 475.00	1035
8170088518	**Principles and Implementation of Data Warehousing**	Rajiv A. Parida	Rs. 295.00	487
817008864X	**DBA Study Guide OCP Prep Guide**	Nazar Abdul	Rs. 295.00	474
8170088658	**Oracle 11i—The Complete Reference**	Rashmi Anandi	Rs. 495.00	975
8131800067	**Toxonomy of Database Management System**	Aditya Kumar Gupta	Rs. 75.00	146
8131800385	**Introduction to SQL and PL/SQL**	Sharad Maheshwari, Ruchin Jain	Rs. 200.00	389
	DOEACC 'O' LEVEL			
8170088089	**DOEACC 'O' Level Model Test Papers**	Ramesh Bangia	Rs. 175.00	296
8170089115	**DOEACC 'O' & 'A' Level Programming & Problem Solving Through 'C' Language (Model Test Paper with Solutions)**	Mukesh Sharma	Rs. 95.00	213
8170089069	**DOEACC 'O' & 'A' Level Business Systems (Model Test Paper with Solutions)**	Mukesh Sharma	Rs. 100.00	252
8170085640	**Programming and Problem Solving Through "C" Language**	Harsha Priya, R. Ranjeet	Rs. 95.00	306

ISBN	TITLE	AUTHOR	PRICE	PAGES
8170084474	**IT Tools and Applications**	Ramesh Bangia	Rs. 145.00	370
8170085594	**Business Systems**	Ramesh Bangia	Rs. 175.00	452
8170089514	**Internet & Web Design**	Ramesh Bangia	Rs. 150.00	300
	ELECTRONIC COMMERCE			
8170085497	**Electronic Commerce**	Pete Loshin, John Vacca	Rs. 295.00	472
817008119X	**E-Commerce**	Mamta Bhusry	Rs. 95.00	215
8170083524	**Marketing in the Cyber Age**	Kurt Rohner	Rs. 295.00	223
	HARDWARE/EMBEDDED SYSTEMS			
8170087473	**Essential Electronics for PC Technicians**	John W. Farber	Rs. 295.00	546
8170086264	**Grid Computing: A Practical Guide to Technology and Applications**	Ahmar Abbas	Rs. 295.00	408
8170088186	**CD Cracking Uncovered Protection Against Unsanctioned CD Copy**	Kris Kaspersky	Rs. 295.00	422
8170083435	**Practical Linux Programming: Device Drivers, Embedded Systems and the Internet**	Ashfaq A. Khan	Rs. 295.00	420
8170083575	**TCP/IP Application Layer Protocols for Embedded Systems**	M. Tim Jones	Rs. 295.00	460
8131800520	**PC Repair and Maintenance : A Practical Guide**	Joel Rosenthal, Kevin Irwin	Rs. 195.00	362
8131800768	**The A+ Certification and PC Repair Handbook**	Christopher A Crayton, Joel Z. Rosenthal	Rs. 495.00	888
	INTERNET & WEB TECHNOLOGY			
8170083206	**The Internet Handbook for Writers, Students and Teachers**	Mary McGuire, Linda Stilborne	Rs. 195.00	276
8170084776	**Way in-Internet Getting Started**	Elizabeth Bramire	Rs. 95.00	165
8170088976	**Web Technology**	Ramesh Bangia	Rs. 250.00	560
8170087163	**Web Design with Macromedia Studio MX 2004**	Eric Hunley	Rs. 295.00	558
8170083400	**Professional Web Design (Techniques and Templates)**	Clint Eccher	Rs. 295.00	425
8170088046	**HTML, XHTML, CSS and XML**	Teodoru Gugoiu	Rs. 195.00	355
8170083583	**FrontPage 2000 for Visual Learners**	Chris Charuhas	Rs. 95.00	200
8170083591	**HTML & Java Script for Visual Learners**	Chris Charuhas	Rs. 95.00	200

ISBN	TITLE	AUTHOR	PRICE	PAGES
8170083605	**The Visual Learners Guide to Managing Web Projects**	Chris Charuhas	Rs. 95.00	130
8170083613	**Dreamweaver 4 for Visual Learners**	Chris Charuhas	Rs. 95.00	200
8170084768	**IT Resource-Implementing XML: Managing and Formatting Data**	Johhny Brochard	Rs. 125.00	279
8170089476	**Design Your Web World**	Sunil Jalota	Rs. 75.00	146
	KEEPING AHEAD SERIES			
8170084652	**Keeping Ahead-Exchange 2000 Server**	Philippe Levesque	Rs. 145.00	285
8170084660	**Keeping Ahead-Windows 2000 Professional**	Jose Dardoigne	Rs. 175.00	388
8170084679	**Keeping Ahead-Windows 2000 Server**	Philippe Mathon	Rs. 175.00	360
8170084687	**Keeping Ahead-Linux Administration Kernel Version 2.0 to 2.2**	Bruno Guèrin	Rs. 125.00	240
8170084695	**Keeping Ahead-Using Linux Kernel Version 2.0 to 2.2**	Bruno Guèrin	Rs. 125.00	258
8170084709	**Keeping Ahead-Java 2**	Benjamin Aumaille	Rs. 145.00	284
8170084717	**Keeping Ahead-SQL Server 7**	Joelle Mosset	Rs. 145.00	329
8170084725	**Keeping Ahead-JavaScript and VBScript**	Benjamin Aumaille	Rs. 145.00	313
8170084733	**Keeping Ahead-C++ Programming Language**	Bruno Dubois	Rs. 125.00	234
8170084741	**Keeping Ahead-TCP/IP in the NT Environment**	Bruno Ferec	Rs. 125.00	230
	MCSE			
817008489X	**MCSE-Administering SQL Server 7.0**	Jerome Gabillaud	Rs. 295.00	580
8170084903	**MCSE-Networking Essentials**	Jose Dordoigne	Rs. 245.00	453
8170084911	**MCSE-Windows 2000 Professional**	Jose Dordoigne	Rs. 325.00	665
817008492X	**MCSE-Windows 2000 Server**	Phillippe Mathon	Rs. 345.00	712
	MULTIMEDIA AND ANIMATION			
8170088208	**3DS Max 6 Animation with Character Studio 4 and Plug-Ins**	Boris Kulagin, Dmitry Morozov	Rs. 175.00	216

ISBN	TITLE	AUTHOR	PRICE	PAGES
8170088216	**Adobe Audition: Soundtracks for Digital Video**	Roman Petelin, Yury Petelin	Rs. 195.00	278
8170086205	**Building A Digital Human**	Ken Brilliant	Rs. 295.00	380
8170086213	**Making Digital Videos**	Ben Long	Rs. 295.00	284
8170087171	**Illustrating with Macromedia Flash ™ MX2004**	Robert Firbaugh	Rs. 245.00	366
8170082439	**Multimedia Basics-Technology (Vol. I)**	Andreas Holzinger	Rs. 195.00	312
8170082447	**Multimedia Basics-Learning (Vol. II)**	Andreas Holzinger	Rs. 195.00	326
8170082455	**Multimedia Basics-Design (Vol. III)**	Andreas Holzinger	Rs. 195.00	280
8170083532	**Maya Feature Creature Creations**	Todd Palamar	Rs. 295.00	376
8170083540	**Sound Forge Power**	Scott R. Garrigus	Rs. 195.00	344
8131800288	**Multimedia and Web Technology**	Ramesh Bangia	Rs. 395.00	878
813180044X	**Photoshop CS**	Shruti Lal	Rs. 195.00	434
	NETWORKING			
817008721X	**Networking Essentials**	Jose Dordoigne	Rs. 195.00	453
8170089328	**TCP/IP Distributed System**	Vivek Acharya	Rs. 250.00	474
8170087023	**Computer Networks**	Ajit Kumar Singh	Rs. 95.00	181
8131800148	**The Real—world Network Troubleshooting Manual**	Alan Sugano	Rs. 295.00	396
817008203X	**Telecom & Networking Glossary**	Robert Mastin	Rs. 300.00	250
8170082048	**Data Networking Made Easy**	Karen Patten	Rs. 360.00	350
8170082056	**Digital Convergence**	Andy Covell	Rs. 300.00	234
	OFFICE AUTOMATION			
8170089891	**Desk Top Publishing**	Dinesh Maidasani	Rs. 150.00	311
8170087805	**Learning Computer Fundamentals, MS Office and Internet & Web Technology**	Dinesh Maidasani	Rs. 95.00	301
8170087686	**MS-Word 2000 Thumb-Rules and Details**	Snigdha Banerjee	Rs. 175.00	390
8170089239	**Computer Accounting with Tally 7.2**	Firewall Media	Rs. 195.00	330
	ON YOUR SIDE SERIES			
8170084830	**On your Side-Powerpoint 2002**	Andrew Blackburn	Rs. 145.00	282
8170084849	**On your Side-Excel 2002**	Adrienne Tommy	Rs. 125.00	275

Please write for a free color Firewall Media Catalog for details on the above books.

ISBN	TITLE	AUTHOR	PRICE	PAGES
8170084857	On your Side-Word 2002	Adrienne Tommy	Rs. 125.00	289
8170084865	On your Side-Access 2002	Adrienne Tommy	Rs. 125.00	303
8170084873	On your Side-Frontpage 2002	Andrew Blackburn	Rs. 95.00	245
8170084881	On your Side-Windows XP	Adrienne Tommy	Rs. 125.00	310

OPERATING SYSTEMS

ISBN	TITLE	AUTHOR	PRICE	PAGES
8170087236	Linux—A Practical Approach	B. Mohamed Ibrahim	Rs. 95.00	187
8170088623	Red Hat Linux Study Guide	Vijay Shekhar	Rs. 350.00	635
8170088631	Red Hat Linux-The Complete Bible	Vijay Shekhar	Rs. 545.00	1176
8170089581	Unix and Shell Programming	Archana Verma	Rs. 80.00	137
8170089131	Operating System Concepts	P.S. Gill	Rs. 95.00	181
8170083427	The MS-Windows XP Professional Handbook	Louis Columbus	Rs. 295.00	330
8170084784	Way in-Windows XP Home Edition	Andrew Blackburn	Rs. 95.00	183
8170086221	Cyber Rookies—Operating System Fundamentals	D. Irtegov	Rs. 295.00	498

PROGRAMMING

ISBN	TITLE	AUTHOR	PRICE	PAGES
8170087791	The Art of Programming Through Flowcharts & Algorithms	Anil Bikas Chaudhuri	Rs. 95.00	160
8170086248	Preventative Programming Techniques: Avoid and Correct Common Mistakes	Brian Hawkins	Rs. 295.00	322
8170083443	Learning Computer Programming : It's not about Languages	Mary Farrell	Rs. 295.00	375
8170086256	Object-Oriented Programming: From Problem Solving to Java	José M. Garrido	Rs. 295.00	360
817008931X	Object-Oriented Programming-Concept and Implementation	A. Rajesh	Rs. 95.00	182
8170089107	Java: J2SE-5 A Practical Approach	B. Mohammad Ibrahim	Rs. 175.00	332
8170089409	Advance Java	Gajendra Gupta	Rs. 175.00	305
8170088038	Assembly Language Programming for Intel Processors Family	Vasile Lungu	Rs. 295.00	577
8170088178	The Assembly Programming Master Book	Vlad Pirogov	Rs. 395.00	726
813180075X	Java Messaging	Eric Bruno	Rs. 295.00	480

ISBN	TITLE	AUTHOR	PRICE	PAGES
	PROGRAMMING - C#, C, C++			
8170083702	**The Power of C#**	Rajiv Parida	Rs. 295.00	576
8170085632	**Mastering Graphics Programming in 'C'**	Sudhir Dawra	Rs. 145.00	286
8170088879	**Programming in C and Numerical Analysis**	J.B. Dixit	Rs. 350.00	355
8170087074	**Mastering C Programs**	J.B. Dixit	Rs. 195.00	434
8170081262	**Programming in C**	J.B. Dixit	Rs. 295.00	506
8170087619	**Unix and C Programming**	Ashok Arora, Shefali Bansal	Rs. 295.00	606
817008878X	**C Interview Questions and Answers**	J. Rajaram	Rs. 75.00	139
8170089034	**Pragmatic C**	R.K. Jangda	Rs. 150.00	258
8170086140	**Data Structure for 'C' Programming**	Ajay Kumar	Rs. 145.00	290
8170081270	**Programming in C++**	J.B. Dixit	Rs. 260.00	602
8170088194	**Hackish C++ Pranks & Tricks**	Michael Flenov	Rs. 245.00	326
8170082889	**Basics of C++ Programming**	Nishant Kundalia	Rs. 95.00	168
8170083648	**Mastering C++ Programs**	J.B. Dixit	Rs. 295.00	598
817008623X	**Cyber Rookies—C++ Programming Fundamentals**	Chuck Easttom	Rs. 295.00	417
8131800202	**Data Structure using C++**	N. Jayalakshmi	Rs. 65.00	126
8170089123	**C++ Made Easy**	T.D. Malhotra	Rs. 250.00	449
8131800393	**C++ & Introduction to C#**	T.D. Malhotra, Rajeev A. Parida, A. Rajesh	Rs. 200.00	440
8131800350	**OOPS with C++**	M. Jaya Prasad	Rs. 150.00	317
	SECURITY			
8170083419	**Computer Forensics : Computer Crime Scene Investigation**	John Vacca	Rs. 445.00	731
8131800156	**Computer Evidence (Collection and Preservation)**	Christopher L.T. Brown	Rs. 295.00	394
8170083494	**Firewall Architecture for the Enterprise**	Norbert Pohlmann, Tim Crothers	Rs. 295.00	480
8170086272	**Net Spies**	Andrew Gauntlett	Rs. 195.00	210
3826607546	**Firewall Systems**	Norbert Pohlmann	Rs. 1630.00	544
8131800504	**Homeland Security Techniques and Technologies**	Jesus Mena	Rs. 295.00	346

Please write for a free color Firewall Media Catalog for details on the above books.

ISBN	TITLE	AUTHOR	PRICE	PAGES
	ENGINEERING AND TECHNOLOGY			
817008718X	**Human Aspects of Software Engineering**	James E. Tomayko, Orit Hazzan	Rs. 195.00	338
8131800032	**Management Information Systems**	Avdhesh Gupta, Anurag Malik	Rs. 195.00	400
8170087953	**Human Computer Interaction**	Rajendra Ranjan Kumar	Rs. 95.00	210
8170088097	**Structured System Analysis and Design**	Preeti Gupta	Rs. 125.00	192
817008802X	**Autocad 2005 for Engineers**	Ionel Simion	Rs. 175.00	271
8170088054	**Digital Signal Processing Fundamentals**	Ashfaq A. Khan	Rs. 295.00	391
8131800164	**Digital Communication System Using System VUE**	Dennis Silage	Rs. 295.00	365
8170089719	**Foundations of Computer Science**	Ashok Arora	Rs. 250.00	386
817008363X	**Practical Project Management**	Ivan Bayross	Rs. 195.00	342
8131800806	**Digital Signal Processing using MATLAB and Wavelets**	Michael Weeks	Rs. 350.00	452
8131800792	**Classical Electrodynamics**	Hans C. Dhanian	Rs. 395.00	620
8131800512	**The Software Vulnerability Guide**	Herbert H. Thompson, Scott G. Chase	Rs. 195.00	368
8131800776	**Robot Modelling and Kinematics**	Rachid Manseur	Rs. 295.00	380
8131800369	**System Software**	M. Joseph	Rs. 95.00	185
	STRAIGHT TO THE POINT SERIES			
8170084601	**STTP : Word 2002**	Corinne Hervo	Rs. 45.00	154
817008461X	**STTP : Excel 2002**	Corinne Hervo	Rs. 45.00	153
8170084628	**STTP : Dreamweaver 4**	Corinne Hervo	Rs. 45.00	135
8170084636	**STTP : Flash 5**	Corinne Hervo	Rs. 45.00	183
8170084644	**STTP : Photoshop 6**	Corinne Hervo	Rs. 45.00	152
817008881X	**STTP : MS Office 2000**	Dinesh Maidasani	Rs. 125.00	290
8170086100	**STTP : MS Office 2003**	Dinesh Maidasani	Rs. 145.00	288
8170087651	**STTP : MS Word 2003**	Firewall Media	Rs. 60.00	150
8170088011	**STTP : Photoshop CS**	Firewall Media	Rs. 60.00	150
8170088143	**STTP : MS Excel 2003**	Firewall Media	Rs. 60.00	150
8170088151	**STTP : CorelDraw 12**	Firewall Media	Rs. 60.00	150
8131800105	**STTP : 3ds MAX 7**	Dinesh Maidasani	Rs. 95.00	182
8131800083	**STTP : Auto CAD 2006**	Dinesh Maidasani	Rs. 95.00	190
8131800245	**STTP : CorelDraw X3**	Dinesh Maidasani	Rs. 75.00	188

ISBN	TITLE	AUTHOR	PRICE	PAGES
8131800253	**STTP : Dreamweaver 8**	Dinesh Maidasani	Rs. 75.00	148
8131800237	**STTP : Photoshop CS2**	Dinesh Maidasani	Rs. 75.00	172
8170088380	**STTP : Tally 7.2**	Firewall Media	Rs. 175.00	322
8131800091	**STTP : Flash 8**	Dinesh Maidasani	Rs. 95.00	180
8131800407	**STTP : My SQL 5.0**	Dinesh Maidasani	Rs. 85.00	166
8131800458	**STTP : Microsoft Power Point 2003**	Dinesh Maidasani	Rs. 75.00	142

STUDIO FACTORY

ISBN	TITLE	AUTHOR	PRICE	PAGES
8170084792	**Studio Factory—Photoshop 6**	Christophe Aubry	Rs. 175.00	364
8170084806	**Studio Factory—Flash 5**	Sami Ben Yahiya	Rs. 145.00	314
8170084814	**Studio Factory—Dreamweaver Ultradev 4**	Phillippe Chatellier	Rs. 95.00	240
8170084822	**Studio Factory-–Dreamweaver 4**	Christophe Aubry	Rs. 175.00	373
8170087643	**Studio Factory—Dreamweaver MX**	Christophe Aubry	Rs. 195.00	407
8170087627	**Studio Factory– Flash MX**	Arnaud Blanche	Rs. 145.00	337
817008766X	**Studio Factory—Photoshop 7**	Cyril Guerin	Rs. 195.00	420

LAXMI PUBLICATIONS (P) LTD

113, Golden House, Daryaganj, New Delhi-110002

Phone : **011 - 43 53 25 00**

Fax : **011 - 43 53 25 28**

EMAIL : info@laxmipublications.com

Website : www.laxmipublications.com

BRANCHES

- 129/1, IIIrd Main Road, IX Cross, Chamrajpet, **Bangalore** (*Phone* : 080-26 61 15 61)
- 26, Damodaran Street, T. Nagar, **Chennai** (*Phone* : 044-24 34 47 26)
- 43/1394D, St. Benedict's Road, Ernakulam North, **Cochin** (*Phone* : 0484-239 70 04)
- Pan Bazar, Rani Bari, **Guwahati** (*Phones* : 0361-254 36 69, 251 38 81)
- 4-2-453, Ist Floor, Ramkote, **Hyderabad** (*Phone* : 040-24 75 02 47)
- Adda Tanda Chowk, N.D. 365, **Jalandhar City** (*Phone* : 0181-222 12 72)
- 106/A, Ist Floor, S.N. Banerjee Road, **Kolkata** (*Phones* : 033-22 27 37 73, 22 27 52 47)
- 18, Madan Mohan Malviya Marg, **Lucknow** (*Phone* : 0522-220 95 78)
- 142-C, Victor House, Ground Floor, N.M. Joshi Marg, Lower Parel (W), **Mumbai** (*Phones* : 022-24 91 54 15, 24 92 78 69)
- Radha Govind Street, Tharpagna, **Ranchi** (*Phone* : 0651-230 77 64)